ZeroMQ

Pieter Hintjens

Beijing · Cambridge · Farnham · Köln · Sebastopol · Tokyo

ZeroMQ

by Pieter Hintjens

Printed in the United States of America.

Published by O'Reilly Media, Inc., 1005 Gravenstein Highway North, Sebastopol, CA 95472.

O'Reilly books may be purchased for educational, business, or sales promotional use. Online editions are also available for most titles (*http://my.safaribooksonline.com*). For more information, contact our corporate/institutional sales department: 800-998-9938 or *corporate@oreilly.com*.

Editors: Andy Oram and Maria Gulick	**Indexer:** Angela Howard
Production Editor: Christopher Hearse	**Cover Designer:** Randy Comer
Copyeditor: Gillian McGarvey	**Interior Designer:** David Futato
Proofreader: Rachel Head	**Illustrator:** Rebecca Demarest and Kara Ebrahim

March 2013:   First Edition

Revision History for the First Edition:

2013-03-11:   First release

See *http://oreilly.com/catalog/errata.csp?isbn=9781449334062* for release details.

ISBN: 978-1-449-33406-2

[LSI]

To Noémie, Freeman, and Gregor.

Table of Contents

Part I.   Learning to Work with ØMQ

Part II.   Software Engineering Using ØMQ

Preface

ØMQ in a Hundred Words

ØMQ (also known as ZeroMQ, 0MQ, or zmq) looks like an embeddable networking library, but acts like a concurrency framework. It gives you sockets that carry atomic messages across various transports, like in-process, inter-process, TCP, and multicast. You can connect sockets N-to-N with patterns like fan-out, pub-sub, task distribution, and request-reply. It's fast enough to be the fabric for clustered products. Its asynchronous I/O model gives you scalable multicore applications, built as asynchronous message-processing tasks. It has a score of language APIs and runs on most operating systems. ØMQ is from iMatix (*http://www.imatix.com*) and is LGPLv3 open source.

The Zen of Zero

The Ø in ØMQ is all about trade-offs. On the one hand, this strange name lowers ØMQ's visibility on Google and Twitter. On the other hand, it annoys the heck out of some Danish folk who write us things like "ØMG røtfl", and "Ø is not a funny-looking zero!" and "*Rødgrød med Fløde!*" (which is apparently an insult that means "May your neighbours be the direct descendants of Grendel!"). Seems like a fair trade.

Originally, the zero in ØMQ was meant to signify "zero broker" and (as close to) "zero latency" (as possible). Since then, it has come to encompass different goals: zero administration, zero cost, zero waste. More generally, "zero" refers to the culture of minimalism that permeates the project. We add power by removing complexity rather than by exposing new functionality.

How This Book Came to Be

In the summer of 2010, ØMQ was still a little-known niche library described by its rather terse reference manual and a living but sparse wiki. Martin Sustrik and I were sitting in the bar of the Hotel Kyjev in Bratislava plotting how to make ØMQ more widely popular. Martin had written most of the ØMQ code, and I'd put up the funding and organized the community. Over some Zlatý Bažant, we agreed that ØMQ needed a new, simpler website and a basic guide for new users.

Martin collected some ideas for topics to explain. I'd never written a line of ØMQ code before this, so it became a live learning documentary. As I worked through simple examples to more complex ones, I tried to answer many of the questions I'd seen on the mailing list. Because I'd been building large-scale architectures for 30 years, there were a lot of problems I was keen to throw ØMQ at. Amazingly, the results were mostly simple and elegant, even when working in C. I felt a pure joy learning ØMQ and using it to solve real problems, which brought me back to programming after a few years' pause. And often, not knowing how it was "supposed" to be done, we improved ØMQ as we went along.

From the start, I wanted the guide to be a community project, so I put it onto GitHub and let others contribute with pull requests. This was considered a radical, even vulgar approach by some. We came to a division of labor: I'd do the writing and make the original C examples, and others would help fix the text and translate the examples into other languages.

This worked better than I dared hope. You can now find all the examples in several languages, and many in a dozen languages. It's a kind of programming language Rosetta Stone, and a valuable outcome in itself. We set up a high score: reach 80% translation and your language gets its own guide. PHP, Python, Lua, and Haxe reached this goal. People asked for PDFs, and we created those. People asked for ebooks, and got those. About a hundred people have contributed to the guide to date.

The guide achieved its goal of popularizing ØMQ. The style pleases most and annoys some, which is how it should be. In December 2010, my work on ØMQ and the guide stopped, as I found myself going through late-stage cancer, heavy surgery, and six months of chemotherapy. When I picked up work again in mid-2011, it was to start using ØMQ in anger for one of the largest use-cases imagineable: on the mobile phones and tablets of the world's biggest electronics company.

But the goal of the guide was, from the start, a printed book. So it was exciting to get an email from Bill Lubanovic in January 2012, introducing me to his editor, Andy Oram, at O'Reilly, suggesting a ØMQ book. "Of course!" I said. Where do I sign? How much do I have to pay? Oh, I *get money* for this? All I have to do is finish it?"

Of course, as soon as O'Reilly announced a ØMQ book, other publishers started sending out emails to potential authors. You'll probably see a rash of ØMQ books coming out next year. That's good. Our niche library has hit the mainstream and deserves its six inches of shelf space. My apologies to the other ØMQ authors. We've set the bar horribly high, and my advice is to make your books complementary. Perhaps focus on a specific language, platform, or pattern.

This is the magic and power of communities: be the first community in a space, stay healthy, and you own that space for ever.

Audience

This book is written for professional programmers who want to learn how to make the massively distributed software that will dominate the future of computing. We assume you can read C code, because most of the examples here are in C (even though ØMQ is used in many languages). We assume you care about scale, because ØMQ solves that problem above all others. We assume you need the best possible results with the least possible cost, because otherwise you won't appreciate the trade-offs that ØMQ makes. Other than that basic background, we try to present all the concepts in networking and distributed computing you will need to use ØMQ.

Conventions Used in This Book

We used the following typographical conventions in this book:

Italic
> Indicates new terms, commands and command-line options, URLs, email addresses, filenames, and file extensions.

`Constant width`
> Used for program listings, as well as within paragraphs to refer to program elements such as variable or function names, data types, and environment variables.

`Constant width bold`
> Shows user input at the command line.

`Constant width italic`
> Shows placeholder user input that you should replace with something that makes sense for you.

 This icon signifies a tip, suggestion, or general note.

Using the Code Examples

The code examples are all online in the repository at *https://github.com/imatix/zguide/tree/master/examples/*. You'll find each example translated into several—often a dozen—other languages. The examples are licensed under MIT/X11; see the *LICENSE* file in that directory. The text of the book explains in each case how to run each example.

We appreciate, but do not require, attribution. An attribution usually includes the title, author, publisher, and ISBN. For example: "*ZeroMQ* by Pieter Hintjens (O'Reilly). Copyright 2013 Pieter Hintjens, 978-1-449-33406-2."

If you feel your use of code examples falls outside fair use or the permission given above, feel free to contact us at *permissions@oreilly.com*.

Safari® Books Online

 Safari Books Online (*www.safaribooksonline.com*) is an on-demand digital library that delivers expert content in both book and video form from the world's leading authors in technology and business.

Technology professionals, software developers, web designers, and business and creative professionals use Safari Books Online as their primary resource for research, problem solving, learning, and certification training.

Safari Books Online offers a range of product mixes and pricing programs for organizations, government agencies, and individuals. Subscribers have access to thousands of books, training videos, and prepublication manuscripts in one fully searchable database from publishers like O'Reilly Media, Prentice Hall Professional, Addison-Wesley Professional, Microsoft Press, Sams, Que, Peachpit Press, Focal Press, Cisco Press, John Wiley & Sons, Syngress, Morgan Kaufmann, IBM Redbooks, Packt, Adobe Press, FT Press, Apress, Manning, New Riders, McGraw-Hill, Jones & Bartlett, Course Technology, and dozens more. For more information about Safari Books Online, please visit us online.

How to Contact Us

Please address comments and questions concerning this book to the publisher:

> O'Reilly Media, Inc.
> 1005 Gravenstein Highway North
> Sebastopol, CA 95472
> 800-998-9938 (in the United States or Canada)
> 707-829-0515 (international or local)
> 707-829-0104 (fax)

We have a web page for this book, where we list errata, examples, and any additional information. You can access this page at *http://bit.ly/ZeroMQ-OReilly*.

To comment or ask technical questions about this book, send email to *bookques tions@oreilly.com*.

For more information about our books, courses, conferences, and news, see our website at *http://www.oreilly.com*.

Find us on Facebook: *http://facebook.com/oreilly*

Follow us on Twitter: *http://twitter.com/oreillymedia*

Watch us on YouTube: *http://www.youtube.com/oreillymedia*

Acknowledgments

Thanks to Andy Oram for making this happen at O'Reilly and editing the book.

Thanks to Bill Desmarais, Brian Dorsey, Daniel Lin, Eric Desgranges, Gonzalo Diethelm, Guido Goldstein, Hunter Ford, Kamil Shakirov, Martin Sustrik, Mike Castleman, Naveen Chawla, Nicola Peduzzi, Oliver Smith, Olivier Chamoux, Peter Alexander, Pierre Rouleau, Randy Dryburgh, John Unwin, Alex Thomas, Mihail Minkov, Jeremy Avnet, Michael Compton, Kamil Kisiel, Mark Kharitonov, Guillaume Aubert, Ian Barber, Mike Sheridan, Faruk Akgul, Oleg Sidorov, Lev Givon, Allister MacLeod, Alexander D'Archangel, Andreas Hoelzlwimmer, Han Holl, Robert G. Jakabosky, Felipe Cruz, Marcus McCurdy, Mikhail Kulemin, Dr. Gergö Érdi, Pavel Zhukov, Alexander Else, Giovanni Ruggiero, Rick "Technoweenie", Daniel Lundin, Dave Hoover, Simon Jefford, Benjamin Peterson, Justin Case, Devon Weller, Richard Smith, Alexander Morland, Wadim Grasza, Michael Jakl, Uwe Dauernheim, Sebastian Nowicki, Simone Deponti, Aaron Raddon, Dan Colish, Markus Schirp, Benoit Larroque, Jonathan Palardy, Isaiah Peng, Arkadiusz Orzechowski, Umut Aydin, Matthew Horsfall, Jeremy W. Sherman, Eric Pugh, Tyler Sellon, John E. Vincent, Pavel Mitin, Min RK, Igor Wiedler, Olof Åkesson, Patrick Lucas, Heow Goodman, Senthil Palanisami, John Gallagher, Tomas Roos, Stephen McQuay, Erik Allik, Arnaud Cogoluègnes, Rob Gagnon, Dan Williams, Edward Smith, James Tucker, Kristian Kristensen, Vadim Shalts, Martin Trojer, Tom van Leeuwen, Hiten Pandya, Harm Aarts, Marc Harter, Iskren Ivov Chernev, Jay Han, Sonia Hamilton, Nathan Stocks, Naveen Palli, and Zed Shaw for their contributions to this work.

Thanks to Martin Sustrik for his years of incredible work on ZeroMQ.

Thanks to Stathis Sideris for Ditaa (*http://www.ditaa.org*).

## PART I

Learning to Work with ØMQ

In the first part of this book, you'll learn how to use ØMQ. We'll cover the basics, the API, the different socket types and how they work, reliability, and a host of patterns you can use in your applications. You'll get the best results by working through the examples and text from start to end.

## CHAPTER 1

Basics

Fixing the World

How to explain ØMQ? Some of us start by saying all the wonderful things it does. *It's sockets on steroids. It's like mailboxes with routing. It's fast!* Others try to share their moment of enlightenment, that zap-pow-kaboom satori paradigm-shift moment when it all became obvious. *Things just become simpler. Complexity goes away. It opens the mind.* Others try to explain by comparison. *It's smaller, simpler, but still looks familiar.* Personally, I like to remember why we made ØMQ at all, because that's most likely where you, the reader, still are today.

Programming is a science dressed up as art, because most of us don't understand the physics of software and it's rarely, if ever, taught. The physics of software is not algorithms, data structures, languages, and abstractions. These are just tools we make, use, and throw away. The real physics of software is the physics of people.

Specifically, it's about our limitations when it comes to complexity and our desire to work together to solve large problems in pieces. This is the science of programming: make building blocks that people can understand and use *easily*, and people will work together to solve the very largest problems.

We live in a connected world, and modern software has to navigate this world. So, the building blocks for tomorrow's very largest solutions are connected and massively parallel. It's not enough for code to be "strong and silent" any more. Code has to talk to code. Code has to be chatty, sociable, and well-connected. Code has to run like the human brain; trillions of individual neurons firing off messages to each other, a massively parallel network with no central control, no single point of failure, yet able to solve immensely difficult problems. And it's no accident that the future of code looks like the human brain, because the endpoints of every network are, at some level, human brains.

If you've done any work with threads, protocols, or networks, you'll realize this is pretty much impossible. It's a dream. Even connecting a few programs across a few sockets is plain nasty when you start to handle real-life situations. Trillions? The cost would be unimaginable. Connecting computers is so difficult that creating software and services to do this is a multi-billion dollar business.

So we live in a world where the wiring is years ahead of our ability to use it. We had a software crisis in the 1980s, when leading software engineers like Fred Brooks believed there was no "silver bullet" (*http://en.wikipedia.org/wiki/No_Silver_Bullet*) to "promise even one order of magnitude of improvement in productivity, reliability, or simplicity."

Brooks missed free and open source software, which solved that crisis, enabling us to share knowledge efficiently. Today we face another software crisis, but it's one we don't talk about much. Only the largest, richest firms can afford to create connected applications. There is a cloud, but it's proprietary. Our data and our knowledge are disappearing from our personal computers into clouds that we cannot access and with which we cannot compete. Who owns our social networks? It is like the mainframe-PC revolution in reverse.

We can leave the political philosophy for another book (*http://swsi.info*). The point is that while the Internet offers the potential of massively connected code, the reality is that this is out of reach for most of us, and so large, interesting problems (in health, education, economics, transport, and so on) remain unsolved because there is no way to connect the code, and thus no way to connect the brains that could work together to solve these problems.

There have been many attempts to solve the challenge of connected software. There are thousands of IETF specifications, each solving part of the puzzle. For application developers, HTTP is perhaps the one solution to have been simple enough to work, but it arguably makes the problem worse by encouraging developers and architects to think in terms of big servers and thin, stupid clients.

So today people are still connecting applications using raw UDP and TCP, proprietary protocols, HTTP, and WebSockets. It remains painful, slow, hard to scale, and essentially centralized. Distributed peer-to-peer architectures are mostly for play, not work. How many applications use Skype or BitTorrent to exchange data?

Which brings us back to the science of programming. To fix the world, we needed to do two things. One, to solve the general problem of "how to connect any code to any code, anywhere." Two, to wrap that up in the simplest possible building blocks that people could understand and use *easily*.

It sounds ridiculously simple. And maybe it is. That's kind of the whole point.

Audience for This Book

We assume you are using the latest 3.2 release of ØMQ. We assume you are using a
Linux box or something similar. We assume you can read C code, more or less, as that's
the default language for the examples. We assume that when we write constants like
PUSH or SUBSCRIBE, you can imagine they are really called ZMQ_PUSH or ZMQ_SUB
SCRIBE if the programming language needs it.

Getting the Examples

This book's examples live in the book's Git repository (*https://github.com/imatix/
zguide*). The simplest way to get all the examples is to clone this repository:

```
git clone --depth=1 git://github.com/imatix/zguide.git
```

Next, browse the *examples* subdirectory. You'll find examples by language. If there are
examples missing in a language you use, you're encouraged to submit a translation
(*http://zguide.zeromq.org/main:translate*). This is how this book became so useful,
thanks to the work of many people. All examples are licensed under MIT/X11.

Ask and Ye Shall Receive

So let's start with some code. We'll begin, of course, with a "Hello World" example. We'll
make a client and a server. The client sends "Hello" to the server, which replies with
"World" (Figure 1-1). Example 1-1 presents the code for the server in C, which opens
a ØMQ socket on port 5555, reads requests on it, and replies with "World" to each
request.

Example 1-1. Hello World server (hwserver.c)

```
//
//  Hello World server
//  Binds REP socket to tcp://*:5555
//  Expects "Hello" from client, replies with "World"
//
#include <zmq.h>
#include <stdio.h>
#include <unistd.h>
#include <string.h>

int main (void)
{
    void *context = zmq_ctx_new ();

    //  Socket to talk to clients
    void *responder = zmq_socket (context, ZMQ_REP);
    zmq_bind (responder, "tcp://*:5555");
```

```
    while (1) {
        //  Wait for next request from client
        zmq_msg_t request;
        zmq_msg_init (&request);
        zmq_msg_recv (&request, responder, 0);
        printf ("Received Hello\n");
        zmq_msg_close (&request);

        //  Do some 'work'
        sleep (1);

        //  Send reply back to client
        zmq_msg_t reply;
        zmq_msg_init_size (&reply, 5);
        memcpy (zmq_msg_data (&reply), "World", 5);
        zmq_msg_send (&reply, responder, 0);
        zmq_msg_close (&reply);
    }
    //  We never get here but if we did, this would be how we end
    zmq_close (responder);
    zmq_ctx_destroy (context);
    return 0;
}
```

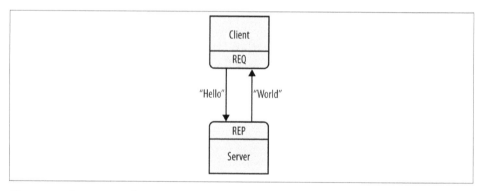

Figure 1-1. Request-reply

The REQ-REP socket pair is in lockstep. The client issues zmq_msg_send() and then
zmq_msg_recv(), in a loop (or once if that's all it needs). Any other sequence (e.g.,
sending two messages in a row) will result in a return code of -1 from the send or recv
call. Similarly, the server issues zmq_msg_recv() and then zmq_msg_send(), in that order, as often as it needs to.

ØMQ uses C as its reference language, and this is the main language we'll use for examples. If you're reading this online, the link below the example takes you to translations
into other programming languages. For print readers, Example 1-2 shows what the same
server looks like in C++.

Example 1-2. Hello World server (hwserver.cpp)

```
//
//  Hello World server in C++
//  Binds REP socket to tcp://*:5555
//  Expects "Hello" from client, replies with "World"
//
#include <zmq.hpp>
#include <string>
#include <iostream>
#include <unistd.h>

int main () {
    //  Prepare our context and socket
    zmq::context_t context (1);
    zmq::socket_t socket (context, ZMQ_REP);
    socket.bind ("tcp://*:5555");

    while (true) {
        zmq::message_t request;

        //  Wait for next request from client
        socket.recv (&request);
        std::cout << "Received Hello" << std::endl;

        //  Do some 'work'
        sleep (1);

        //  Send reply back to client
        zmq::message_t reply (5);
        memcpy ((void *) reply.data (), "World", 5);
        socket.send (reply);
    }
    return 0;
}
```

You can see that the ØMQ API is similar in C and C++. In a language like PHP, we can hide even more and the code becomes even easier to read, as shown in Example 1-3.

Example 1-3. Hello World server (hwserver.php)

```php
<?php
/*
 *  Hello World server
 *  Binds REP socket to tcp://*:5555
 *  Expects "Hello" from client, replies with "World"
 *  @author Ian Barber <ian(dot)barber(at)gmail(dot)com>
 */

$context = new ZMQContext(1);

//  Socket to talk to clients
```

```
$responder = new ZMQSocket($context, ZMQ::SOCKET_REP);
$responder->bind("tcp://*:5555");

while (true) {
    //  Wait for next request from client
    $request = $responder->recv();
    printf ("Received request: [%s]\n", $request);

    //  Do some 'work'
    sleep (1);

    //  Send reply back to client
    $responder->send("World");
}
```

Example 1-4 shows the client code.

Example 1-4. Hello World client (hwclient.c)

```
//
//  Hello World client
//  Connects REQ socket to tcp://localhost:5555
//  Sends "Hello" to server, expects "World" back
//
#include <zmq.h>
#include <string.h>
#include <stdio.h>
#include <unistd.h>

int main (void)
{
    void *context = zmq_ctx_new ();

    //  Socket to talk to server
    printf ("Connecting to hello world server...\n");
    void *requester = zmq_socket (context, ZMQ_REQ);
    zmq_connect (requester, "tcp://localhost:5555");

//      int request_nbr;
//      for (request_nbr = 0; request_nbr != 10; request_nbr++) {
//          zmq_msg_t request;
//          zmq_msg_init_size (&request, 5);
//          memcpy (zmq_msg_data (&request), "Hello", 5);
//          printf ("Sending Hello %d...\n", request_nbr);
//          zmq_msg_send (&request, requester, 0);
//          zmq_msg_close (&request);
//
//          zmq_msg_t reply;
//          zmq_msg_init (&reply);
//          zmq_msg_recv (&reply, requester, 0);
//          printf ("Received World %d\n", request_nbr);
//          zmq_msg_close (&reply);
//      }
```

```
    sleep (2);
    zmq_close (requester);
    zmq_ctx_destroy (context);
    return 0;
}
```

Now this looks too simple to be realistic, but a ØMQ socket is what you get when you take a normal TCP socket, inject it with a mix of radioactive isotopes stolen from a secret Soviet atomic research project, bombard it with 1950s-era cosmic rays, and put it into the hands of a drug-addled comic book author with a badly disguised fetish for bulging muscles clad in spandex (Figure 1-2). Yes, ØMQ sockets are the world-saving super-heroes of the networking world.

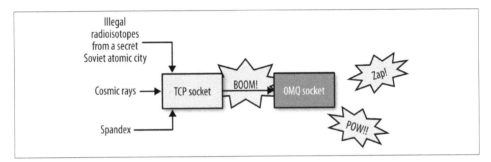

Figure 1-2. There was a terrible accident...

You could throw thousands of clients at this server, all at once, and it would continue to work happily and quickly. For fun, try starting the client and *then* starting the server, see how it all still works, and then think for a second what this means.

Let us explain briefly what these two programs are actually doing. They create a ØMQ context to work with, and a socket. Don't worry what the words mean. You'll pick it up. The server binds its REP (reply) socket to port 5555. It then waits for a request in a loop, and responds each time with a reply. The client sends a request and reads the reply back from the server.

If you kill the server (Ctrl-C) and restart it, the client won't recover properly. Recovering from crashing processes isn't quite that easy. Making a reliable request-reply flow is complex enough that we won't cover it until "Reliable Request-Reply Patterns" in Chapter 4.

There is a lot happening behind the scenes, but what matters to us programmers is how short and sweet the code is and how often it doesn't crash, even under a heavy load. This is the request-reply pattern, probably the simplest way to use ØMQ. It maps to RPC (remote procedure calls) and the classic client/server model.

A Minor Note on Strings

ØMQ doesn't know anything about the data you send except its size in bytes. That means you are responsible for formatting it safely so that applications can read it back. Doing this for objects and complex data types is a job for specialized libraries like protocol buffers. But even for strings, you need to take care.

In C and some other languages, strings are terminated with a null byte. We could send a string like "HELLO" with that extra null byte:

```
zmq_msg_init_data (&request, "Hello", 6, NULL, NULL);
```

However, if you send a string from another language, it probably will not include that null byte. For example, when we send that same string in Python, we do this:

```
socket.send ("Hello")
```

Then what goes onto the wire is a length (one byte for shorter strings) and the string contents as individual characters (Figure 1-3).

Figure 1-3. A ØMQ string

And if you read this from a C program, you will get something that looks like a string, and might by accident act like a string (if by luck the five bytes find themselves followed by an innocently lurking null), but isn't a proper string. When your client and server don't agree on the string format, you will get weird results.

When you receive string data from ØMQ in C, you simply cannot trust that it's safely terminated. Every single time you read a string, you should allocate a new buffer with space for an extra byte, copy the string, and terminate it properly with a null.

So let's establish the rule that *ØMQ strings are length-specified and are sent on the wire* **without** *a trailing null*. In the simplest case (and we'll do this in our examples), a ØMQ string maps neatly to a ØMQ message frame, which looks like the above figure—a length and some bytes.

Here is what we need to do, in C, to receive a ØMQ string and deliver it to the application as a valid C string:

```
// Receive 0MQ string from socket and convert into C string
static char *
s_recv (void *socket) {
    zmq_msg_t message;
    zmq_msg_init (&message);
    int size = zmq_msg_recv (&message, socket, 0);
```

```
        if (size == -1)
            return NULL;
        char *string = malloc (size + 1);
        memcpy (string, zmq_msg_data (&message), size);
        zmq_msg_close (&message);
        string [size] = 0;
        return (string);
    }
```

This makes a very handy helper function. In the spirit of making things we can reuse profitably, we can write a similar **s_send()** function that sends strings in the correct ØMQ format and package this into a header file we can reuse.

The result is *zhelpers.h*, which lets us write sweeter and shorter ØMQ applications in C. It is a fairly long source, and only fun for C developers, so read it at your leisure (*https://github.com/imatix/zguide/blob/master/examples/C/zhelpers.h*).

Version Reporting

ØMQ does come in several versions, and quite often if you hit a problem, it'll be something that's been fixed in a later version. So it's a useful trick to know *exactly* what version of ØMQ you're actually linking with. Example 1-5 is a tiny program that lets you do just that.

Example 1-5. ØMQ version reporting (version.c)

```
//
//  Report 0MQ version
//
#include "zhelpers.h"

int main (void)
{
    int major, minor, patch;
    zmq_version (&major, &minor, &patch);
    printf ("Current 0MQ version is %d.%d.%d\n", major, minor, patch);

    return EXIT_SUCCESS;
}
```

Getting the Message Out

The second classic pattern is one-way data distribution, in which a server pushes updates to a set of clients. Let's look at an example that pushes out weather updates consisting of a zip code, temperature, and relative humidity. We'll generate random values, just like the real weather stations do.

Example 1-6 shows the code for the server. We'll use port 5556 for this application.

Example 1-6. Weather update server (wuserver.c)

```
//
//  Weather update server
//  Binds PUB socket to tcp://*:5556
//  Publishes random weather updates
//
#include "zhelpers.h"

int main (void)
{
    //  Prepare our context and publisher
    void *context = zmq_ctx_new ();
    void *publisher = zmq_socket (context, ZMQ_PUB);
    int rc = zmq_bind (publisher, "tcp://*:5556");
    assert (rc == 0);
    rc = zmq_bind (publisher, "ipc://weather.ipc");
    assert (rc == 0);

    //  Initialize random number generator
    srandom ((unsigned) time (NULL));
    while (1) {
        //  Get values that will fool the boss
        int zipcode, temperature, relhumidity;
        zipcode     = randof (100000);
        temperature = randof (215) - 80;
        relhumidity = randof (50) + 10;

        //  Send message to all subscribers
        char update [20];
        sprintf (update, "%05d %d %d", zipcode, temperature, relhumidity);
        s_send (publisher, update);
    }
    zmq_close (publisher);
    zmq_ctx_destroy (context);
    return 0;
}
```

There's no start and no end to this stream of updates; it's like a never-ending broadcast (Figure 1-4).

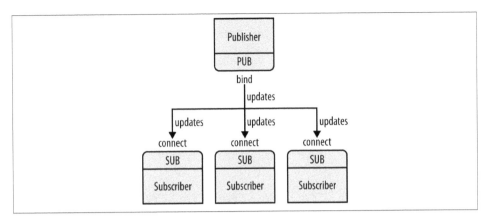

Figure 1-4. Publish-subscribe

Example 1-7 shows the client application, which listens to the stream of updates and grabs anything to do with a specified zip code (by default, New York City, because that's a great place to start any adventure).

Example 1-7. Weather update client (wuclient.c)

```
//
//  Weather update client
//  Connects SUB socket to tcp://localhost:5556
//  Collects weather updates and finds avg temp in zipcode
//
#include "zhelpers.h"

int main (int argc, char *argv [])
{
    void *context = zmq_ctx_new ();

    //  Socket to talk to server
    printf ("Collecting updates from weather server...\n");
    void *subscriber = zmq_socket (context, ZMQ_SUB);
    int rc = zmq_connect (subscriber, "tcp://localhost:5556");
    assert (rc == 0);

    //  Subscribe to zipcode, default is NYC, 10001
    char *filter = (argc > 1)? argv [1]: "10001 ";
    rc = zmq_setsockopt (subscriber, ZMQ_SUBSCRIBE, filter, strlen (filter));
    assert (rc == 0);

    //  Process 100 updates
    int update_nbr;
    long total_temp = 0;
    for (update_nbr = 0; update_nbr < 100; update_nbr++) {
        char *string = s_recv (subscriber);

        int zipcode, temperature, relhumidity;
```

```
        sscanf (string, "%d %d %d",
            &zipcode, &temperature, &relhumidity);
        total_temp += temperature;
        free (string);
    }
    printf ("Average temperature for zipcode '%s' was %dF\n",
        filter, (int) (total_temp / update_nbr));

    zmq_close (subscriber);
    zmq_ctx_destroy (context);
    return 0;
}
```

Note that when you use a SUB socket you *must* set a subscription using `zmq_setsock opt()` and SUBSCRIBE, as in this code. If you don't set any subscription, you won't get any messages. It's a common mistake for beginners. The subscriber can set many subscriptions, which are added together. That is, if an update matches *any* subscription, the subscriber receives it. The subscriber can also cancel specific subscriptions. A subscription is often but not necessarily a printable string. See `zmq_setsockopt()` for how this works.

The PUB-SUB socket pair is asynchronous. The client does `zmq_msg_recv()`, in a loop (or once if that's all it needs). Trying to send a message to a SUB socket will cause an error. Similarly, the service does `zmq_msg_send()` as often as it needs to, but must not do `zmq_msg_recv()` on a PUB socket.

In theory, with ØMQ sockets it does not matter which end connects and which end binds. However, in practice there are undocumented differences that I'll come to later. For now, bind the PUB and connect the SUB, unless your network design makes that impossible.

There is one more important thing to know about PUB-SUB sockets: you do not know precisely when a subscriber starts to get messages. Even if you start a subscriber, wait a while, and then start the publisher, *the subscriber will always miss the first messages that the publisher sends*. This is because as the subscriber connects to the publisher (something that takes a small but nonzero amount of time), the publisher may already be sending messages out.

This "slow joiner" symptom hits enough people, often enough, that we're going to explain it in detail. Remember that ØMQ does asynchronous I/O (i.e., in the background). Say you have two nodes doing this, in this order:

- Subscriber connects to an endpoint and receives and counts messages.
- Publisher binds to an endpoint and immediately sends 1,000 messages.

The subscriber will most likely not receive anything. You'll blink, check that you set a correct filter, and try again, and the subscriber will still not receive anything.

Making a TCP connection involves to and from handshaking that can take several milliseconds (msec), depending on your network and the number of hops between peers. In that time, ØMQ can send very many messages. For the sake of argument, assume it takes 5 msec to establish a connection, and that same link can handle 1M messages per second. During the 5 msec that the subscriber is connecting to the publisher, it takes the publisher only 1 msec to send out those 1K messages.

In Chapter 2, we'll explain how to synchronize a publisher and subscribers so that you don't start to publish data until the subscribers really are connected and ready. There is a simple (and stupid) way to delay the publisher, which is to sleep. Don't do this in a real application, though, because it is extremely fragile as well as inelegant and slow. Use sleeps to prove to yourself what's happening, and then read Chapter 2 to see how to do this right.

The alternative to synchronization is to simply assume that the published data stream is infinite and has no start and no end. One also assumes that the subscriber doesn't care what transpired before it started up. This is how we built our weather client example.

So, the client subscribes to its chosen zip code and collects a thousand updates for that zip code. That means about 10 million updates from the server, if zip codes are randomly distributed. You can start the client, and then the server, and the client will keep working. You can stop and restart the server as often as you like, and the client will keep working. When the client has collected its thousand updates, it calculates the average, prints it, and exits.

Some points about the publish-subscribe pattern:

- A subscriber can connect to more than one publisher, using one connect call each time. Data will then arrive and be interleaved ("fair queued") so that no single publisher drowns out the others.
- If a publisher has no connected subscribers, then it will simply drop all messages.
- If you're using TCP and a subscriber is slow, messages will queue up on the publisher. We'll look at how to protect publishers against this by using the "high-water mark" in the next chapter.
- From ØMQ v3.x, filtering happens on the publisher's side when using a connected protocol (tcp or ipc). Using the epgm protocol, filtering happens on the subscriber's side. In ØMQ v2.x, all filtering happened on the subscriber's side.

This is how long it takes to receive and filter 10M messages on my laptop, which is a 2011-era Intel I7—fast, but nothing special:

```
ph@nb201103:~/work/git/zguide/examples/c$ time wuclient
Collecting updates from weather server...
Average temperature for zipcode '10001 ' was 28F
```

```
real    0m4.470s
user    0m0.000s
sys     0m0.008s
```

Divide and Conquer

As a final example (you are surely getting tired of juicy code and want to delve back into philological discussions about comparative abstractive norms), let's do a little supercomputing. Then, coffee. Our supercomputing application is a fairly typical parallel processing model (Figure 1-5). We have:

- A ventilator that produces tasks that can be done in parallel
- A set of workers that processes tasks
- A sink that collects results back from the worker processes

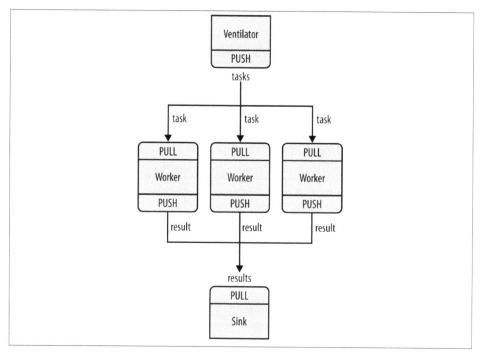

Figure 1-5. Parallel pipeline

In reality, workers run on superfast boxes, perhaps using GPUs (graphic processing units) to do the hard math. Example 1-8 shows the code for the ventilator. It generates 100 tasks, each one a message telling the worker to sleep for some number of milliseconds.

Example 1-8. Parallel task ventilator (taskvent.c)

```
//
//  Task ventilator
//  Binds PUSH socket to tcp://localhost:5557
//  Sends batch of tasks to workers via that socket
//
#include "zhelpers.h"

int main (void)
{
    void *context = zmq_ctx_new ();

    //  Socket to send messages on
    void *sender = zmq_socket (context, ZMQ_PUSH);
    zmq_bind (sender, "tcp://*:5557");

    //  Socket to send start of batch message on
    void *sink = zmq_socket (context, ZMQ_PUSH);
    zmq_connect (sink, "tcp://localhost:5558");

    printf ("Press Enter when the workers are ready: ");
    getchar ();
    printf ("Sending tasks to workers...\n");

    //  The first message is "0" and signals start of batch
    s_send (sink, "0");

    //  Initialize random number generator
    srandom ((unsigned) time (NULL));

    //  Send 100 tasks
    int task_nbr;
    int total_msec = 0;     //  Total expected cost in msec
    for (task_nbr = 0; task_nbr < 100; task_nbr++) {
        int workload;
        //  Random workload from 1 to 100 msec
        workload = randof (100) + 1;
        total_msec += workload;
        char string [10];
        sprintf (string, "%d", workload);
        s_send (sender, string);
    }
    printf ("Total expected cost: %d msec\n", total_msec);
    sleep (1);              //  Give 0MQ time to deliver

    zmq_close (sink);
    zmq_close (sender);
    zmq_ctx_destroy (context);
    return 0;
}
```

The code for the worker application is in Example 1-9. It receives a message, sleeps for that number of seconds, and then signals that it's finished.

Example 1-9. Parallel task worker (taskwork.c)

```
//
//  Task worker
//  Connects PULL socket to tcp://localhost:5557
//  Collects workloads from ventilator via that socket
//  Connects PUSH socket to tcp://localhost:5558
//  Sends results to sink via that socket
//
#include "zhelpers.h"

int main (void)
{
    void *context = zmq_ctx_new ();

    //  Socket to receive messages on
    void *receiver = zmq_socket (context, ZMQ_PULL);
    zmq_connect (receiver, "tcp://localhost:5557");

    //  Socket to send messages to
    void *sender = zmq_socket (context, ZMQ_PUSH);
    zmq_connect (sender, "tcp://localhost:5558");

    //  Process tasks forever
    while (1) {
        char *string = s_recv (receiver);
        //  Simple progress indicator for the viewer
        fflush (stdout);
        printf ("%s.", string);

        //  Do the work
        s_sleep (atoi (string));
        free (string);

        //  Send results to sink
        s_send (sender, "");
    }
     zmq_close (receiver);
    zmq_close (sender);
    zmq_ctx_destroy (context);
    return 0;
}
```

Finally, Example 1-10 shows the sink application. It collects the 100 messages and then calculates how long the overall processing took, so we can confirm that the workers really were running in parallel if there are more than one of them.

Example 1-10. Parallel task sink (tasksink.c)

```c
//
//  Task sink
//  Binds PULL socket to tcp://localhost:5558
//  Collects results from workers via that socket
//
#include "zhelpers.h"

int main (void)
{
    //  Prepare our context and socket
    void *context = zmq_ctx_new ();
    void *receiver = zmq_socket (context, ZMQ_PULL);
    zmq_bind (receiver, "tcp://*:5558");

    //  Wait for start of batch
    char *string = s_recv (receiver);
    free (string);

    //  Start our clock now
    int64_t start_time = s_clock ();

    //  Process 100 confirmations
    int task_nbr;
    for (task_nbr = 0; task_nbr < 100; task_nbr++) {
        char *string = s_recv (receiver);
        free (string);
        if ((task_nbr / 10) * 10 == task_nbr)
            printf (":");
        else
            printf (".");
        fflush (stdout);
    }
    //  Calculate and report duration of batch
    printf ("Total elapsed time: %d msec\n",
        (int) (s_clock () - start_time));

    zmq_close (receiver);
    zmq_ctx_destroy (context);
    return 0;
}
```

The average cost of a batch is five seconds. When we start one, two, and four workers, we get results like this from the sink:

```
#   1 worker
Total elapsed time: 5034 msec
#   2 workers
Total elapsed time: 2421 msec
#   4 workers
Total elapsed time: 1018 msec
```

Let's look at some aspects of this code in more detail:

- The workers connect upstream to the ventilator, and downstream to the sink. This means you can add workers arbitrarily. If the workers bound to their endpoints, you would need (a) more endpoints and (b) to modify the ventilator and/or the sink each time you added a worker. We say that the ventilator and sink are *stable* parts of our architecture and the workers are *dynamic* parts of it.

- We have to synchronize the start of the batch with all workers being up and running. This is a fairly common gotcha in ØMQ, and there is no easy solution. The con nect method takes a certain amount of time, so when a set of workers connect to the ventilator, the first one to successfully connect will get a whole load of messages in that short time while the others are still connecting. If you don't synchronize the start of the batch somehow, the system won't run in parallel at all. Try removing the wait in the ventilator, and see what happens.

- The ventilator's PUSH socket distributes tasks to workers (assuming they are all connected *before* the batch starts going out) evenly. This is called *load balancing*, and it's something we'll look at again in more detail.

- The sink's PULL socket collects results from workers evenly. This is called *fair queuing* (Figure 1-6).

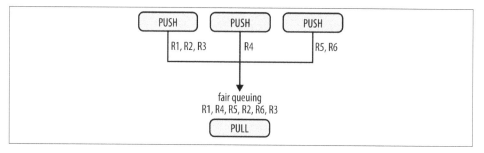

Figure 1-6. Fair queuing

The pipeline pattern also exhibits the "slow joiner" syndrome, leading to accusations that PUSH sockets don't load-balance properly. If you are using PUSH and PULL and one of your workers gets way more messages than the others, it's because that PULL socket has joined faster than the others, and grabs a lot of messages before the others manage to connect.

Programming with ØMQ

Having seen some examples, you must be eager to start using ØMQ in some apps. Before you start that, take a deep breath, chillax, and reflect on some basic advice that will save you much stress and confusion:

- Learn ØMQ step-by-step. It's just one simple API, but it hides a world of possibilities. Take the possibilities slowly and master each one.
- Write nice code. Ugly code hides problems and makes it hard for others to help you. You might get used to meaningless variable names, but people reading your code won't. Use names that are real words, that say something other than "I'm too careless to tell you what this variable is really for." Use consistent indentation and clean layout. Write nice code, and your world will be more comfortable.
- Test what you make as you make it. When your program doesn't work, you should know which five lines are to blame. This is especially true when you do ØMQ magic, which just *won't* work the first few times you try it.
- When you find that things don't work as expected, break your code into pieces, test each one, and see which one is not working. ØMQ lets you make essentially modular code; use that to your advantage.
- Make abstractions (classes, methods, whatever) as you need them. If you copy/paste a lot of code, you're going to copy/paste errors, too.

Getting the Context Right

ØMQ applications always start by creating a *context*, and then using that for creating sockets. In C, it's the zmq_ctx_new() call. You should create and use exactly one context in your process. Technically, the context is the container for all sockets in a single process, and it acts as the transport for inproc sockets, which are the fastest way to connect threads in one process. If at runtime a process has two contexts, these are like separate ØMQ instances. If that's explicitly what you want, that's OK, but otherwise remember:

Do one zmq_ctx_new() at the start of your main code, and one zmq_ctx_destroy() at the end.

If you're using the fork() system call, each process needs its own context. If you do zmq_ctx_new() in the main process before calling fork(), the child processes get their own contexts. In general, you want to do the interesting stuff in the child processes and just manage these from the parent process.

Making a Clean Exit

Classy programmers share the same motto as classy hit men: always clean up when you finish the job. When you use ØMQ in a language like Python, stuff gets automatically freed for you. But when using C, you have to carefully free objects when you're finished with them, or else you get memory leaks, unstable applications, and generally bad karma.

Memory leaks are one thing, but ØMQ is quite finicky about how you exit an application. The reasons are technical and painful, but the upshot is that if you leave any sockets open, the zmq_ctx_destroy() function will hang forever. And even if you close all sockets, zmq_ctx_destroy() will by default wait forever if there are pending connects or sends, unless you set the LINGER to zero on those sockets before closing them.

The ØMQ objects we need to worry about are messages, sockets, and contexts. Luckily, it's quite simple, at least in simple programs:

- Always close a message the moment you are done with it, using zmq_msg_close().
- If you are opening and closing a lot of sockets, that's probably a sign that you need to redesign your application.
- When you exit the program, close your sockets and then call zmq_ctx_destroy(). This destroys the context.

This is at least the case for C development. In a language with automatic object destruction, sockets and contexts will be destroyed as you leave the scope. If you use exceptions you'll have to do the cleanup in something like a "final" block, the same as for any resource.

If you're doing multithreaded work, it gets rather more complex than this. We'll get to multithreading in the next chapter, but because some of you will, despite warnings, try to run before you can safely walk, here is a quick and dirty guide to making a clean exit in a *multithreaded* ØMQ application.

First, do not try to use the same socket from multiple threads. Please don't explain why you think this would be excellent fun; just don't do it. Next, you need to shut down each socket that has ongoing requests. The proper way is to set a low LINGER value (one second), and then close the socket. If your language binding doesn't do this for you automatically when you destroy a context, I'd suggest sending a patch.

Finally, destroy the context. This will cause any blocking receives or polls or sends in attached threads (i.e., which share the same context) to return with an error. Catch that error, and then set LINGER on and close sockets in *that* thread, and exit. Do not destroy the same context twice. The zmq_ctx_destroy() call in the main thread will block until all sockets it knows about are safely closed.

Voilà! It's complex and painful enough that any language binding author worth his or her salt will do this automatically and make the socket closing dance unnecessary.

Why We Needed ØMQ

Now that you've seen ØMQ in action, let's go back to the "why."

Many applications these days consist of components that stretch across some kind of network, either a LAN or the Internet. So, many application developers end up doing some kind of messaging. Some developers use message queuing products, but most of the time they do it themselves, using TCP or UDP. These protocols are not hard to use, but there is a great difference between sending a few bytes from A to B and doing messaging in any kind of reliable way.

Let's look at the typical questions we face when we start to connect pieces using raw TCP. Any reusable messaging layer would need to address all or most of these:

- How do we handle I/O? Does our application block, or do we handle I/O in the background? This is a key design decision. Blocking I/O creates architectures that do not scale well, but background I/O can be very hard to do right.
- How do we handle dynamic components (i.e., pieces that go away temporarily)? Do we formally split components into "clients" and "servers" and mandate that servers cannot disappear? What, then, if we want to connect servers to servers? Do we try to reconnect every few seconds?
- How do we represent a message on the wire? How do we frame data so it's easy to write and read, safe from buffer overflows, and efficient for small messages, yet adequate for the very largest videos of dancing cats wearing party hats?
- How do we handle messages that we can't deliver immediately? Particularly if we're waiting for a component to come back online? Do we discard messages, put them into a database, or put them into a memory queue?
- Where do we store message queues? What happens if the component reading from a queue is very slow and causes our queues to build up? What's our strategy then?
- How do we handle lost messages? Do we wait for fresh data, request a resend, or do we build some kind of reliability layer that ensures messages cannot be lost? What if that layer itself crashes?
- What if we need to use a different network transport? Say, multicast instead of TCP unicast? Or IPv6? Do we need to rewrite the applications, or is the transport abstracted in some layer?
- How do we route messages? Can we send the same message to multiple peers? Can we send replies back to an original requester?

- How do we write an API for another language? Do we reimplement a wire-level protocol, or do we repackage a library? If the former, how can we guarantee efficient and stable stacks? If the latter, how can we guarantee interoperability?

- How do we represent data so that it can be read between different architectures? Do we enforce a particular encoding for data types? To what extent is this the job of the messaging system rather than a higher layer?

- How do we handle network errors? Do we wait and retry, ignore them silently, or abort?

Take a typical open source project like Apache ZooKeeper (*http://zookeep er.apache.org*). Read the C API code in *src/c/src/zookeeper.c* (*http://github.com/apache/ zookeeper/blob/trunk/src/c/src/zookeeper.c*). When I read this code in 2010, it was 3,200 lines of mystery, and in there is an undocumented client/server network communication protocol. I see it's efficient because it uses `poll()` instead of `select()`. But really, Zoo-Keeper should be using a generic messaging layer and an explicitly documented wire-level protocol. It is incredibly wasteful for teams to be building this particular wheel over and over.

But how do we make a reusable messaging layer? Why, when so many projects need this technology, are people still doing it the hard way by driving TCP sockets in their code, and solving the problems in that long list over and over (Figure 1-7)?

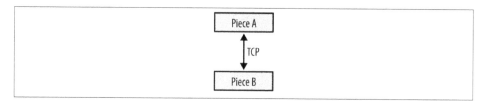

Figure 1-7. Messaging as it starts

It turns out that building reusable messaging systems is really difficult, which is why few free and open source (FOSS) projects ever tried, and why commercial messaging products are complex, expensive, inflexible, and brittle. In 2006, iMatix designed the Advanced Message Queuing Protocol, or AMQP (*http://www.amqp.org*), which started to give FOSS developers perhaps the first reusable recipe for a messaging system. AMQP works better than many other designs, but remains relatively complex, expensive, and brittle (*http://www.imatix.com/articles:whats-wrong-with-amqp*). It takes weeks to learn to use it, and months to create stable architectures that don't crash when things get hairy.

Most messaging projects (like AMQP) that try to solve this long list of problems in a reusable way do so by inventing a new concept, the "broker," that does addressing, routing, and queuing. This results in a client/server protocol or a set of APIs on top of some undocumented protocol that allows applications to speak to this broker. Brokers are an excellent thing in reducing the complexity of large networks. But adding broker-based messaging to a product like ZooKeeper would make it worse, not better. It would mean adding an additional big box, and a new single point of failure. A broker rapidly becomes a bottleneck and a new risk to manage. If the software supports it, we can add a second, third, and fourth broker and make some failover scheme. People do this. However, it creates more moving pieces, more complexity, more things to break.

Also, a broker-centric setup needs its own operations team. You literally need to watch the brokers day and night, and beat them with a stick when they start misbehaving. You need boxes, and you need backup boxes, and you need people to manage those boxes. It is only worth doing for large applications with many moving pieces, built by several teams of people over several years.

So, small to medium application developers are trapped. Either they avoid network programming and make monolithic applications that do not scale, or they jump into network programming and make brittle, complex applications that are hard to maintain. Or they bet on a messaging product, and end up with scalable applications that depend on expensive, easily broken technology. There has been no really good choice, which may be why messaging is largely stuck in the last century and stirs strong emotions—negative ones for users, gleeful joy for those selling support and licenses (Figure 1-8).

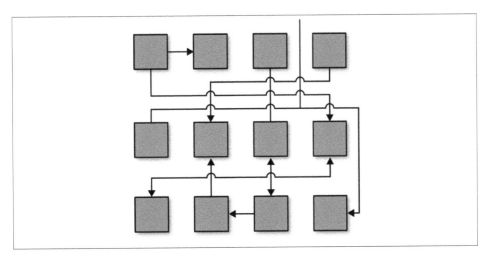

Figure 1-8. Messaging as it becomes

What we need is something that does the job of messaging, but does it in such a simple and cheap way that it can work in any application, with close to zero cost. It should be a library with which you link without any other dependencies. No additional moving pieces, so no additional risk. It should run on any OS and work with any programming language.

And this is ØMQ: an efficient, embeddable library that solves most of the problems an application needs to become nicely elastic across a network, without much cost.

Specifically:

- It handles I/O asynchronously, in background threads. These communicate with application threads using lock-free data structures, so concurrent ØMQ applications need no locks, semaphores, or other wait states.

- Components can come and go dynamically, and ØMQ will automatically reconnect. This means you can start components in any order. You can create "service-oriented architectures" (SOAs) where services can join and leave the network at any time.

- It queues messages automatically when needed. It does this intelligently, pushing messages as close as possible to the receiver before queuing them.

- It has ways of dealing with over-full queues (called the "high-water mark"). When a queue is full, ØMQ automatically blocks senders, or throws away messages, depending on the kind of messaging you are doing (the so-called "pattern").

- It lets your applications talk to each other over arbitrary transports: TCP, multicast, in-process, inter-process. You don't need to change your code to use a different transport.

- It handles slow/blocked readers safely, using different strategies that depend on the messaging pattern.

- It lets you route messages using a variety of patterns, such as request-reply and publish-subscribe. These patterns are how you create the topology, the structure of your network.

- It lets you create proxies to queue, forward, or capture messages with a single call. Proxies can reduce the interconnection complexity of a network.

- It delivers whole messages exactly as they were sent, using a simple framing on the wire. If you write a 10KB message, you will receive a 10KB message.

- It does not impose any format on messages. They are blobs of zero bytes to gigabytes large. When you want to represent data you choose some other product on top, such as Google's protocol buffers, XDR, and others.

- It handles network errors intelligently. Sometimes it retries, sometimes it tells you an operation failed.

- It reduces your carbon footprint. Doing more with less CPU means your boxes use less power, and you can keep your old boxes in use for longer. Al Gore would love ØMQ.

Actually, ØMQ does rather more than this. It has a subversive effect on how you develop network-capable applications. Superficially, it's a socket-inspired API on which you do `zmq_msg_recv()` and `zmq_msg_send()`. But the message processing loop rapidly becomes the central loop, and your application soon breaks down into a set of message processing tasks. It is elegant and natural. And it scales: each of these tasks maps to a node, and the nodes talk to each other across arbitrary transports. Two nodes in one process (node is a thread), two nodes on one box (node is a process), or two boxes on one network (node is a box)—it's all the same, with no application code changes.

Socket Scalability

Let's see ØMQ's scalability in action. Here is a shell script that starts the weather server and then a bunch of clients in parallel:

```
wuserver &
wuclient 12345 &
wuclient 23456 &
wuclient 34567 &
wuclient 45678 &
wuclient 56789 &
```

As the clients run, we take a look at the active processes using top, and we see something like (on a four-core box):

```
  PID USER      PR  NI  VIRT  RES  SHR S %CPU %MEM    TIME+  COMMAND
 7136 ph        20   0 1040m 959m 1156 R  157 12.0 16:25.47 wuserver
 7966 ph        20   0 98608 1804 1372 S   33  0.0  0:03.94 wuclient
 7963 ph        20   0 33116 1748 1372 S   14  0.0  0:00.76 wuclient
 7965 ph        20   0 33116 1784 1372 S    6  0.0  0:00.47 wuclient
 7964 ph        20   0 33116 1788 1372 S    5  0.0  0:00.25 wuclient
 7967 ph        20   0 33072 1740 1372 S    5  0.0  0:00.35 wuclient
```

Let's think for a second about what is happening here. The weather server has a single socket, and yet here we have it sending data to five clients in parallel. We could have thousands of concurrent clients. The server application doesn't see them and doesn't talk to them directly. So the ØMQ socket is acting like a little server, silently accepting client requests and shoving data out to them as fast as the network can handle it. And it's a multithreaded server, squeezing more juice out of your CPU.

Upgrading from ØMQ v2.2 to ØMQ v3.2

In early 2012, ØMQ v3.2 became stable enough for live use, and by the time you're reading this, it's what you really should be using. If you are still using v2.2, here's a quick summary of the changes and instructions on how to migrate your code.

Pub-sub filtering is now done on the publisher side instead of the subscriber side. This improves performance significantly in many pub-sub use cases. You can mix version 3.2 and 2.1/2.2 publishers and subscribers safely.

Most of the API is backward compatible, except a few changes that went into v3.0 with little regard to the cost of breaking existing code. The syntax of zmq_send() and zmq_recv() changed, and ZMQ_NOBLOCK got rebaptized ZMQ_DONTWAIT. So although I'd love to say, "You just recompile your code with the latest libzmq and everything will work," that's not how it is. For what it's worth, we banned such API breakage afterwards.

So, the minimal change for C/C++ apps that use the low-level libzmq API is to replace all calls to zmq_send() with zmq_msg_send(), and zmq_recv() with zmq_msg_recv(). In other languages, your binding author may have done the work already. Note that these two functions now return -1 in case of error, and zero or more according to how many bytes were sent or received.

Other parts of the libzmq API became more consistent. We deprecated zmq_init() and zmq_term(), replacing them with zmq_ctx_new() and zmq_ctx_destroy(). We added zmq_ctx_set() to let you configure a context before starting to work with it.

Finally, we added context monitoring via the zmq_ctx_set_monitor() call, which lets you track connections and disconnections, and other events on sockets.

Warning: Unstable Paradigms!

Traditional network programming is built on the general assumption that one socket talks to one connection, one peer. There are multicast protocols, but these are exotic. When we assume "one socket = one connection," we scale our architectures in certain ways. We create threads of logic where each thread works with one socket, one peer. We place intelligence and state in these threads.

In the ØMQ universe, sockets are doorways to fast little background communications engines that manage a whole set of connections automagically for you. You can't see, work with, open, close, or attach state to these connections. Whether you use blocking send or receive or poll, all you can talk to is the socket, not the connections it manages for you. The connections are private and invisible, and this is the key to ØMQ's scalability.

This is because your code, talking to a socket, can then handle any number of connections across whatever network protocols are around, without change. A messaging pattern sitting in ØMQ can scale more cheaply than a messaging pattern sitting in your application code.

So, the general assumption no longer applies. As you read the code examples, your brain will try to map them to what you know. You will read "socket" and think "Ah, that represents a connection to another node." That is wrong. You will read "thread" and your brain will again think, "Ah, a thread represents a connection to another node," and again your brain will be wrong.

If you're reading this book for the first time, realize that until you actually spend a day or two writing ØMQ code (or maybe three or four days), you may feel confused, especially by how simple ØMQ makes things for you; you may try to impose that general assumption on ØMQ, and it won't work. And then you will experience your moment of enlightenment and trust, that *zap-pow-kaboom* satori paradigm-shift moment when it all becomes clear.

## CHAPTER 2

Sockets and Patterns

In Chapter 1 we took ØMQ for a drive, with some basic examples of the main ØMQ patterns: request-reply, publish-subscribe, and pipeline. In this chapter, we're going to get our hands dirty and start to learn how to use these tools in real programs.

We'll cover:

- How to create and work with ØMQ sockets
- How to send and receive messages on sockets
- How to build your apps around ØMQ's asynchronous I/O model
- How to handle multiple sockets in one thread
- How to handle fatal and nonfatal errors properly
- How to handle interrupt signals like Ctrl-C
- How to shut down a ØMQ application cleanly
- How to check a ØMQ application for memory leaks
- How to send and receive multipart messages
- How to forward messages across networks
- How to build a simple message queuing broker
- How to write multithreaded applications with ØMQ
- How to use ØMQ to signal between threads
- How to use ØMQ to coordinate a network of nodes
- How to create and use message envelopes for publish-subscribe
- How to use the high-water mark (HWM) to protect against memory overflows

The Socket API

To be perfectly honest, ØMQ does a kind of switch-and-bait on you, for which we don't apologize. It's for your own good, and it hurts us more than it hurts you. It presents a familiar socket-based API, which requires great effort for us to hide a bunch of message-processing engines. However, the result will slowly fix your world view about how to design and write distributed software.

Sockets are the de facto standard API for network programming, as well as being useful for stopping your eyes from falling onto your cheeks. One thing that makes ØMQ especially tasty to developers is that it uses sockets and messages instead of some other arbitrary set of concepts. Kudos to Martin Sustrik for pulling this off. It turns "Message Oriented Middleware," a phrase guaranteed to send the whole room off to Catatonia, into "Extra Spicy Sockets!," which leaves us with a strange craving for pizza and a desire to know more.

Like a favorite dish, ØMQ sockets are easy to digest. These sockets have a life in four parts, just like BSD sockets:

- We can create and destroy them, which go together to form a karmic circle of socket life (see zmq_socket(), zmq_close()).
- We can configure them by setting options on them and checking them if necessary (see zmq_setsockopt(), zmq_getsockopt()).
- We can plug them into the network topology by creating ØMQ connections to and from them (see zmq_bind(), zmq_connect()).
- We can use them to carry data by writing and receiving messages on them (see zmq_msg_send(), zmq_msg_recv()).

Note that sockets are always void pointers, and messages (which we'll come to very soon) are structures. So in C you pass sockets as such, but you pass addresses of messages in all functions that work with messages, like zmq_msg_send() and zmq_msg_recv(). As a mnemonic, realize that "in ØMQ, all your sockets are belong to us," but messages are things you actually own in your code.

Creating, destroying, and configuring sockets works as you'd expect for any object. But remember that ØMQ is an asynchronous, elastic fabric. This has some impact on how we plug sockets into the network topology and how we use the sockets after that.

Plugging Sockets into the Topology

To create a connection between two nodes, you use zmq_bind() in one node and zmq_connect() in the other. As a general rule of thumb, the node that does zmq_bind() is a "server," sitting on a well-known network address, and the node that does zmq_connect() is a "client," with unknown or arbitrary network addresses. Thus, we say that we "bind a socket to an endpoint" and "connect a socket to an endpoint," the endpoint being that well-known network address.

ØMQ connections are somewhat different from old-fashioned TCP connections. The main notable differences are:

- They go across an arbitrary transport (inproc, ipc, tcp, pgm, or epgm). See zmq_in proc(), zmq_ipc(), zmq_tcp(), zmq_pgm(), and zmq_epgm().
- One socket may have many outgoing and many incoming connections.
- There is no zmq_accept() method. When a socket is bound to an endpoint, it automatically starts accepting connections.
- The network connection itself happens in the background, and ØMQ will automatically reconnect if the network connection is broken (e.g., if the peer disappears and then comes back).
- Your application code cannot work with these connections directly; they are encapsulated under the socket.

Many architectures follow some kind of client/server model, where the server is the component that is most static, and the clients are the components that are most dynamic—i.e., they come and go the most. There are sometimes issues of addressing: servers will be visible to clients, but not necessarily vice versa. So mostly it's obvious which node should be doing zmq_bind() (the server) and which should be doing zmq_connect() (the client). It also depends on the kind of sockets you're using, with some exceptions for unusual network architectures. We'll look at socket types later.

Now, imagine we start the client *before* we start the server. In traditional networking, we'd get a big red Fail flag. But ØMQ lets us start and stop pieces arbitrarily. As soon as the client node does zmq_connect(), the connection exists and that node can start to write messages to the socket. At some stage (hopefully before messages queue up so much that they start to get discarded, or the client blocks), the server comes alive, does a zmq_bind(), and ØMQ starts to deliver messages.

A server node can bind to many endpoints (that is, a combination of protocol and address), and it can do this using a single socket. This means it will accept connections across different transports:

```
zmq_bind (socket, "tcp://*:5555");
zmq_bind (socket, "tcp://*:9999");
zmq_bind (socket, "inproc://somename");
```

With most transports, you cannot bind to the same endpoint twice (unlike, for example, in UDP). The ipc transport does, however, let one process bind to an endpoint already used by another process. It's meant to allow a process to recover after a crash.

Although ØMQ tries to be neutral about which side binds and which side connects, there are differences. We'll see these in more detail later. The upshot is that you should usually think in terms of "servers" as static parts of your topology that bind to more or less fixed endpoints, and "clients" as dynamic parts that come and go and connect to these endpoints. Then, design your application around this model. The chances that it will "just work" are much better like that.

Sockets have types. The socket type defines the semantics of the socket: its policies for routing messages inwards and outwards, queuing, etc. You can connect certain types of socket together, such as a publisher socket and a subscriber socket. Sockets work together in "messaging patterns." We'll look at this in more detail later.

It's the ability to connect sockets in these different ways that gives ØMQ its basic power as a message queuing system. There are layers on top of this, such as proxies, which we'll get to later. But essentially, with ØMQ you define your network architecture by plugging pieces together like a child's construction toy.

Using Sockets to Carry Data

To send and receive messages, you use the `zmq_msg_send()` and `zmq_msg_recv()` methods. The names are conventional, but ØMQ's I/O model is different enough from the TCP model (Figure 2-1) that you will need time to get your head around it.

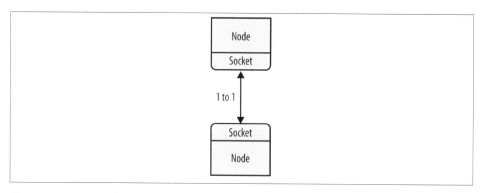

Figure 2-1. TCP sockets are 1-to-1

Let's look at the main differences between TCP sockets and ØMQ sockets when it comes to working with data:

- ØMQ sockets carry messages, like UDP, rather than a stream of bytes as TCP does. A ØMQ message is length-specified binary data. We'll come to messages shortly; their design is optimized for performance and so a little tricky.

- ØMQ sockets do their I/O in a background thread. This means that messages arrive in local input queues and are sent from local output queues, no matter what your application is busy doing.
- ØMQ sockets have 1-to-N routing behavior built in, according to the socket type.

The `zmq_msg_send()` method does not actually send the message to the socket connection(s). It queues the message so that the I/O thread can send it asynchronously. It does not block except in some exception cases. So, the message is not necessarily sent when `zmq_msg_send()` returns to your application.

Unicast Transports

ØMQ provides a set of unicast transports (`inproc`, `ipc`, and `tcp`) and multicast transports (`epgm`, `pgm`). Multicast is an advanced technique that we'll come to later. Don't even start using it unless you know that your fan-out ratios will make 1-to-N unicast impossible.

For most common cases, use `tcp`, which is a *disconnected* TCP transport. It is elastic, portable, and fast enough for most cases. We call this "disconnected" because ØMQ's `tcp` transport doesn't require the endpoint to exist before you connect to it. Clients and servers can connect and bind at any time, can go and come back, and it remains transparent to applications.

The inter-process `ipc` transport is also disconnected. It has one limitation: it does not yet work on Windows. By convention we use endpoint names with an ".ipc" extension to avoid potential conflict with other filenames. On Unix systems, if you use `ipc` endpoints you need to create these with appropriate permissions; otherwise, they may not be shareable between processes running under different user IDs. You must also make sure all processes can access the files, e.g., by running in the same working directory.

The inter-thread transport, `inproc`, is a connected signaling transport. It is much faster than `tcp` or `ipc`. This transport has a specific limitation compared to `tcp` and `ipc`, however *the server must issue a bind request before any client issues a connect*. This is something future versions of ØMQ may fix, but at present this defines how you use `inproc` sockets. We create and bind one socket and start the child threads, which create and connect the other sockets.

ØMQ Is Not a Neutral Carrier

A common question that newcomers to ØMQ ask (it's one I've asked myself) is, "How do I write an XYZ server in ØMQ?" For example, "How do I write an HTTP server in ØMQ?" The implication is that if we use normal sockets to carry HTTP requests and responses, we should be able to use ØMQ sockets to do the same, only much faster and better.

The answer used to be, "This is not how it works." ØMQ is not a neutral carrier; it imposes a framing on the transport protocols it uses. This framing is not compatible with existing protocols, which tend to use their own framing. For example, compare an HTTP request (Figure 2-2) and a ØMQ request (Figure 2-3), both over TCP/IP. The HTTP request uses CRLF (carriage return line feed) as its simplest framing delimiter, whereas ØMQ uses a length-specified frame.

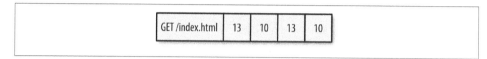

Figure 2-2. HTTP on the wire

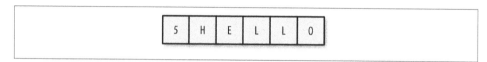

Figure 2-3. ØMQ on the wire

So, you could write an HTTP-like protocol using ØMQ, using for example the request-reply socket pattern. But it would not be HTTP.

Since ØMQ v3.3, however, ØMQ has a socket option called ZMQ_ROUTER_RAW that lets you read and write data without the ØMQ framing. You could use this to read and write proper HTTP requests and responses. Hardeep Singh contributed this change so that he could connect to Telnet servers from his ØMQ application. This is still, at the time of writing, somewhat experimental, but it shows how ØMQ keeps evolving to solve new problems. Maybe the next patch will be yours.

I/O Threads

We said that ØMQ does I/O in a background thread. One I/O thread (for all sockets) is sufficient for all but the most extreme applications. When you create a new context, it starts with one I/O thread. The general rule of thumb is to allow one I/O thread per gigabyte of data in or out per second. To raise the number of I/O threads, use the zmq_ctx_set() call *before* creating any sockets:

```
int io-threads = 4;
void *context = zmq_ctx_new ();
zmq_ctx_set (context, ZMQ_IO_THREADS, io_threads);
assert (zmq_ctx_get (context, ZMQ_IO_THREADS) == io_threads);
```

We've seen that one socket can handle dozens, even thousands of connections at once. This has a fundamental impact on how you write applications. A traditional networked application has one process or one thread per remote connection, and that process or thread handles one socket. ØMQ lets you collapse this entire structure into a single process and then break it up as necessary for scaling.

If you are using ØMQ for inter-thread communications only (i.e., a multithreaded application that does no external socket I/O) you can set the I/O threads to zero. It's not a significant optimization though, more of a curiosity.

Messaging Patterns

Underneath the brown paper wrapping of ØMQ's socket API lies the world of messaging patterns. If you have a background in enterprise messaging, or know UDP well, these will be vaguely familiar. But to most ØMQ newcomers, they are a surprise because we're so used to the TCP paradigm where a socket maps one-to-one to another node.

Let's recap briefly what ØMQ does for you. It delivers blobs of data (messages) to nodes, quickly and efficiently. You can map nodes to threads, processes, or nodes. ØMQ gives your applications a single socket API to work with, no matter what the actual transport is (e.g., in-process, inter-process, TCP, or multicast). It automatically reconnects to peers as they come and go. It queues messages at both sender and receiver, as needed. It manages these queues carefully to ensure processes don't run out of memory, overflowing to disk when appropriate. It handles socket errors. It does all I/O in background threads. It uses lock-free techniques for talking between nodes, so there are never locks, waits, semaphores, or deadlocks.

But cutting through that, it routes and queues messages according to precise recipes called *patterns*. It is these patterns that provide ØMQ's intelligence. They encapsulate our hard-earned experience of the best ways to distribute data and work. ØMQ's patterns are hard-coded, but future versions may allow user-definable patterns.

ØMQ patterns are implemented by pairs of sockets with matching types. In other words, to understand ØMQ patterns you need to understand socket types and how they work together. Mostly, this just takes some studying; there is little that is obvious at this level.

The built-in core ØMQ patterns are:

- *Request-reply*, which connects a set of clients to a set of services. This is a remote procedure call and task distribution pattern.
- *Publish-subscribe*, which connects a set of publishers to a set of subscribers. This is a data distribution pattern.
- *Pipeline*, which connects nodes in a fan-out/fan-in pattern that can have multiple steps and loops. This is a parallel task distribution and collection pattern.

We looked at each of these in the first chapter. There's one more pattern that people tend to try to use when they still think of ØMQ in terms of traditional TCP sockets: *exclusive pair*, which connects two sockets exclusively. This is a pattern you should use only to connect two threads in a process. We'll see an example at the end of this chapter.

The `zmq_socket()` man page is fairly clear about the patterns; it's worth reading it several times until it starts to make sense. These are the socket combinations that are valid for a connect-bind pair (either side can bind):

- PUB and SUB
- REQ and REP
- REQ and ROUTER
- DEALER and REP
- DEALER and ROUTER
- DEALER and DEALER
- ROUTER and ROUTER
- PUSH and PULL
- PAIR and PAIR

You'll also see references to XPUB and XSUB sockets, which we'll come to later (they're like raw versions of PUB and SUB). Any other combination will produce undocumented and unreliable results, and future versions of ØMQ will probably return errors if you try them. You can and will, of course, bridge other socket types via code (i.e., read from one socket type and write to another).

High-Level Messaging Patterns

These four core patterns are cooked into ØMQ. They are part of the ØMQ API, implemented in the core C++ library, and are guaranteed to be available in all fine retail stores.

On top of those, we add *high-level patterns*. We build these high-level patterns on top of ØMQ and implement them in whatever language we're using for our application. They are not part of the core library, do not come with the ØMQ package, and exist in their own space as part of the ØMQ community. For example, the Majordomo pattern, which we explore in Chapter 4 sits in the GitHub Majordomo project in the ØMQ organization.

One of the things we aim to provide you with in this book is a set of such high-level patterns, both small (how to handle messages sanely) and large (how to make a reliable publish-subscribe architecture).

Working with Messages

On the wire, ØMQ messages are blobs of any size, from zero upwards, that fit in memory. You do your own serialization using protobufs, msgpack, JSON, or whatever else your applications need to speak. It's wise to choose a data representation that is portable and fast, but you can make your own decisions about trade-offs.

In memory, ØMQ messages are `zmq_msg_t` structures (or classes, depending on your language). Here are the basic ground rules for using ØMQ messages in C:

- You create and pass around `zmq_msg_t` objects, not blocks of data.
- To read a message, you use `zmq_msg_init()` to create an empty message, and then you pass that to `zmq_msg_recv()`.
- To write a message from new data, you use `zmq_msg_init_size()` to create a message and at the same time allocate a block of data of some size. You then fill that data using `memcpy()`, and pass the message to `zmq_msg_send()`.
- To release (not destroy) a message, you call `zmq_msg_close()`. This drops a reference, and eventually ØMQ will destroy the message.
- To access the message content, you use `zmq_msg_data()`. To know how much data the message contains, use `zmq_msg_size()`.
- Do not use `zmq_msg_move()`, `zmq_msg_copy()`, or `zmq_msg_init_data()` unless you've read the manual pages and know precisely why you need these.

Here is a typical chunk of code working with messages that should be familiar if you have been paying attention. This is from the *zhelpers.h* file we use in all the examples:

```
//  Receive 0MQ string from socket and convert into C string
static char *
s_recv (void *socket) {
    zmq_msg_t message;
    zmq_msg_init (&message);
    int size = zmq_msg_recv (&message, socket, 0);
    if (size == -1)
        return NULL;
    char *string = malloc (size + 1);
    memcpy (string, zmq_msg_data (&message), size);
    zmq_msg_close (&message);
    string [size] = 0;
    return (string);
}

//  Convert C string to 0MQ string and send to socket
static int
s_send (void *socket, char *string) {
    zmq_msg_t message;
    zmq_msg_init_size (&message, strlen (string));
```

```
        memcpy (zmq_msg_data (&message), string, strlen (string));
        int size = zmq_msg_send (&message, socket, 0);
        zmq_msg_close (&message);
        return (size);
    }
```

You can easily extend this code to send and receive blobs of arbitrary length.

> After you pass a message to zmq_msg_send(), ØMQ will clear the mes-
> sage (i.e., set the size to zero). You cannot send the same message twice,
> and you cannot access the message data after sending it.
>
> If you want to send the same message more than once, create a second
> message, initialize it using zmq_msg_init(), and then use
> zmq_msg_copy() to create a copy of the first message. This does not
> copy the data, but rather the reference. You can then send the message
> twice (or more, if you create more copies), and the message will only
> be finally destroyed when the last copy is sent or closed.

ØMQ also supports *multipart* messages, which let you send or receive a list of frames
as a single on-the-wire message. This is widely used in real applications, as we'll see later
in this chapter and in Chapter 3.

Frames (also called "message parts" in the ØMQ reference manual pages) are the basic
wire format for ØMQ messages. A frame is a length-specified block of data. The length
can be from zero upwards. If you've done any TCP programming you'll appreciate why
frames are a useful answer to the question, "How much data am I supposed to read off
this network socket now?"

> There is a wire-level protocol called ZMTP (*http://rfc.zeromq.org/spec:
> 15*) that defines how ØMQ reads and writes frames on a TCP connec-
> tion. If you're interested in how this works, the spec is quite short.

Originally, a ØMQ message was one frame, like UDP. We later extended this with multipart messages, which are quite simply series of frames with a "more" bit set to one,
followed by one with that bit set to zero. The ØMQ API then lets you write messages
with a "more" flag, and when you read messages, it lets you check if there's "more."

In the low-level ØMQ API and the reference manual, therefore, there's some fuzziness
about messages versus parts. So here's a useful lexicon:

- A message can be one or more parts.
- These parts are also called *frames*.

- Each part is a `zmq_msg_t` object.
- You send and receive each part separately, in the low-level API.
- Higher-level APIs provide wrappers to send entire multipart messages.

Some other things that are worth knowing about messages:

- You may send zero-length messages, e.g., for sending a signal from one thread to another.
- ØMQ guarantees to deliver all the parts (one or more) of a message, or none of them.
- ØMQ does not send the message (single or multipart) right away, but at some indeterminate later time. A multipart message must therefore fit in memory.
- A single-part message must also fit in memory. If you want to send files of arbitrary sizes, you should break them into pieces and send each piece as separate single-part messages.
- You must call `zmq_msg_close()` when finished with a message, in languages that don't automatically destroy objects when a scope closes.

And to be necessarily repetitive, do not use `zmq_msg_init_data()` yet. This is a zero-copy method and is guaranteed to create trouble for you. There are far more important things to learn about ØMQ before you start to worry about shaving off microseconds.

Handling Multiple Sockets

The main loop of most examples so far has been:

1. Wait for message on socket.
2. Process message.
3. Repeat.

What if we want to read from multiple endpoints at the same time? The simplest way is to connect one socket to all the endpoints and get ØMQ to do the fan-in for us. This is legal if the remote endpoints are in the same pattern, but it would be wrong to connect a PULL socket to a PUB endpoint, for example.

To actually read from multiple sockets all at once, use `zmq_poll()`. An even better way might be to wrap `zmq_poll()` in a framework that turns it into a nice event-driven *reactor*, but that involves significantly more work than we want to cover here.

Let's start with a dirty hack, partly for the fun of not doing it right, but mainly because it lets me show you how to do non-blocking socket reads. Example 2-1 is a simple example of reading from two sockets using non-blocking reads. This rather confused program acts both as a subscriber to weather updates, and a worker for parallel tasks.

Example 2-1. Multiple socket reader (msreader.c)

```
//
//  Reading from multiple sockets
//  This version uses a simple recv loop
//
#include "zhelpers.h"

int main (void)
{
    //  Prepare our context and sockets
    void *context = zmq_ctx_new ();

    //  Connect to task ventilator
    void *receiver = zmq_socket (context, ZMQ_PULL);
    zmq_connect (receiver, "tcp://localhost:5557");

    //  Connect to weather server
    void *subscriber = zmq_socket (context, ZMQ_SUB);
    zmq_connect (subscriber, "tcp://localhost:5556");
    zmq_setsockopt (subscriber, ZMQ_SUBSCRIBE, "10001 ", 6);

    //  Process messages from both sockets
    //  We prioritize traffic from the task ventilator
    while (1) {
        //  Process any waiting tasks
        int rc;
        for (rc = 0; !rc; ) {
            zmq_msg_t task;
            zmq_msg_init (&task);
            if ((rc = zmq_msg_recv (&task, receiver, ZMQ_DONTWAIT)) != -1) {
                //  Process task
            }
            zmq_msg_close (&task);
        }
        //  Process any waiting weather updates
        for (rc = 0; !rc; ) {
            zmq_msg_t update;
            zmq_msg_init (&update);
            if ((rc = zmq_msg_recv (&update, subscriber, ZMQ_DONTWAIT)) != -1) {
                //  Process weather update
            }
            zmq_msg_close (&update);
        }
        //  No activity, so sleep for 1 msec
        s_sleep (1);
    }
    //  We never get here, but clean up anyhow
    zmq_close (receiver);
```

```
    zmq_close (subscriber);
    zmq_ctx_destroy (context);
    return 0;
}
```

The cost of this approach is some additional latency on the first message (the sleep at the end of the loop, when there are no waiting messages to process). This would be a problem in applications where submillisecond latency was vital. Also, you need to check the documentation for nanosleep() (or whatever function you use) to make sure it does not busy-loop.

You can treat the sockets fairly by reading first from one, then the second, rather than prioritizing them as we did in this example.

Example 2-2 shows the same little senseless application done right, using zmq_poll().

Example 2-2. Multiple socket poller (mspoller.c)

```
//
//  Reading from multiple sockets
//  This version uses zmq_poll()
//
#include "zhelpers.h"

int main (void)
{
    void *context = zmq_ctx_new ();

    //  Connect to task ventilator
    void *receiver = zmq_socket (context, ZMQ_PULL);
    zmq_connect (receiver, "tcp://localhost:5557");

     //  Connect to weather server
    void *subscriber = zmq_socket (context, ZMQ_SUB);
    zmq_connect (subscriber, "tcp://localhost:5556");
    zmq_setsockopt (subscriber, ZMQ_SUBSCRIBE, "10001 ", 6);

    //  Initialize poll set
    zmq_pollitem_t items [] = {
        { receiver, 0, ZMQ_POLLIN, 0 },
        { subscriber, 0, ZMQ_POLLIN, 0 }
    };
    //  Process messages from both sockets
    while (1) {
        zmq_msg_t message;
        zmq_poll (items, 2, -1);
        if (items [0].revents & ZMQ_POLLIN) {
            zmq_msg_init (&message);
            zmq_msg_recv (&message, receiver, 0);
            //  Process task
            zmq_msg_close (&message);
        }
```

```
        if (items [1].revents & ZMQ_POLLIN) {
            zmq_msg_init (&message);
            zmq_msg_recv (&message, subscriber, 0);
            //  Process weather update
            zmq_msg_close (&message);
        }
    }
    //  We never get here
    zmq_close (receiver);
    zmq_close (subscriber);
    zmq_ctx_destroy (context);
    return 0;
}
```

The items structure has these four members:

```
typedef struct {
    void *socket;       //  0MQ socket to poll on
    int fd;             //  OR, native file handle to poll on
    short events;       //  Events to poll on
    short revents;      //  Events returned after poll
} zmq_pollitem_t;
```

Multipart Messages

ØMQ lets us compose a message out of several frames, giving us a "multipart message." Realistic applications use multipart messages heavily, both for wrapping messages with address information and for simple serialization. We'll look at reply envelopes later. What we'll learn now is simply how to safely (but blindly) read and write multipart messages in any application (like a proxy) that needs to forward messages without inspecting them.

When you work with multipart messages, each part is a zmq_msg item. For example, if you are sending a message with five parts, you must construct, send, and destroy five zmq_msg items. You can do this in advance (and store the zmq_msg items in an array or structure), or as you send them, one by one.

Here is how we send the frames in a multipart message (we receive each frame into a message object):

```
zmq_msg_send (socket, &message, ZMQ_SNDMORE);
...
zmq_msg_send (socket, &message, ZMQ_SNDMORE);
...
zmq_msg_send (socket, &message, 0);
```

Here is how we receive and process all the parts in a message, be it single part or multipart:

```
while (1) {
    zmq_msg_t message;
```

```
    zmq_msg_init (&message);
    zmq_msg_recv (socket, &message, 0);
    //  Process the message frame
    zmq_msg_close (&message);
    int more;
    size_t more_size = sizeof (more);
    zmq_getsockopt (socket, ZMQ_RCVMORE, &more, &more_size);
    if (!more)
        break;        //  Last message frame
}
```

Some things to know about multipart messages:

- When you send a multipart message, the first part and all following parts are only actually sent on the wire when you send the final part.
- If you are using `zmq_poll()`, when you receive the first part of a message, all the rest has also arrived.
- You will receive all parts of a message, or none at all.
- Each part of a message is a separate `zmq_msg` item.
- You will receive all parts of a message whether or not you set the RCVMORE option.
- On sending, ØMQ queues message frames in memory until the last is received, and then sends them all.
- There is no way to cancel a partially sent message, except by closing the socket.

Intermediaries and Proxies

ØMQ aims for decentralized intelligence, but that doesn't mean your network is empty space in the middle. It's filled with message-aware infrastructure, and quite often, you build that infrastructure with ØMQ. The ØMQ plumbing can range from tiny pipes to full-blown service-oriented brokers. The messaging industry calls this *intermediation*, meaning that the stuff in the middle deals with either side. In ØMQ, we call these proxies, queues, forwarders, devices, or brokers, depending on the context.

This pattern is extremely common in the real world and is why our societies and economies are filled with intermediaries who have no other real function than to reduce the complexity and scaling costs of larger networks. Real-world intermediaries are typically called wholesalers, distributors, managers, and so on.

The Dynamic Discovery Problem

One of the problems you will hit as you design larger distributed architectures is discovery. That is, how do pieces know about each other? It's especially difficult if pieces come and go; thus, we can call this the "dynamic discovery problem."

There are several solutions to dynamic discovery. The simplest is to entirely avoid it by hard-coding (or configuring) the network architecture so discovery is done by hand. That is, when you add a new piece, you reconfigure the network to know about it.

In practice, this leads to increasingly fragile and unwieldy architectures. Let's say you have one publisher and a hundred subscribers. You connect each subscriber to the publisher by configuring a publisher endpoint in each subscriber. That's easy (Figure 2-4). Subscribers are dynamic; the publisher is static. Now say you add more publishers. Suddenly, it's not so easy any more. If you continue to connect each subscriber to each publisher, the cost of avoiding dynamic discovery gets higher and higher.

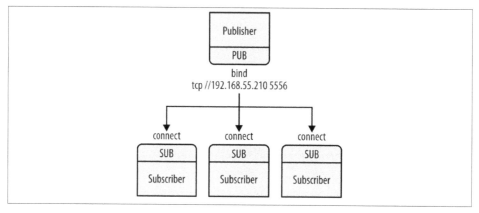

Figure 2-4. Small-scale pub-sub network

There are quite a few solutions to this problem, but the very simplest is to add an intermediary; that is, a static point in the network to which all other nodes connect. In classic messaging, this is the job of the message broker. ØMQ doesn't come with a message broker as such, but it lets us build intermediaries quite easily.

You might wonder, if all networks eventually get large enough to need intermediaries, why don't we simply have a message broker in place for all applications? For beginners, it's a fair compromise. Just always use a star topology, forget about performance, and things will usually work. However, message brokers are greedy things; in their role as central intermediaries, they become too complex, too stateful, and eventually a problem.

It's better to think of intermediaries as simple stateless message switches. The best analogy is an HTTP proxy; it's there, but doesn't have any special role. Adding a pub-sub proxy solves the dynamic discovery problem in our example. We set the proxy in the "middle" of the network (Figure 2-5). The proxy opens an XSUB socket and an XPUB socket, and binds each to well-known IP addresses and ports. Then, all other processes connect to the proxy, instead of to each other. It becomes trivial to add more subscribers or publishers.

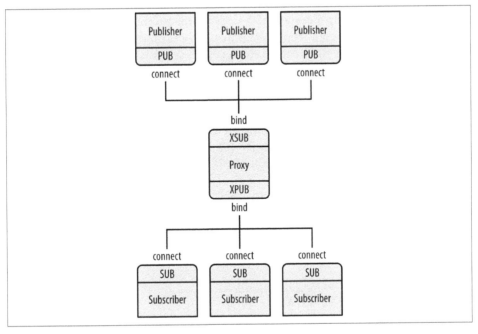

Figure 2-5. Pub-sub network with a proxy

We need XPUB and XSUB sockets because ØMQ does subscription forwarding: SUB sockets actually send subscriptions to PUB sockets as special messages. The proxy has to forward these as well, by reading them from the XPUB socket and writing them to the XSUB socket. This is the main use case for XSUB and XPUB (Figure 2-6).

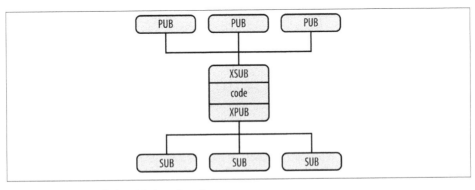

Figure 2-6. Extended publish-subscribe

Shared Queue (DEALER and ROUTER Sockets)

In the "Hello World" client/server application, we have one client that talks to one service. However, in real cases we usually need to allow multiple services as well as multiple clients. This lets us scale up the power of the service (many threads or processes or nodes rather than just one). The only constraint is that services must be stateless, with all state being in the request or in some shared storage, such as a database.

There are two ways to connect multiple clients to multiple servers. The brute-force way is to connect each client socket to multiple service endpoints. One client socket can connect to multiple service sockets, and the REQ socket will then distribute requests among these services. Let's say you connect a client socket to three service endpoints: A, B, and C. The client makes requests R1, R2, R3, R4. R1 and R4 go to service A, R2 goes to B, and R3 goes to service C (Figure 2-7).

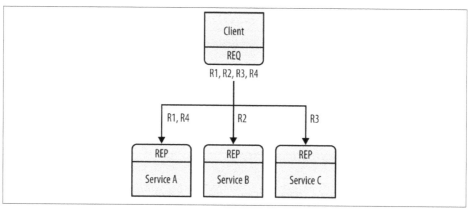

Figure 2-7. Request distribution

This design lets you add more clients cheaply. You can also add more services. Each client will distribute its requests to the services. But each client has to know the service topology. If you have 100 clients and then you decide to add three more services, you need to reconfigure and restart all 100 clients in order for the clients to know about the three new services.

That's clearly not the kind of thing we want to be doing at 3 a.m. when our supercomputing cluster has run out of resources and we desperately need to add a couple of hundred of new service nodes. Too many static pieces are like liquid concrete: knowledge is distributed, and the more static pieces you have, the more effort it is to change the topology. What we want is something sitting in between clients and services that centralizes all knowledge of the topology. Ideally, we should be able to add and remove services or clients at any time without touching any other part of the topology.

So, we'll write a little message queuing broker that gives us this flexibility. The broker binds to two endpoints, a frontend for clients and a backend for services. It then uses zmq_poll() to monitor these two sockets for activity, and when it has some, it shuttles messages between its two sockets. It doesn't actually manage any queues explicitly— ØMQ does that automatically on each socket.

When you use REQ to talk to REP, you get a strictly synchronous request-reply dialog. The client sends a request. The service reads the request and sends a reply. The client then reads the reply. If either the client or the service tries to do anything else (e.g., sending two requests in a row without waiting for a response), it will get an error.

But our broker has to be non-blocking. Obviously, we can use zmq_poll() to wait for activity on either socket, but we can't use REP and REQ.

Luckily, there are two sockets called DEALER and ROUTER that let you do non-blocking request-response. You'll see in Chapter 3 how DEALER and ROUTER sockets let you build all kinds of asynchronous request-reply flows. For now, we're just going to see how DEALER and ROUTER let us extend REQ-REP across an intermediary— that is, our little broker.

In this simple extended request-reply pattern, REQ talks to ROUTER and DEALER talks to REP. In between the DEALER and ROUTER, we have to have code (like our broker) that pulls messages off one socket and shoves them onto the other (Figure 2-8).

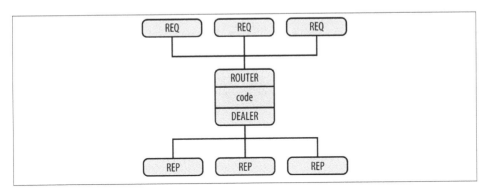

Figure 2-8. Extended request-reply

The request-reply broker binds to two endpoints, one for clients to connect to (the frontend socket) and one for workers to connect to (the backend). To test this broker, you will want to change your workers so they connect to the backend socket. Example 2-3 is a client that shows what I mean.

Example 2-3. Request-reply client (rrclient.c)

```
//
//  Hello World client
//  Connects REQ socket to tcp://localhost:5559
//  Sends "Hello" to server, expects "World" back
//
#include "zhelpers.h"

int main (void)
{
    void *context = zmq_ctx_new ();

    //  Socket to talk to server
    void *requester = zmq_socket (context, ZMQ_REQ);
    zmq_connect (requester, "tcp://localhost:5559");

    int request_nbr;
    for (request_nbr = 0; request_nbr != 10; request_nbr++) {
        s_send (requester, "Hello");
        char *string = s_recv (requester);
        printf ("Received reply %d [%s]\n", request_nbr, string);
        free (string);
    }
    zmq_close (requester);
    zmq_ctx_destroy (context);
    return 0;
}
```

The code for the worker is in Example 2-4.

Example 2-4. Request-reply worker (rrworker.c)

```
//
//  Hello World worker
//  Connects REP socket to tcp://*:5560
//  Expects "Hello" from client, replies with "World"
//
#include "zhelpers.h"

int main (void)
{
    void *context = zmq_ctx_new ();

    //  Socket to talk to clients
    void *responder = zmq_socket (context, ZMQ_REP);
    zmq_connect (responder, "tcp://localhost:5560");
```

```
while (1) {
    //  Wait for next request from client
    char *string = s_recv (responder);
    printf ("Received request: [%s]\n", string);
    free (string);

    //  Do some 'work'
    sleep (1);

    //  Send reply back to client
    s_send (responder, "World");
}
//  We never get here, but clean up anyhow
zmq_close (responder);
zmq_ctx_destroy (context);
return 0;
}
```

And finally, the code for the broker, which properly handles multipart messages, is in
Example 2-5.

Example 2-5. Request-reply broker (rrbroker.c)

```
//
//  Simple request-reply broker
//
#include "zhelpers.h"

int main (void)
{
    //  Prepare our context and sockets
    void *context = zmq_ctx_new ();
    void *frontend = zmq_socket (context, ZMQ_ROUTER);
    void *backend  = zmq_socket (context, ZMQ_DEALER);
    zmq_bind (frontend, "tcp://*:5559");
    zmq_bind (backend,  "tcp://*:5560");

    //  Initialize poll set
    zmq_pollitem_t items [] = {
        { frontend, 0, ZMQ_POLLIN, 0 },
        { backend,  0, ZMQ_POLLIN, 0 }
    };
    //  Switch messages between sockets
    while (1) {
        zmq_msg_t message;
        int more;              //  Multipart detection

        zmq_poll (items, 2, -1);
        if (items [0].revents & ZMQ_POLLIN) {
            while (1) {
                //  Process all parts of the message
```

```
            zmq_msg_init (&message);
            zmq_msg_recv (&message, frontend, 0);
            size_t more_size = sizeof (more);
            zmq_getsockopt (frontend, ZMQ_RCVMORE, &more, &more_size);
            zmq_msg_send (&message, backend, more? ZMQ_SNDMORE: 0);
            zmq_msg_close (&message);
            if (!more)
                break;      //  Last message part
        }
    }
    if (items [1].revents & ZMQ_POLLIN) {
        while (1) {
            //  Process all parts of the message
            zmq_msg_init (&message);
            zmq_msg_recv (&message, backend, 0);
            size_t more_size = sizeof (more);
            zmq_getsockopt (backend, ZMQ_RCVMORE, &more, &more_size);
            zmq_msg_send (&message, frontend, more? ZMQ_SNDMORE: 0);
            zmq_msg_close (&message);
            if (!more)
                break;      //  Last message part
        }
    }
}
//  We never get here, but clean up anyhow
zmq_close (frontend);
zmq_close (backend);
zmq_ctx_destroy (context);
return 0;
}
```

Using a request-reply broker makes your client/server architectures easier to scale, because clients don't see workers and workers don't see clients. The only static node is the broker in the middle (Figure 2-9).

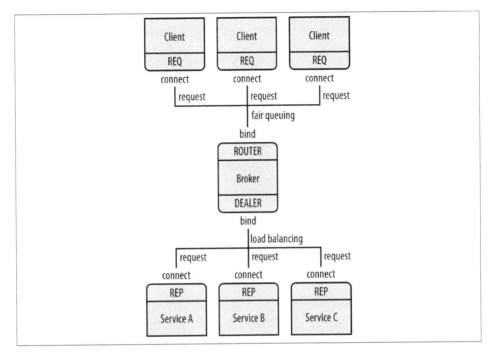

Figure 2-9. Request-reply broker

ØMQ's Built-in Proxy Function

It turns out that the core loop in the previous section's *rrbroker* is very useful, and reusable. It lets us build pub-sub forwarders and shared queues and other little intermediaries with very little effort. ØMQ wraps this up in a single method, zmq_proxy():

```
zmq_proxy (frontend, backend, capture);
```

The two sockets (or three if we want to capture data) must be properly connected, bound, and configured. When we call the zmq_proxy() method, it's exactly like starting the main loop of *rrbroker*. Let's rewrite the request-reply broker to call zmq_proxy(), and re-badge this as an expensive-sounding "message queue" (people have charged houses for code that did less). Example 2-6 shows the result.

Example 2-6. Message queue broker (msgqueue.c)

```
//
//  Simple message queuing broker
//  Same as request-reply broker but using QUEUE device
//
#include "zhelpers.h"

int main (void)
{
```

```
    void *context = zmq_ctx_new ();

    //  Socket facing clients
    void *frontend = zmq_socket (context, ZMQ_ROUTER);
    int rc = zmq_bind (frontend, "tcp://*:5559");
    assert (rc == 0);

    //  Socket facing services
    void *backend = zmq_socket (context, ZMQ_DEALER);
    rc = zmq_bind (backend, "tcp://*:5560");
    assert (rc == 0);

    //  Start the proxy
    zmq_proxy (frontend, backend, NULL);

    //  We never get here...
    zmq_close (frontend);
    zmq_close (backend);
    zmq_ctx_destroy (context);
    return 0;
}
```

If you're like most ØMQ users, at this stage you're starting to think, "What kind of evil stuff can I do if I plug random socket types into the proxy?" The short answer is: try it and work out what is happening. In practice, you would usually stick to ROUTER/ DEALER, XSUB/XPUB, or PULL/PUSH.

Transport Bridging

A frequent request from ØMQ users is, "How do I connect my ØMQ network with technology X?" where X is some other networking or messaging technology. The simple answer is to build a "bridge." A bridge is a small application that speaks one protocol at one socket, and converts to/from a second protocol at another socket. A protocol interpreter, if you like. A common bridging problem in ØMQ is to bridge two transports or networks.

As an example, we're going to write a little proxy (Example 2-7) that sits in between a publisher and a set of subscribers, bridging two networks. The frontend socket (SUB) faces the internal network where the weather server is sitting, and the backend (PUB) faces subscribers on the external network. It subscribes to the weather service on the frontend socket, and republishes its data on the backend socket (Figure 2-10).

Example 2-7. Weather update proxy (wuproxy.c)

```
//
//  Weather proxy device
//
#include "zhelpers.h"

int main (void)
```

```
{
    void *context = zmq_ctx_new ();

    //  This is where the weather server sits
    void *frontend = zmq_socket (context, ZMQ_XSUB);
    zmq_connect (frontend, "tcp://192.168.55.210:5556");

    //  This is our public endpoint for subscribers
    void *backend = zmq_socket (context, ZMQ_XPUB);
    zmq_bind (backend, "tcp://10.1.1.0:8100");

    //  Run the proxy until the user interrupts us
    zmq_proxy (frontend, backend, NULL);

    zmq_close (frontend);
    zmq_close (backend);
    zmq_ctx_destroy (context);
    return 0;
}
```

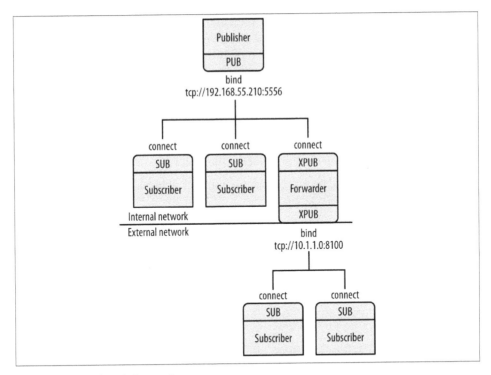

Figure 2-10. Pub-sub forwarder proxy

It looks very similar to the earlier proxy example, but the key part is that the frontend and backend sockets are on two different networks. We can use this model, for example, to connect a multicast network (pgm transport) to a TCP publisher.

Handling Errors and ETERM

ØMQ's error handling philosophy is a mix of fail fast and resilience. Processes, we believe, should be as vulnerable as possible to internal errors, and as robust as possible against external attacks and errors. To give an analogy, a living cell will self-destruct if it detects a single internal error, yet it will resist attack from the outside by all means possible.

Assertions, which pepper the ØMQ code, are absolutely vital to robust code; they just have to be on the right side of the cellular wall. And there should be such a wall. If it is unclear whether a fault is internal or external, that is a design flaw to be fixed. In C/C++, assertions stop the application immediately with an error. In other languages, you may get exceptions or halts.

When ØMQ detects an external fault, it returns an error to the calling code. In some rare cases, it drops messages silently if there is no obvious strategy for recovering from the error.

In most of the C examples we've seen so far, there's been no error handling. *Real code should do error handling on every single ØMQ call.* If you're using a language binding other than C, the binding may handle errors for you. In C, you do need to do this yourself. There are some simple rules, starting with POSIX conventions:

- Methods that create objects return NULL if they fail.
- Methods that process data may return the number of bytes processed, or -1 on an error or failure.
- Other methods return 0 on success and -1 on an error or failure.
- The error code is provided in errno or zmq_errno().
- Descriptive error text for logging is provided by zmq_strerror().

For example:

```
void *context = zmq_ctx_new ();
assert (context);
void *socket = zmq_socket (context, ZMQ_REP);
assert (socket);
int rc = zmq_bind (socket, "tcp://*:5555");
if (rc != 0) {
    printf ("E: bind failed: %s\n", strerror (errno));
    return -1;
}
```

There are two main exceptional conditions that you may want to handle as nonfatal:

- When a thread calls `zmq_msg_recv()` with the `ZMQ_DONTWAIT` option and there is no waiting data, ØMQ will return `-1` and set `errno` to `EAGAIN`.
- When a thread calls `zmq_ctx_destroy()` and other threads are doing blocking work, the `zmq_ctx_destroy()` call closes the context and all blocking calls exit with `-1` and `errno` set to `ETERM`.

In C/C++, asserts can be removed entirely in optimized code, so don't make the mistake of wrapping the whole ØMQ call in an `assert()`. It looks neat; then the optimizer removes all the asserts and the calls you want to make, and your application breaks in impressive ways.

Let's see how to shut down a process cleanly. We'll take the parallel pipeline example from the previous section. If we've started a whole lot of workers in the background, we now want to kill them when the batch is finished. Let's do this by sending a kill message to the workers. The best place to do this is the sink, because it really knows when the batch is done.

How do we connect the sink to the workers? The PUSH/PULL sockets are one-way only. The standard ØMQ answer is: create a new socket flow for each type of problem you need to solve. We'll use a publish-subscribe model to send kill messages to the workers:

- The sink creates a PUB socket on a new endpoint.
- Workers bind their input sockets to this endpoint.
- When the sink detects the end of the batch, it sends a kill to its PUB socket.
- When a worker detects this kill message, it exits.

It doesn't take much new code in the sink:

```
void *control = zmq_socket (context, ZMQ_PUB);
zmq_bind (control, "tcp://*:5559");
...
//  Send kill signal to workers
zmq_msg_init_data (&message, "KILL", 5);
zmq_msg_send (control, &message, 0);
zmq_msg_close (&message);
```

Figure 2-11 illustrates the resulting configuration.

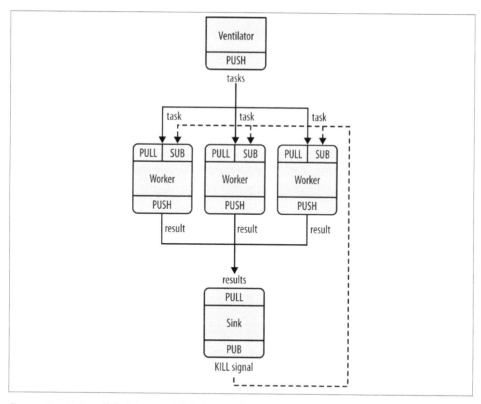

Figure 2-11. Parallel pipeline with kill signaling

Example 2-8 contains the code for the worker process, which manages two sockets (a PULL socket getting tasks, and a SUB socket getting control commands) using the zmq_poll() technique we saw earlier.

Example 2-8. Parallel task worker with kill signaling (taskwork2.c)

```
//
//  Task worker - design 2
//  Adds pub-sub flow to receive and respond to kill signal
//
#include "zhelpers.h"

int main (void)
{
    void *context = zmq_ctx_new ();

    //  Socket to receive messages on
    void *receiver = zmq_socket (context, ZMQ_PULL);
    zmq_connect (receiver, "tcp://localhost:5557");

    //  Socket to send messages to
```

```
    void *sender = zmq_socket (context, ZMQ_PUSH);
    zmq_connect (sender, "tcp://localhost:5558");

    //  Socket for control input
    void *controller = zmq_socket (context, ZMQ_SUB);
    zmq_connect (controller, "tcp://localhost:5559");
    zmq_setsockopt (controller, ZMQ_SUBSCRIBE, "", 0);

    //  Process messages from receiver and controller
    zmq_pollitem_t items [] = {
        { receiver, 0, ZMQ_POLLIN, 0 },
        { controller, 0, ZMQ_POLLIN, 0 }
    };
    //  Process messages from both sockets
    while (1) {
        zmq_msg_t message;
        zmq_poll (items, 2, -1);
        if (items [0].revents & ZMQ_POLLIN) {
            zmq_msg_init (&message);
            zmq_msg_recv (&message, receiver, 0);

            //  Do the work
            s_sleep (atoi ((char *) zmq_msg_data (&message)));

            //  Send results to sink
            zmq_msg_init (&message);
            zmq_msg_send (&message, sender, 0);

            //  Simple progress indicator for the viewer
            printf (".");
            fflush (stdout);

            zmq_msg_close (&message);
        }
        //  Any waiting controller command acts as 'KILL'
        if (items [1].revents & ZMQ_POLLIN)
            break;                          //  Exit loop
    }
    //  Finished
    zmq_close (receiver);
    zmq_close (sender);
    zmq_close (controller);
    zmq_ctx_destroy (context);
    return 0;
}
```

Example 2-9 shows the modified sink application. When it's finished collecting results, it broadcasts a kill message to all workers.

Example 2-9. Parallel task sink with kill signaling (tasksink2.c)

```
//
//  Task sink - design 2
//  Adds pub-sub flow to send kill signal to workers
//
#include "zhelpers.h"

int main (void)
{
    void *context = zmq_ctx_new ();

    //  Socket to receive messages on
    void *receiver = zmq_socket (context, ZMQ_PULL);
    zmq_bind (receiver, "tcp://*:5558");

    //  Socket for worker control
    void *controller = zmq_socket (context, ZMQ_PUB);
    zmq_bind (controller, "tcp://*:5559");

    //  Wait for start of batch
    char *string = s_recv (receiver);
    free (string);

    //  Start our clock now
    int64_t start_time = s_clock ();

    //  Process 100 confirmations
    int task_nbr;
    for (task_nbr = 0; task_nbr < 100; task_nbr++) {
        char *string = s_recv (receiver);
        free (string);
        if ((task_nbr / 10) * 10 == task_nbr)
            printf (":");
        else
            printf (".");
        fflush (stdout);
    }
    printf ("Total elapsed time: %d msec\n",
        (int) (s_clock () - start_time));

    //  Send kill signal to workers
    s_send (controller, "KILL");

    //  Finished
    sleep (1);                  //  Give 0MQ time to deliver

    zmq_close (receiver);
    zmq_close (controller);
    zmq_ctx_destroy (context);
    return 0;
}
```

Handling Interrupt Signals

Realistic applications need to shut down cleanly when interrupted with Ctrl-C or another signal, such as SIGTERM. By default, these simply kill the process, meaning messages won't be flushed, files won't be closed cleanly, and so on.

Example 2-10 shows how we handle signals in various languages.

Example 2-10. Handling Ctrl-C cleanly (interrupt.c)

```
//
//  Shows how to handle Ctrl-C
//
#include <zmq.h>
#include <stdio.h>
#include <signal.h>


//  ----------------------------------------------------------------
//  Signal handling
//
//  Call s_catch_signals() in your application at startup, and then exit
//  your main loop if s_interrupted is ever 1. Works especially well with
//  zmq_poll.

static int s_interrupted = 0;
static void s_signal_handler (int signal_value)
{
    s_interrupted = 1;
}

static void s_catch_signals (void)
{
    struct sigaction action;
    action.sa_handler = s_signal_handler;
    action.sa_flags = 0;
    sigemptyset (&action.sa_mask);
    sigaction (SIGINT, &action, NULL);
    sigaction (SIGTERM, &action, NULL);
}

int main (void)
{
    void *context = zmq_ctx_new ();
    void *socket = zmq_socket (context, ZMQ_REP);
    zmq_bind (socket, "tcp://*:5555");

    s_catch_signals ();
    while (1) {
        //  Blocking read will exit on a signal
        zmq_msg_t message;
        zmq_msg_init (&message);
        zmq_msg_recv (&message, socket, 0);
```

```
            if (s_interrupted) {
                printf ("W: interrupt received, killing server...\n");
                break;
            }
        }
        zmq_close (socket);
        zmq_ctx_destroy (context);
        return 0;
    }
```

The program provides s_catch_signals(), which traps Ctrl-C (SIGINT) and SIG
TERM. When either of these signals arrive, the s_catch_signals() handler sets the global
variable s_interrupted. Thanks to your signal handler, your application will not die
automatically. Instead, you have a chance to clean up and exit gracefully. You have to
now explicitly check for an interrupt and handle it properly. Do this by calling
s_catch_signals() (copy this from *interrupt.c*) at the start of your main code. This
sets up the signal handling. The interrupt will affect ØMQ calls as follows:

- If your code is blocking in zmq_msg_recv(), zmq_poll(), or zmq_msg_send(), when
  a signal arrives, the call will return with EINTR.

- Wrappers like s_recv() return NULL if they are interrupted.

So, check for an EINTR return code, a NULL return, and/or s_interrupted.

Here is a typical code fragment:

```
    s_catch_signals ();
    client = zmq_socket (...);
    while (!s_interrupted) {
        char *message = s_recv (client);
        if (!message)
            break;          // Ctrl-C used
    }
    zmq_close (client);
```

If you call s_catch_signals() and don't test for interrupts, your application will become immune to Ctrl-C and SIGTERM, which may be useful but is usually not.

Detecting Memory Leaks

Any long-running application has to manage memory correctly, or eventually it'll use
up all available memory and crash. If you use a language that handles this automatically
for you, congratulations. If you program in C or C++ or any other language where you're
responsible for memory management, here's a short tutorial on using *valgrind* (*http://
valgrind.org*), which, among other things, will report on any leaks your programs have:

- To install valgrind, such as on Ubuntu or Debian, issue:

```
sudo apt-get install valgrind
```

- By default, ØMQ will cause valgrind to complain a lot. To remove these warnings, create a file called *valgrind.supp* that contains this:

```
{
    <socketcall_sendto>
    Memcheck:Param
    socketcall.sendto(msg)
    fun:send
    ...
}
{
    <socketcall_sendto>
    Memcheck:Param
    socketcall.send(msg)
    fun:send
    ...
}
```

- Fix your applications to exit cleanly after Ctrl-C. For any application that exits by itself, that's not needed, but for long-running applications, this is essential. Otherwise, valgrind will complain about all currently allocated memory.
- Build your application with *-DDEBUG*, if it's not your default setting. That ensures valgrind can tell you exactly where memory is being leaked.
- Finally, run valgrind as follows (all on one line)

```
valgrind --tool=memcheck --leak-check=full --suppressions=valgrind.supp
                            someprog
```

After fixing any errors it reports, you should get the pleasant message:

```
==30536== ERROR SUMMARY: 0 errors from 0 contexts...
```

Multithreading with ØMQ

ØMQ is perhaps the nicest way ever to write multithreaded (MT) applications. Whereas ØMQ sockets require some readjustment if you are used to traditional sockets, ØMQ multithreading will take everything you know about writing MT applications, throw it into a heap in the garden, pour gasoline over it, and set it alight. It's a rare book that deserves burning, but most books on concurrent programming do.

To make utterly perfect MT programs (and I mean that literally), *we don't need mutexes, locks, or any other form of inter-thread communication except messages sent across ØMQ sockets.*

By "perfect" MT programs, I mean code that's easy to write and understand, that works with the same design approach in any programming language and on any operating system, and that scales across any number of CPUs with zero wait states and no point of diminishing returns.

If you've spent years learning tricks to make your MT code work at all, let alone rapidly, with locks and semaphores and critical sections, you will be disgusted when you realize it was all for nothing. If there's one lesson we've learned from 30+ years of concurrent programming, it is: *just don't share state*. It's like two drunkards trying to share a beer. It doesn't matter if they're good buddies. Sooner or later, they're going to get into a fight. And the more drunkards you add to the table, the more they fight each other over the beer. The tragic majority of MT applications look like drunken bar fights.

The list of weird problems that you need to fight as you write classic shared-state MT code would be hilarious if it didn't translate directly into stress and risk, as code that seems to work suddenly fails under pressure. A few years ago, a large firm with world-beating experience in buggy code released its list of "11 Likely Problems in Your Mul-tithreaded Code," which covers forgotten synchronization, incorrect granularity, read and write tearing, lock-free reordering, lock convoys, the two-step dance, and priority inversion.

Yeah, we counted seven problems, not eleven. That's not the point, though. The point is, do you really want code running the power grid or stock market to start getting two-step lock convoys at 3 p.m. on a busy Thursday? Who cares what the terms actually mean? This is not what turned us on to programming, fighting ever more complex side effects with ever more complex hacks.

Some widely used models, despite being the basis for entire industries, are fundamen-tally broken, and shared state concurrency is one of them. Code that wants to scale without limit does it like the Internet does, by sending messages and sharing nothing except a common contempt for broken programming models.

You should follow some rules to write happy multithreaded code with ØMQ:

- You must not access the same data from multiple threads. Using classic MT tech-niques like mutexes is an anti-pattern in ØMQ applications. The only exception to this is a ØMQ context object, which is threadsafe.

- You must create a ØMQ context for your process, and pass that to all threads that you want to connect via `inproc` sockets.

- You may treat threads as separate tasks with their own context, but these threads cannot communicate over `inproc`. However, they will be easier to break into stand-alone processes afterwards.

- You must not share ØMQ sockets between threads. ØMQ sockets are not thread-safe. Technically it's possible to do this, but it demands semaphores, locks, or mutexes. This will make your application slow and fragile. The only place where it's remotely sane to share sockets between threads is in language bindings that need to do magic like garbage collection on sockets.

If you need to start more than one proxy in an application, for example, you will want to run each in its own thread. It is easy to make the error of creating the proxy frontend and backend sockets in one thread, and then passing the sockets to the proxy in another thread. This may appear to work but will fail randomly. Remember: *do not use or close sockets except in the thread that created them.*

If you follow these rules, you can quite easily split threads into separate processes when you need to. Application logic can sit in threads, processes or nodes: whatever your scale needs.

ØMQ uses native OS threads rather than virtual "green" threads. The advantages are that you don't need to learn any new threading API, and that ØMQ threads map cleanly to your operating system. You can use standard tools like Intel's ThreadChecker to see what your application is doing. The disadvantages are that your code, when it for instance starts new threads, won't be portable, and that if you have a huge number of threads (in the thousands), some operating systems will get stressed.

Let's see how this works in practice. We'll turn our old Hello World server into something more capable. The original server ran in a single thread. If the work per request is low, that's fine: one ØMQ thread can run at full speed on a CPU core, with no waits, doing an awful lot of work. But realistic servers have to do nontrivial work per request. A single core may not be enough when 10,000 clients hit the server all at once. So a realistic server must start multiple worker threads. It then accepts requests as fast as it can and distributes these to its worker threads. The worker threads grind through the work and eventually send their replies back.

You can, of course, do all this using a proxy broker and external worker processes, but often it's easier to start one process that gobbles up 16 cores than 16 processes, each gobbling up one core. Further, running workers as threads will cut out a network hop, latency, and network traffic.

The MT version of the Hello World service in Example 2-11 basically collapses the broker and workers into a single process. We use `pthreads` because it's the most widespread standard for multithreading.

Example 2-11. Multithreaded service (mtserver.c)

```
//
//  Multithreaded Hello World server
//
#include "zhelpers.h"
#include <pthread.h>
```

```
static void *
worker_routine (void *context) {
    //  Socket to talk to dispatcher
    void *receiver = zmq_socket (context, ZMQ_REP);
    zmq_connect (receiver, "inproc://workers");

    while (1) {
        char *string = s_recv (receiver);
        printf ("Received request: [%s]\n", string);
        free (string);
        //  Do some 'work'
        sleep (1);
        //  Send reply back to client
        s_send (receiver, "World");
    }
    zmq_close (receiver);
    return NULL;
}

int main (void)
{
    void *context = zmq_ctx_new ();

    //  Socket to talk to clients
    void *clients = zmq_socket (context, ZMQ_ROUTER);
    zmq_bind (clients, "tcp://*:5555");

    //  Socket to talk to workers
    void *workers = zmq_socket (context, ZMQ_DEALER);
    zmq_bind (workers, "inproc://workers");

    //  Launch pool of worker threads
    int thread_nbr;
    for (thread_nbr = 0; thread_nbr < 5; thread_nbr++) {
        pthread_t worker;
        pthread_create (&worker, NULL, worker_routine, context);
    }
    //  Connect work threads to client threads via a queue proxy
    zmq_proxy (clients, workers, NULL);

    //  We never get here, but clean up anyhow
    zmq_close (clients);
    zmq_close (workers);
    zmq_ctx_destroy (context);
    return 0;
}
```

All the code should be recognizable to you by now. Here's how it works:

- The server starts a set of worker threads. Each worker thread creates a REP socket and then processes requests on this socket. Worker threads are just like single-threaded servers. The only differences are the transport (`inproc` instead of `tcp`) and the bind-connect direction.

- The server creates a ROUTER socket to talk to clients and binds this to its external interface (over `tcp`).

- The server creates a DEALER socket to talk to the workers and binds this to its internal interface (over `inproc`).

- The server starts a proxy that connects the two sockets. The proxy pulls incoming requests fairly from all clients and distributes those out to workers. It also routes replies back to their origin.

Note that creating threads is not portable in most programming languages. The POSIX library is `pthreads`, but on Windows you have to use a different API. In our example, the `pthread_create()` call starts up a new thread running the `worker_routine()` function we defined. We'll see in Chapter 3 how to wrap this in a portable API.

Here, the "work" is just a one-second pause. We could do anything in the workers, though, including talking to other nodes. Figure 2-12 shows what the MT server looks like in terms of ØMQ sockets and nodes. Note how the request-reply chain is REQ-ROUTER-queue-DEALER-REP.

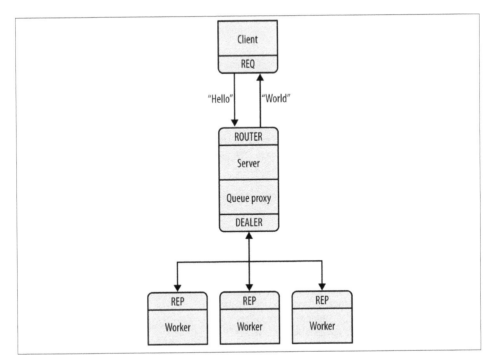

Figure 2-12. Multithreaded server

Signaling Between Threads (PAIR Sockets)

When you start making multithreaded applications with ØMQ, you'll encounter the question of how to coordinate your threads. Though you might be tempted to insert "sleep" statements, or use multithreading techniques such as semaphores or mutexes, *the only mechanism that you should use is ØMQ messages.* Remember the story of the drunkards and the beer.

Let's make three threads that signal each other when they are ready (Figure 2-13). In Example 2-12, we use PAIR sockets over the `inproc` transport.

Example 2-12. Multithreaded relay (mtrelay.c)

```
//
//  Multithreaded relay
//
#include "zhelpers.h"
#include <pthread.h>

static void *
step1 (void *context) {
    //  Connect to step2 and tell it we're ready
    void *xmitter = zmq_socket (context, ZMQ_PAIR);
    zmq_connect (xmitter, "inproc://step2");
    printf ("Step 1 ready, signaling step 2\n");
    s_send (xmitter, "READY");
    zmq_close (xmitter);

    return NULL;
}

static void *
step2 (void *context) {
    //  Bind inproc socket before starting step1
    void *receiver = zmq_socket (context, ZMQ_PAIR);
    zmq_bind (receiver, "inproc://step2");
    pthread_t thread;
    pthread_create (&thread, NULL, step1, context);

    //  Wait for signal and pass it on
    char *string = s_recv (receiver);
    free (string);
    zmq_close (receiver);

    //  Connect to step3 and tell it we're ready
    void *xmitter = zmq_socket (context, ZMQ_PAIR);
    zmq_connect (xmitter, "inproc://step3");
    printf ("Step 2 ready, signaling step 3\n");
    s_send (xmitter, "READY");
    zmq_close (xmitter);
```

```
        return NULL;
}

int main (void)
{
    void *context = zmq_ctx_new ();

    //  Bind inproc socket before starting step2
    void *receiver = zmq_socket (context, ZMQ_PAIR);
    zmq_bind (receiver, "inproc://step3");
    pthread_t thread;
    pthread_create (&thread, NULL, step2, context);

    //  Wait for signal
    char *string = s_recv (receiver);
    free (string);
    zmq_close (receiver);

    printf ("Test successful!\n");
    zmq_ctx_destroy (context);
    return 0;
}
```

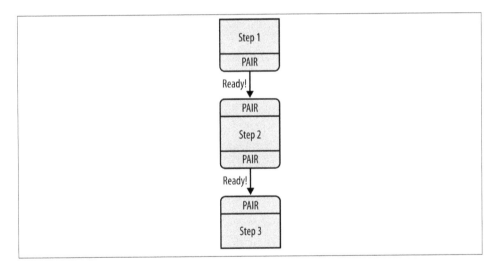

Figure 2-13. The relay race

This is a classic pattern for multithreading with ØMQ:

1. Two threads communicate over inproc, using a shared context.

2. The parent thread creates one socket, binds it to an inproc endpoint, and *then* starts the child thread, passing the context to it.

3. The child thread creates the second socket, connects it to that `inproc` endpoint, and *then* signals to the parent thread that it's ready.

Note that multithreading code using this pattern is not scalable out to processes. If you use `inproc` and socket pairs, you are building a tightly bound application; i.e., one where your threads are structurally interdependent. Do this when low latency is really vital. The other design pattern is a loosely bound application, where threads have their own context and communicate over `ipc` or `tcp`. You can easily break loosely bound threads into separate processes.

This is the first time we've shown an example using PAIR sockets. Why use PAIR? Other socket combinations might seem to work, but they all have side effects that could interfere with signaling:

- You can use PUSH for the sender and PULL for the receiver. This looks simple and will work, but remember that PUSH will distribute messages to all available receivers. If you by accident start two receivers (e.g., you already have one running and you start a second), you'll "lose" half of your signals. PAIR has the advantage of refusing more than one connection; the pair is *exclusive*.

- You can use DEALER for the sender and ROUTER for the receiver. ROUTER, however, wraps your message in an "envelope," meaning your zero-size signal turns into a multipart message. If you don't care about the data and treat anything as a valid signal, and if you don't read more than once from the socket, that won't matter. If, however, you decide to send real data, you will suddenly find ROUTER providing you with "wrong" messages. DEALER also distributes outgoing messages, giving the same risk as PUSH.

- You can use PUB for the sender and SUB for the receiver. This will correctly deliver your messages exactly as you sent them, and PUB does not distribute as PUSH or DEALER do. However, you need to configure the subscriber with an empty subscription, which is annoying. Worse, the reliability of the PUB-SUB link is timing-dependent, and messages can get lost if the SUB socket is connecting while the PUB socket is sending its messages.

For these reasons, PAIR makes the best choice for coordination between pairs of threads.

Node Coordination

When you want to coordinate nodes, PAIR sockets won't work well any more. This is one of the few areas where the strategies for threads and nodes are different. Principally, nodes come and go whereas threads are static. PAIR sockets do not automatically reconnect if the remote node goes away and comes back.

The second significant difference between threads and nodes is that you typically have a fixed number of threads but a more variable number of nodes. Let's take one of our earlier scenarios (the weather server and clients) and use node coordination to ensure that subscribers don't lose data when starting up.

This is how the application will work:

- The publisher knows in advance how many subscribers it expects. This is just a magic number it gets from somewhere.
- The publisher starts up and waits for all subscribers to connect. This is the node coordination part. Each subscriber subscribes and then tells the publisher it's ready via another socket.
- When the publisher has all subscribers connected, it starts to publish data.

In this case, we'll use a REQ-REP socket flow to synchronize the subscribers and the publisher (Figure 2-14). The code for the publisher is in Example 2-13.

Example 2-13. Synchronized publisher (syncpub.c)

```
//
//  Synchronized publisher
//
#include "zhelpers.h"

//  We wait for 10 subscribers
#define SUBSCRIBERS_EXPECTED  10

int main (void)
{
    void *context = zmq_ctx_new ();

    //  Socket to talk to clients
    void *publisher = zmq_socket (context, ZMQ_PUB);
    zmq_bind (publisher, "tcp://*:5561");

    //  Socket to receive signals
    void *syncservice = zmq_socket (context, ZMQ_REP);
    zmq_bind (syncservice, "tcp://*:5562");

    //  Get synchronization from subscribers
    printf ("Waiting for subscribers\n");
    int subscribers = 0;
    while (subscribers < SUBSCRIBERS_EXPECTED) {
        //  - wait for synchronization request
        char *string = s_recv (syncservice);
        free (string);
        //  - send synchronization reply
        s_send (syncservice, "");
        subscribers++;
    }
```

```
    //  Now broadcast exactly 1M updates followed by END
    printf ("Broadcasting messages\n");
    int update_nbr;
    for (update_nbr = 0; update_nbr < 1000000; update_nbr++)
        s_send (publisher, "Rhubarb");

    s_send (publisher, "END");

    zmq_close (publisher);
    zmq_close (syncservice);
    zmq_ctx_destroy (context);
    return 0;
}
```

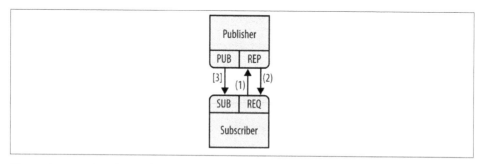

Figure 2-14. Pub-sub synchronization

The code for the subscriber is in Example 2-14.

Example 2-14. Synchronized subscriber (syncsub.c)

```
//
//  Synchronized subscriber
//
#include "zhelpers.h"

int main (void)
{
    void *context = zmq_ctx_new ();

    //  First, connect our subscriber socket
    void *subscriber = zmq_socket (context, ZMQ_SUB);
    zmq_connect (subscriber, "tcp://localhost:5561");
    zmq_setsockopt (subscriber, ZMQ_SUBSCRIBE, "", 0);

    //  0MQ is so fast, we need to wait a while...
    sleep (1);

    //  Second, synchronize with publisher
    void *syncclient = zmq_socket (context, ZMQ_REQ);
    zmq_connect (syncclient, "tcp://localhost:5562");
```

```
//  - send a synchronization request
s_send (syncclient, "");

//  - wait for synchronization reply
char *string = s_recv (syncclient);
free (string);

//  Third, get our updates and report how many we got
int update_nbr = 0;
while (1) {
    char *string = s_recv (subscriber);
    if (strcmp (string, "END") == 0) {
        free (string);
        break;
    }
    free (string);
    update_nbr++;
}
printf ("Received %d updates\n", update_nbr);

zmq_close (subscriber);
zmq_close (syncclient);
zmq_ctx_destroy (context);
return 0;
}
```

This Bash shell script will start 10 subscribers and then the publisher:

```
echo "Starting subscribers..."
for ((a=0; a<10; a++)); do
    syncsub &
done
echo "Starting publisher..."
syncpub
```

Which gives us this satisfying output:

```
Starting subscribers...
Starting publisher...
Received 1000000 updates
Received 1000000 updates
Received 1000000 updates
Received 1000000 updates
Received 1000000 updates
Received 1000000 updates
Received 1000000 updates
Received 1000000 updates
Received 1000000 updates
Received 1000000 updates
```

We can't assume that the SUB connect will be finished by the time the REQ/REP dialog is complete. There are no guarantees that outbound connects will finish in any order whatsoever, if you're using any transport except `inproc`. So, the example does a brute-force sleep of one second between subscribing and sending the REQ/REP synchronization.

A more robust model could be:

- Publisher opens PUB socket and starts sending "Hello" messages (not data).
- Subscribers connect to SUB socket, and when they receive a "Hello" message, they tell the publisher via a REQ/REP socket pair.
- When the publisher has had all the necessary confirmations, it starts to send real data.

Zero-Copy

ØMQ's message API lets you send and receive messages directly to and from application buffers without copying data. We call it *zero-copy*, and it can improve performance in some applications. Like all optimizations, use this when you know it helps, and measure before and after. Zero-copy makes your code more complex.

To do zero-copy, you use `zmq_msg_init_data()` to create a message that refers to a block of data already allocated on the heap with `malloc()`, and then you pass that to `zmq_msg_send()`. When you create the message, you also pass a function that ØMQ will call to free the block of data, when it has finished sending the message. This is the simplest example, assuming "buffer" is a block of 1,000 bytes allocated on the heap:

```
void my_free (void *data, void *hint) {
    free (data);
}
// Send message from buffer, which we allocate and ØMQ will free for us
zmq_msg_t message;
zmq_msg_init_data (&message, buffer, 1000, my_free, NULL);
zmq_msg_send (socket, &message, 0);
```

There is no way to do zero-copy on receive: ØMQ delivers you a buffer that you can store as long as you wish, but it will not write data directly into application buffers.

On writing, ØMQ's multipart messages work nicely together with zero-copy. In traditional messaging, you need to marshal different buffers together into one buffer that you can send. That means copying data. With ØMQ, you can send multiple buffers coming from different sources as individual message frames. Send each field as a length-delimited frame. To the application it looks like a series of send and receive calls, but internally the multiple parts get written to the network and read back with single system calls, so it's very efficient.

Pub-Sub Message Envelopes

In the pub-sub pattern, we can split the key into a separate message frame that we call an *envelope*. If you want to use pub-sub envelopes, make them yourself. It's optional, and in previous pub-sub examples, we didn't do this. Using a pub-sub envelope is a little more work for simple cases, but it's cleaner, especially for real cases, where the key and the data are naturally separate things.

Figure 2-15 shows is what a publish-subscribe message with an envelope looks like.

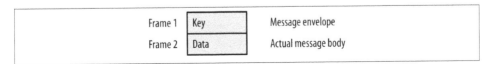

Figure 2-15. Pub-sub envelope with separate key

Recall that subscriptions do a prefix match. That is, they look for "all messages starting with XYZ." The obvious question is: how to delimit keys from data so that the prefix match doesn't accidentally match data. The best answer is to use an envelope, because the match won't cross a frame boundary.

Here is a minimalist example of how pub-sub envelopes look in code. This publisher (Example 2-15) sends messages of two types, A and B. The envelope holds the message type.

Example 2-15. Pub-sub envelope publisher (psenvpub.c)

```
//
//  Pub-sub envelope publisher
//  Note that the zhelpers.h file also provides s_sendmore
//
#include "zhelpers.h"

int main (void)
{
    //  Prepare our context and publisher
    void *context = zmq_ctx_new ();
    void *publisher = zmq_socket (context, ZMQ_PUB);
    zmq_bind (publisher, "tcp://*:5563");

    while (1) {
        //  Write two messages, each with an envelope and content
        s_sendmore (publisher, "A");
        s_send (publisher, "We don't want to see this");
        s_sendmore (publisher, "B");
        s_send (publisher, "We would like to see this");
        sleep (1);
    }
    //  We never get here, but clean up anyhow
```

```
    zmq_close (publisher);
    zmq_ctx_destroy (context);
    return 0;
}
```

The subscriber, shown in Example 2-16, wants only messages of type B.

Example 2-16. Pub-sub envelope subscriber (psenvsub.c)

```
//
//  Pub-sub envelope subscriber
//
#include "zhelpers.h"

int main (void)
{
    //  Prepare our context and subscriber
    void *context = zmq_ctx_new ();
    void *subscriber = zmq_socket (context, ZMQ_SUB);
    zmq_connect (subscriber, "tcp://localhost:5563");
    zmq_setsockopt (subscriber, ZMQ_SUBSCRIBE, "B", 1);

    while (1) {
        //  Read envelope with address
        char *address = s_recv (subscriber);
        //  Read message contents
        char *contents = s_recv (subscriber);
        printf ("[%s] %s\n", address, contents);
        free (address);
        free (contents);
    }
    //  We never get here, but clean up anyhow
    zmq_close (subscriber);
    zmq_ctx_destroy (context);
    return 0;
}
```

When you run the two programs, the subscriber should show you this:

```
[B] We would like to see this
[B] We would like to see this
[B] We would like to see this
[B] We would like to see this
...
```

This example shows that the subscription filter rejects or accepts the entire multipart message (key plus data). You won't get part of a multipart message, ever.

If you subscribe to multiple publishers and you want to know their addresses so that you can send them data via another socket (and this is a typical use case), create a three-part message, as illustrated in Figure 2-16.

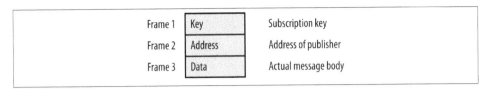

Frame 1	Key	Subscription key
Frame 2	Address	Address of publisher
Frame 3	Data	Actual message body

Figure 2-16. Pub-sub envelope with sender address

High-Water Marks

When you can send messages rapidly from process to process, you soon discover that memory is a precious resource, and one that can be trivially filled up. A few seconds of delay somewhere in a process can turn into a backlog that blows up a server unless you understand the problem and take precautions.

The problem is this: if you have process A sending messages to process B, which suddenly gets very busy (garbage collection, CPU overload, whatever), then what happens to the messages that process A wants to send? Some will sit in B's network buffers. Some will sit on the Ethernet wire itself. Some will sit in A's network buffers. And the rest will accumulate in A's memory. If you don't take some precaution, A can easily run out of memory and crash. It is a consistent, classic problem with message brokers.

What are the answers? One is to pass the problem upstream. A is getting the messages from somewhere else, so tell that process to stop, and so on up the line. This is called *flow control*. It sounds great, but what if you're sending out a Twitter feed? Do you tell the whole world to stop tweeting while B gets its act together?

Flow control works in some cases, but not in others. The transport layer can't tell the application layer to "stop" any more than a subway system can tell a large business, "Please keep your staff at work for another half an hour. I'm too busy."

The answer for messaging is to set limits on the size of buffers, and then, when we reach those limits, to take some sensible action. In some cases (not for a subway system, though), the answer is to throw away messages. In a others, the best strategy is to wait.

ØMQ uses the concept of *high-water mark* (HWM) to define the capacity of its internal pipes. Each connection out of a socket or into a socket has its own pipe, and HWM, for sending and/or receiving, depending on the socket type. Some sockets (PUB, PUSH) only have send buffers. Some (SUB, PULL, REQ, REP) only have receive buffers. Some (DEALER, ROUTER, PAIR) have both send and receive buffers.

In ØMQ v2.x, the HWM was infinite by default. In ØMQ v3.x, it's set to 1,000 by default, which is more sensible. If you're still using ØMQ v2.x, you should always set an HWM on your sockets, be it 1,000 to match ØMQ v3.x, or another figure that takes into account your message sizes.

When your socket reaches its HWM, it will either block or drop data, depending on the socket type. PUB and ROUTER sockets will drop data if they reach their HWM, while other socket types will block.

Over the `inproc` transport, the sender and receiver share the same buffers, so the real HWM is the sum of the HWMs set by both sides.

Lastly, the high-water marks are counted in *message parts*, not whole messages. If you are sending two-part messages, the default HWM is 500. When you use the ROUTER socket type (discussed in detail in the next chapter), every message is at least two parts.

Missing Message Problem Solver

As you build applications with ØMQ, you will come across this problem more than once: losing messages that you expect to receive. We have put together a diagram (Figure 2-17) that walks through the most common causes for this.

If you're using ØMQ in a context where failures are expensive, you'll want to plan properly. First, build prototypes that let you learn and test the different aspects of your design. Stress them until they break, so that you know exactly how strong your designs are. Second, invest in testing. This means building test frameworks, ensuring you have access to realistic setups with sufficient computer power, and taking the time or getting help to actually test seriously. Ideally, one team writes the code and a second team tries to break it. Lastly, do get your organization to contact iMatix (*http://www.imatix.com/contact*) to discuss how we can help to make sure things work properly, and can be fixed rapidly if they break.

In short, if you have not proven that an architecture works in realistic conditions, it will most likely break at the worst possible moment.

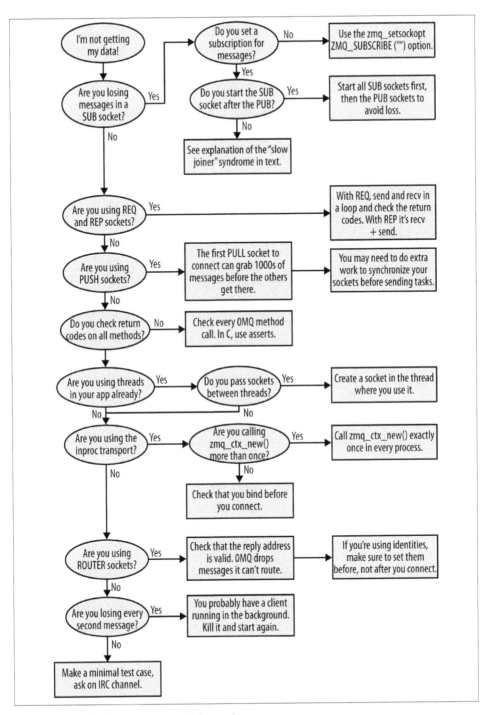

Figure 2-17. Missing message problem solver

## CHAPTER 3

Advanced Request-Reply Patterns

In Chapter 2, we worked through the basics of using ØMQ by developing a series of small applications, each time exploring new aspects of ØMQ. We'll continue this approach in this chapter as we explore advanced patterns built on top of ØMQ's core request-reply pattern.

We'll cover:

- How the request-reply mechanisms work
- How to combine REQ, REP, DEALER, and ROUTER sockets
- How ROUTER sockets work, in detail
- The load-balancing pattern
- Building a simple load-balancing message broker
- Designing a high-level API for ØMQ
- Building an asynchronous request-reply server
- A detailed inter-broker routing example

The Request-Reply Mechanisms

We already looked briefly at multipart messages. Let's now look at a major use case, which is *reply message envelopes*. An envelope is a way of safely packaging up data with an address, without touching the data itself. By separating reply addresses into an envelope, we make it possible to write general-purpose intermediaries such as APIs and proxies that create, read, and remove addresses no matter what the message payload or structure is.

In the request-reply pattern, the envelope holds the return address for replies. It is how a ØMQ network with no state can create round-trip request-reply dialogs.

When you use REQ and REP sockets, you don't even see envelopes; these sockets deal with them automatically. But for most of the interesting request-reply patterns, you'll want to understand envelopes and ROUTER sockets. We'll work through this step-by-step.

The Simple Reply Envelope

A request-reply exchange consists of a *request* message, and an eventual *reply* message. In the simple request-reply pattern there's one reply for each request. In more advanced patterns, requests and replies can flow asynchronously. However, the reply envelope always works the same way.

The ØMQ reply envelope formally consists of zero or more reply addresses, followed by an empty frame (the envelope delimiter), followed by the message body (zero or more frames). The envelope is created by multiple sockets working together in a chain. We'll break this down.

We'll start by sending "Hello" through a REQ socket. The REQ socket creates the simplest possible reply envelope, which has no addresses, just an empty delimiter frame and the message frame containing the "Hello" string. This is a two-frame message (Figure 3-1).

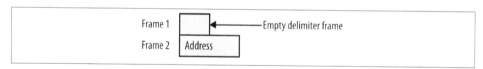

Figure 3-1. Request with minimal envelope

The REP socket does the matching work: it strips off the envelope, up to and including the delimiter frame, saves the whole envelope, and passes the "Hello" string up the application. Thus, our original "Hello World" example used request-reply envelopes internally, but the application never saw them.

If you spy on the network data flowing between *hwclient* and *hwserver*, this is what you'll see: every request and every reply is in fact two frames, an empty frame and then the body. This may not seem to make much sense for a simple REQ-REP dialog, but you'll see the reason when we explore how ROUTER and DEALER handle envelopes.

The Extended Reply Envelope

Now let's extend the REQ-REP pair with a ROUTER-DEALER proxy in the middle and see how this affects the reply envelope. This is the *extended request-reply pattern* we already saw in Chapter 2. We can, in fact, insert any number of proxy steps (Figure 3-2). The mechanics are the same.

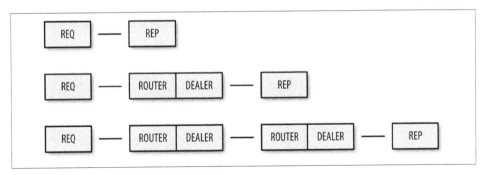

Figure 3-2. Extended request-reply pattern

The proxy does this, in pseudo-code:

```
prepare context, frontend and backend sockets
while true:
    poll on both sockets
    if frontend had input:
        read all frames from frontend
        send to backend
    if backend had input:
        read all frames from backend
        send to frontend
```

The ROUTER socket, unlike other sockets, tracks every connection it has, and tells the caller about these. The way it tells the caller is by sticking the connection *identity* in front of each message received. An identity, sometimes called an *address*, is just a binary string with no meaning except "this is a unique handle to the connection." Then, when you send a message via a ROUTER socket, you first send an identity frame.

The zmq_socket() man page describes it thusly:

> When receiving messages, a ZMQ_ROUTER socket shall prepend a message part containing the identity of the originating peer to the message before passing it to the application. Messages received are fair-queued from among all connected peers. When sending messages a ZMQ_ROUTER socket shall remove the first part of the message and use it to determine the identity of the peer the message shall be routed to.

As a historical note, ØMQ v2.2 and earlier use universally unique identifiers (UUIDs) as identities, and ØMQ v3.0 and later use short integers. There's some impact on network performance, but only when you use multiple proxy hops, which is rare.

It's a difficult concept to understand, but it's essential if you want to become a ØMQ expert. The ROUTER socket *invents* a random identity for each connection with which it works. If there are three REQ sockets connected to a ROUTER socket, it will invent three random identities, one for each REQ socket.

So, if we continue our worked example, let's say the REQ socket has identity 02. Internally, this means the ROUTER socket keeps a hash table where it can search for 02 and find the TCP connection for the REQ socket.

When we receive the message off the ROUTER socket, we get three frames (Figure 3-3).

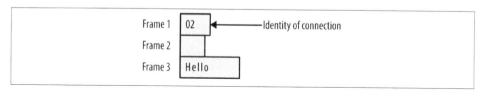

Figure 3-3. Request with one address

The core of the proxy loop is "read from one socket, write to the other," so we literally send these three frames out on the DEALER socket. If you now sniffed the network traffic, you would see these three frames flying from the DEALER socket to the REP socket. The REP socket does as before: strips off the whole envelope, including the new reply address, and once again delivers the "Hello" to the caller.

Incidentally, the REP socket can only deal with one request-reply exchange at a time, which is why if you try to read multiple requests or send multiple replies without sticking to a strict recv-send cycle, it gives an error.

You should now be able to visualize the return path. When hwserver sends "World" back, the REP socket wraps that with the envelope it saved and sends a three-frame reply message across the wire to the DEALER socket (Figure 3-4).

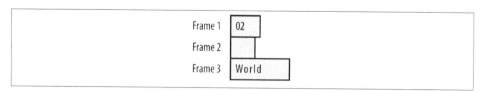

Figure 3-4. Reply with one address

Now the DEALER reads these three frames and sends all three out via the ROUTER socket. The ROUTER takes the first frame of the message, which is the 02 identity, and looks up the connection for this. If it finds that, it then pumps the next two frames out onto the wire (Figure 3-5).

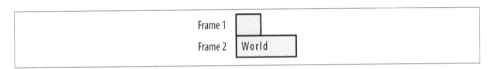

| Frame 1 | |
| Frame 2 | World |

Figure 3-5. Reply with minimal envelope

The REQ socket picks up this message and checks that the first frame is the empty delimiter, which it is. It then discards that frame and passes "World" to the calling application, which prints it out, to the amazement of those of us looking at ØMQ for the first time.

What's This Good For?

To be honest, the use cases for strict request-reply or extended request-reply are somewhat limited. For one thing, there's no easy way to recover from common failures like the server crashing due to buggy application code (we'll see more about this in Chapter 4). However, once you grasp the way these four sockets deal with envelopes, and how they talk to each other, you can do very useful things. We saw how ROUTER uses the reply envelope to decide which client REQ socket to route a reply back to. Now let's express this another way:

- Each time ROUTER gives you a message, it tells you what peer that message came from, as an identity.
- You can use this with a hash table (with the identity as the key) to track new peers as they arrive.
- ROUTER will route messages asynchronously to any peer connected to it, if you prefix the identity as the first frame of the message.

ROUTER sockets don't care about the whole envelope. They don't know anything about the empty delimiter. All they care about is that one identity frame that lets them figure out which connection to send a message to.

Recap of Request-Reply Sockets

Let's recap this:

- The REQ socket sends to the network an empty delimiter frame in front of the message data. REQ sockets are synchronous: they always send one request and then wait for one reply. REQ sockets talk to one peer at a time. If you connect a REQ socket to multiple peers, requests are distributed to and replies expected from each peer in turn, one at a time.
- The REP socket reads and saves all identity frames up to and including the empty delimiter, then passes the following frame or frames to the caller. REP sockets are

synchronous and talk to one peer at a time. If you connect a REP socket to multiple peers, requests are read from peers in fair fashion, and replies are always sent to the same peer that made the last request.

- The DEALER socket is oblivious to the reply envelope and handles this like any multipart message. DEALER sockets are asynchronous, like PUSH and PULL combined. They distribute sent messages among all connections, and fair-queue received messages from all connections.

- The ROUTER socket is oblivious to the reply envelope, like DEALER. It creates identities for its connections and passes these identities to the caller as a first frame in any received message. Conversely, when the caller sends a message, it uses the first message frame as an identity to look up the connection to send to. ROUTERs are asynchronous.

Request-Reply Combinations

We have four request-reply sockets, each with a certain behavior. We've seen how they connect in simple and extended request-reply patterns. But these sockets are building blocks that you can use to solve many problems.

These are the legal combinations:

- REQ to REP
- DEALER to REP
- REQ to ROUTER
- DEALER to ROUTER
- DEALER to DEALER
- ROUTER to ROUTER

And these combinations are invalid (I'll explain why):

- REQ to REQ
- REQ to DEALER
- REP to REP
- REP to ROUTER

Here are some tips for remembering the semantics. DEALER is like an asynchronous REQ socket, and ROUTER is like an asynchronous REP socket. Where we use a REQ socket, we can use a DEALER; we just have to read and write the envelope ourselves. Where we use a REP socket, we can stick a ROUTER; we just need to manage the identities ourselves.

Think of REQ and DEALER sockets as "clients" and REP and ROUTER sockets as "servers." Mostly, you'll want to bind REP and ROUTER sockets, and connect REQ and DEALER sockets to them. It's not always going to be this simple, but it is a clean and memorable place to start.

The REQ to REP Combination

We've already covered a REQ client talking to a REP server, but there's one important aspect to mention here: the REQ client *must* initiate the message flow. A REP server cannot talk to a REQ client that hasn't first sent it a request. Technically, it's not even possible, and the API also returns an EFSM error if you try it.

The DEALER to REP Combination

Now, let's replace the REQ client with a DEALER. This gives us an asynchronous client that can talk to multiple REP servers. If we rewrote our "Hello World" client using DEALER, we'd be able to send off any number of "Hello" requests without waiting for replies.

When we use a DEALER to talk to a REP socket, we *must* accurately emulate the envelope that the REQ socket would have sent, or the REP socket will discard the message as invalid. So, to send a message, we:

1. Send an empty message frame with the MORE flag set.
2. Send the message body.

And when we receive a message, we:

1. Receive the first frame and, if it's not empty, discard the whole message.
2. Receive the next frame and pass that to the application.

The REQ to ROUTER Combination

In the same way as we can replace REQ with DEALER, we can replace REP with ROUTER. This gives us an asynchronous server that can talk to multiple REQ clients at the same time. If we rewrote our "Hello World" server using ROUTER, we'd be able to process any number of "Hello" requests in parallel. We saw this in the *mtserver* example in Chapter 2.

We can use ROUTER in two distinct ways:

- As a proxy that switches messages between frontend and backend sockets
- As an application that reads the message and acts on it

In the first case, the ROUTER simply reads all frames, including the artificial identity frame, and passes them on blindly. In the second case, the ROUTER *must* know the format of the reply envelope it's being sent. As the other peer is a REQ socket, the ROUTER gets the identity frame, an empty frame, and then the data frame.

The DEALER to ROUTER Combination

Now we can switch out both REQ and REP with DEALER and ROUTER to get the most powerful socket combination, which is DEALER talking to ROUTER. It gives us asynchronous clients talking to asynchronous servers, where both sides have full control over the message formats.

Because both DEALER and ROUTER can work with arbitrary message formats, if you hope to use these safely, you have to become a little bit of a protocol designer. At the very least, you must decide whether you wish to emulate the REQ/REP reply envelope. (It depends on whether you actually need to send replies or not.)

The DEALER to DEALER Combination

You can swap a REP with a ROUTER, but you can also swap a REP with a DEALER, if the DEALER is talking to one and only one peer.

When you replace a REP with a DEALER, your worker can suddenly go fully asynchronous, sending any number of replies back. The cost is that you have to manage the reply envelopes yourself, and get them right, or nothing at all will work. We'll see a worked example later. Let's just say for now that DEALER to DEALER is one of the trickier patterns to get right, and happily it's rare that we need it.

The ROUTER to ROUTER Combination

This sounds perfect for N-to-N connections, but it's the most difficult combination to use. You should avoid it until you are well advanced with ØMQ. We'll see one example of it in the Freelance pattern in Chapter 4, and an alternative DEALER to ROUTER design for peer-to-peer work in Chapter 8.

Invalid Combinations

Mostly, trying to connect clients to clients, or servers to servers, is a bad idea and won't work. Rather than give general vague warnings, I'll explain in detail what's wrong with each of the following combinations:

REQ to REQ
Both sides want to start by sending messages to each other, and this could only work if you timed things so that both peers exchanged messages at exactly the same time. It hurts my brain to even think about it.

REQ to DEALER

You could in theory do this, but it would break if you added a second REQ because DEALER has no way of sending a reply to the original peer. Thus, the REQ socket would get confused, and/or return messages meant for another client.

REP to REP

Both sides would wait for the other to send the first message.

REP to ROUTER

The ROUTER socket can in theory initiate the dialog and send a properly formatted request, if it knows the REP socket has connected *and* it knows the identity of that connection. It's messy, though, and adds nothing over DEALER to ROUTER.

The common thread in this valid versus invalid breakdown is that a ØMQ socket connection is always biased toward one peer that binds to an endpoint, and another that connects to that. Further, which side binds and which side connects is not arbitrary, but follows natural patterns. The side we expect to "be there" binds: it'll be a server, a broker, a publisher, a collector. The side that "comes and goes" connects: it'll be clients or workers. Remembering this will help you design better ØMQ architectures.

Exploring ROUTER Sockets

Let's look at ROUTER sockets a little closer. We've already seen how they work by routing individual messages to specific connections. I'll explain in more detail how we identify those connections, and what a ROUTER socket does when it can't send a message.

Identities and Addresses

The *identity* concept in ØMQ refers specifically to ROUTER sockets and how they identify the connections they have to other sockets. More broadly, identities are used as addresses in the reply envelope. In most cases, the identity is arbitrary and local to the ROUTER socket: it's a lookup key in a hash table. Independently, a peer can have an address that is physical (a network endpoint like "tcp://192.168.55.117:5670") or logical (a UUID or email address or other unique key).

An application that uses a ROUTER socket to talk to specific peers can convert a logical address to an identity if it has built the necessary hash table. Because ROUTER sockets only announce the identity of a connection (to a specific peer) when that peer sends a message, you can only really reply to a message, not spontaneously talk to a peer.

This is true even if you flip the rules and make the ROUTER connect to the peer rather than wait for the peer to connect to the ROUTER.

However, you can force the ROUTER socket to use a logical address in place of its identity. The `zmq_setsockopt()` reference page calls this *setting the socket identity*. It works as follows:

- The peer application sets the ZMQ_IDENTITY option of its peer socket (DEALER or REQ) *before* binding or connecting.

- Usually the peer then connects to the already bound ROUTER socket, but the ROUTER can also connect to the peer.

- At connection time, the peer socket tells the router socket, "Please use this identity for this connection."

- If the peer socket doesn't say that, the router generates its usual arbitrary random identity for the connection.

- The ROUTER socket now provides this logical address to the application as a prefix identity frame for any messages coming in from that peer.

- The ROUTER also expects the logical address as the prefix identity frame for any outgoing messages to that peer.

Example 3-1 is a simple example of two peers that connect to a ROUTER socket, one of which imposes the logical address "PEER2."

Example 3-1. Identity check (identity.c)

```
//
//  Demonstrate identities as used by the request-reply pattern.  Run this
//  program by itself.  Note that the utility functions s_ are provided by
//  zhelpers.h.  It gets boring for everyone to keep repeating this code.
//
#include "zhelpers.h"

int main (void)
{
    void *context = zmq_ctx_new ();

    void *sink = zmq_socket (context, ZMQ_ROUTER);
    zmq_bind (sink, "inproc://example");

    //  First allow 0MQ to set the identity
    void *anonymous = zmq_socket (context, ZMQ_REQ);
    zmq_connect (anonymous, "inproc://example");
    s_send (anonymous, "ROUTER uses a generated UUID");
    s_dump (sink);

    //  Then set the identity ourselves
    void *identified = zmq_socket (context, ZMQ_REQ);
    zmq_setsockopt (identified, ZMQ_IDENTITY, "PEER2", 5);
    zmq_connect (identified, "inproc://example");
    s_send (identified, "ROUTER socket uses REQ's socket identity");
    s_dump (sink);

    zmq_close (sink);
    zmq_close (anonymous);
```

```
    zmq_close (identified);
    zmq_ctx_destroy (context);
    return 0;
}
```

Here is what the program prints:

```
----------------------------------------
[005] 006B8B4567
[000]
[026] ROUTER uses a generated UUID
----------------------------------------
[005] PEER2
[000]
[038] ROUTER uses REQ's socket identity
```

ROUTER Error Handling

ROUTER sockets do have a somewhat brutal way of dealing with messages they can't send anywhere: they drop them silently. It's an attitude that makes sense in working code, but it makes debugging hard. The "send identity as first frame" approach is tricky enough that we often get this wrong when we're learning, and the ROUTER's stony silence when we mess up isn't very constructive.

Since ØMQ v3.2, there's a socket option you can set to catch this error: ZMQ_ROUT ER_MANDATORY. Set that on the ROUTER socket, and when you provide an unroutable identity on a send call, the socket will signal an EHOSTUNREACH error.

The Load-Balancing Pattern

Let's now look at some code. We'll see how to connect a ROUTER socket to a REQ socket, and then to a DEALER socket. These two examples follow the same logic, which is a *load-balancing* pattern. This pattern is our first exposure to using the ROUTER socket for deliberate routing, rather than it simply acting as a reply channel.

The load-balancing pattern is very common and we'll see it several times in this book. It solves the main problem with simple round-robin routing (as PUSH and DEALER offer), which is that round robin becomes inefficient if tasks do not all take roughly the same time.

It's the post office analogy: if you have one queue per counter, and you have some people buying stamps (a fast, simple transaction), and some people opening new accounts (a very slow transaction), you will find stamp buyers getting unfairly stuck in queues. And just as in a post office, if your messaging architecture is unfair, people will get annoyed.

The solution in the post office is to create a single queue so that even if one or two counters get stuck with slow work, other counters will continue to serve clients on a first-come, first-serve basis.

One reason PUSH and DEALER use this simplistic approach is sheer performance. If you arrive in any major US airport, you'll find long queues of people waiting at immigration. The border patrol officials will send people in advance to queue up at each counter, rather than using a single queue. Having people walk 50 yards in advance saves a minute or two per passenger. And since every passport check takes roughly the same time, it's more or less fair. This is the strategy for PUSH and DEALER: send workloads ahead of time so that there is less travel distance.

This is a recurring theme with ØMQ: the world's problems are diverse and you can really benefit from solving different problems each in the right way. The airport isn't the post office, and "one size" fits no one really well.

Let's return to the scenario of a worker (DEALER or REQ) connected to a broker (ROUTER). The broker has to know when the worker is ready, and keep a list of workers so that it can take the *least recently used* worker each time.

The solution is really simple, in fact: workers send a "ready" message when they start, and after they finish each task. The broker reads these messages one by one. Each time it reads a message, it is from the last-used worker. And since we're using a ROUTER socket, we get an identity that we can then use to send a task back to the worker.

It's a twist on request-reply because the task is sent with the reply, and any response for the task is sent as a new request. The following code examples should make it clearer.

ROUTER Broker and REQ Workers

Example 3-2 is an example of the load-balancing pattern using a ROUTER broker talking to a set of REQ workers.

Example 3-2. ROUTER-to-REQ (rtreq.c)

```
//
//  ROUTER-to-REQ example
//
#include "zhelpers.h"
#include <pthread.h>

#define NBR_WORKERS 10

static void *
worker_task (void *args)
{
    void *context = zmq_ctx_new ();
    void *worker = zmq_socket (context, ZMQ_REQ);
    s_set_id (worker);          //  Set a printable identity
    zmq_connect (worker, "tcp://localhost:5671");

    int total = 0;
    while (1) {
```

```
    //  Tell the broker we're ready for work
    s_send (worker, "Hi Boss");

    //  Get workload from broker, until finished
    char *workload = s_recv (worker);
    int finished = (strcmp (workload, "Fired!") == 0);
    free (workload);
    if (finished) {
        printf ("Completed: %d tasks\n", total);
        break;
    }
    total++;

    //  Do some random work
    s_sleep (randof (500) + 1);
    }
    zmq_close (worker);
    zmq_ctx_destroy (context);
    return NULL;
}
```

While this example runs in a single process, that is only to make it easier to start and stop. Each thread has its own context and conceptually acts as a separate process. Example 3-3 shows the main task.

Example 3-3. ROUTER-to-REQ (rtreq.c): main task

```
int main (void)
{
    void *context = zmq_ctx_new ();
    void *broker = zmq_socket (context, ZMQ_ROUTER);

    zmq_bind (broker, "tcp://*:5671");
    srandom ((unsigned) time (NULL));

    int worker_nbr;
    for (worker_nbr = 0; worker_nbr < NBR_WORKERS; worker_nbr++) {
        pthread_t worker;
        pthread_create (&worker, NULL, worker_task, NULL);
    }
    //  Run for five seconds and then tell workers to end
    int64_t end_time = s_clock () + 5000;
    int workers_fired = 0;
    while (1) {
        //  Next message gives us least recently used worker
        char *identity = s_recv (broker);
        s_sendmore (broker, identity);
        free (identity);
        free (s_recv (broker));     //  Envelope delimiter
        free (s_recv (broker));     //  Response from worker
        s_sendmore (broker, "");
```

```
    // Encourage workers until it's time to fire them
    if (s_clock () < end_time)
        s_send (broker, "Work harder");
    else {
        s_send (broker, "Fired!");
        if (++workers_fired == NBR_WORKERS)
            break;
    }
}
zmq_close (broker);
zmq_ctx_destroy (context);
return 0;
}
```

The example runs for five seconds, and then each worker prints how many tasks it handled. If the routing worked, we'd expect a fair distribution of work:

```
Completed: 20 tasks
Completed: 18 tasks
Completed: 21 tasks
Completed: 23 tasks
Completed: 19 tasks
Completed: 21 tasks
Completed: 17 tasks
Completed: 17 tasks
Completed: 25 tasks
Completed: 19 tasks
```

To talk to the workers in this example, we have to create a REQ-friendly envelope consisting of an identity plus an empty envelope delimiter frame (Figure 3-6).

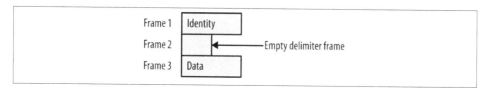

Figure 3-6. Routing envelope for REQ

ROUTER Broker and DEALER Workers

Anywhere you can use REQ, you can use DEALER. There are two specific differences:

- The REQ socket always sends an empty delimiter frame before any data frames; the DEALER does not.

- The REQ socket will send only one message before it receives a reply; the DEALER is fully asynchronous.

The synchronous versus asynchronous behavior has no effect on our example since we're doing strict request-reply. It is more relevant when we come to recovering from failures, which we'll address in Chapter 4.

Now let's look at exactly the same example, but with the REQ socket replaced by a DEALER socket (Example 3-4).

Example 3-4. ROUTER-to-DEALER (rtdealer.c)

```
//
//  ROUTER-to-DEALER example
//
#include "zhelpers.h"
#include <pthread.h>

#define NBR_WORKERS 10

static void *
worker_task (void *args)
{
    void *context = zmq_ctx_new ();
    void *worker = zmq_socket (context, ZMQ_DEALER);
    s_set_id (worker);          // Set a printable identity
    zmq_connect (worker, "tcp://localhost:5671");

    int total = 0;
    while (1) {
        // Tell the broker we're ready for work
        s_sendmore (worker, "");
        s_send (worker, "Hi Boss");

        // Get workload from broker, until finished
        free (s_recv (worker));     // Envelope delimiter
        char *workload = s_recv (worker);
...
```

The code is almost identical, except that the worker uses a DEALER socket and reads and writes that empty frame before the data frame. This is the approach I use when I want to maintain compatibility with REQ workers.

However, remember the reason for that empty delimiter frame: it's to allow multihop extended requests that terminate in a REP socket, which uses that delimiter to split off the reply envelope so it can hand the data frames to its application.

If we never need to pass the message along to a REP socket, we can simply drop the empty delimiter frame at both sides, which makes things simpler. This is usually the design I use for pure DEALER to ROUTER protocols.

A Load-Balancing Message Broker

The previous example is half-complete. It can manage a set of workers with dummy requests and replies, but it has no way to talk to clients.

If we add a second *frontend* ROUTER socket that accepts client requests, and turn our example into a proxy that can switch messages from frontend to backend, we get a useful and reusable tiny load-balancing message broker (Figure 3-7).

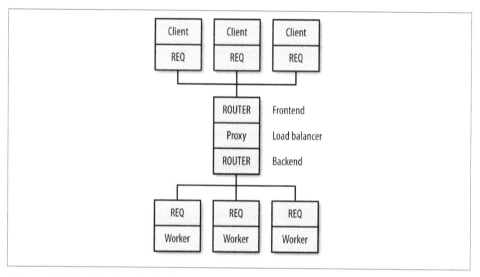

Figure 3-7. Load-balancing broker

This broker does the following:

- Accepts connections from a set of clients
- Accepts connections from a set of workers
- Accepts requests from clients and holds these in a single queue
- Sends these requests to workers using the load-balancing pattern
- Receives replies back from workers
- Sends these replies back to the original requesting client

The broker code (listed in Example 3-5) is fairly long, but worth understanding.

Example 3-5. Load-balancing broker (lbbroker.c)

```
//
//  Load-balancing broker
//  Clients and workers are shown here in-process
//
```

```
#include "zhelpers.h"
#include <pthread.h>

#define NBR_CLIENTS 10
#define NBR_WORKERS 3

//  Dequeue operation for queue implemented as array of anything
#define DEQUEUE(q) memmove (&(q)[0], &(q)[1], sizeof (q) - sizeof (q [0]))

//  Basic request-reply client using REQ socket.
//  Since s_send and s_recv can't handle 0MQ binary identities we
//  set a printable text identity to allow routing.
//
static void *
client_task (void *args)
{
    void *context = zmq_ctx_new ();
    void *client = zmq_socket (context, ZMQ_REQ);
    s_set_id (client);          //  Set a printable identity
    zmq_connect (client, "ipc://frontend.ipc");

    //  Send request, get reply
    s_send (client, "HELLO");
    char *reply = s_recv (client);
    printf ("Client: %s\n", reply);
    free (reply);
    zmq_close (client);
    zmq_ctx_destroy (context);
    return NULL;
}
```

While this example runs in a single process, that is just to make it easier to start and stop. Each thread has its own context and conceptually acts as a separate process. Example 3-6 shows the worker task, using a REQ socket to do load balancing. Since s_send() and s_recv() can't handle ØMQ binary identities, we set a printable text identity to allow routing.

Example 3-6. Load-balancing broker (lbbroker.c): worker task

```
static void *
worker_task (void *args)
{
    void *context = zmq_ctx_new ();
    void *worker = zmq_socket (context, ZMQ_REQ);
    s_set_id (worker);          //  Set a printable identity
    zmq_connect (worker, "ipc://backend.ipc");

    //  Tell broker we're ready for work
    s_send (worker, "READY");

    while (1) {
        //  Read and save all frames until we get an empty frame
```

```
    //  In this example there is only 1 but there could be more
    char *identity = s_recv (worker);
    char *empty = s_recv (worker);
    assert (*empty == 0);
    free (empty);

    //  Get request, send reply
    char *request = s_recv (worker);
    printf ("Worker: %s\n", request);
    free (request);

    s_sendmore (worker, identity);
    s_sendmore (worker, "");
    s_send      (worker, "OK");
    free (identity);
    }
    zmq_close (worker);
    zmq_ctx_destroy (context);
    return NULL;
}
```

The main task starts the clients and workers, and then routes requests between the two layers (Example 3-7). Workers signal "ready" when they start; after that, we treat them as ready when they reply with a response back to a client. The load-balancing data structure is just a queue of next available workers.

Example 3-7. Load-balancing broker (lbbroker.c): main task

```
int main (void)
{
    //  Prepare our context and sockets
    void *context = zmq_ctx_new ();
    void *frontend = zmq_socket (context, ZMQ_ROUTER);
    void *backend  = zmq_socket (context, ZMQ_ROUTER);
    zmq_bind (frontend, "ipc://frontend.ipc");
    zmq_bind (backend,  "ipc://backend.ipc");

    int client_nbr;
    for (client_nbr = 0; client_nbr < NBR_CLIENTS; client_nbr++) {
        pthread_t client;
        pthread_create (&client, NULL, client_task, NULL);
    }
    int worker_nbr;
    for (worker_nbr = 0; worker_nbr < NBR_WORKERS; worker_nbr++) {
        pthread_t worker;
        pthread_create (&worker, NULL, worker_task, NULL);
    }
```

Example 3-8 shows the main loop for the least-recently-used queue. It has two sockets: a frontend for clients and a backend for workers. It polls the backend in all cases, and polls the frontend only when there are one or more workers ready. This is a neat way to use ØMQ's own queues to hold messages we're not ready to process yet. When we get a client reply, we pop the next available worker and send the request to it, including the originating client's identity. When a worker replies, we requeue that worker and forward the reply to the original client using the reply envelope.

Example 3-8. Load-balancing broker (lbbroker.c): main task body

```
// Queue of available workers
int available_workers = 0;
char *worker_queue [10];

while (1) {
    zmq_pollitem_t items [] = {
        { backend,  0, ZMQ_POLLIN, 0 },
        { frontend, 0, ZMQ_POLLIN, 0 }
    };
    // Poll frontend only if we have available workers
    int rc = zmq_poll (items, available_workers ? 2 : 1, -1);
    if (rc == -1)
        break;              // Interrupted

    // Handle worker activity on backend
    if (items [0].revents & ZMQ_POLLIN) {
        // Queue worker identity for load-balancing
        char *worker_id = s_recv (backend);
        assert (available_workers < NBR_WORKERS);
        worker_queue [available_workers++] = worker_id;

        // Second frame is empty
        char *empty = s_recv (backend);
        assert (empty [0] == 0);
        free (empty);

        // Third frame is READY or else a client reply identity
        char *client_id = s_recv (backend);

        // If client reply, send rest back to frontend
        if (strcmp (client_id, "READY") != 0) {
            empty = s_recv (backend);
            assert (empty [0] == 0);
            free (empty);
            char *reply = s_recv (backend);
            s_sendmore (frontend, client_id);
            s_sendmore (frontend, "");
            s_send     (frontend, reply);
            free (reply);
            if (--client_nbr == 0)
                break;     // Exit after N messages
        }
        free (client_id);
    }
```

Example 3-9 shows how we handle a client request.

Example 3-9. Load-balancing broker (lbbroker.c): handling a client request

```
        if (items [1].revents & ZMQ_POLLIN) {
            //  Now get next client request, route to last-used worker
            //  Client request is [identity][empty][request]
            char *client_id = s_recv (frontend);
            char *empty = s_recv (frontend);
            assert (empty [0] == 0);
            free (empty);
            char *request = s_recv (frontend);

            s_sendmore (backend, worker_queue [0]);
            s_sendmore (backend, "");
            s_sendmore (backend, client_id);
            s_sendmore (backend, "");
            s_send      (backend, request);

            free (client_id);
            free (request);

            //  Dequeue and drop the next worker identity
            free (worker_queue [0]);
            DEQUEUE (worker_queue);
            available_workers--;
        }
    }
    zmq_close (frontend);
    zmq_close (backend);
    zmq_ctx_destroy (context);
    return 0;
}
```

The difficult parts of this program are the envelopes that each socket reads and writes, and the load-balancing algorithm. We'll take these in turn, starting with the message envelope formats.

Let's walk through a full request-reply chain from client to worker and back. In this code we set the identity of the client and worker sockets to make it easier to trace the message frames. In reality we'd allow the ROUTER sockets to invent identities for connections. Let's assume the client's identity is "CLIENT" and the worker's identity is "WORKER." The client application sends a single frame containing "HELLO" (Figure 3-8).

Figure 3-8. Message that client sends

Since the REQ socket adds its empty delimiter frame and the ROUTER socket adds its connection identity, the proxy reads three frames off the frontend ROUTER socket: the client address, the empty delimiter frame, and the data part (Figure 3-9).

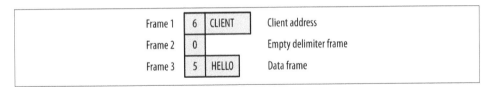

Figure 3-9. Message coming in on frontend

The broker sends this to the worker, prefixed by the address of the chosen worker, plus an additional empty part to keep the REQ at the other end happy (Figure 3-10).

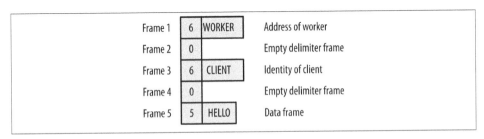

Figure 3-10. Message sent to backend

This complex envelope stack gets chewed up first by the backend ROUTER socket, which removes the first frame. Then the REQ socket in the worker removes the empty part, and provides the rest to the worker application (Figure 3-11).

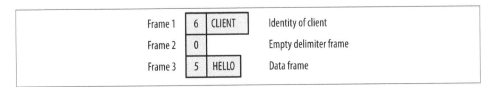

Figure 3-11. Message delivered to worker

The worker has to save the envelope (which is all the parts up to and including the empty message frame), and then it can do what's needed with the data part. Note that a REP socket would do this automatically, but we're using the REQ-ROUTER pattern so that we can get proper load balancing.

On the return path, the messages are the same as when they come in; i.e., the backend socket gives the broker a message in five parts, the broker sends the frontend socket a message in three parts, and the client gets a message in one part.

Now let's look at the load-balancing algorithm. It requires that both clients and workers use REQ sockets, and that workers correctly store and replay the envelopes on messages they get. The algorithm is:

- Create a poll set that always polls the backend, and polls the frontend only if there are one or more workers available.

- Poll for activity with infinite timeout.

- If there is activity on the backend, we either have a "ready" message or a reply for a client. In either case, we store the worker address (the first part) on our worker queue, and if the rest is a client reply, we send it back to that client via the frontend.

- If there is activity on the frontend, we take the client request, pop the next worker (which is the last used), and send the request to the backend. This means sending the worker address, the empty part, and then the three parts of the client request.

You should now see that you can reuse and extend the load-balancing algorithm with variations based on the information the worker provides in its initial "ready" message. For example, workers might start up and do a performance self-test, then tell the broker how fast they are. The broker can then choose the fastest available worker rather than the oldest.

A High-Level API for ØMQ

We're going to push request-reply onto the stack now and open a different area, which is the ØMQ API itself. There's a reason for this detour: as we write more complex examples, the low-level ØMQ API starts to look increasingly clumsy. Look at the core of the worker thread from our load-balancing broker:

```
while (true) {
    //  Read and save all frames until we get an empty frame
    //   In this example there is only 1 but there could be more
    char *address = s_recv (worker);
    char *empty = s_recv (worker);
    assert (*empty == 0);
    free (empty);

    //  Get request, send reply
    char *request = s_recv (worker);
    printf ("Worker: %s\n", request);
    free (request);

    s_sendmore (worker, address);
    s_sendmore (worker, "");
```

```
        s_send    (worker, "OK");
        free (address);
    }
```

That code isn't even reusable because it can only handle one reply address in the enve-lope, and it already does some wrapping around the ØMQ API. If we used the libzmq API directly, this is what we'd have to write:

```
while (true) {
    //  Read and save all frames until we get an empty frame
    //  In this example there is only 1 but there could be more
    zmq_msg_t address;
    zmq_msg_init (&address);
    zmq_msg_recv (worker, &address, 0);

    zmq_msg_t empty;
    zmq_msg_init (&empty);
    zmq_msg_recv (worker, &empty, 0);

    //  Get request, send reply
    zmq_msg_t payload;
    zmq_msg_init (&payload);
    zmq_msg_recv (worker, &payload, 0);

    int char_nbr;
    printf ("Worker: ");
    for (char_nbr = 0; char_nbr < zmq_msg_size (&payload); char_nbr++)
        printf ("%c", *(char *) (zmq_msg_data (&payload) + char_nbr));
    printf ("\n");

    zmq_msg_init_size (&payload, 2);
    memcpy (zmq_msg_data (&payload), "OK", 2);

    zmq_msg_send (worker, &address, ZMQ_SNDMORE);
    zmq_close (&address);
    zmq_msg_send (worker, &empty, ZMQ_SNDMORE);
    zmq_close (&empty);
    zmq_msg_send (worker, &payload, 0);
    zmq_close (&payload);
}
```

And when code is too long to write quickly, it's also too long to understand. Up to now, I've stuck to the native API because, as ØMQ users, we need to know that intimately. But when it gets in our way, we have to treat it as a problem to solve.

I'm not proposing changing the ØMQ API, which is a documented public contract on which thousands of people agree and depend. What I'm proposing is to construct a higher-level API on top that is based on our experience so far—more specifically, our experience from writing more complex request-reply patterns.

What we want is an API that lets us receive and send an entire message in one shot, including the reply envelope with any number of reply addresses—one that lets us do what we want with the absolute fewest lines of code.

Making a good message API is fairly difficult. We have a problem of terminology: ØMQ uses "message" to describe both multipart messages and individual message frames. We have a problem of expectations: sometimes it's natural to see message content as printable string data, sometimes as binary blobs. And we have technical challenges, especially if we want to avoid copying data around too much.

The challenge of making a good API affects all languages, though my specific use case is C. Whatever language you use, think about how you could contribute to your language binding to make it as good as (or better than) the C binding I'm going to describe.

Features of a Higher-Level API

My solution is to use three fairly natural and obvious concepts: *string* helpers (already the basis for our s_send() and s_recv()), *frames* (a message frame), and *messages* (a list of one or more frames). Here is the worker code, rewritten onto an API using these concepts:

```
while (true) {
    zmsg_t *msg = zmsg_recv (worker);
    zframe_reset (zmsg_last (msg), "OK", 2);
    zmsg_send (&msg, worker);
}
```

Cutting the amount of code we need to read and write complex messages is great: the results are easy to read and understand. Let's continue this process for other aspects of working with ØMQ. Here's a wish list of things I'd like in a higher-level API, based on my experience with ØMQ so far:

- *Automatic handling of sockets.* I find it cumbersome to have to close sockets manually, and to have to explicitly define the linger timeout in some (but not all) cases. It'd be great to have a way to close sockets automatically when I close the context.

- *Portable thread management.* Every nontrivial ØMQ application uses threads, but POSIX threads aren't portable. A decent high-level API should hide this under a portable layer.

- *Portable clocks.* Even getting the time to a millisecond resolution, or sleeping for some milliseconds, is not portable. Realistic ØMQ applications need portable clocks, so our API should provide them.

- *A reactor to replace zmq_poll().* The poll loop is simple, but clumsy. Writing a lot of these, we end up doing the same work over and over: calculating timers, and calling code when sockets are ready. A simple reactor with socket readers and timers would save a lot of repeated work.

- *Proper handling of Ctrl-C.* We already saw how to catch an interrupt. It would be useful if this happened in all applications.

The CZMQ High-Level API

Turning this wish list into reality for the C language gives us CZMQ (*http://zero.mq/c*), a ØMQ language binding for C. This high-level binding, in fact, was developed out of earlier versions of this book. It combines nicer semantics for working with ØMQ with some portability layers, and (importantly for C, but less for other languages) containers like hashes and lists. CZMQ also uses an elegant object model that leads to frankly lovely code.

Example 3-10 shows the load-balancing broker rewritten to use a higher-level API (CZMQ for the C case).

Example 3-10. Load-balancing broker using high-level API (lbbroker2.c)

```
//
//  Load-balancing broker
//  Demonstrates use of the CZMQ API
//
#include "czmq.h"

#define NBR_CLIENTS 10
#define NBR_WORKERS 3
#define WORKER_READY    "\001"      //  Signals worker is ready

//  Basic request-reply client using REQ socket
//
static void *
client_task (void *args)
{
    zctx_t *ctx = zctx_new ();
    void *client = zsocket_new (ctx, ZMQ_REQ);
    zsocket_connect (client, "ipc://frontend.ipc");

    //  Send request, get reply
    while (true) {
        zstr_send (client, "HELLO");
        char *reply = zstr_recv (client);
        if (!reply)
            break;
        printf ("Client: %s\n", reply);
        free (reply);
        sleep (1);
    }
    zctx_destroy (&ctx);
    return NULL;
}
```

```
// Worker using REQ socket to do load balancing
//
static void *
worker_task (void *args)
{
    zctx_t *ctx = zctx_new ();
    void *worker = zsocket_new (ctx, ZMQ_REQ);
    zsocket_connect (worker, "ipc://backend.ipc");

    // Tell broker we're ready for work
    zframe_t *frame = zframe_new (WORKER_READY, 1);
    zframe_send (&frame, worker, 0);

    // Process messages as they arrive
    while (true) {
        zmsg_t *msg = zmsg_recv (worker);
        if (!msg)
            break;              // Interrupted
        zframe_reset (zmsg_last (msg), "OK", 2);
        zmsg_send (&msg, worker);
    }
    zctx_destroy (&ctx);
    return NULL;
}
```

Now we come to the main task (Example 3-11). This has identical functionality to the previous *lbbroker* example, but it uses CZMQ to start child threads, to hold the list of workers, and to read and send messages.

Example 3-11. Load-balancing broker using high-level API (lbbroker2.c): main task

```
int main (void)
{
    zctx_t *ctx = zctx_new ();
    void *frontend = zsocket_new (ctx, ZMQ_ROUTER);
    void *backend = zsocket_new (ctx, ZMQ_ROUTER);
    zsocket_bind (frontend, "ipc://frontend.ipc");
    zsocket_bind (backend, "ipc://backend.ipc");

    int client_nbr;
    for (client_nbr = 0; client_nbr < NBR_CLIENTS; client_nbr++)
        zthread_new (client_task, NULL);
    int worker_nbr;
    for (worker_nbr = 0; worker_nbr < NBR_WORKERS; worker_nbr++)
        zthread_new (worker_task, NULL);

    // Queue of available workers
    zlist_t *workers = zlist_new ();
```

The main loop for the load balancer is shown in Example 3-12. It works the same way as the previous example, but is a lot shorter because CZMQ gives us an API that does more with fewer calls.

Example 3-12. Load-balancing broker using high-level API (lbbroker2.c): main load-balancer loop

```
        zmq_pollitem_t items [] = {
            { backend,  0, ZMQ_POLLIN, 0 },
            { frontend, 0, ZMQ_POLLIN, 0 }
        };
        //  Poll frontend only if we have available workers
        int rc = zmq_poll (items, zlist_size (workers)? 2: 1, -1);
        if (rc == -1)
            break;                  //  Interrupted

        //  Handle worker activity on backend
        if (items [0].revents & ZMQ_POLLIN) {
            //  Use worker identity for load balancing
            zmsg_t *msg = zmsg_recv (backend);
            if (!msg)
                break;              //  Interrupted
            zframe_t *identity = zmsg_unwrap (msg);
            zlist_append (workers, identity);

            //  Forward message to client if it's not a READY
            zframe_t *frame = zmsg_first (msg);
            if (memcmp (zframe_data (frame), WORKER_READY, 1) == 0)
                zmsg_destroy (&msg);
            else
                zmsg_send (&msg, frontend);
        }
        if (items [1].revents & ZMQ_POLLIN) {
            //  Get client request, route to first available worker
            zmsg_t *msg = zmsg_recv (frontend);
            if (msg) {
                zmsg_wrap (msg, (zframe_t *) zlist_pop (workers));
                zmsg_send (&msg, backend);
            }
        }
    }
    //  When we're done, clean up properly
    while (zlist_size (workers)) {
        zframe_t *frame = (zframe_t *) zlist_pop (workers);
        zframe_destroy (&frame);
    }
    zlist_destroy (&workers);
    zctx_destroy (&ctx);
    return 0;
}
```

One thing CZMQ provides is clean interrupt handling. This means that Ctrl-C will cause any blocking ØMQ call to exit with a return code of -1 and errno set to EINTR. The high-level recv methods will return NULL in such cases. So, you can cleanly exit a loop like this:

```
while (true) {
    zstr_send (client, "HELLO");
    char *reply = zstr_recv (client);
    if (!reply)
        break;              // Interrupted
    printf ("Client: %s\n", reply);
    free (reply);
    sleep (1);
}
```

Or, if you're calling zmq_poll(), test on the return code:

```
if (zmq_poll (items, 2, 1000 * 1000) == -1)
    break;              // Interrupted
```

The previous example still uses zmq_poll(). So how about reactors? The CZMQ zloop reactor is simple but functional. It lets you:

- Set a reader on any socket (i.e., code that is called whenever the socket has input).
- Cancel a reader on a socket.
- Set a timer that goes off once or multiple times at specific intervals.
- Cancel a timer.

zloop, of course, uses zmq_poll() internally. It rebuilds its poll set each time you add or remove readers, and it calculates the poll timeout to match the next timer. Then it calls the reader and timer handlers for each socket and timer that need attention.

When we use a reactor pattern, our code turns inside out. The main logic looks like this:

```
zloop_t *reactor = zloop_new ();
zloop_reader (reactor, self->backend, s_handle_backend, self);
zloop_start (reactor);
zloop_destroy (&reactor);
```

The actual handling of messages sits inside dedicated functions or methods. You may not like the style—it's a matter of taste. What it does help with is mixing timers and socket activity. In the rest of this text, we'll use zmq_poll() in simpler cases, and zloop in more complex examples.

Example 3-13 shows the load-balancing broker rewritten once again, this time to use zloop.

Example 3-13. Load-balancing broker using zloop (lbbroker3.c)

```
//
//  Load-balancing broker
//  Demonstrates use of the CZMQ API and reactor style
//
//  The client and worker tasks are identical to the previous example
...
//  Our load-balancer structure, passed to reactor handlers
```

```
typedef struct {
    void *frontend;             //  Listen to clients
    void *backend;              //  Listen to workers
    zlist_t *workers;           //  List of ready workers
} lbbroker_t;
```

In the reactor design, each time a message arrives on a socket, the reactor passes it to a handler function. We have two handlers, one for the frontend and one for the backend, and as seen in Example 3-14.

Example 3-14. Load-balancing broker using zloop (lbbroker3.c): reactor design

```
//  Handle input from client, on frontend
int s_handle_frontend (zloop_t *loop, zmq_pollitem_t *poller, void *arg)
{
    lbbroker_t *self = (lbbroker_t *) arg;
    zmsg_t *msg = zmsg_recv (self->frontend);
    if (msg) {
        zmsg_wrap (msg, (zframe_t *) zlist_pop (self->workers));
        zmsg_send (&msg, self->backend);

        //  Cancel reader on frontend if we went from 1 to 0 workers
        if (zlist_size (self->workers) == 0) {
            zmq_pollitem_t poller = { self->frontend, 0, ZMQ_POLLIN };
            zloop_poller_end (loop, &poller);
        }
    }
    return 0;
}

//  Handle input from worker, on backend
int s_handle_backend (zloop_t *loop, zmq_pollitem_t *poller, void *arg)
{
    //  Use worker identity for load balancing
    lbbroker_t *self = (lbbroker_t *) arg;
    zmsg_t *msg = zmsg_recv (self->backend);
    if (msg) {
        zframe_t *identity = zmsg_unwrap (msg);
        zlist_append (self->workers, identity);

        //  Enable reader on frontend if we went from 0 to 1 workers
        if (zlist_size (self->workers) == 1) {
            zmq_pollitem_t poller = { self->frontend, 0, ZMQ_POLLIN };
            zloop_poller (loop, &poller, s_handle_frontend, self);
        }
        //  Forward message to client if it's not a READY
        zframe_t *frame = zmsg_first (msg);
        if (memcmp (zframe_data (frame), WORKER_READY, 1) == 0)
            zmsg_destroy (&msg);
        else
            zmsg_send (&msg, self->frontend);
    }
```

```
        return 0;
}
```

The main task (Example 3-15) now sets up child tasks and then starts its reactor. If you press Ctrl-C, the reactor exits and the main task shuts down. Because the reactor is a CZMQ class, this example may not translate into all languages equally well.

Example 3-15. Load-balancing broker using zloop (lbbroker3.c): main task

```
int main (void)
{
    zctx_t *ctx = zctx_new ();
    lbbroker_t *self = (lbbroker_t *) zmalloc (sizeof (lbbroker_t));
    self->frontend = zsocket_new (ctx, ZMQ_ROUTER);
    self->backend = zsocket_new (ctx, ZMQ_ROUTER);
    zsocket_bind (self->frontend, "ipc://frontend.ipc");
    zsocket_bind (self->backend, "ipc://backend.ipc");

    int client_nbr;
    for (client_nbr = 0; client_nbr < NBR_CLIENTS; client_nbr++)
        zthread_new (client_task, NULL);
    int worker_nbr;
    for (worker_nbr = 0; worker_nbr < NBR_WORKERS; worker_nbr++)
        zthread_new (worker_task, NULL);

    //  Queue of available workers
    self->workers = zlist_new ();

    //  Prepare reactor and fire it up
    zloop_t *reactor = zloop_new ();
    zmq_pollitem_t poller = { self->backend, 0, ZMQ_POLLIN };
    zloop_poller (reactor, &poller, s_handle_backend, self);
    zloop_start  (reactor);
    zloop_destroy (&reactor);

    //  When we're done, clean up properly
    while (zlist_size (self->workers)) {
        zframe_t *frame = (zframe_t *) zlist_pop (self->workers);
        zframe_destroy (&frame);
    }
    zlist_destroy (&self->workers);
    zctx_destroy (&ctx);
    free (self);
    return 0;
}
```

Getting applications to shut down properly when you send them Ctrl-C can be tricky. If you use the zctx class it'll automatically set up signal handling, but your code still has to cooperate. You must break any loop if zmq_poll() returns -1 or if any of the zstr_recv(), zframe_recv(), or zmsg_recv() methods returns NULL. If you have nested loops, it can be useful to make the outer ones conditional on !zctx_interrupted.

The Asynchronous Client/Server Pattern

In the ROUTER to DEALER example, we saw a 1-to-N use case where one server talks asynchronously to multiple workers. We can turn this upside down to get a very useful N-to-1 architecture where various clients talk to a single server, and do this asynchronously (Figure 3-12).

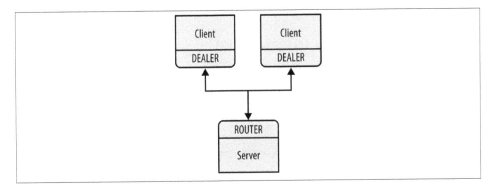

Figure 3-12. Asynchronous client/server

Here's how it works:

- Clients connect to the server and send requests.
- For each request, the server sends 0 or more replies.
- Clients can send multiple requests without waiting for a reply.
- Servers can send multiple replies without waiting for new requests.

Example 3-16 shows how this works.

Example 3-16. Asynchronous client/server (asyncsrv.c)

```
//
//  Asynchronous client-to-server (DEALER to ROUTER)
//
//  While this example runs in a single process, that is only to make
//  it easier to start and stop the example. Each task has its own
//  context and conceptually acts as a separate process.

#include "czmq.h"
```

```
// --------------------------------------------------------------------
// This is our client task.
// It connects to the server, and then sends a request once per second.
// It collects responses as they arrive, and it prints them out. We will
// run several client tasks in parallel, each with a different random ID.

static void *
client_task (void *args)
{
    zctx_t *ctx = zctx_new ();
    void *client = zsocket_new (ctx, ZMQ_DEALER);

    // Set random identity to make tracing easier
    char identity [10];
    sprintf (identity, "%04X-%04X", randof (0x10000), randof (0x10000));
    zsockopt_set_identity (client, identity);
    zsocket_connect (client, "tcp://localhost:5570");

    zmq_pollitem_t items [] = { { client, 0, ZMQ_POLLIN, 0 } };
    int request_nbr = 0;
    while (true) {
        // Tick once per second, pulling in arriving messages
        int centitick;
        for (centitick = 0; centitick < 100; centitick++) {
            zmq_poll (items, 1, 10 * ZMQ_POLL_MSEC);
            if (items [0].revents & ZMQ_POLLIN) {
                zmsg_t *msg = zmsg_recv (client);
                zframe_print (zmsg_last (msg), identity);
                zmsg_destroy (&msg);
            }
        }
        zstr_sendf (client, "request #%d", ++request_nbr);
    }
    zctx_destroy (&ctx);
    return NULL;
}
```

Our server task is presented in Example 3-17. It uses the multithreaded server model
to deal requests out to a pool of workers and route replies back to clients. One worker
can handle one request at a time, but one client can talk to multiple workers at once.

Example 3-17. Asynchronous client/server (asyncsrv.c): server task

```
static void server_worker (void *args, zctx_t *ctx, void *pipe);

void *server_task (void *args)
{
    zctx_t *ctx = zctx_new ();

    // Frontend socket talks to clients over TCP
```

```
void *frontend = zsocket_new (ctx, ZMQ_ROUTER);
zsocket_bind (frontend, "tcp://*:5570");


// Backend socket talks to workers over inproc
void *backend = zsocket_new (ctx, ZMQ_DEALER);
zsocket_bind (backend, "inproc://backend");

// Launch pool of worker threads, precise number is not critical
int thread_nbr;
for (thread_nbr = 0; thread_nbr < 5; thread_nbr++)
    zthread_fork (ctx, server_worker, NULL);

// Connect backend to frontend via a proxy
zmq_proxy (frontend, backend, NULL);

zctx_destroy (&ctx);
return NULL;
}
```

Each worker task works on one request at a time and sends back a random number of replies, with random delays between replies, as illustrated in Example 3-18.

Example 3-18. Asynchronous client/server (asyncsrv.c): worker task

```
static void
server_worker (void *args, zctx_t *ctx, void *pipe)
{
    void *worker = zsocket_new (ctx, ZMQ_DEALER);
    zsocket_connect (worker, "inproc://backend");

    while (true) {
        // The DEALER socket gives us the reply envelope and message
        zmsg_t *msg = zmsg_recv (worker);
        zframe_t *identity = zmsg_pop (msg);
        zframe_t *content = zmsg_pop (msg);
        assert (content);
        zmsg_destroy (&msg);

        // Send 0..4 replies back
        int reply, replies = randof (5);
        for (reply = 0; reply < replies; reply++) {
            // Sleep for some fraction of a second
            zclock_sleep (randof (1000) + 1);
            zframe_send (&identity, worker, ZFRAME_REUSE + ZFRAME_MORE);
            zframe_send (&content, worker, ZFRAME_REUSE);
        }
        zframe_destroy (&identity);
        zframe_destroy (&content);
    }
}
```

```
//  The main thread simply starts several clients and a server, and then
//  waits for the server to finish.

int main (void)
{
    zthread_new (client_task, NULL);
    zthread_new (client_task, NULL);
    zthread_new (client_task, NULL);
    zthread_new (server_task, NULL);

    //  Run for 5 seconds then quit
    zclock_sleep (5 * 1000);
    return 0;
}
```

The example runs in one process, with multiple threads simulating a real multiprocess architecture. When you run the example, you'll see three clients (each with a random ID), printing out the replies they get from the server. Look carefully and you'll see each client task gets zero or more replies per request.

Some comments on this code:

- The clients send a request once per second, and get zero or more replies back. To make this work using zmq_poll(), we can't simply poll with a 1-second timeout, or we'd end up sending a new request only one second *after we received the last reply*. So we poll at a high frequency (100 times at 1/100th of a second per poll), which is approximately accurate.

- The server uses a pool of worker threads, each processing one request synchronously. It connects these to its frontend socket using an internal queue. It connects the frontend and backend sockets using a zmq_proxy() call.

Figure 3-13 shows a detailed view of the architecture of this example. Note that we're doing DEALER to ROUTER dialog between the clients and the server, but internally between the server's main thread and workers, we're doing DEALER to DEALER. If the workers were strictly synchronous, we'd use REP, but since we want to send multiple replies we need an async socket. We do *not* want to route replies; they always go to the single server thread that sent us the request.

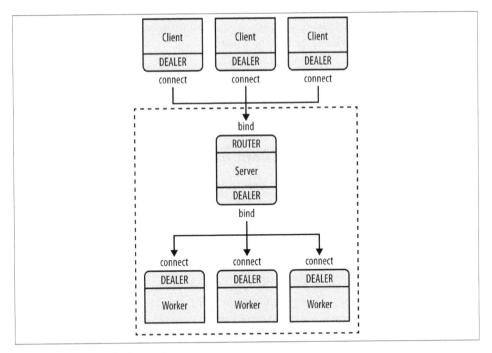

Figure 3-13. Detail of asynchronous server

Let's think about the routing envelope. The client sends a simple message. The server thread receives a two-part message (real message prefixed by client identity). We send this on to the worker, which treats it as a normal reply envelope and returns that to us. We can then use it to route the reply back to the right client:

```
      client              server      frontend      worker
   [ DEALER ]<---->[ ROUTER <----> DEALER <----> DEALER ]
             1 part        2 parts       2 parts
```

Now for the sockets: we could use the load-balancing ROUTER to DEALER pattern to talk to workers, but it's extra work. In this case, a DEALER to DEALER pattern is probably fine: the trade-off is lower latency for each request, but higher risk of unbalanced work distribution. Simplicity wins in this case.

When you build servers that maintain stateful conversations with clients, you will run into a classic problem. If the server keeps some state per client, and clients keep coming and going, eventually the server will run out of resources. Even if the same clients keep connecting, if you're using default identities, each connection will look like a new one.

We cheat in this example by keeping state only for a very short time (the time it takes a worker to process a request) and then throwing away the state. But that's not practical for many cases. To properly manage client state in a stateful asynchronous server, you have to:

- Do heartbeating from client to server. In our example, we send a request once per second, which can reliably be used as a heartbeat.

- Store state using the client identity (whether generated or explicit) as the key.

- Detect a stopped heartbeat. If there's no request from a client within, say, two seconds, the server can detect this and destroy any state it's holding for that client.

Worked Example: Inter-Broker Routing

Let's take everything we've seen so far and scale things up to a real application. We'll build this step-by-step over several iterations.

Suppose our best client calls us urgently and asks for a design of a large cloud computing facility. He has this vision of a cloud that spans many data centers, each a cluster of clients and workers, and that works together as a whole.

Because we're smart enough to know that practice always beats theory, we propose to make a working simulation using ØMQ. Our client, eager to lock down the budget before his own boss changes his mind, and having read great things about ØMQ on Twitter, agrees.

Establishing the Details

Several espressos later, we want to jump into writing code, but a little voice tells us to get more details before making a sensational solution to entirely the wrong problem. "What kind of work is the cloud doing?" we ask. The client explains:

- Workers run on various kinds of hardware, but they are all able to handle any task. There are several hundred workers per cluster, and as many as a dozen clusters in total.

- Clients create tasks for workers. Each task is an independent unit of work, and all the client wants is to find an available worker and send it the task as soon as possible. There will be a lot of clients and they'll come and go arbitrarily.

- The real difficulty is to be able to add and remove clusters at any time. A cluster can leave or join the cloud instantly, bringing all its workers and clients with it.

- If there are no workers in its own cluster, a client's tasks will go off to other available workers in the cloud.

- Clients send out one task at a time, waiting for a reply. If they don't get an answer within X seconds, they'll just send out the task again. This isn't our concern; the client API does it already.

- Workers process one task at a time; they are very simple beasts. If they crash, they get restarted by whatever script started them.

So we double-check to make sure that we understood this correctly:

- "There will be some kind of super-duper network interconnect between clusters, right?" we ask. The client says, "Yes, of course, we're not idiots."
- "What kind of volumes are we talking about?" we ask. The client replies, "Up to a thousand clients per cluster, each doing at most 10 requests per second. Requests are small, and replies are also small, no more than 1K bytes each."

So we do a little calculation and see that this will work nicely over plain TCP. 2,500 clients * 10/second * 1,000 bytes * 2 directions = 50 MB/sec or 400 Mb/sec, not a problem for a 1 Gb network.

It's a straightforward problem that requires no exotic hardware or protocols, just some clever routing algorithms and careful design. We start by designing one cluster (one data center) and then we figure out how to connect clusters together.

Architecture of a Single Cluster

Workers and clients are synchronous. We want to use the load-balancing pattern to route tasks to workers. Workers are all identical; our facility has no notion of different services. Workers are anonymous; clients never address them directly. We make no attempt here to provide guaranteed delivery, retries, and so on.

For reasons we already examined, clients and workers won't speak to each other directly. This makes it impossible to add or remove nodes dynamically. So, our basic model consists of the request-reply message broker we saw earlier (Figure 3-14).

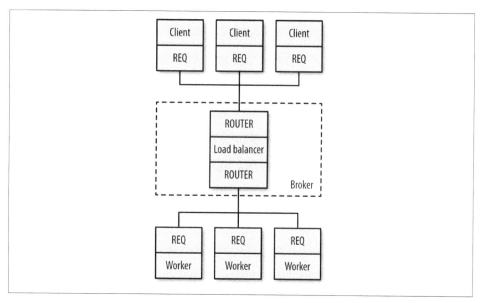

Figure 3-14. Cluster architecture

Scaling to Multiple Clusters

Now we scale this out to more than one cluster. Each cluster has a set of clients and workers, and a broker that joins these together, as illustrated in Figure 3-15.

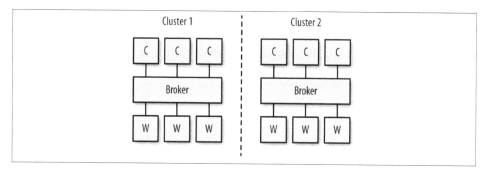

Figure 3-15. Multiple clusters

The question is, how do we get the clients of each cluster talking to the workers of the other cluster? There are a few possibilities, each with pros and cons:

- Clients could connect directly to both brokers. The advantage here is that we don't need to modify the brokers or workers. However, the clients get more complex and become aware of the overall topology. If we want to add a third or fourth cluster, for example, the clients are affected. In effect, we have to move routing and failover logic into the clients, and that's not nice.

- Workers might connect directly to both brokers. But REQ workers can't do that; they can only reply to one broker. We might use REPs, but REPs don't give us customizable broker-to-worker routing like load balancing does, only the built-in load balancing. That's a fail; if we want to distribute work to idle workers, we precisely need load balancing. One solution would be to use ROUTER sockets for the worker nodes. Let's label this "Idea #1."

- Brokers could connect to each other. This looks the neatest because it creates the fewest additional connections. We can't add clusters on the fly, but that is probably out of our scope anyway. With this solution, clients and workers remain ignorant of the real network topology, and brokers tell each other when they have spare capacity. Let's label this "Idea #2."

Let's explore Idea #1. In this model, we have workers connecting to both brokers and accepting jobs from either one (Figure 3-16).

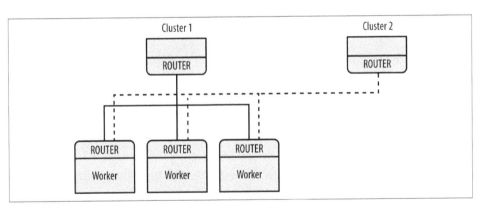

Figure 3-16. Idea 1: cross-connected workers

It looks feasible. However, it doesn't provide what we wanted, which was that clients get local workers if possible and remote workers only if it's better than waiting. Also, workers will signal "ready" to both brokers and so can get two jobs at once, while other workers remain idle. It seems this design fails because again we're putting routing logic at the edges.

So, Idea #2 then. We interconnect the brokers and don't touch the clients or workers, which are REQs like we're used to (Figure 3-17).

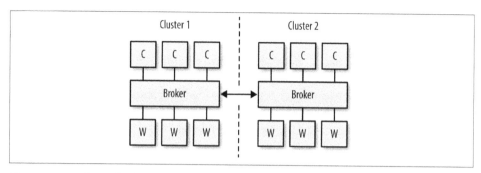

Figure 3-17. Idea 2: brokers talking to each other

This design is appealing because the problem is solved in one place, invisible to the rest of the world. Basically, brokers open secret channels to each other and whisper, like camel traders, "Hey, I've got some spare capacity. If you have too many clients give me a shout and we'll deal."

In effect, it is just a more sophisticated routing algorithm: brokers become subcontractors for each other. There are other things to like about this design, even before we play with real code:

- It treats the common case (clients and workers on the same cluster) as the default and does extra work for the exceptional case (shuffling jobs between clusters).

- It lets us use different message flows for the different types of work. That means we can handle them differently, for example using different types of network connection.

- It feels like it would scale smoothly. Interconnecting three or more brokers doesn't get overly complex. If we find this to be a problem, it's easy to solve by adding a super-broker.

We'll now make a worked example. We'll pack an entire cluster into one process. That is obviously not realistic, but it makes it simple to simulate, and the simulation can accurately scale to real processes. This is the beauty of ØMQ—you can design at the micro level and scale that up to the macro level. Threads become processes, and then become boxes, and the patterns and logic remain the same. Each of our "cluster" processes contains client threads, worker threads, and a broker thread.

We know the basic model well by now:

- The REQ client (REQ) threads create workloads and pass them to the broker (ROUTER).

- The REQ worker (REQ) threads process workloads and return the results to the broker (ROUTER).

- The broker queues and distributes workloads using the load-balancing pattern.

Federation Versus Peering

There are several possible ways to interconnect brokers. What we want is to be able to tell other brokers, "We have capacity," and then receive multiple tasks. We also need to be able to tell other brokers, "Stop, we're full." It doesn't need to be perfect; sometimes we may accept jobs we can't process immediately, but we'll do them as soon as possible.

The simplest interconnect is *federation*, in which brokers simulate clients and workers for each other. We would do this by connecting our frontend to the other broker's backend socket (Figure 3-18). Note that it is legal to both bind a socket to an endpoint and connect it to other endpoints.

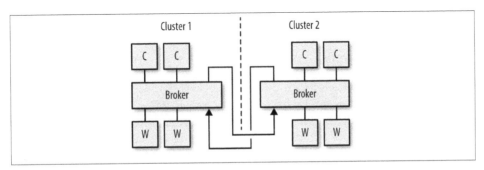

Figure 3-18. Cross-connected brokers in federation model

This would give us simple logic in both brokers and a reasonably good mechanism: when there are no clients, tell the other broker "ready," and accept one job from it. The problem is that it is *too* simple for this problem. A federated broker would be able to handle only one task at a time. If the broker emulates a lock-step client and worker, it will by definition also be lock-step, and if it has lots of available workers, they won't be used. Our brokers need to be connected in a fully asynchronous fashion.

The federation model is perfect for other kinds of routing, especially service-oriented architectures (SOAs), which route by service name and proximity rather than load balancing or round robin. So don't dismiss it as useless; it's just not right for all use cases.

Instead of federation, let's look at a *peering* approach in which brokers are explicitly aware of each other and talk over privileged channels. Let's break this down, assuming we want to interconnect N brokers. Each broker has (N – 1) peers, and all brokers are using exactly the same code and logic. There are two distinct flows of information between brokers:

- Each broker needs to tell its peers how many workers it has available at any time. This can be fairly simple information—just a quantity that is updated regularly. The obvious (and correct) socket pattern for this is publish-subscribe: every broker opens a PUB socket and publishes state information on that, and every broker also opens a SUB socket and connects that to the PUB socket of every other broker, to get state information from its peers.

- Each broker needs a way to delegate tasks to a peer and get replies back, asynchronously. We'll do this using ROUTER sockets; no other combination works. Each broker has two such sockets: one for tasks it receives and one for tasks it delegates. If we didn't use two sockets, it would be more work to know whether we were reading a request or a reply each time. That would mean adding more information to the message envelope.

And there is also the flow of information between a broker and its local clients and workers.

The Naming Ceremony

Three flows * two sockets for each flow = six sockets that we have to manage in the broker. Choosing good names is vital to keeping a multisocket juggling act reasonably coherent in our minds. Sockets *do* something, and what they do should form the basis for their names. It's about being able to read the code several weeks later on a cold Monday morning before coffee, and not feel any pain.

Let's do a shamanistic naming ceremony for the sockets. The three flows are:

- A *local* request-reply flow between the broker and its clients and workers
- A *cloud* request-reply flow between the broker and its peer brokers
- A *state* flow between the broker and its peer brokers

Finding meaningful names that are all the same length means our code will align nicely. It's not a big thing, but attention to detail helps. For each flow, the broker has two sockets that we can orthogonally call the *frontend* and *backend*. We've used these names quite often. A frontend receives information or tasks. A backend sends those out to other peers. The conceptual flow is from front to back (with replies going in the opposite direction, from back to front).

So, in all the code we write for this tutorial, we will use these socket names:

- `localfe` and `localbe` for the local flow
- `cloudfe` and `cloudbe` for the cloud flow
- `statefe` and `statebe` for the state flow

For our transport, because we're simulating the whole thing on one box, we'll use `ipc` for everything. This has the advantage of working like `tcp` in terms of connectivity (i.e., it's a disconnected transport, unlike `inproc`), yet we don't need IP addresses or DNS names, which would be a pain here. Instead, we will use `ipc` endpoints called `something-local`, `something-cloud`, and `something-state`, where `something` is the name of our simulated cluster.

You might be thinking that this is a lot of work for some names. Why not call them `s1`, `s2`, `s3`, `s4`, etc.? The answer is that if your brain is not a perfect machine, you need a lot of help when reading code, and we'll see that these names do help. It's easier to remember "three flows, two directions" than "six different sockets" (Figure 3-19).

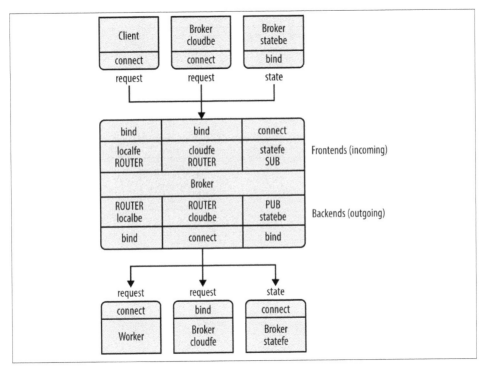

Figure 3-19. Broker socket arrangement

Note that we connect the `cloudbe` in each broker to the `cloudfe` in every other broker, and likewise we connect the `statebe` in each broker to the `statefe` in every other broker.

Prototyping the State Flow

Because each socket flow has its own little traps for the unwary, we will test them in real code one by one, rather than trying to throw the whole lot into code in one go. When we're happy with each flow, we can put them together into a full program. We'll start with the state flow (Figure 3-20).

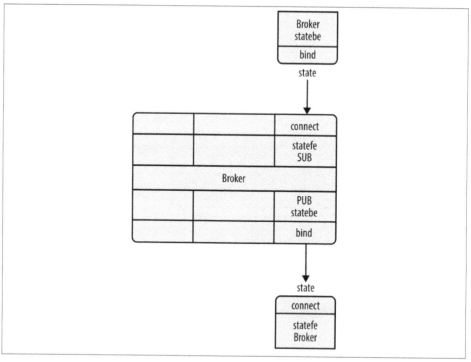

Figure 3-20. The state flow

Example 3-19 shows how this works in code.

Example 3-19. Prototype state flow (peering1.c)

```
//
//  Broker peering simulation (part 1)
//  Prototypes the state flow
//
#include "czmq.h"

int main (int argc, char *argv [])
{
    //  First argument is this broker's name
    //  Other arguments are our peers' names
    //
    if (argc < 2) {
        printf ("syntax: peering1 me {you}...\n");
        exit (EXIT_FAILURE);
    }
    char *self = argv [1];
```

```
    printf ("I: preparing broker at %s...\n", self);
    srandom ((unsigned) time (NULL));

    zctx_t *ctx = zctx_new ();

    //  Bind state backend to endpoint
    void *statebe = zsocket_new (ctx, ZMQ_PUB);
    zsocket_bind (statebe, "ipc://%s-state.ipc", self);

    //  Connect statefe to all peers
    void *statefe = zsocket_new (ctx, ZMQ_SUB);
    zsockopt_set_subscribe (statefe, "");
    int argn;
    for (argn = 2; argn < argc; argn++) {
        char *peer = argv [argn];
        printf ("I: connecting to state backend at '%s'\n", peer);
        zsocket_connect (statefe, "ipc://%s-state.ipc", peer);
    }
```

The main loop (Example 3-20) sends out status messages to peers and collects status messages back from peers. The zmq_poll() timeout defines our own heartbeat.

Example 3-20. Prototype state flow (peering1.c): main loop

```
    while (true) {
        //  Poll for activity, or 1-second timeout
        zmq_pollitem_t items [] = { { statefe, 0, ZMQ_POLLIN, 0 } };
        int rc = zmq_poll (items, 1, 1000 * ZMQ_POLL_MSEC);
        if (rc == -1)
            break;              //  Interrupted

        //  Handle incoming status messages
        if (items [0].revents & ZMQ_POLLIN) {
            char *peer_name = zstr_recv (statefe);
            char *available = zstr_recv (statefe);
            printf ("%s - %s workers free\n", peer_name, available);
            free (peer_name);
            free (available);
        }
        else {
            //  Send random values for worker availability
            zstr_sendm (statebe, self);
            zstr_sendf (statebe, "%d", randof (10));
        }
    }
    zctx_destroy (&ctx);
    return EXIT_SUCCESS;
}
```

Notes about this code:

- Each broker has an identity that we use to construct `ipc` endpoint names. A real broker would need to work with TCP and a more sophisticated configuration scheme. We'll look at such schemes later in this book, but for now, using generated `ipc` names lets us ignore the problem of where to get TCP/IP addresses or names.

- We use a `zmq_poll()` loop as the core of the program. This processes incoming messages and sends out state messages. We send a state message *only* if we did not get any incoming messages *and* we waited for a second. If we send out a state message each time we get one in, we'll get message storms.

- We use a two-part pub-sub message consisting of sender address and data. Note that we will need to know the address of the publisher in order to send it tasks, and the only way to send this explicitly is as a part of the message.

- We don't set identities on subscribers, because if we did we'd get outdated state information when connecting to running brokers.

- We don't set an HWM on the publisher, yet if we were using ØMQ v2.x, that would be a wise idea.

We can build this little program and run it three times to simulate three clusters. Let's call them DC1, DC2, and DC3 (the names are arbitrary). Run these three commands, each in a separate window:

```
peering1 DC1 DC2 DC3  #  Start DC1 and connect to DC2 and DC3
peering1 DC2 DC1 DC3  #  Start DC2 and connect to DC1 and DC3
peering1 DC3 DC1 DC2  #  Start DC3 and connect to DC1 and DC2
```

You'll see each cluster report the state of its peers, and after a few seconds they will all happily be printing random numbers once per second. Try this and satisfy yourself that the three brokers all match up and synchronize to per-second state updates.

In real life, we would not send out state messages at regular intervals, but rather whenever we had a state change—i.e., whenever a worker became available or unavailable. That may seem like a lot of traffic, but state messages are small and we've established that the inter-cluster connections are superfast.

If we wanted to send state messages at precise intervals, we'd create a child thread and open the `statebe` socket in that thread. We'd then send irregular state updates to that child thread from our main thread and allow the child thread to conflate them into regular outgoing messages. This is more work than we need here, though.

Prototyping the Local and Cloud Flows

Let's now prototype the flow of tasks via the local and cloud sockets (Figure 3-21). This code pulls requests from clients and then distributes them to local workers and cloud peers on a random basis.

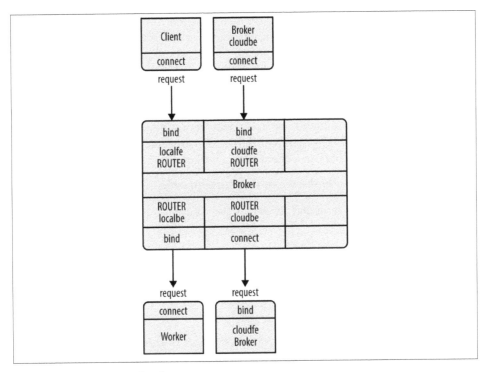

Figure 3-21. The flow of tasks

Before we jump into the code, which is getting a little complex, let's sketch the core routing logic and break it down into a simple but robust design.

We need two queues, one for requests from local clients and one for requests from cloud clients. One option would be to pull messages off the local and cloud frontends and pump these onto their respective queues. But this is kind of pointless, because ØMQ sockets *are* queues already. So let's use the ØMQ socket buffers as queues.

This was the technique we used in the load-balancing broker earlier in this chapter, and it worked nicely. We only read from the two frontends when there is somewhere to send the requests. We can always read from the backends, as they give us replies to route back. As long as the backends aren't talking to us, there's no point in even looking at the frontends.

So, our main loop becomes:

- Poll the backends for activity. When we get a message, it may be "ready" from a worker or it may be a reply. If it's a reply, we route it back via the local or cloud frontend.
- If a worker has replied, it has become available, so we queue it and count it.

- While there are workers available, we take a request (if there are any) from either frontend and route it either to a local worker or randomly to a cloud peer.

Randomly sending tasks to a peer broker rather than a worker simulates work distribution across the cluster. It's dumb, but that is fine for this stage.

We use broker identities to route messages between brokers. Each broker has a name that we provide on the command line in this simple prototype. As long as these names don't overlap with the ØMQ-generated UUIDs used for client nodes, we can figure out whether to route a reply back to a client or to a broker.

Examples 3-21 through 3-26 show how this works in code.

Example 3-21. Prototype local and cloud flow (peering2.c)

```
//
//  Broker peering simulation (part 2)
//  Prototypes the request-reply flow
//
#include "czmq.h"

#define NBR_CLIENTS 10
#define NBR_WORKERS 3
#define WORKER_READY   "\001"      //  Signals worker is ready

//  Our own name; in practice this would be configured per node
static char *self;
```

The client task, shown in Example 3-22, implements a request-reply dialog using a standard synchronous REQ socket.

Example 3-22. Prototype local and cloud flow (peering2.c): client task

```
static void *
client_task (void *args)
{
    zctx_t *ctx = zctx_new ();
    void *client = zsocket_new (ctx, ZMQ_REQ);
    zsocket_connect (client, "ipc://%s-localfe.ipc", self);

    while (true) {
        //  Send request, get reply
        zstr_send (client, "HELLO");
        char *reply = zstr_recv (client);
        if (!reply)
            break;                 //  Interrupted
        printf ("Client: %s\n", reply);
        free (reply);
        sleep (1);
    }
    zctx_destroy (&ctx);
```

```
        return NULL;
}
```

The worker task, shown in Example 3-23, plugs into the load balancer using a REQ
socket.

Example 3-23. Prototype local and cloud flow (peering2.c): worker task

```
static void *
worker_task (void *args)
{
    zctx_t *ctx = zctx_new ();
    void *worker = zsocket_new (ctx, ZMQ_REQ);
    zsocket_connect (worker, "ipc://%s-localbe.ipc", self);

    // Tell broker we're ready for work
    zframe_t *frame = zframe_new (WORKER_READY, 1);
    zframe_send (&frame, worker, 0);

    // Process messages as they arrive
    while (true) {
        zmsg_t *msg = zmsg_recv (worker);
        if (!msg)
            break;              // Interrupted

        zframe_print (zmsg_last (msg), "Worker: ");
        zframe_reset (zmsg_last (msg), "OK", 2);
        zmsg_send (&msg, worker);
    }
    zctx_destroy (&ctx);
    return NULL;
}
```

The main task begins by setting up its frontend and backend sockets and then starting
its client and worker tasks (Example 3-24).

Example 3-24. Prototype local and cloud flow (peering2.c): main task

```
int main (int argc, char *argv [])
{
    // First argument is this broker's name
    // Other arguments are our peers' names
    //
    if (argc < 2) {
        printf ("syntax: peering2 me {you}...\n");
        exit (EXIT_FAILURE);
    }
    self = argv [1];
    printf ("I: preparing broker at %s...\n", self);
    srandom ((unsigned) time (NULL));

    zctx_t *ctx = zctx_new ();
```

```
// Bind cloud frontend to endpoint
void *cloudfe = zsocket_new (ctx, ZMQ_ROUTER);
zsockopt_set_identity (cloudfe, self);
zsocket_bind (cloudfe, "ipc://%s-cloud.ipc", self);

// Connect cloud backend to all peers
void *cloudbe = zsocket_new (ctx, ZMQ_ROUTER);
zsockopt_set_identity (cloudbe, self);
int argn;
for (argn = 2; argn < argc; argn++) {
    char *peer = argv [argn];
    printf ("I: connecting to cloud frontend at '%s'\n", peer);
    zsocket_connect (cloudbe, "ipc://%s-cloud.ipc", peer);
}
// Prepare local frontend and backend
void *localfe = zsocket_new (ctx, ZMQ_ROUTER);
zsocket_bind (localfe, "ipc://%s-localfe.ipc", self);
void *localbe = zsocket_new (ctx, ZMQ_ROUTER);
zsocket_bind (localbe, "ipc://%s-localbe.ipc", self);

// Get user to tell us when we can start...
printf ("Press Enter when all brokers are started: ");
getchar ();

// Start local workers
int worker_nbr;
for (worker_nbr = 0; worker_nbr < NBR_WORKERS; worker_nbr++)
    zthread_new (worker_task, NULL);

// Start local clients
int client_nbr;
for (client_nbr = 0; client_nbr < NBR_CLIENTS; client_nbr++)
    zthread_new (client_task, NULL);
```

Next, we handle the request-reply flow (Example 3-25). We're using load balancing to poll workers at all times, and clients only when there are one or more workers available.

Example 3-25. Prototype local and cloud flow (peering2.c): request-reply handling

```
// Least recently used queue of available workers
int capacity = 0;
zlist_t *workers = zlist_new ();

while (true) {
    // First, route any waiting replies from workers
    zmq_pollitem_t backends [] = {
        { localbe, 0, ZMQ_POLLIN, 0 },
        { cloudbe, 0, ZMQ_POLLIN, 0 }
    };
    // If we have no workers, wait indefinitely
    int rc = zmq_poll (backends, 2,
        capacity? 1000 * ZMQ_POLL_MSEC: -1);
```

```
        if (rc == -1)
            break;              //  Interrupted

        //  Handle reply from local worker
        zmsg_t *msg = NULL;
        if (backends [0].revents & ZMQ_POLLIN) {
            msg = zmsg_recv (localbe);
            if (!msg)
                break;          //  Interrupted
            zframe_t *identity = zmsg_unwrap (msg);
            zlist_append (workers, identity);
            capacity++;

            //  If it's READY, don't route the message any further
            zframe_t *frame = zmsg_first (msg);
            if (memcmp (zframe_data (frame), WORKER_READY, 1) == 0)
                zmsg_destroy (&msg);
        }
        //  Or handle reply from peer broker
        else
        if (backends [1].revents & ZMQ_POLLIN) {
            msg = zmsg_recv (cloudbe);
            if (!msg)
                break;          //  Interrupted
            //  We don't use peer broker identity for anything
            zframe_t *identity = zmsg_unwrap (msg);
            zframe_destroy (&identity);
        }
        //  Route reply to cloud if it's addressed to a broker
        for (argn = 2; msg && argn < argc; argn++) {
            char *data = (char *) zframe_data (zmsg_first (msg));
            size_t size = zframe_size (zmsg_first (msg));
            if (size == strlen (argv [argn])
            &&  memcmp (data, argv [argn], size) == 0)
                zmsg_send (&msg, cloudfe);
        }
        //  Route reply to client if we still need to
        if (msg)
            zmsg_send (&msg, localfe);
```

Now we route as many client requests as we have worker capacity for, as illustrated in
Example 3-26. We may reroute requests from our local frontend, but not from the cloud
frontend. We'll reroute randomly for now, just to test things out. In the next version,
we'll do this properly by calculating cloud capacity.

Example 3-26. Prototype local and cloud flow (peering2.c): route client requests

```
        while (capacity) {
            zmq_pollitem_t frontends [] = {
                { localfe, 0, ZMQ_POLLIN, 0 },
                { cloudfe, 0, ZMQ_POLLIN, 0 }
            };
```

```
            rc = zmq_poll (frontends, 2, 0);
            assert (rc >= 0);
            int reroutable = 0;
            //  We'll do peer brokers first, to prevent starvation
            if (frontends [1].revents & ZMQ_POLLIN) {
                msg = zmsg_recv (cloudfe);
                reroutable = 0;
            }
            else
            if (frontends [0].revents & ZMQ_POLLIN) {
                msg = zmsg_recv (localfe);
                reroutable = 1;
            }
            else
                break;      //  No work, go back to backends

            //  If reroutable, send to cloud 20% of the time
            //  Here we'd normally use cloud status information
            //
            if (reroutable && argc > 2 && randof (5) == 0) {
                //  Route to random broker peer
                int random_peer = randof (argc - 2) + 2;
                zmsg_pushmem (msg, argv [random_peer], strlen (argv [random_peer]));
                zmsg_send (&msg, cloudbe);
            }
            else {
                zframe_t *frame = (zframe_t *) zlist_pop (workers);
                zmsg_wrap (msg, frame);
                zmsg_send (&msg, localbe);
                capacity--;
            }
        }
    }
    //  When we're done, clean up properly
    while (zlist_size (workers)) {
        zframe_t *frame = (zframe_t *) zlist_pop (workers);
        zframe_destroy (&frame);
    }
    zlist_destroy (&workers);
    zctx_destroy (&ctx);
    return EXIT_SUCCESS;
}
```

Run this by, for instance, starting two instances of the broker in two windows:

```
peering2 me you
peering2 you me
```

Some comments on this code:

- In the C code at least, using the zmsg class makes life much easier, and our code much shorter. It's obviously an abstraction that works. If you build ØMQ applications in C, you should use CZMQ.

- Because we're not getting any state information from peers, we naively assume they are running. The code prompts us to confirm when we've started all the brokers. In the real case, we wouldn't send anything to brokers who had not told us they exist.

You can satisfy yourself that the code works by watching it run forever. If there were any misrouted messages, clients would end up blocking, and the brokers would stop printing trace information. You can prove that by killing either of the brokers. The other broker tries to send requests to the cloud, and one by one its clients block, waiting for an answer.

Putting It All Together

Let's put this together into a single package. As before, we'll run an entire cluster as one process. We're going to take the two previous examples and merge them into one properly working design that lets us simulate any number of clusters.

This code is the size of both previous prototypes together, at 270 lines of code. That's pretty good for a simulation of a cluster that includes clients and workers and cloud workload distribution. The code is presented in the following series of examples, beginning with Example 3-27.

Example 3-27. Full cluster simulation (peering3.c)

```
//
//  Broker peering simulation (part 3)
//  Prototypes the full flow of status and tasks
//
#include "czmq.h"

#define NBR_CLIENTS 10
#define NBR_WORKERS 5
#define WORKER_READY   "\001"     //  Signals worker is ready

//  Our own name; in practice this would be configured per node
static char *self;
```

Example 3-28 shows the client task. It issues a burst of requests and then sleeps for a few seconds. This simulates sporadic activity; when a number of clients are active at once, the local workers should be overloaded. The client uses a REQ socket for requests and also pushes statistics to the monitor socket.

Example 3-28. Full cluster simulation (peering3.c): client task

```c
static void *
client_task (void *args)
{
    zctx_t *ctx = zctx_new ();
    void *client = zsocket_new (ctx, ZMQ_REQ);
    zsocket_connect (client, "ipc://%s-localfe.ipc", self);
    void *monitor = zsocket_new (ctx, ZMQ_PUSH);
    zsocket_connect (monitor, "ipc://%s-monitor.ipc", self);

    while (true) {
        sleep (randof (5));
        int burst = randof (15);
        while (burst--) {
            char task_id [5];
            sprintf (task_id, "%04X", randof (0x10000));

            //  Send request with random hex ID
            zstr_send (client, task_id);

            //  Wait max 10 seconds for a reply, then complain
            zmq_pollitem_t pollset [1] = { { client, 0, ZMQ_POLLIN, 0 } };
            int rc = zmq_poll (pollset, 1, 10 * 1000 * ZMQ_POLL_MSEC);
            if (rc == -1)
                break;          //  Interrupted

            if (pollset [0].revents & ZMQ_POLLIN) {
                char *reply = zstr_recv (client);
                if (!reply)
                    break;              //  Interrupted
                //  Worker is supposed to answer us with our task ID
                assert (streq (reply, task_id));
                zstr_sendf (monitor, "%s", reply);
                free (reply);
            }
            else {
                zstr_sendf (monitor,
                    "E: CLIENT EXIT - lost task %s", task_id);
                return NULL;
            }
        }
    }
    zctx_destroy (&ctx);
    return NULL;
}
```

The worker task, which uses a REQ socket to plug into the load balancer, is shown in
Example 3-29. It's the same stub worker task that you've seen in other examples.

Example 3-29. Full cluster simulation (peering3.c): worker task

```
static void *
worker_task (void *args)
{
    zctx_t *ctx = zctx_new ();
    void *worker = zsocket_new (ctx, ZMQ_REQ);
    zsocket_connect (worker, "ipc://%s-localbe.ipc", self);

    //  Tell broker we're ready for work
    zframe_t *frame = zframe_new (WORKER_READY, 1);
    zframe_send (&frame, worker, 0);

    //  Process messages as they arrive
    while (true) {
        zmsg_t *msg = zmsg_recv (worker);
        if (!msg)
            break;                  //  Interrupted

        //  Workers are busy for 0/1 seconds
        sleep (randof (2));
        zmsg_send (&msg, worker);
    }
    zctx_destroy (&ctx);
    return NULL;
}
```

The main task begins by setting up all its sockets (Example 3-30). The local frontend talks to clients, and our local backend talks to workers. The cloud frontend talks to peer brokers as if they were clients, and the cloud backend talks to peer brokers as if they were workers. The state backend publishes regular state messages, and the state frontend subscribes to all state backends to collect these messages. Finally, we use a PULL monitor socket to collect printable messages from tasks.

Example 3-30. Full cluster simulation (peering3.c): main task

```
int main (int argc, char *argv [])
{
    //  First argument is this broker's name
    //  Other arguments are our peers' names
    //
    if (argc < 2) {
        printf ("syntax: peering3 me {you}...\n");
        exit (EXIT_FAILURE);
    }
    self = argv [1];
    printf ("I: preparing broker at %s...\n", self);
    srandom ((unsigned) time (NULL));

    zctx_t *ctx = zctx_new ();

    //  Prepare local frontend and backend
```

```
void *localfe = zsocket_new (ctx, ZMQ_ROUTER);
zsocket_bind (localfe, "ipc://%s-localfe.ipc", self);

void *localbe = zsocket_new (ctx, ZMQ_ROUTER);
zsocket_bind (localbe, "ipc://%s-localbe.ipc", self);

//  Bind cloud frontend to endpoint
void *cloudfe = zsocket_new (ctx, ZMQ_ROUTER);
zsockopt_set_identity (cloudfe, self);
zsocket_bind (cloudfe, "ipc://%s-cloud.ipc", self);

//  Connect cloud backend to all peers
void *cloudbe = zsocket_new (ctx, ZMQ_ROUTER);
zsockopt_set_identity (cloudbe, self);
int argn;
for (argn = 2; argn < argc; argn++) {
    char *peer = argv [argn];
    printf ("I: connecting to cloud frontend at '%s'\n", peer);
    zsocket_connect (cloudbe, "ipc://%s-cloud.ipc", peer);
}
//  Bind state backend to endpoint
void *statebe = zsocket_new (ctx, ZMQ_PUB);
zsocket_bind (statebe, "ipc://%s-state.ipc", self);

//  Connect state frontend to all peers
void *statefe = zsocket_new (ctx, ZMQ_SUB);
zsockopt_set_subscribe (statefe, "");
for (argn = 2; argn < argc; argn++) {
    char *peer = argv [argn];
    printf ("I: connecting to state backend at '%s'\n", peer);
    zsocket_connect (statefe, "ipc://%s-state.ipc", peer);
}
//  Prepare monitor socket
void *monitor = zsocket_new (ctx, ZMQ_PULL);
zsocket_bind (monitor, "ipc://%s-monitor.ipc", self);
```

After binding and connecting all our sockets, we start our child tasks—workers and clients—as shown in Example 3-31.

Example 3-31. Full cluster simulation (peering3.c): start child tasks

```
int worker_nbr;
for (worker_nbr = 0; worker_nbr < NBR_WORKERS; worker_nbr++)
    zthread_new (worker_task, NULL);

//  Start local clients
int client_nbr;
for (client_nbr = 0; client_nbr < NBR_CLIENTS; client_nbr++)
    zthread_new (client_task, NULL);

//  Queue of available workers
int local_capacity = 0;
```

```
int cloud_capacity = 0;
zlist_t *workers = zlist_new ();
```

The main loop (Example 3-32) has two parts. First, we poll workers and our two service sockets (statefe and monitor), in any case. If we have no ready workers, then there's no point in looking at incoming requests. These can remain on their internal ØMQ queues.

Example 3-32. Full cluster simulation (peering3.c): main loop

```
while (true) {
    zmq_pollitem_t primary [] = {
        { localbe, 0, ZMQ_POLLIN, 0 },
        { cloudbe, 0, ZMQ_POLLIN, 0 },
        { statefe, 0, ZMQ_POLLIN, 0 },
        { monitor, 0, ZMQ_POLLIN, 0 }
    };
    //  If we have no workers ready, wait indefinitely
    int rc = zmq_poll (primary, 4,
        local_capacity? 1000 * ZMQ_POLL_MSEC: -1);
    if (rc == -1)
        break;              //  Interrupted

    //  Track if capacity changes during this iteration
    int previous = local_capacity;

    //  Handle reply from local worker
    zmsg_t *msg = NULL;

    if (primary [0].revents & ZMQ_POLLIN) {
        msg = zmsg_recv (localbe);
        if (!msg)
            break;          //  Interrupted
        zframe_t *identity = zmsg_unwrap (msg);
        zlist_append (workers, identity);
        local_capacity++;

        //  If it's READY, don't route the message any further
        zframe_t *frame = zmsg_first (msg);
        if (memcmp (zframe_data (frame), WORKER_READY, 1) == 0)
            zmsg_destroy (&msg);
    }
    //  Or handle reply from peer broker
    else
    if (primary [1].revents & ZMQ_POLLIN) {
        msg = zmsg_recv (cloudbe);
        if (!msg)
            break;          //  Interrupted
        //  We don't use peer broker identity for anything
        zframe_t *identity = zmsg_unwrap (msg);
        zframe_destroy (&identity);
    }
```

```
//  Route reply to cloud if it's addressed to a broker
for (argn = 2; msg && argn < argc; argn++) {
    char *data = (char *) zframe_data (zmsg_first (msg));
    size_t size = zframe_size (zmsg_first (msg));
    if (size == strlen (argv [argn])
    &&  memcmp (data, argv [argn], size) == 0)
        zmsg_send (&msg, cloudfe);
}
//  Route reply to client if we still need to
if (msg)
    zmsg_send (&msg, localfe);
```

If we have input messages on our statefe or monitor sockets, we can process these immediately, as shown in Example 3-33.

Example 3-33. Full cluster simulation (peering3.c): handle state messages

```
if (primary [2].revents & ZMQ_POLLIN) {
    char *peer = zstr_recv (statefe);
    char *status = zstr_recv (statefe);
    cloud_capacity = atoi (status);
    free (peer);
    free (status);
}
if (primary [3].revents & ZMQ_POLLIN) {
    char *status = zstr_recv (monitor);
    printf ("%s\n", status);
    free (status);
}
```

Now we route as many clients requests as we can handle, as illustrated in Example 3-34. If we have local capacity, we poll both localfe and cloudfe. If we have cloud capacity only, we poll just localfe. We route any request locally if we can, or else we route it to the cloud.

Example 3-34. Full cluster simulation (peering3.c): route client requests

```
while (local_capacity + cloud_capacity) {
    zmq_pollitem_t secondary [] = {
        { localfe, 0, ZMQ_POLLIN, 0 },
        { cloudfe, 0, ZMQ_POLLIN, 0 }
    };
    if (local_capacity)
        rc = zmq_poll (secondary, 2, 0);
    else
        rc = zmq_poll (secondary, 1, 0);
    assert (rc >= 0);

    if (secondary [0].revents & ZMQ_POLLIN)
        msg = zmsg_recv (localfe);
    else
    if (secondary [1].revents & ZMQ_POLLIN)
```

```
            msg = zmsg_recv (cloudfe);
        else
            break;        //  No work, go back to primary

        if (local_capacity) {
            zframe_t *frame = (zframe_t *) zlist_pop (workers);
            zmsg_wrap (msg, frame);
            zmsg_send (&msg, localbe);
            local_capacity--;
        }
        else {
            //  Route to random broker peer
            int random_peer = randof (argc - 2) + 2;
            zmsg_pushmem (msg, argv [random_peer], strlen (argv [random_peer]));
            zmsg_send (&msg, cloudbe);
        }
    }
```

We broadcast capacity messages to other peers, as shown in Example 3-35; to reduce chatter, we do this only if our capacity has changed.

Example 3-35. Full cluster simulation (peering3.c): broadcast capacity

```
        if (local_capacity != previous) {
            //  We stick our own identity onto the envelope
            zstr_sendm (statebe, self);
            //  Broadcast new capacity
            zstr_sendf (statebe, "%d", local_capacity);
        }
    }
    //  When we're done, clean up properly
    while (zlist_size (workers)) {
        zframe_t *frame = (zframe_t *) zlist_pop (workers);
        zframe_destroy (&frame);
    }
    zlist_destroy (&workers);
    zctx_destroy (&ctx);
    return EXIT_SUCCESS;
}
```

It's a nontrivial program and took about a day to get working. These are the highlights:

- The client threads detect and report a failed request. They do this by polling for a response and, if none arrives after a while (10 seconds), printing an error message.

- Client threads don't print directly, but instead send a message to a monitor socket (PUSH) that the main loop collects (PULL) and prints off. This is the first case we've seen of using ØMQ sockets for monitoring and logging; this is a big use case that we'll come back to later.

- Clients simulate varying loads to get the cluster to 100% at random moments, so that tasks are shifted over to the cloud. The number of clients and workers and delays in the client and worker threads control this. Feel free to play with them to see if you can make a more realistic simulation.

- The main loop uses two poll sets. It could in fact use three: information, backends, and frontends. As in the earlier prototype, there is no point in taking a frontend message if there is no backend capacity.

These are some of the problems that arose during development of this program:

- Clients would freeze, due to requests or replies getting lost somewhere. Recall that the ROUTER socket drops messages it can't route. The first tactic here was to modify the client thread to detect and report such problems. Secondly, I put zmsg_dump() calls after every receive and before every send in the main loop, until the origins of the problems were clear.

- The main loop was mistakenly reading from more than one ready socket. This caused the first message to be lost. I fixed that by reading only from the first ready socket.

- The zmsg class was not properly encoding UUIDs as C strings. This caused UUIDs that contain 0 bytes to be corrupted. I fixed this by modifying zmsg to encode UUIDs as printable hex strings.

This simulation does not detect the disappearance of a cloud peer. If you start several peers and stop one, and that peer was broadcasting capacity to the others, they will continue to send it work even after it's gone. You can try this, and you will get clients that complain of lost requests. The solution is twofold. First, only keep the capacity information for a short time, so that if a peer does disappear its capacity is quickly set to zero. Second, add reliability to the request-reply chain. We'll look at reliability in the next chapter.

## CHAPTER 4

Reliable Request-Reply Patterns

Chapter 3 covered advanced uses of ØMQ's request-reply pattern with working examples. This chapter looks at the general question of reliability and builds a set of reliable messaging patterns on top of ØMQ's core request-reply pattern.

In this chapter, we focus heavily on user-space request-reply patterns, which are reusable models that help you design your own ØMQ architectures:

- The *Lazy Pirate* pattern: reliable request-reply from the client side
- The *Simple Pirate* pattern: reliable request-reply using load balancing
- The *Paranoid Pirate* pattern: reliable request-reply with heartbeating
- The *Majordomo* pattern: service-oriented reliable queuing
- The *Titanic* pattern: disk-based/disconnected reliable queuing
- The *Binary Star* pattern: primary backup server failover
- The *Freelance* pattern: brokerless reliable request-reply

What Is "Reliability"?

Most people who speak of "reliability" don't really know what they mean by it. We can only define reliability in terms of failure. That is, if we can handle a certain set of well-defined and understood failures, we are reliable with respect to those failures. No more, no less. So let's look at the possible causes of failure in a distributed ØMQ application, in roughly descending order of probability:

1. Application code is the worst offender. It can crash and exit, freeze and stop responding to input, run too slowly for its input, exhaust all memory, and so on.

2. System code (such as brokers we write using ØMQ) can die for the same reasons as application code. System code *should* be more reliable than application code, but it can still crash and burn, and especially run out of memory if it tries to queue messages for slow clients.

3. Message queues can overflow, typically in system code that has learned to deal brutally with slow clients. When a queue overflows, it starts to discard messages, so we get "lost" messages.

4. Networks can fail (e.g., WiFi gets switched off or goes out of range). ØMQ will automatically reconnect in such cases, but in the meantime, messages may get lost.

5. Hardware can fail and take with it all the processes running on that box.

6. Networks can fail in exotic ways; e.g., some ports on a switch may die and those parts of the network become inaccessible.

7. Entire data centers can be struck by lightning, earthquakes, fire, or more mundane power or cooling failures.

Making a software system fully reliable against *all* of these possible failures is an enormously difficult and expensive job and goes beyond the scope of this modest tome.

Because the first five cases in the preceding list cover 99.9% of real-world requirements outside large companies (according to a highly scientific study I just ran, which also told me that 78% of statistics are made up on the spot), that's what we'll examine here. If you're a large company with money to spend on the last two cases, contact my company immediately! There's a large hole behind my beach house waiting to be converted into an executive swimming pool.

Designing Reliability

So, to make things brutally simple, reliability is "keeping things working properly when code freezes or crashes," a situation we'll shorten to "when code dies." However, the things we want to keep working properly are more complex than just messages. We need to take each core ØMQ messaging pattern and see how to make it work (if we can) even when code dies.

Let's take them one by one:

Request-reply:
> If the server dies while processing a request, the client can figure that out because it won't get an answer back. Then it can give up in a huff, wait and try again later, find another server, etc. As for the client dying, we can brush that off as "someone else's problem" for now.

Publish-subscribe

If the client dies (having gotten some data), the server won't know about it. Pub-sub doesn't send any information back from the client to the server. However, the client can contact the server out-of-band—e.g., via request-reply—and say, "Please resend everything I missed." As for the server dying, that's outside the scope of this discussion. Subscribers can also self-verify that they're not running too slowly, and take action (e.g., warn the operator and die) if they are.

Pipeline

If a worker dies (while working), the ventilator doesn't know about it. Pipelines, like pub-sub and the grinding gears of time, only work in one direction. But the downstream collector can detect that one task didn't get done, and send a message back to the ventilator saying, "Hey, resend task 324!" If the ventilator or collector dies, whatever upstream client originally sent the work batch can get tired of waiting and resend the whole lot. It's not elegant, but system code should really not die often enough for this to matter.

In this chapter we'll focus just on request-reply, which is the low-hanging fruit of reliable messaging.

The basic request-reply pattern (a REQ client socket doing a blocking send/receive to a REP server socket) scores low on handling the most common types of failure. If the server crashes while processing the request, the client just hangs forever. Similarly, if the network loses the request or the reply, the client hangs forever.

Request-reply is still much better than TCP, thanks to ØMQ's ability to reconnect peers silently, to load-balance messages, and so on. But it's still not good enough for real work. The only case where you can really trust the basic request-reply pattern is between two threads in the same process where there's no network or separate server process to die.

However, with a little extra work, this humble pattern becomes a good basis for real work across a distributed network, and we get a set of reliable request-reply (RRR) patterns that I like to call the *Pirate* patterns (you'll eventually get the joke, I hope).

There are, in my experience, roughly three ways to connect clients to servers. Each needs a specific approach to reliability:

1. Multiple clients talking directly to a single server. Use case: a single well-known server to which clients need to talk. Types of failure we aim to handle: server crashes and restarts, and network disconnects.

2. Multiple clients talking to a broker proxy that distributes work to multiple workers. Use case: service-oriented transaction processing. Types of failure we aim to handle: worker crashes and restarts, worker busy looping, worker overload, queue crashes and restarts, and network disconnects.

3. Multiple clients talking to multiple servers with no intermediary proxies. Use case: distributed services such as name resolution. Types of failure we aim to handle: service crashes and restarts, service busy looping, service overload, and network disconnects.

Each of these approaches has its trade-offs, and often you'll mix them. We'll look at all three in detail.

Client-Side Reliability (Lazy Pirate Pattern)

We can get very simple, reliable request-reply with some changes to the client. We call this the Lazy Pirate pattern (Figure 4-1). Rather than doing a blocking receive, we:

- Poll the REQ socket and receive from it only when it's sure a reply has arrived.
- Resend a request, if no reply has arrived within a timeout period.
- Abandon the transaction if there is still no reply after several requests.

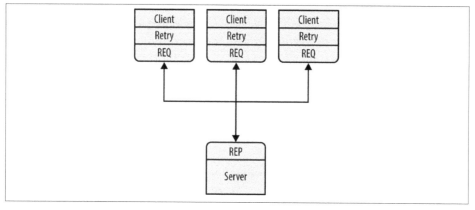

Figure 4-1. The Lazy Pirate pattern

If we try to use a REQ socket in anything other than a strict send/receive fashion, we'll get an error (technically, the REQ socket implements a small finite-state machine to enforce the send/receive ping-pong, so the error code is called "EFSM"). This is slightly annoying when we want to use REQ in a Pirate pattern, because we may send several requests before getting a reply, as you can see in Example 4-1. The pretty good brute-force solution is to close and reopen the REQ socket after an error.

Example 4-1. Lazy Pirate client (lpclient.c)

```
//
//  Lazy Pirate client
//  Use zmq_poll to do a safe request-reply
```

```
//  To run, start lpserver and then randomly kill/restart it
//
#include "czmq.h"

#define REQUEST_TIMEOUT     2500    //  msec (> 1000!)
#define REQUEST_RETRIES     3       //  Before we abandon
#define SERVER_ENDPOINT     "tcp://localhost:5555"

int main (void)
{
    zctx_t *ctx = zctx_new ();
    printf ("I: connecting to server...\n");
    void *client = zsocket_new (ctx, ZMQ_REQ);
    assert (client);
    zsocket_connect (client, SERVER_ENDPOINT);

    int sequence = 0;
    int retries_left = REQUEST_RETRIES;
    while (retries_left && !zctx_interrupted) {
        //  We send a request, then we work to get a reply
        char request [10];
        sprintf (request, "%d", ++sequence);
        zstr_send (client, request);

        int expect_reply = 1;
        while (expect_reply) {
            //  Poll socket for a reply, with timeout
            zmq_pollitem_t items [] = { { client, 0, ZMQ_POLLIN, 0 } };
            int rc = zmq_poll (items, 1, REQUEST_TIMEOUT * ZMQ_POLL_MSEC);
            if (rc == -1)
                break;          //  Interrupted
```

Example 4-2 shows how we process a server reply and exit our loop if the reply is valid.
If we didn't receive a reply, we close the client socket and resend the request. We try a
number of times before finally abandoning.

Example 4-2. Lazy Pirate client (lpclient.c): process server reply

```
            if (items [0].revents & ZMQ_POLLIN) {
                //  We got a reply from the server, must match sequence
                char *reply = zstr_recv (client);
                if (!reply)
                    break;      //  Interrupted
                if (atoi (reply) == sequence) {
                    printf ("I: server replied OK (%s)\n", reply);
                    retries_left = REQUEST_RETRIES;
                    expect_reply = 0;
                }
                else
                    printf ("E: malformed reply from server: %s\n",
                        reply);
```

```
            free (reply);
        }
        else
        if (--retries_left == 0) {
            printf ("E: server seems to be offline, abandoning\n");
            break;
        }
        else {
            printf ("W: no response from server, retrying...\n");
            //  Old socket is confused; close it and open a new one
            zsocket_destroy (ctx, client);
            printf ("I: reconnecting to server...\n");
            client = zsocket_new (ctx, ZMQ_REQ);
            zsocket_connect (client, SERVER_ENDPOINT);
            //  Send request again, on new socket
            zstr_send (client, request);
        }
    }
}
zctx_destroy (&ctx);
return 0;
}
```

We run this together with the matching server, shown in Example 4-3.

Example 4-3. Lazy Pirate server (lpserver.c)

```
//
//  Lazy Pirate server
//  Binds REQ socket to tcp://*:5555
//  Like hwserver except:
//   - echoes request as-is
//   - randomly runs slowly, or exits to simulate a crash.
//
#include "zhelpers.h"

int main (void)
{
    srandom ((unsigned) time (NULL));

    void *context = zmq_ctx_new ();
    void *server = zmq_socket (context, ZMQ_REP);
    zmq_bind (server, "tcp://*:5555");

    int cycles = 0;
    while (1) {
        char *request = s_recv (server);
        cycles++;

        //  Simulate various problems, after a few cycles
        if (cycles > 3 && randof (3) == 0) {
            printf ("I: simulating a crash\n");
            break;
```

```
        }
        else
        if (cycles > 3 && randof (3) == 0) {
            printf ("I: simulating CPU overload\n");
            sleep (2);
        }
        printf ("I: normal request (%s)\n", request);
        sleep (1);                 // Do some heavy work
        s_send (server, request);
        free (request);
    }
    zmq_close (server);
    zmq_ctx_destroy (context);
    return 0;
}
```

To run this test case, start the client and the server in two console windows. The server will randomly misbehave after a few messages. You can check the client's response. Here is typical output from the server:

```
I: normal request (1)
I: normal request (2)
I: normal request (3)
I: simulating CPU overload
I: normal request (4)
I: simulating a crash
```

And here is the client's response:

```
I: connecting to server...
I: server replied OK (1)
I: server replied OK (2)
I: server replied OK (3)
W: no response from server, retrying...
I: connecting to server...
W: no response from server, retrying...
I: connecting to server...
E: server seems to be offline, abandoning
```

The client sequences each message and checks that replies come back exactly in order: that no requests or replies are lost, and no replies come back more than once or out of order. Run the test a few times until you're convinced that this mechanism actually works. You don't need sequence numbers in a production application; they just help us trust our design.

The client uses a REQ socket, and it does the brute-force close/reopen because REQ sockets impose that strict send/receive cycle. You might be tempted to use a DEALER instead, but it would not be a good decision. First, it would mean emulating the secret sauce that REQ does with envelopes (if you've forgotten what that is, it's a good sign you don't want to have to do it). Second, it would mean potentially getting back replies that you didn't expect.

Handling failures only at the client works when we have a set of clients talking to a single server. This design can handle a server crash, but only if recovery means restarting that same server. If there's a permanent error, such as a dead power supply on the server hardware, this approach won't work. Because the application code in servers is usually the biggest source of failures in any architecture, depending on a single server is not a great idea.

So, the pros and cons are:

- Pro: simple to understand and implement.
- Pro: works easily with existing client and server application code.
- Pro: ØMQ automatically retries the actual reconnection until it works.
- Con: doesn't do failover to backup or alternate servers.

Basic Reliable Queuing (Simple Pirate Pattern)

Our second approach extends the Lazy Pirate pattern with a queue proxy that lets us talk, transparently, to multiple servers, which we can more accurately call "workers." We'll develop this in stages, starting with a minimal working model, the Simple Pirate pattern.

In all these Pirate patterns, workers are stateless. If the application requires some shared state, such as a shared database, we don't know about it as we design our messaging framework. Having a queue proxy means workers can come and go without clients knowing anything about it. If one worker dies, another takes over. This is a nice, simple topology with only one real weakness: the central queue itself, which can become a problem to manage and is a single point of failure.

The basis for the queue proxy is the load-balancing broker from Chapter 3. What is the very *minimum* we need to do to handle dead or blocked workers? Turns out, it's surprisingly little. We already have a retry mechanism in the client, so using the load-balancing pattern will work pretty well. This fits with ØMQ's philosophy that we can extend a peer-to-peer pattern like request-reply by plugging naive proxies in the middle (Figure 4-2).

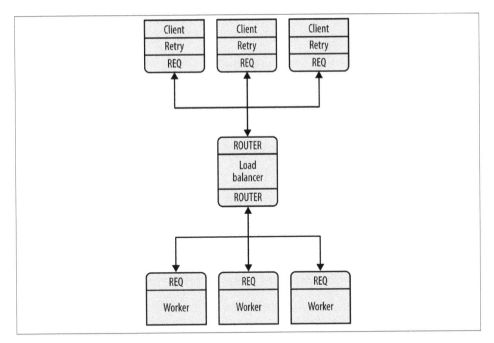

Figure 4-2. The Simple Pirate pattern

We don't need a special client; we're still using the Lazy Pirate client. Example 4-4 presents is the queue, which is identical to the main task of the load-balancing broker.

Example 4-4. Simple Pirate queue (spqueue.c)

```
//
//  Simple Pirate broker
//  This is identical to load-balancing pattern, with no reliability
//  mechanisms. It depends on the client for recovery. Runs forever.
//
#include "czmq.h"

#define WORKER_READY    "\001"      //  Signals worker is ready

int main (void)
{
    zctx_t *ctx = zctx_new ();
    void *frontend = zsocket_new (ctx, ZMQ_ROUTER);
    void *backend = zsocket_new (ctx, ZMQ_ROUTER);
    zsocket_bind (frontend, "tcp://*:5555");    //  For clients
    zsocket_bind (backend,  "tcp://*:5556");    //  For workers

    //  Queue of available workers
    zlist_t *workers = zlist_new ();

    //  The body of this example is exactly the same as lbbroker2
```

```
    ...
}
```

Example 4-5 shows the worker, which takes the Lazy Pirate server and adapts it for the load-balancing pattern (using the REQ "ready" signaling).

Example 4-5. Simple Pirate worker (spworker.c)

```
//
//  Simple Pirate worker
//  Connects REQ socket to tcp://*:5556
//  Implements worker part of load balancing
//
#include "czmq.h"
#define WORKER_READY   "\001"      //  Signals worker is ready

int main (void)
{
    zctx_t *ctx = zctx_new ();
    void *worker = zsocket_new (ctx, ZMQ_REQ);

    //  Set random identity to make tracing easier
    srandom ((unsigned) time (NULL));
    char identity [10];
    sprintf (identity, "%04X-%04X", randof (0x10000), randof (0x10000));
    zmq_setsockopt (worker, ZMQ_IDENTITY, identity, strlen (identity));
    zsocket_connect (worker, "tcp://localhost:5556");

    //  Tell broker we're ready for work
    printf ("I: (%s) worker ready\n", identity);
    zframe_t *frame = zframe_new (WORKER_READY, 1);
    zframe_send (&frame, worker, 0);

    int cycles = 0;
    while (true) {
        zmsg_t *msg = zmsg_recv (worker);
        if (!msg)
            break;                  //  Interrupted

        //  Simulate various problems, after a few cycles
        cycles++;
        if (cycles > 3 && randof (5) == 0) {
            printf ("I: (%s) simulating a crash\n", identity);
            zmsg_destroy (&msg);
            break;
        }
        else
        if (cycles > 3 && randof (5) == 0) {
            printf ("I: (%s) simulating CPU overload\n", identity);
            sleep (3);
            if (zctx_interrupted)
                break;
```

```
    }
    printf ("I: (%s) normal reply\n", identity);
    sleep (1);              //  Do some heavy work
    zmsg_send (&msg, worker);
  }
  zctx_destroy (&ctx);
  return 0;
}
```

To test this, start a handful of workers, a Lazy Pirate client, and the queue, in any order. You'll see that the workers eventually all crash and burn, and the client retries and then gives up. The queue never stops, and you can restart workers and clients ad nauseum. This model works with any number of clients and workers.

Robust Reliable Queuing (Paranoid Pirate Pattern)

The Simple Pirate queue pattern works pretty well, especially because it's just a combination of two existing patterns. Still, it does have some weaknesses:

- It's not robust in the face of a queue crash and restart. The client will recover, but the workers won't. While ØMQ will reconnect workers' sockets automatically, as far as the newly started queue is concerned the workers haven't signaled ready, so they don't exist. To fix this we have to do heartbeating from queue to worker so that the worker can detect when the queue has gone away.

- The queue does not detect worker failure, so if a worker dies while idle, the queue can't remove it from its worker queue until the queue sends it a request. The client waits and retries for nothing. It's not a critical problem, but it's not nice. To make this work properly, we need to do heartbeating from worker to queue, so that the queue can detect a lost worker at any stage.

We'll fix these issues in a properly pedantic Paranoid Pirate pattern.

We previously used a REQ socket for the worker. For the Paranoid Pirate worker, we'll switch to a DEALER socket (Figure 4-3). This has the advantage of letting us send and receive messages at any time, rather than the lock-step send/receive that REQ imposes. The downside of DEALER is that we have to do our own envelope management (re-read Chapter 3 for background on this concept).

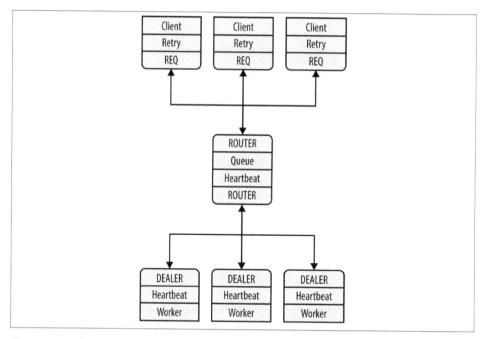

Figure 4-3. The Paranoid Pirate pattern

We're still using the Lazy Pirate client. The Paranoid Pirate queue proxy is shown in Example 4-6.

Example 4-6. Paranoid Pirate queue (ppqueue.c)

```
//
//  Paranoid Pirate queue
//
#include "czmq.h"

#define HEARTBEAT_LIVENESS  3       //  3-5 is reasonable
#define HEARTBEAT_INTERVAL  1000    //  msec

//  Paranoid Pirate Protocol constants
#define PPP_READY       "\001"      //  Signals worker is ready
#define PPP_HEARTBEAT   "\002"      //  Signals worker heartbeat
```

Example 4-7 defines the worker class: a structure and a set of functions that act as constructor, destructor, and methods on worker objects.

Example 4-7. Paranoid Pirate queue (ppqueue.c): worker class structure

```
typedef struct {
    zframe_t *identity;         //  Identity of worker
    char *id_string;            //  Printable identity
    int64_t expiry;             //  Expires at this time
```

```
} worker_t;

// Construct new worker
static worker_t *
s_worker_new (zframe_t *identity)
{
    worker_t *self = (worker_t *) zmalloc (sizeof (worker_t));
    self->identity = identity;
    self->id_string = zframe_strdup (identity);
    self->expiry = zclock_time () + HEARTBEAT_INTERVAL * HEARTBEAT_LIVENESS;
    return self;
}

// Destroy specified worker object, including identity frame
static void
s_worker_destroy (worker_t **self_p)
{
    assert (self_p);
    if (*self_p) {
        worker_t *self = *self_p;
        zframe_destroy (&self->identity);
        free (self->id_string);
        free (self);
        *self_p = NULL;
    }
}
```

The ready method (Example 4-8) puts a worker at the end of the ready list.

Example 4-8. Paranoid Pirate queue (ppqueue.c): worker ready method

```
static void
s_worker_ready (worker_t *self, zlist_t *workers)
{
    worker_t *worker = (worker_t *) zlist_first (workers);
    while (worker) {
        if (streq (self->id_string, worker->id_string)) {
            zlist_remove (workers, worker);
            s_worker_destroy (&worker);
            break;
        }
        worker = (worker_t *) zlist_next (workers);
    }
    zlist_append (workers, self);
}
```

The next method, shown in Example 4-9, returns the next available worker's identity.

Example 4-9. Paranoid Pirate queue (ppqueue.c): get next available worker method

```
static zframe_t *
s_workers_next (zlist_t *workers)
{
```

```
        worker_t *worker = zlist_pop (workers);
        assert (worker);
        zframe_t *frame = worker->identity;
        worker->identity = NULL;
        s_worker_destroy (&worker);
        return frame;
}
```

The purge method (Example 4-10) looks for and kills expired workers. We hold workers from oldest to most recent, so we stop at the first alive worker.

Example 4-10. Paranoid Pirate queue (ppqueue.c): purge expired workers method

```
static void
s_workers_purge (zlist_t *workers)
{
    worker_t *worker = (worker_t *) zlist_first (workers);
    while (worker) {
        if (zclock_time () < worker->expiry)
            break;                    //  Worker is alive, we're done here

        zlist_remove (workers, worker);
        s_worker_destroy (&worker);
        worker = (worker_t *) zlist_first (workers);
    }
}
```

The main task is a load balancer with heartbeating on workers so we can detect crashed or blocked worker tasks, as shown in Example 4-11.

Example 4-11. Paranoid Pirate queue (ppqueue.c): main task

```
int main (void)
{
    zctx_t *ctx = zctx_new ();
    void *frontend = zsocket_new (ctx, ZMQ_ROUTER);
    void *backend = zsocket_new (ctx, ZMQ_ROUTER);
    zsocket_bind (frontend, "tcp://*:5555");    //  For clients
    zsocket_bind (backend,  "tcp://*:5556");    //  For workers

    //  List of available workers
    zlist_t *workers = zlist_new ();

    //  Send out heartbeats at regular intervals
    uint64_t heartbeat_at = zclock_time () + HEARTBEAT_INTERVAL;

    while (true) {
        zmq_pollitem_t items [] = {
            { backend,  0, ZMQ_POLLIN, 0 },
            { frontend, 0, ZMQ_POLLIN, 0 }
        };
        //  Poll frontend only if we have available workers
        int rc = zmq_poll (items, zlist_size (workers)? 2: 1,
```

```
        HEARTBEAT_INTERVAL * ZMQ_POLL_MSEC);
    if (rc == -1)
        break;                  //  Interrupted

    //  Handle worker activity on backend
    if (items [0].revents & ZMQ_POLLIN) {
        //  Use worker identity for load balancing
        zmsg_t *msg = zmsg_recv (backend);
        if (!msg)
            break;              //  Interrupted

        //  Any sign of life from worker means it's ready
        zframe_t *identity = zmsg_unwrap (msg);
        worker_t *worker = s_worker_new (identity);
        s_worker_ready (worker, workers);

        //  Validate control message, or return reply to client
        if (zmsg_size (msg) == 1) {
            zframe_t *frame = zmsg_first (msg);
            if (memcmp (zframe_data (frame), PPP_READY, 1)
            &&  memcmp (zframe_data (frame), PPP_HEARTBEAT, 1)) {
                printf ("E: invalid message from worker");
                zmsg_dump (msg);
            }
            zmsg_destroy (&msg);
        }
        else
            zmsg_send (&msg, frontend);
    }
    if (items [1].revents & ZMQ_POLLIN) {
        //  Now get next client request, route to next worker
        zmsg_t *msg = zmsg_recv (frontend);
        if (!msg)
            break;              //  Interrupted
        zmsg_push (msg, s_workers_next (workers));
        zmsg_send (&msg, backend);
    }
```

We handle heartbeating after any socket activity. As shown in Example 4-12, first, we send heartbeats to any idle workers if it's time, then we purge any dead workers.

Example 4-12. Paranoid Pirate queue (ppqueue.c): handle heartbeating

```
    if (zclock_time () >= heartbeat_at) {
        worker_t *worker = (worker_t *) zlist_first (workers);
        while (worker) {
            zframe_send (&worker->identity, backend,
                        ZFRAME_REUSE + ZFRAME_MORE);
            zframe_t *frame = zframe_new (PPP_HEARTBEAT, 1);
            zframe_send (&frame, backend, 0);
            worker = (worker_t *) zlist_next (workers);
        }
```

```
        heartbeat_at = zclock_time () + HEARTBEAT_INTERVAL;
    }
    s_workers_purge (workers);
}

// When we're done, clean up properly
while (zlist_size (workers)) {
    worker_t *worker = (worker_t *) zlist_pop (workers);
    s_worker_destroy (&worker);
}
zlist_destroy (&workers);
zctx_destroy (&ctx);
return 0;
}
```

The queue extends the load-balancing pattern with heartbeating of workers. Heartbeating is one of those "simple" things that can be difficult to get right. I'll explain more about that in the next section; for now, back to the code.

Take a look at the Paranoid Pirate worker in Example 4-13.

Example 4-13. Paranoid Pirate worker (ppworker.c)

```
//
//  Paranoid Pirate worker
//
#include "czmq.h"

#define HEARTBEAT_LIVENESS  3       // 3-5 is reasonable
#define HEARTBEAT_INTERVAL  1000    // msec
#define INTERVAL_INIT       1000    // Initial reconnect
#define INTERVAL_MAX        32000   // After exponential backoff

//  Paranoid Pirate Protocol constants
#define PPP_READY       "\001"      // Signals worker is ready
#define PPP_HEARTBEAT   "\002"      // Signals worker heartbeat

//  Helper function that returns a new configured socket
//  connected to the Paranoid Pirate queue

static void *
s_worker_socket (zctx_t *ctx) {
    void *worker = zsocket_new (ctx, ZMQ_DEALER);
    zsocket_connect (worker, "tcp://localhost:5556");

    //  Tell queue we're ready for work
    printf ("I: worker ready\n");
    zframe_t *frame = zframe_new (PPP_READY, 1);
    zframe_send (&frame, worker, 0);

    return worker;
}
```

We have a single task that implements the worker side of the Paranoid Pirate Protocol (PPP). The heartbeating code in Example 4-14 lets the worker detect if the queue has died, and vice versa.

Example 4-14. Paranoid Pirate worker (ppworker.c): main task

```
int main (void)
{
    zctx_t *ctx = zctx_new ();
    void *worker = s_worker_socket (ctx);

    //  If liveness hits zero, queue is considered disconnected
    size_t liveness = HEARTBEAT_LIVENESS;
    size_t interval = INTERVAL_INIT;

    //  Send out heartbeats at regular intervals
    uint64_t heartbeat_at = zclock_time () + HEARTBEAT_INTERVAL;

    srandom ((unsigned) time (NULL));
    int cycles = 0;
    while (true) {
        zmq_pollitem_t items [] = { { worker,  0, ZMQ_POLLIN, 0 } };
        int rc = zmq_poll (items, 1, HEARTBEAT_INTERVAL * ZMQ_POLL_MSEC);
        if (rc == -1)
            break;              //  Interrupted

        if (items [0].revents & ZMQ_POLLIN) {
            //  Get message
            //  - 3-part envelope + content -> request
            //  - 1-part HEARTBEAT -> heartbeat
            zmsg_t *msg = zmsg_recv (worker);
            if (!msg)
                break;          //  Interrupted
```

To test the robustness of the queue implementation, we simulate various typical problems, such as the worker crashing or running very slowly. We do this after a few cycles so that the architecture can get up and running first. The problem simulation code is in Example 4-15.

Example 4-15. Paranoid Pirate worker (ppworker.c): simulating problems

```
            cycles++;
            if (cycles > 3 && randof (5) == 0) {
                printf ("I: simulating a crash\n");
                zmsg_destroy (&msg);
                break;
            }
            else
            if (cycles > 3 && randof (5) == 0) {
                printf ("I: simulating CPU overload\n");
                sleep (3);
                if (zctx_interrupted)
```

```
                    break;
            }
            printf ("I: normal reply\n");
            zmsg_send (&msg, worker);
            liveness = HEARTBEAT_LIVENESS;
            sleep (1);                    // Do some heavy work
            if (zctx_interrupted)
                break;
        }
        else
```

When we get a heartbeat message from the queue, it means the queue is (or rather, was recently) alive, so we must reset our liveness indicator. The code in Example 4-16 handles the heartbeats.

Example 4-16. Paranoid Pirate worker (ppworker.c): handle heartbeats

```
            zframe_t *frame = zmsg_first (msg);
            if (memcmp (zframe_data (frame), PPP_HEARTBEAT, 1) == 0)
                liveness = HEARTBEAT_LIVENESS;
            else {
                printf ("E: invalid message\n");
                zmsg_dump (msg);
            }
            zmsg_destroy (&msg);
        }
        else {
            printf ("E: invalid message\n");
            zmsg_dump (msg);
        }
        interval = INTERVAL_INIT;
    }
    else
```

If the queue hasn't sent us heartbeats in a while, we destroy the socket and reconnect, as shown in Example 4-17. This is the simplest and most brutal way of discarding any messages we might have sent in the meantime.

Example 4-17. Paranoid Pirate worker (ppworker.c): detecting a dead queue

```
        printf ("W: heartbeat failure, can't reach queue\n");
        printf ("W: reconnecting in %zd msec...\n", interval);
        zclock_sleep (interval);

        if (interval < INTERVAL_MAX)
            interval *= 2;
        zsocket_destroy (ctx, worker);
        worker = s_worker_socket (ctx);
        liveness = HEARTBEAT_LIVENESS;
    }

    // Send heartbeat to queue if it's time
```

```
        if (zclock_time () > heartbeat_at) {
            heartbeat_at = zclock_time () + HEARTBEAT_INTERVAL;
            printf ("I: worker heartbeat\n");
            zframe_t *frame = zframe_new (PPP_HEARTBEAT, 1);
            zframe_send (&frame, worker, 0);
        }
    }
    zctx_destroy (&ctx);
    return 0;
}
```

Some comments about this example:

- The code includes simulation of failures, as before. This makes it (a) very hard to debug, and (b) dangerous to reuse. When you want to debug this code, disable the failure simulation.

- The worker uses a reconnect strategy similar to the one we designed for the Lazy Pirate client, with two major differences: it does an exponential backoff, and it retries indefinitely (whereas the client retries a few times before reporting a failure).

You can try the client, queue, and workers by using a script like this:

```
ppqueue &
for i in 1 2 3 4; do
    ppworker &
    sleep 1
done
lpclient &
```

You should see the workers die one by one as they simulate a crash, and the client eventually give up. You can stop and restart the queue, and both the client and the workers will reconnect and carry on. And no matter what you do to queues and workers, the client will never get an out-of-order reply: either the whole chain works, or the client abandons.

Heartbeating

Heartbeating solves the problem of knowing whether a peer is alive or dead. This is not an issue specific to ØMQ. TCP has a long timeout (30 minutes or so), which means that it can be impossible to know whether a peer has died, been disconnected, or gone on a weekend trip to Prague with a case of vodka, a redhead, and a large expense account.

It's not easy to get heartbeating right. When writing the Paranoid Pirate examples, it took me about five hours to get the heartbeating working properly. The rest of the request-reply chain took perhaps 10 minutes. It is especially easy to create "false failures"; i.e., when peers decide that they are disconnected because the heartbeats aren't sent properly.

In this section, we'll look at the three main solutions people use for heartbeating with ØMQ.

Shrugging It Off

The most common approach is to do no heartbeating at all and hope for the best. Many, if not most, ØMQ applications do this. ØMQ encourages this by hiding peers in many cases. What problems does this approach cause?

- When we use a ROUTER socket in an application that tracks peers, as peers disconnect and reconnect, the application will leak memory (resources that the application holds for each peer) and get slower and slower.

- When we use SUB- or DEALER-based data recipients, we can't tell the difference between good silence (there's no data) and bad silence (the other end has died). When a recipient knows the other side has died, it can for example switch over to a backup route.

- If we use a TCP connection that stays silent for a long while, it will, in some networks, just die. Sending something (technically, a "keep alive" more than a heartbeat) will keep the network alive.

One-Way Heartbeats

A second option is to send a heartbeat message from each node to its peers every second or so. When one node hears nothing from another within some timeout (several seconds, typically), it will treat that peer as dead. Sounds good, right? Sadly, no. This works in some cases but has nasty edge cases in others.

For pub-sub, this approach does work, and it's the only model you can use. SUB sockets cannot talk back to PUB sockets, but PUB sockets can happily send "I'm alive" messages to their subscribers.

As an optimization, you can send heartbeats only when there is no real data to send. Furthermore, you can send heartbeats at progressively longer intervals, if network activity is an issue (e.g., on mobile networks where activity drains the battery). As long as the recipient can detect a failure (a sharp stop in activity), that's fine.

Here are the typical problems with this design:

- It can be inaccurate when we send large amounts of data, as heartbeats will be delayed behind that data. If heartbeats are delayed, you can get false timeouts and disconnections due to network congestion. Thus, always treat *any* incoming data as a heartbeat, whether or not the sender optimizes out heartbeats.

- While the pub-sub pattern will drop messages for disappeared recipients, PUSH and DEALER sockets will queue them. So if you've send heartbeats to a dead peer and it comes back to life, it will get all the heartbeats you've sent, which can be thousands. Whoa, whoa!
- This design assumes that heartbeat timeouts are the same across the whole network. But that won't be accurate. Some peers will want very aggressive heartbeating in order to detect faults rapidly. And some will want very relaxed heartbeating in order to let sleeping networks lie and save power.

Ping-Pong Heartbeats

The third option is to use a ping-pong dialog. One peer sends a *ping* command to the other, which replies with a *pong* command. Neither command has any payload. Pings and pongs are not correlated. Because the roles of "client" and "server" are arbitrary in some networks, we usually specify that either peer can in fact send a *ping* and expect a *pong* in response. However, as the timeouts depend on network topologies known best to dynamic clients, it is usually the client that pings the server.

This works for all ROUTER-based brokers. The same optimizations we used in the second model make this work even better: treat any incoming data as a *pong*, and only send a *ping* when not otherwise sending data.

Heartbeating for Paranoid Pirate

For Paranoid Pirate, we chose the second approach. It might not have been the simplest option: if designing this today, I'd probably try a ping-pong approach instead. However, the principles are similar. The heartbeat messages flow asynchronously in both directions, and either peer can decide the other is "dead" and stop talking to it.

In the worker, this is how we handle heartbeats from the queue:

- We calculate a *liveness*, which is how many heartbeats we can still miss before deciding the queue is dead. It starts at three and we decrement it each time we miss a heartbeat.
- We wait in the zmq_poll() loop for one second each time, which is our heartbeat interval.
- If there's any message from the queue during that time, we reset our liveness to three.
- If there's no message during that time, we count down our liveness.
- If the liveness reaches zero, we consider the queue dead.
- If the queue is dead, we destroy our socket, create a new one, and reconnect.

- To avoid opening and closing too many sockets, we wait for a certain interval before reconnecting, and we double the interval each time until it reaches 32 seconds.

And this is how we handle heartbeats *to* the queue:

- We calculate when to send the next heartbeat; this is a single variable because we're talking to one peer, the queue.
- In the zmq_poll() loop, whenever we pass this time, we send a heartbeat to the queue.

Here's the essential heartbeating code for the worker:

```
#define HEARTBEAT_LIVENESS  3       //  3-5 is reasonable
#define HEARTBEAT_INTERVAL  1000    //  msec
#define INTERVAL_INIT       1000    //  Initial reconnect
#define INTERVAL_MAX        32000   //  After exponential backoff

...

//  If liveness hits zero, queue is considered disconnected
size_t liveness = HEARTBEAT_LIVENESS;
size_t interval = INTERVAL_INIT;

//  Send out heartbeats at regular intervals
uint64_t heartbeat_at = zclock_time () + HEARTBEAT_INTERVAL;

while (true) {
    zmq_pollitem_t items [] = { { worker,  0, ZMQ_POLLIN, 0 } };
    int rc = zmq_poll (items, 1, HEARTBEAT_INTERVAL * ZMQ_POLL_MSEC);

    if (items [0].revents & ZMQ_POLLIN) {
        //  Receive any message from queue
        liveness = HEARTBEAT_LIVENESS;
        interval = INTERVAL_INIT;
    }
    else
    if (--liveness == 0) {
        zclock_sleep (interval);
        if (interval < INTERVAL_MAX)
            interval *= 2;
        zsocket_destroy (ctx, worker);
        ...
        liveness = HEARTBEAT_LIVENESS;
    }
    //  Send heartbeat to queue if it's time
    if (zclock_time () > heartbeat_at) {
        heartbeat_at = zclock_time () + HEARTBEAT_INTERVAL;
        //  Send heartbeat message to queue
    }
}
```

The queue does the same, but manages an expiration time for each worker.

Here are some tips for your own heartbeating implementation:

- Use `zmq_poll()` or a reactor as the core of your application's main task.
- Start by building the heartbeating between peers, test it by simulating failures, and *then* build the rest of the message flow. Adding heartbeating afterwards is much trickier.
- Use simple tracing (i.e., print to console) to get this working. To help you trace the flow of messages between peers, use a dump method such as the one `zmsg` offers, and number your messages incrementally so you can see if there are gaps.
- In a real application, heartbeating must be configurable and usually negotiated with the peer. Some peers will want aggressive heartbeating, as low as 10 msec. Other peers will be far away and want heartbeating as high as 30 seconds.
- If you have different heartbeat intervals for different peers, your poll timeout should be the lowest (shortest time) of these. Do not use an infinite timeout.
- Do heartbeating on the same socket you use for messages, so your heartbeats also act as a *keep alive* to stop the network connection from going stale (some firewalls can be unkind to silent connections).

Contracts and Protocols

If you're paying attention, you'll realize that Paranoid Pirate is not interoperable with Simple Pirate, because of the heartbeats. But how do we define "interoperable"? To guarantee interoperability, we need a kind of contract, an agreement that lets different teams in different times and places write code that is guaranteed to work together. We call this a "protocol."

It's fun to experiment without specifications, but that's not a sensible basis for real applications. What happens if we want to write a worker in another language? Do we have to read code to see how things work? What if we want to change the protocol for some reason? Even a simple protocol will, if it's successful, evolve and become more complex.

Lack of contracts is a sure sign of a disposable application. So let's write a contract for this protocol. How do we do that?

There's a wiki at *http://rfc.zeromq.org* that we made especially as a home for public ØMQ contracts.

To create a new specification, register and follow the instructions. It's fairly straightforward, though writing technical texts is not everyone's cup of tea.

It took me about 15 minutes to draft the new Pirate Pattern Protocol (*http://rfc.zeromq.org/spec:6*). It's not a big specification, but it does capture enough to act as the basis for arguments ("Your queue isn't PPP compatible; please fix it!").

Turning PPP into a real protocol would take more work:

- There should be a protocol version number in the READY command so that it's possible to distinguish between different versions of PPP.
- Right now, READY and HEARTBEAT are not entirely distinct from requests and replies. To make them distinct, we would need a message structure that includes a "message type" part.

Service-Oriented Reliable Queuing (Majordomo Pattern)

The nice thing about progress is how fast it happens when lawyers and committees aren't involved. Just a few sentences ago, we were dreaming of a better protocol that would fix the world. And here we have it: the Majordomo Protocol (*http://rfc.zeromq.org/spec:7*).

This one-page specification turns PPP into something more solid (Figure 4-4). This is how we should design complex architectures: start by writing down the contracts, and only *then* write software to implement them.

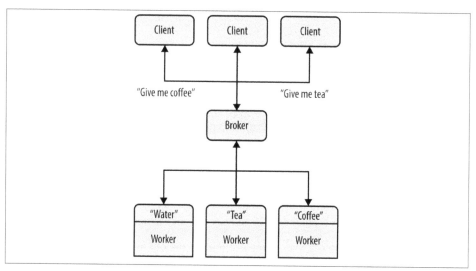

Figure 4-4. The Majordomo pattern

The Majordomo Protocol (MDP) extends and improves on PPP in one interesting way: it adds a "service name" to requests that the client sends, and asks workers to register for specific services. Adding service names turns our Paranoid Pirate queue into a service-oriented broker. The nice thing about MDP is that it came out of working code, a simpler ancestor protocol (PPP), and a precise set of improvements. This made it easy to draft.

To implement Majordomo, we need to write a framework for clients and workers. It's really not sane to ask every application developer to read the spec and make it work, when they could be using a simpler API built and tested just once.

So while our first contract (MDP itself) defines how the pieces of our distributed architecture talk to each other, our second contract defines how user applications talk to the technical framework we're going to design.

Majordomo has two halves, a client side and a worker side. Since we'll write both client and worker applications, we will need two APIs. Here is a sketch for the client API, using a simple object-oriented approach:

```
mdcli_t *mdcli_new     (char *broker);
void     mdcli_destroy (mdcli_t **self_p);
zmsg_t  *mdcli_send    (mdcli_t *self, char *service, zmsg_t **request_p);
```

That's it. We open a session to the broker, send a request message, get a reply message back, and eventually close the connection. Here's a sketch for the worker API:

```
mdwrk_t *mdwrk_new     (char *broker,char *service);
void     mdwrk_destroy (mdwrk_t **self_p);
zmsg_t  *mdwrk_recv    (mdwrk_t *self, zmsg_t *reply);
```

It's more or less symmetrical, but the worker dialog is a little different. The first time a worker does a recv(), it passes a null reply. Thereafter, it passes the current reply and gets a new request.

The client and worker APIs were fairly simple to construct because they're heavily based on the Paranoid Pirate code we already developed. The client API is shown in Example 4-18.

Example 4-18. Majordomo client API (mdcliapi.c)

```
/*  =====================================================================
 *  mdcliapi.c - Majordomo Protocol Client API
 *  Implements the MDP/Worker spec at http://rfc.zeromq.org/spec:7.
 *  ===================================================================== */

#include "mdcliapi.h"

//  Structure of our class
//  We access these properties only via class methods

struct _mdcli_t {
    zctx_t *ctx;                //  Our context
    char *broker;
    void *client;               //  Socket to broker
    int verbose;                //  Print activity to stdout
    int timeout;                //  Request timeout
    int retries;                //  Request retries
};
```

```
//  -------------------------------------------------------------------
//  Connect or reconnect to broker

void s_mdcli_connect_to_broker (mdcli_t *self)
{
    if (self->client)
        zsocket_destroy (self->ctx, self->client);
    self->client = zsocket_new (self->ctx, ZMQ_REQ);
    zmq_connect (self->client, self->broker);
    if (self->verbose)
        zclock_log ("I: connecting to broker at %s...", self->broker);
}
```

Example 4-19 presents the constructor and destructor for our mdcli class.

Example 4-19. Majordomo client API (mdcliapi.c): constructor and destructor

```
//  -------------------------------------------------------------------
//  Constructor

mdcli_t *
mdcli_new (char *broker, int verbose)
{
    assert (broker);

    mdcli_t *self = (mdcli_t *) zmalloc (sizeof (mdcli_t));
    self->ctx = zctx_new ();
    self->broker = strdup (broker);
    self->verbose = verbose;
    self->timeout = 2500;        //  msec
    self->retries = 3;           //  Before we abandon

    s_mdcli_connect_to_broker (self);
    return self;
}


//  -------------------------------------------------------------------
//  Destructor

void
mdcli_destroy (mdcli_t **self_p)
{
    assert (self_p);
    if (*self_p) {
        mdcli_t *self = *self_p;
        zctx_destroy (&self->ctx);
        free (self->broker);
        free (self);
        *self_p = NULL;
    }
}
```

These are the class methods. We can set the request timeout and number of retry attempts before sending requests, as shown in Example 4-20.

Example 4-20. Majordomo client API (mdcliapi.c): configure retry behavior

```
//  ----------------------------------------------------------------------
//  Set request timeout

void
mdcli_set_timeout (mdcli_t *self, int timeout)
{
    assert (self);
    self->timeout = timeout;
}



//  ----------------------------------------------------------------------
//  Set request retries

void
mdcli_set_retries (mdcli_t *self, int retries)
{
    assert (self);
    self->retries = retries;
}
```

Example 4-21 and 4-22 show the send method. It sends a request to the broker and gets a reply even if it has to retry several times. It takes ownership of the request message, and destroys it when sent. It returns the reply message, or NULL if there was no reply after multiple attempts.

Example 4-21. Majordomo client API (mdcliapi.c): send request and wait for reply

```
zmsg_t *
mdcli_send (mdcli_t *self, char *service, zmsg_t **request_p)
{
    assert (self);
    assert (request_p);
    zmsg_t *request = *request_p;

    //  Prefix request with protocol frames
    //  Frame 1: "MDPCxy" (six bytes, MDP/Client x.y)
    //  Frame 2: Service name (printable string)
    zmsg_pushstr (request, service);
    zmsg_pushstr (request, MDPC_CLIENT);
    if (self->verbose) {
        zclock_log ("I: send request to '%s' service:", service);
        zmsg_dump (request);
    }
    int retries_left = self->retries;
    while (retries_left && !zctx_interrupted) {
        zmsg_t *msg = zmsg_dup (request);
```

```
    zmsg_send (&msg, self->client);

    zmq_pollitem_t items [] = {
        { self->client, 0, ZMQ_POLLIN, 0 }
    };
```

On any blocking call, libzmq will return -1 if there was an error. We could in theory check for different error codes, but in practice it's okay to assume it was EINTR (Ctrl-C). The body of our send method is shown in Example 4-22.

Example 4-22. Majordomo client API (mdcliapi.c): body of send

```
        int rc = zmq_poll (items, 1, self->timeout * ZMQ_POLL_MSEC);
        if (rc == -1)
            break;          //  Interrupted

        //  If we got a reply, process it
        if (items [0].revents & ZMQ_POLLIN) {
            zmsg_t *msg = zmsg_recv (self->client);
            if (self->verbose) {
                zclock_log ("I: received reply:");
                zmsg_dump (msg);
            }
            //  We would handle malformed replies better in real code
            assert (zmsg_size (msg) >= 3);

            zframe_t *header = zmsg_pop (msg);
            assert (zframe_streq (header, MDPC_CLIENT));
            zframe_destroy (&header);

            zframe_t *reply_service = zmsg_pop (msg);
            assert (zframe_streq (reply_service, service));
            zframe_destroy (&reply_service);

            zmsg_destroy (&request);
            return msg;     //  Success
        }
        else
        if (--retries_left) {
            if (self->verbose)
                zclock_log ("W: no reply, reconnecting...");
            s_mdcli_connect_to_broker (self);
        }
        else {
            if (self->verbose)
                zclock_log ("W: permanent error, abandoning");
            break;          //  Give up
        }
    }
    if (zctx_interrupted)
        printf ("W: interrupt received, killing client...\n");
    zmsg_destroy (&request);
```

```
        return NULL;
}
```

Let's see how the client API looks in action, with an example test program (Example 4-23) that does 100K request-reply cycles.

Example 4-23. Majordomo client application (mdclient.c)

```
//
//  Majordomo Protocol client example
//  Uses the mdcli API to hide all MDP aspects
//

//  Lets us build this source without creating a library
#include "mdcliapi.c"

int main (int argc, char *argv [])
{
    int verbose = (argc > 1 && streq (argv [1], "-v"));
    mdcli_t *session = mdcli_new ("tcp://localhost:5555", verbose);

    int count;
    for (count = 0; count < 100000; count++) {
        zmsg_t *request = zmsg_new ();
        zmsg_pushstr (request, "Hello world");
        zmsg_t *reply = mdcli_send (session, "echo", &request);
        if (reply)
            zmsg_destroy (&reply);
        else
            break;              //  Interrupt or failure
    }
    printf ("%d requests/replies processed\n", count);
    mdcli_destroy (&session);
    return 0;
}
```

The worker API is presented in Example 4-24 through 4-30.

Example 4-24. Majordomo worker API (mdwrkapi.c)

```
/*  =========================================================================
 *  mdwrkapi.c - Majordomo Protocol Worker API
 *  Implements the MDP/Worker spec at http://rfc.zeromq.org/spec:7.
 *  ========================================================================= */

#include "mdwrkapi.h"

//  Reliability parameters
#define HEARTBEAT_LIVENESS  3       //  3-5 is reasonable
```

Example 4-25 shows is the structure of a worker API instance. We use a pseudo object-oriented approach in a lot of the C examples, as well as the CZMQ binding.

Example 4-25. Majordomo worker API (mdwrkapi.c): worker class structure

```
//  Structure of our class
//  We access these properties only via class methods

struct _mdwrk_t {
    zctx_t *ctx;                    //  Our context
    char *broker;
    char *service;
    void *worker;                   //  Socket to broker
    int verbose;                    //  Print activity to stdout

    //  Heartbeat management
    uint64_t heartbeat_at;          //  When to send HEARTBEAT
    size_t liveness;                //  How many attempts left
    int heartbeat;                  //  Heartbeat delay, in msec
    int reconnect;                  //  Reconnect delay, in msec

    int expect_reply;               //  Zero only at start
    zframe_t *reply_to;             //  Return identity, if any
};
```

We have two utility functions, to send a message to the broker and to (re)connect to the broker, as you can see in Example 4-26.

Example 4-26. Majordomo worker API (mdwrkapi.c): utility functions

```
//  ----------------------------------------------------------------------
//  Send message to broker
//  If no msg is provided, creates one internally

static void
s_mdwrk_send_to_broker (mdwrk_t *self, char *command, char *option,
                        zmsg_t *msg)
{
    msg = msg? zmsg_dup (msg): zmsg_new ();

    //  Stack protocol envelope to start of message
    if (option)
        zmsg_pushstr (msg, option);
    zmsg_pushstr (msg, command);
    zmsg_pushstr (msg, MDPW_WORKER);
    zmsg_pushstr (msg, "");

    if (self->verbose) {
        zclock_log ("I: sending %s to broker",
            mdps_commands [(int) *command]);
        zmsg_dump (msg);
    }
    zmsg_send (&msg, self->worker);
}
```

```
//  -----------------------------------------------------------------
//  Connect or reconnect to broker

void s_mdwrk_connect_to_broker (mdwrk_t *self)
{
    if (self->worker)
        zsocket_destroy (self->ctx, self->worker);
    self->worker = zsocket_new (self->ctx, ZMQ_DEALER);
    zmq_connect (self->worker, self->broker);
    if (self->verbose)
        zclock_log ("I: connecting to broker at %s...", self->broker);

    //  Register service with broker
    s_mdwrk_send_to_broker (self, MDPW_READY, self->service, NULL);

    //  If liveness hits zero, queue is considered disconnected
    self->liveness = HEARTBEAT_LIVENESS;
    self->heartbeat_at = zclock_time () + self->heartbeat;
}
```

Example 4-27 presents the constructor and destructor for our mdwrk class.

Example 4-27. Majordomo worker API (mdwrkapi.c): constructor and destructor

```
//  -----------------------------------------------------------------
//  Constructor

mdwrk_t *
mdwrk_new (char *broker,char *service, int verbose)
{
    assert (broker);
    assert (service);

    mdwrk_t *self = (mdwrk_t *) zmalloc (sizeof (mdwrk_t));
    self->ctx = zctx_new ();
    self->broker = strdup (broker);
    self->service = strdup (service);
    self->verbose = verbose;
    self->heartbeat = 2500;     //  msec
    self->reconnect = 2500;     //  msec

    s_mdwrk_connect_to_broker (self);
    return self;
}


//  -----------------------------------------------------------------
//  Destructor

void
mdwrk_destroy (mdwrk_t **self_p)
{
    assert (self_p);
```

```
        if (*self_p) {
            mdwrk_t *self = *self_p;
            zctx_destroy (&self->ctx);
            free (self->broker);
            free (self->service);
            free (self);
            *self_p = NULL;
        }
}
```

We provide two methods to configure the worker API. You can set the heartbeat interval
and retries to match the expected network performance (Example 4-28).

Example 4-28. Majordomo worker API (mdwrkapi.c): configure worker

```
//  ---------------------------------------------------------------------
//  Set heartbeat delay

void
mdwrk_set_heartbeat (mdwrk_t *self, int heartbeat)
{
    self->heartbeat = heartbeat;
}



//  ---------------------------------------------------------------------
//  Set reconnect delay

void
mdwrk_set_reconnect (mdwrk_t *self, int reconnect)
{
    self->reconnect = reconnect;
}
```

Example 4-29 shows the recv method; it's a little misnamed since it first sends any reply
and then waits for a new request. If you have a better name for this, let me know!

Example 4-29. Majordomo worker API (mdwrkapi.c): recv method

```
//  ---------------------------------------------------------------------
//  Send reply, if any, to broker and wait for next request.

zmsg_t *
mdwrk_recv (mdwrk_t *self, zmsg_t **reply_p)
{
    //  Format and send the reply if we were provided one
    assert (reply_p);
    zmsg_t *reply = *reply_p;
    assert (reply || !self->expect_reply);
    if (reply) {
        assert (self->reply_to);
        zmsg_wrap (reply, self->reply_to);
        s_mdwrk_send_to_broker (self, MDPW_REPLY, NULL, reply);
```

```
    zmsg_destroy (reply_p);
}
self->expect_reply = 1;

while (true) {
    zmq_pollitem_t items [] = {
        { self->worker,   0, ZMQ_POLLIN, 0 } };
    int rc = zmq_poll (items, 1, self->heartbeat * ZMQ_POLL_MSEC);
    if (rc == -1)
        break;              //  Interrupted

    if (items [0].revents & ZMQ_POLLIN) {
        zmsg_t *msg = zmsg_recv (self->worker);
        if (!msg)
            break;          //  Interrupted
        if (self->verbose) {
            zclock_log ("I: received message from broker:");
            zmsg_dump (msg);
        }
        self->liveness = HEARTBEAT_LIVENESS;

        //  Don't try to handle errors, just assert noisily
        assert (zmsg_size (msg) >= 3);

        zframe_t *empty = zmsg_pop (msg);
        assert (zframe_streq (empty, ""));
        zframe_destroy (&empty);

        zframe_t *header = zmsg_pop (msg);
        assert (zframe_streq (header, MDPW_WORKER));
        zframe_destroy (&header);

        zframe_t *command = zmsg_pop (msg);
        if (zframe_streq (command, MDPW_REQUEST)) {
            //  We should pop and save as many addresses as there are
            //  up to a null part, but for now, just save one...
            self->reply_to = zmsg_unwrap (msg);
            zframe_destroy (&command);
```

Finally, here is where we actually have a message to process; as shown in
Example 4-30, we return it to the caller application.

Example 4-30. Majordomo worker API (mdwrkapi.c): process message

```
            return msg;     //  We have a request to process
        }
        else
        if (zframe_streq (command, MDPW_HEARTBEAT))
            ;                       //  Do nothing for heartbeats
        else
        if (zframe_streq (command, MDPW_DISCONNECT))
            s_mdwrk_connect_to_broker (self);
```

```
            else {
                zclock_log ("E: invalid input message");
                zmsg_dump (msg);
            }
            zframe_destroy (&command);
            zmsg_destroy (&msg);
        }
        else
        if (--self->liveness == 0) {
            if (self->verbose)
                zclock_log ("W: disconnected from broker - retrying...");
            zclock_sleep (self->reconnect);
            s_mdwrk_connect_to_broker (self);
        }
        //  Send HEARTBEAT if it's time
        if (zclock_time () > self->heartbeat_at) {
            s_mdwrk_send_to_broker (self, MDPW_HEARTBEAT, NULL, NULL);
            self->heartbeat_at = zclock_time () + self->heartbeat;
        }
    }
    if (zctx_interrupted)
        printf ("W: interrupt received, killing worker...\n");
    return NULL;
}
```

Let's see how the worker API looks in action with an example test program
(Example 4-31) that implements an echo service.

Example 4-31. Majordomo worker application (mdworker.c)

```
//
//  Majordomo Protocol worker example
//  Uses the mdwrk API to hide all MDP aspects
//

//  Lets us build this source without creating a library
#include "mdwrkapi.c"

int main (int argc, char *argv [])
{
    int verbose = (argc > 1 && streq (argv [1], "-v"));
    mdwrk_t *session = mdwrk_new (
        "tcp://localhost:5555", "echo", verbose);

    zmsg_t *reply = NULL;
    while (true) {
        zmsg_t *request = mdwrk_recv (session, &reply);
        if (request == NULL)
            break;              //  Worker was interrupted
        reply = request;        //  Echo is complex... :-)
    }
    mdwrk_destroy (&session);
```

```
    return 0;
}
```

Here are some things to note about the worker API code:

- The APIs are single-threaded. This means, for example, that the worker won't send heartbeats in the background. Happily, this is exactly what we want: if the worker application gets stuck, heartbeats will stop and the broker will stop sending requests to the worker.
- The worker API doesn't do an exponential backoff; it's not worth the extra complexity.
- The APIs don't do any error reporting. If something isn't as expected, they raise an assertion (or exception, depending on the language). This is ideal for a reference implementation, so any protocol errors show immediately. For real applications, the API should be robust against invalid messages.

You might wonder why the worker API is manually closing its socket and opening a new one, when ØMQ will automatically reconnect a socket if the peer disappears and comes back. Look back at the Simple Pirate and Paranoid Pirate workers to understand. Although ØMQ will automatically reconnect workers if the broker dies and comes back up, this isn't sufficient to re-register the workers with the broker. I know of at least two solutions. The simplest, which we use here, is for the worker to monitor the connection using heartbeats and, if it decides the broker is dead, to close its socket and start afresh with a new socket. The alternative is for the broker to challenge unknown workers when it gets a heartbeat from them and ask them to re-register. That would require protocol support.

Now let's design the Majordomo broker. Its core structure is a set of queues, one per service. We will create these queues as workers appear (we could delete them as workers disappear, but forget that for now because it gets complex). Additionally, we will keep a queue of workers per service.

The code for the broker is shown in Example 4-32.

Example 4-32. Majordomo broker (mdbroker.c)

```
//
//  Majordomo Protocol broker
//  A minimal C implementation of the Majordomo Protocol as defined in
//  http://rfc.zeromq.org/spec:7 and http://rfc.zeromq.org/spec:8.
//
#include "czmq.h"
#include "mdp.h"

//  We'd normally pull these from config data

#define HEARTBEAT_LIVENESS  3       //  3-5 is reasonable
```

```
#define HEARTBEAT_INTERVAL  2500     // msec
#define HEARTBEAT_EXPIRY     HEARTBEAT_INTERVAL * HEARTBEAT_LIVENESS
```

The broker class (Example 4-33) defines a single broker instance.

Example 4-33. Majordomo broker (mdbroker.c): broker class structure

```
typedef struct {
    zctx_t *ctx;                // Our context
    void *socket;               // Socket for clients & workers
    int verbose;                // Print activity to stdout
    char *endpoint;             // Broker binds to this endpoint
    zhash_t *services;          // Hash of known services
    zhash_t *workers;           // Hash of known workers
    zlist_t *waiting;           // List of waiting workers
    uint64_t heartbeat_at;      // When to send HEARTBEAT
} broker_t;

static broker_t *
    s_broker_new (int verbose);
static void
    s_broker_destroy (broker_t **self_p);
static void
    s_broker_bind (broker_t *self, char *endpoint);
static void
    s_broker_worker_msg (broker_t *self, zframe_t *sender, zmsg_t *msg);
static void
    s_broker_client_msg (broker_t *self, zframe_t *sender, zmsg_t *msg);
static void
    s_broker_purge (broker_t *self);
```

The service class (Example 4-34) defines a single service instance.

Example 4-34. Majordomo broker (mdbroker.c): service class structure

```
typedef struct {
    broker_t *broker;           // Broker instance
    char *name;                 // Service name
    zlist_t *requests;          // List of client requests
    zlist_t *waiting;           // List of waiting workers
    size_t workers;             // How many workers we have
} service_t;

static service_t *
    s_service_require (broker_t *self, zframe_t *service_frame);
static void
    s_service_destroy (void *argument);
static void
    s_service_dispatch (service_t *service, zmsg_t *msg);
```

The worker class (Example 4-35) defines a single worker, idle or active.

Example 4-35. Majordomo broker (mdbroker.c): worker class structure

```
typedef struct {
    broker_t *broker;            //  Broker instance
    char *id_string;             //  Identity of worker as string
    zframe_t *identity;          //  Identity frame for routing
    service_t *service;          //  Owning service, if known
    int64_t expiry;              //  When a worker expires, if no heartbeat
} worker_t;

static worker_t *
    s_worker_require (broker_t *self, zframe_t *identity);
static void
    s_worker_delete (worker_t *self, int disconnect);
static void
    s_worker_destroy (void *argument);
static void
    s_worker_send (worker_t *self, char *command, char *option,
                   zmsg_t *msg);
static void
    s_worker_waiting (worker_t *self);
```

The constructor and destructor for the broker are shown in Example 4-36.

Example 4-36. Majordomo broker (mdbroker.c): broker constructor and destructor

```
static broker_t *
s_broker_new (int verbose)
{
    broker_t *self = (broker_t *) zmalloc (sizeof (broker_t));

    //  Initialize broker state
    self->ctx = zctx_new ();
    self->socket = zsocket_new (self->ctx, ZMQ_ROUTER);
    self->verbose = verbose;
    self->services = zhash_new ();
    self->workers = zhash_new ();
    self->waiting = zlist_new ();
    self->heartbeat_at = zclock_time () + HEARTBEAT_INTERVAL;
    return self;
}

static void
s_broker_destroy (broker_t **self_p)
{
    assert (self_p);
    if (*self_p) {
        broker_t *self = *self_p;
        zctx_destroy (&self->ctx);
        zhash_destroy (&self->services);
        zhash_destroy (&self->workers);
        zlist_destroy (&self->waiting);
        free (self);
```

```
        *self_p = NULL;
    }
}
```

The `bind` method, shown in Example 4-37, binds the broker instance to an endpoint.
We can call this multiple times. Note that MDP uses a single socket for both clients and
workers.

Example 4-37. Majordomo broker (mdbroker.c): broker bind method

```
void
s_broker_bind (broker_t *self, char *endpoint)
{
    zsocket_bind (self->socket, endpoint);
    zclock_log ("I: MDP broker/0.2.0 is active at %s", endpoint);
}
```

The `worker_msg` method shown in Example 4-38 processes one READY, REPLY,
HEARTBEAT, or DISCONNECT message sent to the broker by a worker.

Example 4-38. Majordomo broker (mdbroker.c): broker worker_msg method

```
static void
s_broker_worker_msg (broker_t *self, zframe_t *sender, zmsg_t *msg)
{
    assert (zmsg_size (msg) >= 1);      //  At least, command

    zframe_t *command = zmsg_pop (msg);
    char *id_string = zframe_strhex (sender);
    int worker_ready = (zhash_lookup (self->workers, id_string) != NULL);
    free (id_string);
    worker_t *worker = s_worker_require (self, sender);

    if (zframe_streq (command, MDPW_READY)) {
        if (worker_ready)                    //  Not first command in session
            s_worker_delete (worker, 1);
        else
        if (zframe_size (sender) >= 4  //  Reserved service name
        && memcmp (zframe_data (sender), "mmi.", 4) == 0)
            s_worker_delete (worker, 1);
        else {
            //  Attach worker to service and mark as idle
            zframe_t *service_frame = zmsg_pop (msg);
            worker->service = s_service_require (self, service_frame);
            worker->service->workers++;
            s_worker_waiting (worker);
            zframe_destroy (&service_frame);
        }
    }
    else
    if (zframe_streq (command, MDPW_REPLY)) {
        if (worker_ready) {
```

```
        //  Remove and save client return envelope and insert the
        //  protocol header and service name, then rewrap envelope
        zframe_t *client = zmsg_unwrap (msg);
        zmsg_pushstr (msg, worker->service->name);
        zmsg_pushstr (msg, MDPC_CLIENT);
        zmsg_wrap (msg, client);
        zmsg_send (&msg, self->socket);
        s_worker_waiting (worker);
    }
    else
        s_worker_delete (worker, 1);
}
else
if (zframe_streq (command, MDPW_HEARTBEAT)) {
    if (worker_ready)
        worker->expiry = zclock_time () + HEARTBEAT_EXPIRY;
    else
        s_worker_delete (worker, 1);
}
else
if (zframe_streq (command, MDPW_DISCONNECT))
    s_worker_delete (worker, 0);
else {
    zclock_log ("E: invalid input message");
    zmsg_dump (msg);
}
free (command);
zmsg_destroy (&msg);
}
```

Example 4-39 shows how we process a request coming from a client. We implement
Majordomo Management Interface (MMI) requests directly here (at present, only the
mmi.service request).

Example 4-39. Majordomo broker (mdbroker.c): broker client_msg method

```
static void
s_broker_client_msg (broker_t *self, zframe_t *sender, zmsg_t *msg)
{
    assert (zmsg_size (msg) >= 2);     //  Service name + body

    zframe_t *service_frame = zmsg_pop (msg);
    service_t *service = s_service_require (self, service_frame);

    //  Set reply return identity to client sender
    zmsg_wrap (msg, zframe_dup (sender));

    //  If we got an MMI service request, process that internally
    if (zframe_size (service_frame) >= 4
    &&  memcmp (zframe_data (service_frame), "mmi.", 4) == 0) {
        char *return_code;
        if (zframe_streq (service_frame, "mmi.service")) {
```

```
            char *name = zframe_strdup (zmsg_last (msg));
            service_t *service =
                (service_t *) zhash_lookup (self->services, name);
            return_code = service && service->workers? "200": "404";
            free (name);
        }
        else
            return_code = "501";

        zframe_reset (zmsg_last (msg), return_code, strlen (return_code));

        //  Remove & save client return envelope and insert the
        //  protocol header and service name, then rewrap envelope
        zframe_t *client = zmsg_unwrap (msg);
        zmsg_push (msg, zframe_dup (service_frame));
        zmsg_pushstr (msg, MDPC_CLIENT);
        zmsg_wrap (msg, client);
        zmsg_send (&msg, self->socket);
    }
    else
        //  Else dispatch the message to the requested service
        s_service_dispatch (service, msg);
    zframe_destroy (&service_frame);
}
```

The purge method, shown in Example 4-40, deletes any idle workers that haven't pinged us in a while. We hold workers in order from oldest to most recent, so we can stop scanning whenever we find a live worker. This means we'll mainly stop at the first worker, which is essential when we have large numbers of workers (because we call this method in our critical path).

Example 4-40. Majordomo broker (mdbroker.c): broker purge method

```
static void
s_broker_purge (broker_t *self)
{
    worker_t *worker = (worker_t *) zlist_first (self->waiting);
    while (worker) {
        if (zclock_time () < worker->expiry)
            break;                  //  Worker is alive, we're done here
        if (self->verbose)
            zclock_log ("I: deleting expired worker: %s",
                        worker->id_string);

        s_worker_delete (worker, 0);
        worker = (worker_t *) zlist_first (self->waiting);
    }
}
```

Example 4-41 shows the implementation of the methods that work on a service.

Example 4-41. Majordomo broker (mdbroker.c): service methods

```
//  Lazy constructor that locates a service by name, or creates a new
//  service if there is no service already with that name

static service_t *
s_service_require (broker_t *self, zframe_t *service_frame)
{
    assert (service_frame);
    char *name = zframe_strdup (service_frame);

    service_t *service =
        (service_t *) zhash_lookup (self->services, name);
    if (service == NULL) {
        service = (service_t *) zmalloc (sizeof (service_t));
        service->broker = self;
        service->name = name;
        service->requests = zlist_new ();
        service->waiting = zlist_new ();
        zhash_insert (self->services, name, service);
        zhash_freefn (self->services, name, s_service_destroy);
        if (self->verbose)
            zclock_log ("I: added service: %s", name);
    }
    else
        free (name);

    return service;
}

//  Service destructor is called automatically whenever the service is
//  removed from broker->services

static void
s_service_destroy (void *argument)
{
    service_t *service = (service_t *) argument;
    while (zlist_size (service->requests)) {
        zmsg_t *msg = zlist_pop (service->requests);
        zmsg_destroy (&msg);
    }
    zlist_destroy (&service->requests);
    zlist_destroy (&service->waiting);
    free (service->name);
    free (service);
}
```

The dispatch method, shown in Example 4-42, sends requests to waiting workers.

Example 4-42. Majordomo broker (mdbroker.c): service dispatch method

```
static void
s_service_dispatch (service_t *self, zmsg_t *msg)
```

```
{
    assert (self);
    if (msg)                        //  Queue message, if any
        zlist_append (self->requests, msg);

    s_broker_purge (self->broker);
    while (zlist_size (self->waiting) && zlist_size (self->requests)) {
        worker_t *worker = zlist_pop (self->waiting);
        zlist_remove (self->broker->waiting, worker);
        zmsg_t *msg = zlist_pop (self->requests);
        s_worker_send (worker, MDPW_REQUEST, NULL, msg);
        zmsg_destroy (&msg);
    }
}
```

Example 4-43 shows the implementation of the methods that work on a worker.

Example 4-43. Majordomo broker (mdbroker.c): worker methods

```
//  Lazy constructor that locates a worker by identity, or creates a new
//  worker if there is no worker already with that identity

static worker_t *
s_worker_require (broker_t *self, zframe_t *identity)
{
    assert (identity);

    //  self->workers is keyed off worker identity
    char *id_string = zframe_strhex (identity);
    worker_t *worker =
        (worker_t *) zhash_lookup (self->workers, id_string);

    if (worker == NULL) {
        worker = (worker_t *) zmalloc (sizeof (worker_t));
        worker->broker = self;
        worker->id_string = id_string;
        worker->identity = zframe_dup (identity);
        zhash_insert (self->workers, id_string, worker);
        zhash_freefn (self->workers, id_string, s_worker_destroy);
        if (self->verbose)
            zclock_log ("I: registering new worker: %s", id_string);
    }
    else
        free (id_string);
    return worker;
}

//  The delete method deletes the current worker

static void
s_worker_delete (worker_t *self, int disconnect)
{
    assert (self);
```

```
    if (disconnect)
        s_worker_send (self, MDPW_DISCONNECT, NULL, NULL);

    if (self->service) {
        zlist_remove (self->service->waiting, self);
        self->service->workers--;
    }
    zlist_remove (self->broker->waiting, self);
    //  This implicitly calls s_worker_destroy
    zhash_delete (self->broker->workers, self->id_string);
}

//  Worker destructor is called automatically whenever the worker is
//  removed from broker->workers

static void
s_worker_destroy (void *argument)
{
    worker_t *self = (worker_t *) argument;
    zframe_destroy (&self->identity);
    free (self->id_string);
    free (self);
}
```

The send method (Example 4-44) formats and sends a command to a worker. The caller may also provide a command option and a message payload.

Example 4-44. Majordomo broker (mdbroker.c): worker send method

```
static void
s_worker_send (worker_t *self, char *command, char *option, zmsg_t *msg)
{
    msg = msg? zmsg_dup (msg): zmsg_new ();

    //  Stack protocol envelope to start of message
    if (option)
        zmsg_pushstr (msg, option);
    zmsg_pushstr (msg, command);
    zmsg_pushstr (msg, MDPW_WORKER);

    //  Stack routing envelope to start of message
    zmsg_wrap (msg, zframe_dup (self->identity));

    if (self->broker->verbose) {
        zclock_log ("I: sending %s to worker",
            mdps_commands [(int) *command]);
        zmsg_dump (msg);
    }
    zmsg_send (&msg, self->broker->socket);
}

//  This worker is now waiting for work
```

```
static void
s_worker_waiting (worker_t *self)
{
    //  Queue to broker and service waiting lists
    assert (self->broker);
    zlist_append (self->broker->waiting, self);
    zlist_append (self->service->waiting, self);
    self->expiry = zclock_time () + HEARTBEAT_EXPIRY;
    s_service_dispatch (self->service, NULL);
}
```

Finally, here is the main task. In Example 4-45, we create a new broker instance and then process messages on the broker socket.

Example 4-45. Majordomo broker (mdbroker.c): main task

```
int main (int argc, char *argv [])
{
    int verbose = (argc > 1 && streq (argv [1], "-v"));

    broker_t *self = s_broker_new (verbose);
    s_broker_bind (self, "tcp://*:5555");

    //  Get and process messages forever or until interrupted
    while (true) {
        zmq_pollitem_t items [] = {
            { self->socket,  0, ZMQ_POLLIN, 0 } };
        int rc = zmq_poll (items, 1, HEARTBEAT_INTERVAL * ZMQ_POLL_MSEC);
        if (rc == -1)
            break;              //  Interrupted

        //  Process next input message, if any
        if (items [0].revents & ZMQ_POLLIN) {
            zmsg_t *msg = zmsg_recv (self->socket);
            if (!msg)
                break;          //  Interrupted
            if (self->verbose) {
                zclock_log ("I: received message:");
                zmsg_dump (msg);
            }
            zframe_t *sender = zmsg_pop (msg);
            zframe_t *empty  = zmsg_pop (msg);
            zframe_t *header = zmsg_pop (msg);

            if (zframe_streq (header, MDPC_CLIENT))
                s_broker_client_msg (self, sender, msg);
            else
            if (zframe_streq (header, MDPW_WORKER))
                s_broker_worker_msg (self, sender, msg);
            else {
                zclock_log ("E: invalid message:");
```

```
                zmsg_dump (msg);
                zmsg_destroy (&msg);
            }
            zframe_destroy (&sender);
            zframe_destroy (&empty);
            zframe_destroy (&header);
        }
        //  Disconnect and delete any expired workers
        //  Send heartbeats to idle workers if needed
        if (zclock_time () > self->heartbeat_at) {
            s_broker_purge (self);
            worker_t *worker = (worker_t *) zlist_first (self->waiting);
            while (worker) {
                s_worker_send (worker, MDPW_HEARTBEAT, NULL, NULL);
                worker = (worker_t *) zlist_next (self->waiting);
            }
            self->heartbeat_at = zclock_time () + HEARTBEAT_INTERVAL;
        }
    }
    if (zctx_interrupted)
        printf ("W: interrupt received, shutting down...\n");

    s_broker_destroy (&self);
    return 0;
}
```

This is by far the most complex example we've seen. It's almost 500 lines of code; writing this and making it somewhat robust took two days. However, this is still a relatively short piece of code for a full service-oriented broker.

Notes on this code:

- The Majordomo Protocol lets us handle both clients and workers on a single socket. This is nicer for those deploying and managing the broker: it just sits on one ØMQ endpoint rather than the two that most proxies need.

- The broker implements all of MDP/0.1 properly (as far as I know), including disconnection if the broker sends invalid commands, heartbeating, and the rest.

- It can be extended to run multiple threads, each managing one socket and one set of clients and workers. This could be interesting for segmenting large architectures. The C code is already organized around a broker class to make this trivial.

- A primary/failover or live/live broker reliability model is easy, as the broker essentially has no state except service presence. It's up to clients and workers to choose another broker if their first choice isn't up and running.

- The examples use five-second heartbeats, mainly to reduce the amount of output when you enable tracing. Realistic values would be lower for most LAN applications. However, any retry has to be slow enough to allow for a service to restart, say 10 seconds at least.

We later improved and extended the protocol and the Majordomo implementation, which now sits in its own GitHub project. If you want a properly usable Majordomo stack, use the GitHub project.

Asynchronous Majordomo Pattern

The Majordomo implementation in the previous section is simple and stupid. The client is just the original Simple Pirate, wrapped up in a sexy API. When I fire up a client, broker, and worker on a test box, it can process 100,000 requests in about 14 seconds. That is partially due to the code, which cheerfully copies message frames around as if CPU cycles were free. But the real problem is that we're doing network round-trips. ØMQ disables Nagle's algorithm (*http://en.wikipedia.org/wiki/Nagles_algorithm*), but round-tripping is still slow.

Theory is great in theory, but in practice, practice is better. Let's measure the actual cost of round-tripping with a simple test program. This sends a bunch of messages, first waiting for a reply to each message, and second as a batch, reading all the replies back as a batch. Both approaches do the same work, but they give very different results. We mock up a client, broker, and worker. The client task is shown in Example 4-46.

Example 4-46. Round-trip demonstrator (tripping.c)

```
//
//  Round-trip demonstrator
//
//  While this example runs in a single process, that is just to make
//  it easier to start and stop the example. The client task signals to
//  main when it's ready.
//
#include "czmq.h"

static void
client_task (void *args, zctx_t *ctx, void *pipe)
{
    void *client = zsocket_new (ctx, ZMQ_DEALER);
    zsocket_connect (client, "tcp://localhost:5555");
    printf ("Setting up test...\n");
    zclock_sleep (100);

    int requests;
    int64_t start;

    printf ("Synchronous round-trip test...\n");
    start = zclock_time ();
    for (requests = 0; requests < 10000; requests++) {
        zstr_send (client, "hello");
```

```
        char *reply = zstr_recv (client);
        free (reply);
    }
    printf (" %d calls/second\n",
        (1000 * 10000) / (int) (zclock_time () - start));

    printf ("Asynchronous round-trip test...\n");
    start = zclock_time ();
    for (requests = 0; requests < 100000; requests++)
        zstr_send (client, "hello");
    for (requests = 0; requests < 100000; requests++) {
        char *reply = zstr_recv (client);
        free (reply);
    }
    printf (" %d calls/second\n",
        (1000 * 100000) / (int) (zclock_time () - start));
    zstr_send (pipe, "done");
}
```

The worker task is in Example 4-47. All it does is receive a message, and bounce it back
the way it came.

Example 4-47. Round-trip demonstrator (tripping.c): worker task

```
static void *
worker_task (void *args)
{
    zctx_t *ctx = zctx_new ();
    void *worker = zsocket_new (ctx, ZMQ_DEALER);
    zsocket_connect (worker, "tcp://localhost:5556");

    while (true) {
        zmsg_t *msg = zmsg_recv (worker);
        zmsg_send (&msg, worker);
    }
    zctx_destroy (&ctx);
    return NULL;
}
```

Example 4-48 shows the broker task. It uses the `zmq_proxy()` function to switch messages between the frontend and backend.

Example 4-48. Round-trip demonstrator (tripping.c): broker task

```
static void *
broker_task (void *args)
{
    //  Prepare our context and sockets
    zctx_t *ctx = zctx_new ();
    void *frontend = zsocket_new (ctx, ZMQ_DEALER);
    zsocket_bind (frontend, "tcp://*:5555");
    void *backend = zsocket_new (ctx, ZMQ_DEALER);
    zsocket_bind (backend, "tcp://*:5556");
```

```
    zmq_proxy (frontend, backend, NULL);
    zctx_destroy (&ctx);
    return NULL;
}
```

Finally, Example 4-49 presents the main task, which starts the client, worker, and broker, and then runs until the client signals it to stop.

Example 4-49. Round-trip demonstrator (tripping.c): main task

```
int main (void)
{
    //  Create threads
    zctx_t *ctx = zctx_new ();
    void *client = zthread_fork (ctx, client_task, NULL);
    zthread_new (worker_task, NULL);
    zthread_new (broker_task, NULL);

    //  Wait for signal on client pipe
    char *signal = zstr_recv (client);
    free (signal);

    zctx_destroy (&ctx);
    return 0;
}
```

On my development box, running this program results in:

```
Setting up test...
Synchronous round-trip test...
 9057 calls/second
Asynchronous round-trip test...
 173010 calls/second
```

Note that the client thread does a small pause before starting. This is to get around one of the "features" of the router socket: if you send a message with the address of a peer that's not yet connected, the message gets discarded. In this example we don't use the load-balancing mechanism, so without the sleep, if the worker thread is too slow to connect it will lose messages, making a mess of our test.

As we see, round-tripping in the simplest case is 20 times slower than the asynchronous, "shove it down the pipe as fast as it'll go" approach. Let's see if we can apply this to Majordomo to make it faster.

First, we modify the client API to send and receive in two separate methods:

```
    mdcli_t *mdcli_new    (char *broker);
    void     mdcli_destroy (mdcli_t **self_p);
    int      mdcli_send   (mdcli_t *self, char *service, zmsg_t **request_p);
    zmsg_t *mdcli_recv    (mdcli_t *self);
```

It's literally a few minutes' work to refactor the synchronous client API to become asynchronous, as shown in Example 4-50.

Example 4-50. Majordomo asynchronous client API (mdcliapi2.c)

```
/*  =========================================================================
 *  mdcliapi2.c - Majordomo Protocol Client API
 *  Implements the MDP/Worker spec at http://rfc.zeromq.org/spec:7.
 *  ========================================================================= */

#include "mdcliapi2.h"

//  Structure of our class
//  We access these properties only via class methods

struct _mdcli_t {
    zctx_t *ctx;                //  Our context
    char *broker;
    void *client;               //  Socket to broker
    int verbose;                //  Print activity to stdout
    int timeout;                //  Request timeout
};

//  ---------------------------------------------------------------------
//  Connect or reconnect to broker. In this asynchronous class, we use a
//  DEALER socket instead of a REQ socket; this lets us send any number
//  of requests without waiting for a reply.

void s_mdcli_connect_to_broker (mdcli_t *self)
{
    if (self->client)
        zsocket_destroy (self->ctx, self->client);
    self->client = zsocket_new (self->ctx, ZMQ_DEALER);
    zmq_connect (self->client, self->broker);
    if (self->verbose)
        zclock_log ("I: connecting to broker at %s...", self->broker);
}


//  The constructor and destructor are the same as in mdcliapi, except
//  we don't do retries, so there's no retries property.
...
...
```

The differences are:

- We use a DEALER socket instead of REQ, so we emulate REQ with an empty delimiter frame before each request and each response.
- We don't retry requests; if the application needs to retry, it can do this itself.
- We break the synchronous send method into separate send and recv methods.

- The send method is asynchronous and returns immediately after sending. The caller can thus send a number of messages before getting a response.

- The recv method waits for (with a timeout) one response and returns that to the caller.

The corresponding client test program, which sends 100,000 messages and then receives 100,000 back, is shown in Example 4-51.

Example 4-51. Majordomo client application (mdclient2.c)

```
//
//  Majordomo Protocol client example - asynchronous
//  Uses the mdcli API to hide all MDP aspects
//
//  Lets us build this source without creating a library
#include "mdcliapi2.c"

int main (int argc, char *argv [])
{
    int verbose = (argc > 1 && streq (argv [1], "-v"));
    mdcli_t *session = mdcli_new ("tcp://localhost:5555", verbose);

    int count;
    for (count = 0; count < 100000; count++) {
        zmsg_t *request = zmsg_new ();
        zmsg_pushstr (request, "Hello world");
        mdcli_send (session, "echo", &request);
    }
    for (count = 0; count < 100000; count++) {
        zmsg_t *reply = mdcli_recv (session);
        if (reply)
            zmsg_destroy (&reply);
        else
            break;              //  Interrupted by Ctrl-C
    }
    printf ("%d replies received\n", count);
    mdcli_destroy (&session);
    return 0;
}
```

The broker and worker are unchanged because we haven't modified the protocol at all. We see an immediate improvement in performance. Here's the synchronous client chugging through 100K request-reply cycles:

```
$ time mdclient
100000 requests/replies processed

real    0m14.088s
user    0m1.310s
sys     0m2.670s
```

And here's the asynchronous client, with a single worker:

```
$ time mdclient2
100000 replies received

real    0m8.730s
user    0m0.920s
sys     0m1.550s
```

Twice as fast. Not bad, but let's fire up 10 workers and see how it handles the traffic:

```
$ time mdclient2
100000 replies received

real    0m3.863s
user    0m0.730s
sys     0m0.470s
```

It isn't fully asynchronous because workers get their messages on a strict last-used basis, but it will scale better with more workers. On my PC, after eight or so workers, it doesn't get any faster. Four cores only stretches so far. But we got a 4x improvement in throughput with just a few minutes' work. The broker is still unoptimized. It spends most of its time copying message frames around, instead of doing zero-copy, which it could. But we're getting 25K reliable request-reply calls a second, with pretty low effort.

However, the asynchronous Majordomo pattern isn't all roses. It has a fundamental weakness, namely that it cannot survive a broker crash without more work. If you look at the mdcliapi2 code you'll see it does not attempt to reconnect after a failure. A proper reconnect would require the following:

- A number on every request and a matching number on every reply, which would ideally require a change to the protocol to enforce
- Tracking and holding onto all outstanding requests in the client API (i.e., those for which no reply has yet been received)
- In case of fail over, for the client API to *resend* all outstanding requests to the broker

It's not a deal breaker, but it does show that performance often means complexity. Is this worth doing for Majordomo? It depends on your use case. For a name lookup service you call once per session, no. For a web frontend serving thousands of clients, probably yes.

Service Discovery

So, we have a nice service-oriented broker, but we have no way of knowing whether a particular service is available or not. We know when a request fails, but we don't know why. It would be useful to be able to ask the broker questions like, "Is the echo service running?" The most obvious way to implement this would be to modify our MDP/Client protocol to add commands to ask such questions. But MDP/Client has the great charm of being simple. Adding service discovery to it would make it as complex as the MDP/Worker protocol.

Another option is to do what email servers do, and ask that undeliverable requests be returned. This can work well in an asynchronous world, but it also adds complexity. We need ways to distinguish returned requests from replies and to handle these properly.

Let's try to use what we've already built, building on top of MDP instead of modifying it. Service discovery is, itself, a service. It might indeed be one of several management services, such as "disable service X," "provide statistics," and so on. What we want is a general, extensible solution that doesn't affect the protocol or existing applications.

There's a small RFC that layers this on top of MDP: the Majordomo Management Interface (MMI) (*http://rfc.zeromq.org/spec:8*). We already implemented it in the broker, though unless you read the whole thing you probably missed that. I'll explain how it works in the broker:

- When a client requests a service that starts with mmi., instead of routing this request to a worker, we handle it internally.

- We handle just one service in our broker, which is mmi.service, the service discovery service.

- The payload for the request is the name of an external service (a real one, provided by a worker).

- The broker returns "200" (OK) or "404" (Not found), depending on whether there are workers registered for that service or not.

Example 4-52 shows how we use the service discovery in an application.

Example 4-52. Service discovery over Majordomo (mmiecho.c)

```
//
//  MMI echo query example
//

//  Lets us build this source without creating a library
#include "mdcliapi.c"

int main (int argc, char *argv [])
{
    int verbose = (argc > 1 && streq (argv [1], "-v"));
    mdcli_t *session = mdcli_new ("tcp://localhost:5555", verbose);

    //  This is the service we want to look up
    zmsg_t *request = zmsg_new ();
    zmsg_addstr (request, "echo");

    //  This is the service to which we send our request
```

```
zmsg_t *reply = mdcli_send (session, "mmi.service", &request);

if (reply) {
    char *reply_code = zframe_strdup (zmsg_first (reply));
    printf ("Lookup echo service: %s\n", reply_code);
    free (reply_code);
    zmsg_destroy (&reply);
}
else
    printf ("E: no response from broker, make sure it's running\n");

mdcli_destroy (&session);
return 0;
}
```

Try this with and without a worker running, and you should see the little program report "200" or "404" accordingly.

The implementation of MMI in our example broker is flimsy. For example, if a worker disappears, services remain "present." In practice, a broker should remove services that have no workers after some configurable timeout.

Idempotent Services

Idempotency is not something you take a pill for. What it means is that it's safe to repeat an operation. Checking the clock is idempotent. Lending one's credit card to one's children is not. While many client-to-server use cases are idempotent, some are not. Examples of idempotent use cases include:

- Stateless task distribution—i.e., a pipeline where the servers are stateless workers that compute a reply based purely on the state provided by a request. In such a case, it's safe (though inefficient) to execute the same request many times.
- A name service that translates logical addresses into endpoints to bind or connect to. In such a case it's safe to make the same lookup request many times.

And here are examples of non-idempotent use cases:

- A logging service. One does not want the same log information recorded more than once.
- Any service that has an impact on downstream nodes (e.g., sends information on to other nodes). If that service gets the same request more than once, downstream nodes will get duplicate information.
- Any service that modifies shared data in some non-idempotent way; e.g., a service that debits a bank account is definitely not idempotent.

When our server applications are not idempotent, we have to think more carefully about when exactly they might crash. If an application dies when it's idle, or while it's processing a request, that's usually fine. We can use database transactions to make sure a debit and a credit are always done together, if at all. If the server dies while sending its reply, however, that's a problem, because as far as it's concerned, it has done its work.

If the network dies just as the reply is making its way back to the client, the same problem arises. The client will think the server died and will resend the request, and the server will do the same work twice, which is not what we want.

To handle non-idempotent operations, we use the fairly standard solution of detecting and rejecting duplicate requests. This means:

- The client must stamp every request with a unique client identifier and a unique message number.
- The server, before sending back a reply, stores it using the combination of client ID and message number as a key.
- The server, when getting a request from a given client, first checks whether it has a reply for that client ID and message number. If so, it does not process the request, but just resends the reply.

Disconnected Reliability (Titanic Pattern)

Once you realize that Majordomo is a "reliable" message broker, you might be tempted to add some spinning rust (that is, ferrous-based hard disk platters). After all, this works for all the enterprise messaging systems. It's such a tempting idea that it's a little sad to have to be negative toward it. But brutal cynicism is one of my specialties. So, some reasons you don't want rust-based brokers sitting in the center of your architecture are:

- As you've seen, the Lazy Pirate client performs surprisingly well. It works across a whole range of architectures, from direct client-to-server to distributed queue proxies. It does tend to assume that workers are stateless and idempotent, but we can work around that limitation without resorting to rust.
- Rust brings a whole set of problems, from slow performance to additional pieces that you have to manage, repair, and handle 6 a.m. panics from, as they inevitably break at the start of daily operations. The beauty of the Pirate patterns in general is their simplicity. They won't crash. And if you're still worried about the hardware, you can move to a peer-to-peer pattern that has no broker at all (I'll explain that later in this chapter).

Having said this, however, there is one sane use case for rust-based reliability, which is an asynchronous disconnected network. It solves a major problem with Pirate, namely that a client has to wait for an answer in real time. If clients and workers are only sporadically connected (think of email as an analogy), we can't use a stateless network between clients and workers. We have to put state in the middle.

So, here's the Titanic pattern (Figure 4-5), in which we write messages to disk to ensure they never get lost, no matter how sporadically clients and workers are connected. As we did for service discovery, we're going to layer Titanic on top of MDP rather than extend it. It's wonderfully lazy because it means we can implement our fire-and-forget reliability in a specialized worker, rather than in the broker. This is excellent for several reasons:

- It is *much* easier because we divide and conquer: the broker handles message routing and the worker handles reliability.
- It lets us mix brokers written in one language with workers written in another.
- It lets us evolve the fire-and-forget technology independently.

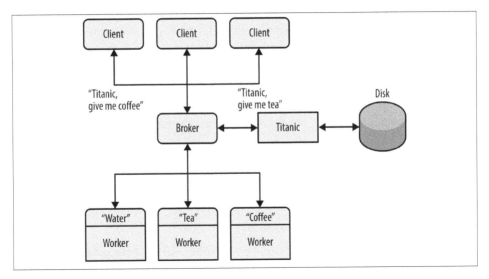

Figure 4-5. The Titanic pattern

The only downside is that there's an extra network hop between broker and hard disk. The benefits are easily worth it.

There are many ways to make a persistent request-reply architecture. We'll aim for one that is simple and painless. The simplest design I could come up with, after playing with this for a few hours, was a "proxy service." That is, Titanic doesn't affect workers at all. If a client wants a reply immediately, it talks directly to a service and hopes the service is available. If a client is happy to wait a while, it talks to Titanic instead and asks, "Hey, buddy, would you take care of this for me while I go buy my groceries?"

Titanic is thus both a worker and a client. The dialog between the client and Titanic goes along these lines:

- Client: "Please accept this request for me." Titanic: "OK, done."
- Client: "Do you have a reply for me?" Titanic: "Yes, here it is." (Or, "No, not yet".)
- Client: "OK, you can wipe that request now, I'm happy." Titanic: "OK, done."

Whereas the dialog between Titanic and the broker and worker goes like this:

- Titanic: "Hey, Broker, is there a coffee service?"
- Broker: "Um, yeah, seems like there is."
- Titanic: "Hey, coffee service, please handle this for me."
- Coffee: "Sure, here you are."
- Titanic: "Sweeeeet!"

You can work through these and the possible failure scenarios. If a worker crashes while processing a request, Titanic retries, indefinitely. If a reply gets lost somewhere, Titanic will retry. If the request gets processed but the client doesn't get the reply, it will ask again. If Titanic crashes while processing a request or a reply, the client will try again. As long as requests are fully committed to safe storage, work can't get lost.

The handshaking is pedantic, but can be pipelined; i.e., clients can use the asynchronous Majordomo pattern to do a lot of work and then get the responses later.

We need some way for a client to request *its* replies. We'll have many clients asking for the same services, and clients may disappear and reappear with different identities. Here is a simple, reasonably secure solution:

- Every request generates a universally unique ID (UUID), which Titanic returns to the client after it has queued the request.
- When a client asks for a reply, it must specify the UUID for the original request.

In a realistic case, the client would want to store its request UUIDs safely, such as in a local database.

Before we jump off and write yet another formal specification (fun, fun!), let's consider how the client talks to Titanic. One way is to use a single service and send it three different request types. Another way, which seems simpler, is to use three services:

`titanic.request`
    Stores a request message, and return a UUID for the request.

`titanic.reply`
    Fetches a reply, if available, for a given request UUID.

---

titanic.close

Confirms that a reply has been stored and processed.

We'll just make a multithreaded worker, which, as we've seen from our multithreading experience with ØMQ, is trivial. However, let's first sketch what Titanic would look like in terms of ØMQ messages and frames. This gives us the Titanic Service Protocol (TSP) (*http://rfc.zeromq.org/spec:9*).

Using TSP is clearly more work for client applications than accessing a service directly via MDP. The shortest robust "echo" client example is presented in Example 4-53.

Example 4-53. Titanic client example (ticlient.c)

```
//
//  Titanic client example
//  Implements client side of http://rfc.zeromq.org/spec:9

//  Lets us build this source without creating a library
#include "mdcliapi.c"

//  Calls a TSP service
//  Returns response if successful (status code 200 OK), else NULL
//
static zmsg_t *
s_service_call (mdcli_t *session, char *service, zmsg_t **request_p)
{
    zmsg_t *reply = mdcli_send (session, service, request_p);
    if (reply) {
        zframe_t *status = zmsg_pop (reply);
        if (zframe_streq (status, "200")) {
            zframe_destroy (&status);
            return reply;
        }
        else
        if (zframe_streq (status, "400")) {
            printf ("E: client fatal error, aborting\n");
            exit (EXIT_FAILURE);
        }
        else
        if (zframe_streq (status, "500")) {
            printf ("E: server fatal error, aborting\n");
            exit (EXIT_FAILURE);
        }
    }
    else
        exit (EXIT_SUCCESS);    //  Interrupted or failed

    zmsg_destroy (&reply);
    return NULL;        //  Didn't succeed; don't care why not
}
```

The main task (Example 4-54) tests our service call by sending an echo request.

Example 4-54. Titanic client example (ticlient.c): main task

```
int main (int argc, char *argv [])
{
    int verbose = (argc > 1 && streq (argv [1], "-v"));
    mdcli_t *session = mdcli_new ("tcp://localhost:5555", verbose);

    //  1. Send 'echo' request to Titanic
    zmsg_t *request = zmsg_new ();
    zmsg_addstr (request, "echo");
    zmsg_addstr (request, "Hello world");
    zmsg_t *reply = s_service_call (
        session, "titanic.request", &request);

    zframe_t *uuid = NULL;
    if (reply) {
        uuid = zmsg_pop (reply);
        zmsg_destroy (&reply);
        zframe_print (uuid, "I: request UUID ");
    }

    //  2. Wait until we get a reply
    while (!zctx_interrupted) {
        zclock_sleep (100);
        request = zmsg_new ();
        zmsg_add (request, zframe_dup (uuid));
        zmsg_t *reply = s_service_call (
            session, "titanic.reply", &request);

        if (reply) {
            char *reply_string = zframe_strdup (zmsg_last (reply));
            printf ("Reply: %s\n", reply_string);
            free (reply_string);
            zmsg_destroy (&reply);

            //  3. Close request
            request = zmsg_new ();
            zmsg_add (request, zframe_dup (uuid));
            reply = s_service_call (session, "titanic.close", &request);
            zmsg_destroy (&reply);
            break;
        }
        else {
            printf ("I: no reply yet, trying again...\n");
            zclock_sleep (5000);     //  Try again in 5 seconds
        }
    }
    zframe_destroy (&uuid);
    mdcli_destroy (&session);
    return 0;
}
```

Of course, this can be, and should be, wrapped up in some kind of framework or API. It's not healthy to ask average application developers to learn the full details of messaging: it hurts their brains, costs time, and offers too many ways to introduce buggy complexity. Additionally, it makes it hard to add intelligence.

For example, this client blocks on each request, whereas in a real application we'd want to be doing useful work while tasks are executed. It requires some nontrivial plumbing to build a background thread and talk to that cleanly. This is the kind of thing you want to wrap in a nice simple API that the average developer cannot misuse. It's the same approach that we used for Majordomo.

The Titanic implementation is shown in Example 4-55 through 4-60. This server handles the three services using three threads, as proposed. It does full persistence to disk using the most brutal approach possible: one file per message. It's so simple, it's scary. The only complex part is that it keeps a separate queue of all requests in order to avoid reading the directory over and over.

Example 4-55. Titanic broker example (titanic.c)

```
//
//  Titanic service
//
//  Implements server side of http://rfc.zeromq.org/spec:9

//  Lets us build this source without creating a library
#include "mdwrkapi.c"
#include "mdcliapi.c"

#include "zfile.h"
#include <uuid/uuid.h>

//  Return a new UUID as a printable character string
//  Caller must free returned string when finished with it

static char *
s_generate_uuid (void)
{
    char hex_char [] = "0123456789ABCDEF";
    char *uuidstr = zmalloc (sizeof (uuid_t) * 2 + 1);
    uuid_t uuid;
    uuid_generate (uuid);
    int byte_nbr;
    for (byte_nbr = 0; byte_nbr < sizeof (uuid_t); byte_nbr++) {
        uuidstr [byte_nbr * 2 + 0] = hex_char [uuid [byte_nbr] >> 4];
        uuidstr [byte_nbr * 2 + 1] = hex_char [uuid [byte_nbr] & 15];
    }
    return uuidstr;
}

//  Returns freshly allocated request filename for given UUID
```

```
#define TITANIC_DIR ".titanic"

static char *
s_request_filename (char *uuid) {
    char *filename = malloc (256);
    snprintf (filename, 256, TITANIC_DIR "/%s.req", uuid);
    return filename;
}

//  Returns freshly allocated reply filename for given UUID

static char *
s_reply_filename (char *uuid) {
    char *filename = malloc (256);
    snprintf (filename, 256, TITANIC_DIR "/%s.rep", uuid);
    return filename;
}
```

The titanic.request task (Example 4-56) waits for requests to this service. It writes each request to disk and returns a UUID to the client. The client picks up the reply asynchronously using the titanic.reply service.

Example 4-56. Titanic broker example (titanic.c): Titanic request service
```
static void
titanic_request (void *args, zctx_t *ctx, void *pipe)
{
    mdwrk_t *worker = mdwrk_new (
        "tcp://localhost:5555", "titanic.request", 0);
    zmsg_t *reply = NULL;

    while (true) {
        //  Send reply if it's not null
        //  And then get next request from broker
        zmsg_t *request = mdwrk_recv (worker, &reply);
        if (!request)
            break;      //  Interrupted, exit

        //  Ensure message directory exists
        zfile_mkdir (TITANIC_DIR);

        //  Generate UUID and save message to disk
        char *uuid = s_generate_uuid ();
        char *filename = s_request_filename (uuid);
        FILE *file = fopen (filename, "w");
        assert (file);
        zmsg_save (request, file);
        fclose (file);
        free (filename);
        zmsg_destroy (&request);
```

```
        //  Send UUID through to message queue
        reply = zmsg_new ();
        zmsg_addstr (reply, uuid);
        zmsg_send (&reply, pipe);

        //  Now send UUID back to client
        //  Done by the mdwrk_recv() at the top of the loop
        reply = zmsg_new ();
        zmsg_addstr (reply, "200");
        zmsg_addstr (reply, uuid);
        free (uuid);
    }
    mdwrk_destroy (&worker);
}
```

The `titanic.reply` task, shown in Example 4-57, checks if there's a reply for the specified request (by UUID), and returns a 200 (OK), 300 (Pending), or 400 (Unknown)
accordingly.

Example 4-57. Titanic broker example (titanic.c): Titanic reply service

```
static void *
titanic_reply (void *context)
{
    mdwrk_t *worker = mdwrk_new (
        "tcp://localhost:5555", "titanic.reply", 0);
    zmsg_t *reply = NULL;

    while (true) {
        zmsg_t *request = mdwrk_recv (worker, &reply);
        if (!request)
            break;      //  Interrupted, exit

        char *uuid = zmsg_popstr (request);
        char *req_filename = s_request_filename (uuid);
        char *rep_filename = s_reply_filename (uuid);
        if (zfile_exists (rep_filename)) {
            FILE *file = fopen (rep_filename, "r");
            assert (file);
            reply = zmsg_load (NULL, file);
            zmsg_pushstr (reply, "200"): // OK
            fclose (file);
        }
        else {
            reply = zmsg_new ();
            if (zfile_exists (req_filename))
                zmsg_pushstr (reply, "300"); // Pending
            else
                zmsg_pushstr (reply, "400"); // Unknown
        }
        zmsg_destroy (&request);
        free (uuid);
```

```
        free (req_filename);
        free (rep_filename);
    }
    mdwrk_destroy (&worker);
    return 0;
}
```

The `titanic.close` task, shown in Example 4-58, removes any waiting replies for the request (specified by UUID). It's idempotent, so it is safe to call it more than once in a row.

Example 4-58. Titanic broker example (titanic.c): Titanic close task

```
static void *
titanic_close (void *context)
{
    mdwrk_t *worker = mdwrk_new (
        "tcp://localhost:5555", "titanic.close", 0);
    zmsg_t *reply = NULL;

    while (true) {
        zmsg_t *request = mdwrk_recv (worker, &reply);
        if (!request)
            break;      //  Interrupted, exit

        char *uuid = zmsg_popstr (request);
        char *req_filename = s_request_filename (uuid);
        char *rep_filename = s_reply_filename (uuid);
        zfile_delete (req_filename);
        zfile_delete (rep_filename);
        free (uuid);
        free (req_filename);
        free (rep_filename);

        zmsg_destroy (&request);
        reply = zmsg_new ();
        zmsg_addstr (reply, "200");
    }
    mdwrk_destroy (&worker);
    return 0;
}
```

Example 4-59 shows the main thread for the Titanic worker. It starts three child threads, for the request, reply, and close services. It then dispatches requests to workers using a simple brute-force disk queue. It receives request UUIDs from the `titanic.request` service, saves these to a disk file, and then throws each request at MDP workers until it gets a response.

Example 4-59. Titanic broker example (titanic.c): worker task

```
static int s_service_success (char *uuid);
```

```
int main (int argc, char *argv [])
{
    int verbose = (argc > 1 && streq (argv [1], "-v"));
    zctx_t *ctx = zctx_new ();

    void *request_pipe = zthread_fork (ctx, titanic_request, NULL);
    zthread_new (titanic_reply, NULL);
    zthread_new (titanic_close, NULL);

    //  Main dispatcher loop
    while (true) {
        //  We'll dispatch once per second, if there's no activity
        zmq_pollitem_t items [] = { { request_pipe, 0, ZMQ_POLLIN, 0 } };
        int rc = zmq_poll (items, 1, 1000 * ZMQ_POLL_MSEC);
        if (rc == -1)
            break;              //  Interrupted
        if (items [0].revents & ZMQ_POLLIN) {
            //  Ensure message directory exists
            zfile_mkdir (TITANIC_DIR);

            //  Append UUID to queue, prefixed with '-' for pending
            zmsg_t *msg = zmsg_recv (request_pipe);
            if (!msg)
                break;          //  Interrupted
            FILE *file = fopen (TITANIC_DIR "/queue", "a");
            char *uuid = zmsg_popstr (msg);
            fprintf (file, "-%s\n", uuid);
            fclose (file);
            free (uuid);
            zmsg_destroy (&msg);
        }
        //  Brute force dispatcher
        char entry [] = "?......:......:......:......:";
        FILE *file = fopen (TITANIC_DIR "/queue", "r+");
        while (file && fread (entry, 33, 1, file) == 1) {
            //  UUID is prefixed with '-' if still waiting
            if (entry [0] == '-') {
                if (verbose)
                    printf ("I: processing request %s\n", entry + 1);
                if (s_service_success (entry + 1)) {
                    //  Mark queue entry as processed
                    fseek (file, -33, SEEK_CUR);
                    fwrite ("+", 1, 1, file);
                    fseek (file, 32, SEEK_CUR);
                }
            }
            //  Skip end of line, LF, or CRLF
            if (fgetc (file) == '\r')
                fgetc (file);
            if (zctx_interrupted)
                break;
        }
    }
```

```
        if (file)
            fclose (file);
    }
    return 0;
}
```

In the final part of the broker code (Example 4-60), we first check if the requested MDP service is defined or not, using an MMI lookup to the Majordomo broker. If the service exists, we send a request and wait for a reply using the conventional MDP client API. This is not meant to be fast, just very simple.

Example 4-60. Titanic broker example (titanic.c): try to call a service

```
static int
s_service_success (char *uuid)
{
    //  Load request message, service will be first frame
    char *filename = s_request_filename (uuid);
    FILE *file = fopen (filename, "r");
    free (filename);

    //  If client already closed request, treat as successful
    if (!file)
        return 1;

    zmsg_t *request = zmsg_load (NULL, file);
    fclose (file);
    zframe_t *service = zmsg_pop (request);
    char *service_name = zframe_strdup (service);

    //  Create MDP client session with short timeout
    mdcli_t *client = mdcli_new ("tcp://localhost:5555", FALSE);
    mdcli_set_timeout (client, 1000);  //  1 sec
    mdcli_set_retries (client, 1);     //  only 1 retry

    //  Use MMI protocol to check if service is available
    zmsg_t *mmi_request = zmsg_new ();
    zmsg_add (mmi_request, service);
    zmsg_t *mmi_reply = mdcli_send (client, "mmi.service", &mmi_request);
    int service_ok = (mmi_reply
        && zframe_streq (zmsg_first (mmi_reply), "200"));
    zmsg_destroy (&mmi_reply);

    int result = 0;
    if (service_ok) {
        zmsg_t *reply = mdcli_send (client, service_name, &request);
        if (reply) {
            filename = s_reply_filename (uuid);
            FILE *file = fopen (filename, "w");
            assert (file);
            zmsg_save (reply, file);
            fclose (file);
```

```
        free (filename);
        result = 1;
    }
    zmsg_destroy (&reply);
}
else
    zmsg_destroy (&request);

mdcli_destroy (&client);
free (service_name);
return result;
}
```

To test this, start mdbroker and titanic, and then run ticlient. Now start mdworker
arbitrarily, and you should see the client getting a response and exiting happily.

Some notes about this code:

- Note that some loops start by sending, and others by receiving messages. This is
  because Titanic acts both as a client and a worker in different roles.
- The Titanic broker uses the MMI service discovery protocol to send requests only
  to services that appear to be running. Since the MMI implementation in our little
  Majordomo broker is quite poor, this won't work all the time.
- We use an inproc connection to send new request data from the titanic.re
  quest service through to the main dispatcher. This saves the dispatcher from having
  to scan the disk directory, load all request files, and sort them by date/time.

The important thing about this example is not its performance (which, although I haven't tested it, is surely terrible), but how well it implements the reliability contract. To
try it, start the *mdbroker* and *titanic* programs. Then start the *ticlient*, and then start the
mdworker echo service. You can run all four of these using the -*v* option to do verbose
activity tracing. You can stop and restart any piece *except the client*, and nothing will
get lost.

If you want to use Titanic in real cases, you'll rapidly be asking, "How do we make this
faster?" Here's what I'd do, starting with the example implementation:

- Use a single disk file for all data, rather than multiple files. Operating systems are
  usually better at handling a few large files than many smaller ones.
- Organize that disk file as a circular buffer so that new requests can be written con-
  tiguously (with very occasional wraparound). One thread, writing full speed to a
  disk file, can work rapidly.
- Keep the index in memory and rebuild the index at startup time, from the disk
  buffer. This saves the extra disk head flutter needed to keep the index fully safe on

disk. You would want an `fsync` after every message, or every N milliseconds if you were prepared to lose the last M messages in case of a system failure.

- Use a solid-state drive rather than spinning iron oxide platters.
- Preallocate the entire file, or allocate it in large chunks, which allows the circular buffer to grow and shrink as needed. This avoids fragmentation and ensures that most reads and writes are contiguous.

And so on. What I'd not recommend is storing messages in a database, not even a "fast" key/value store, unless you really like a specific database and don't have performance worries. You will pay a steep price for the abstraction—10 to 1,000 times over a raw disk file.

If you want to make Titanic *even more reliable*, duplicate the requests to a second server, and place it in a second location just far away enough to survive a nuclear attack on your primary location, yet not so far that you get too much latency.

If you want to make Titanic *much faster but less reliable*, store requests and replies purely in memory. This will give you the functionality of a disconnected network, but requests won't survive a crash of the Titanic server itself.

High-Availability Pair (Binary Star Pattern)

The Binary Star pattern configures two servers as a primary/backup high-availability pair (Figure 4-6). At any given time, one of these (the active server) accepts connections from client applications. The other (the passive server) does nothing, but the two servers monitor each other. If the active one disappears from the network, after a certain time the passive one takes over as active.

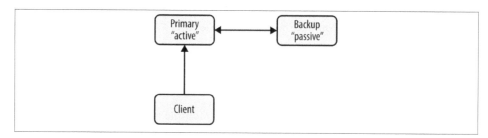

Figure 4-6. High-availability pair, normal operation

We developed the Binary Star pattern at iMatix for our OpenAMQ server (*http://www.openamq.org*). We designed it:

- To provide a straightforward high-availability solution
- To be simple enough to actually understand and use

- To fail over reliably when needed, and only when needed

Assuming we have a Binary Star pair running, here are the different scenarios that will result in a failover (Figure 4-7):

- The hardware running the primary server has a fatal problem (power supply explodes, machine catches fire, or someone simply unplugs it by mistake), and disappears. Applications see this and reconnect to the backup server.
- The network segment on which the primary server sits crashes—perhaps because a router gets hit by a power spike—and applications start to reconnect to the backup server.
- The primary server crashes or is killed by the operator and does not restart automatically.

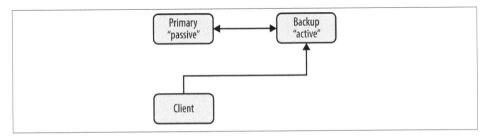

Figure 4-7. High-availability pair during failover

Recovery from failover works as follows:

- The operators restart the primary server and fix whatever problems were causing it to disappear from the network.
- The operators stop the backup server at a moment when it will cause minimal disruption to applications.
- When applications have reconnected to the primary server, the operators restart the backup server.

Recovery (to using the primary server as the active one) is a manual operation. Painful experience has taught us that automatic recovery is undesirable. There are several reasons:

- Failover creates an interruption of service to applications, possibly lasting 10–30 seconds. If there is a real emergency, this is much better than total outage. But if recovery creates a further such outage, it is better that this happens off-peak, when users have gone off the network.

- When there is an emergency, the absolute first priority is certainty for those trying to fix things. Automatic recovery creates uncertainty for system administrators, who can no longer be sure which server is in charge without double-checking.

- Automatic recovery can create situations where networks fail over and then recover, placing operators in the difficult position of analyzing what happened. There was an interruption of service, but the cause isn't clear.

Having said this, the Binary Star pattern will automatically fail back to the primary server if this is running (again) and the backup server fails. In fact, this is how we provoke recovery.

The shutdown process for a Binary Star pair is to do one of the following:

1. Stop the passive server and then stop the active server at any later time.
2. Stop both servers in any order, but within a few seconds of each other.

Stopping the active and then the passive server with any delay longer than the failover timeout will cause applications to disconnect, then reconnect, and then disconnect again, which may disturb users.

Detailed Requirements

The Binary Star pattern is as simple as it can be, while still working accurately. In fact, the current design is the third complete redesign. Each of the previous designs we found to be too complex, trying to do too much, and we stripped out functionality until we came to a design that was understandable, easy to use, and reliable enough to be worth using.

These are our requirements for a high-availability architecture:

- The failover is meant to provide insurance against catastrophic system failures, such as hardware breakdown, fire, accident, and so on. There are simpler ways to recover from ordinary server crashes, and we already covered these.

- Failover time should be under 60 seconds, and preferably under 10 seconds.

- Failover has to happen automatically, whereas recovery must happen manually. We want applications to switch over to the backup server automatically, but we do not want them to switch back to the primary server except when the operators have fixed whatever problem there was and decided that it is a good time to interrupt applications again.

- The semantics for client applications should be simple and easy for developers to understand. Ideally, they should be hidden in the client API.

- There should be clear instructions for network architects on how to avoid designs that could lead to "split-brain syndrome," in which both servers in a Binary Star pair think they are the active server.
- There should be no dependencies on the order in which the two servers are started.
- It must be possible to make planned stops and restarts of either server without stopping client applications (though they may be forced to reconnect).
- Operators must be able to monitor both servers at all times.
- It must be possible to connect the two servers using a high-speed dedicated network connection. That is, failover synchronization must be able to use a specific IP route.

We make the following assumptions:

- A single backup server provides enough insurance; we don't need multiple levels of backup.
- The primary and backup servers are equally capable of carrying the application load. We do not attempt to balance load across the servers.
- There is sufficient budget to cover a fully redundant backup server that does nothing almost all the time.

We don't attempt to cover the following:

- The use of an active backup server or load balancing. In a Binary Star pair, the backup server is inactive and does no useful work until the primary server goes off-line.
- The handling of persistent messages or transactions in any way. We assume the existence of a network of unreliable (and probably untrusted) servers or Binary Star pairs.
- Any automatic exploration of the network. The Binary Star pair is manually and explicitly defined in the network and is known to applications (at least in their configuration data).
- Replication of state or messages between servers. All server-side state must be re-created by applications when they fail over.

Here is the key terminology that we use in Binary Star:

Primary
    The server that is normally or initially active.

Backup
    The server that is normally passive. It will become active if and when the primary server disappears from the network, and when client applications ask the backup server to connect.

Active

The server that accepts client connections. There is at most one active server.

Passive

The server that takes over if the active server disappears. Note that when a Binary Star pair is running normally, the primary server is active, and the backup is passive. When a failover has happened, the roles are switched.

To configure a Binary Star pair, you need to:

1. Tell the primary server where the backup server is located.
2. Tell the backup server where the primary server is located.
3. Optionally, tune the failover response times, which must be the same for both servers.

The main tuning concern is how frequently you want the servers to check their peering status, and how quickly you want to activate failover. In our example, the failover time-out value defaults to 2,000 msec. If you reduce this, the backup server will take over as active more rapidly, but may take over in cases where the primary server could recover. For example, you may have wrapped the primary server in a shell script that restarts it if it crashes. In that case, the timeout should be higher than the time needed to restart the primary server.

For client applications to work properly with a Binary Star pair, they must:

1. Know both server addresses.
2. Try to connect to the primary server and if, that fails, to the backup server.
3. Detect a failed connection, typically using heartbeating.
4. Try to reconnect to the primary, and then the backup (in that order), with a delay between retries that is at least as high as the server failover timeout.
5. Recreate all of the required state.
6. Retransmit messages lost during a failover, if messages need to be reliable.

It's not trivial work, and we'd usually wrap this in an API that hides it from real end-user applications.

These are the main limitations of the Binary Star pattern:

- A server process cannot be part of more than one Binary Star pair.
- A primary server can have a single backup server, and no more.
- The passive server does no useful work, and is thus "wasted."
- The backup server must be capable of handling full application loads.

- Failover configuration cannot be modified at runtime.
- Client applications must do some work to benefit from failover.

Preventing Split-Brain Syndrome

Split-brain syndrome occurs when different parts of a cluster think they are active at the same time. It causes applications to stop seeing each other. Binary Star has an algorithm for detecting and eliminating split brain, which is based on a three-way decision mechanism (a server will not decide to become active until it gets application connection requests and it cannot see its peer server).

However, it is still possible to (mis)design a network to fool this algorithm. A typical scenario would be a Binary Star pair that is distributed between two buildings, where each building also had a set of applications and where there was a single network link between both buildings. Breaking this link would create two sets of client applications, each with half of the Binary Star pair, and each failover server would become active.

To prevent split-brain situations, we must connect a Binary Star pair using a dedicated network link, which can be as simple as plugging them both into the same switch or, better, using a crossover cable directly between two machines.

We must not split a Binary Star architecture into two islands, each with a set of applications. While this may be a common type of network architecture, we should use federation, not high-availability failover, in such cases.

A suitably paranoid network configuration would use two private cluster interconnects, rather than a single one. Further, the network cards used for the cluster would be different from those used for message traffic, and possibly even on different PCI paths on the server hardware. The goal is to separate possible failures in the network from possible failures in the cluster. Network ports have a relatively high failure rate.

Binary Star Implementation

Without further ado, here is a proof-of-concept implementation of the Binary Star server, beginning with Example 4-61. The primary and backup servers run the same code, and their roles are chosen by the invoker.

Example 4-61. Binary Star server (bstarsrv.c)

```
//
//  Binary Star server proof-of-concept implementation. This server does no
//  real work; it just demonstrates the Binary Star failover model.

#include "czmq.h"

//  States in which we can be at any point in time
```

```
typedef enum {
    STATE_PRIMARY = 1,          //  Primary, waiting for peer to connect
    STATE_BACKUP = 2,           //  Backup, waiting for peer to connect
    STATE_ACTIVE = 3,           //  Active - accepting connections
    STATE_PASSIVE = 4           //  Passive - not accepting connections
} state_t;

//  Events, which start with the states our peer can be in
typedef enum {
    PEER_PRIMARY = 1,           //  HA peer is pending primary
    PEER_BACKUP = 2,            //  HA peer is pending backup
    PEER_ACTIVE = 3,            //  HA peer is active
    PEER_PASSIVE = 4,           //  HA peer is passive
    CLIENT_REQUEST = 5          //  Client makes request
} event_t;

//  Our finite-state machine
typedef struct {
    state_t state;              //  Current state
    event_t event;              //  Current event
    int64_t peer_expiry;        //  When peer is considered "dead"
} bstar_t;

//  We send state information this often
//  If peer doesn't respond in two heartbeats, it is "dead"
#define HEARTBEAT 1000          //  In msec
```

The heart of the Binary Star design is its finite-state machine (FSM). The FSM runs one event at a time. We apply an event to the current state, which checks if the event is accepted, and if so sets a new state (Example 4-62).

Example 4-62. Binary Star server (bstarsrv.c): Binary Star state machine

```
static Bool
s_state_machine (bstar_t *fsm)
{
    Bool exception = FALSE;

    //  These are the PRIMARY and BACKUP states; we're waiting to become
    //  ACTIVE or PASSIVE depending on events we get from our peer
    if (fsm->state == STATE_PRIMARY) {
        if (fsm->event == PEER_BACKUP) {
            printf ("I: connected to backup (passive), ready as active\n");
            fsm->state = STATE_ACTIVE;
        }
        else
        if (fsm->event == PEER_ACTIVE) {
            printf ("I: connected to backup (active), ready as passive\n");
            fsm->state = STATE_PASSIVE;
        }
        //  Accept client connections
    }
```

```
    else
    if (fsm->state == STATE_BACKUP) {
        if (fsm->event == PEER_ACTIVE) {
            printf ("I: connected to primary (active), ready as passive\n");
            fsm->state = STATE_PASSIVE;
        }
        else
        // Reject client connections when acting as backup
        if (fsm->event == CLIENT_REQUEST)
            exception = TRUE;
    }
    else
```

The ACTIVE and PASSIVE states are laid out in Example 4-63.

Example 4-63. Binary Star server (bstarsrv.c): active and passive states

```
    if (fsm->state == STATE_ACTIVE) {
        if (fsm->event == PEER_ACTIVE) {
            // Two actives would mean split-brain
            printf ("E: fatal error - dual actives, aborting\n");
            exception = TRUE;
        }
    }
    else
    // Server is passive
    // CLIENT_REQUEST events can trigger failover if peer looks dead
    if (fsm->state == STATE_PASSIVE) {
        if (fsm->event == PEER_PRIMARY) {
            // Peer is restarting - become active, peer will go passive
            printf ("I: primary (passive) is restarting, ready as active\n");
            fsm->state = STATE_ACTIVE;
        }
        else
        if (fsm->event == PEER_BACKUP) {
            // Peer is restarting - become active, peer will go passive
            printf ("I: backup (passive) is restarting, ready as active\n");
            fsm->state = STATE_ACTIVE;
        }
        else
        if (fsm->event == PEER_PASSIVE) {
            // Two passives would mean cluster would be nonresponsive
            printf ("E: fatal error - dual passives, aborting\n");
            exception = TRUE;
        }
        else
        if (fsm->event == CLIENT_REQUEST) {
            // Peer becomes active if timeout has passed
            // It's the client request that triggers the failover
            assert (fsm->peer_expiry > 0);
            if (zclock_time () >= fsm->peer_expiry) {
                // If peer is dead, switch to the active state
                printf ("I: failover successful, ready as active\n");
```

```
                    fsm->state = STATE_ACTIVE;
            }
            else
                //  If peer is alive, reject connections
                exception = TRUE;
        }
    }
    return exception;
}
```

Example 4-64 shows our main task. First we bind/connect our sockets with our peer and make sure we will get state messages correctly. We use three sockets: one to publish state, one to subscribe to state, and one for client requests/replies.

Example 4-64. Binary Star server (bstarsrv.c): main task

```
int main (int argc, char *argv [])
{
    //  Arguments can be either of:
    //      -p  primary server, at tcp://localhost:5001
    //      -b  backup server, at tcp://localhost:5002
    zctx_t *ctx = zctx_new ();
    void *statepub = zsocket_new (ctx, ZMQ_PUB);
    void *statesub = zsocket_new (ctx, ZMQ_SUB);
    zsockopt_set_subscribe (statesub, "");
    void *frontend = zsocket_new (ctx, ZMQ_ROUTER);
    bstar_t fsm = { 0 };

    if (argc == 2 && streq (argv [1], "-p")) {
        printf ("I: Primary active, waiting for backup (passive)\n");
        zsocket_bind (frontend, "tcp://*:5001");
        zsocket_bind (statepub, "tcp://*:5003");
        zsocket_connect (statesub, "tcp://localhost:5004");
        fsm.state = STATE_PRIMARY;
    }
    else
    if (argc == 2 && streq (argv [1], "-b")) {
        printf ("I: Backup passive, waiting for primary (active)\n");
        zsocket_bind (frontend, "tcp://*:5002");
        zsocket_bind (statepub, "tcp://*:5004");
        zsocket_connect (statesub, "tcp://localhost:5003");
        fsm.state = STATE_BACKUP;
    }
    else {
        printf ("Usage: bstarsrv { -p | -b }\n");
        zctx_destroy (&ctx);
        exit (0);
    }
```

We now process events on our two input sockets, and process these events one at a time via our finite-state machine (Example 4-65). Our "work" for a client request is simply to echo it back.

Example 4-65. Binary Star server (bstarsrv.c): handling socket input

```
//  Set timer for next outgoing state message
int64_t send_state_at = zclock_time () + HEARTBEAT;
while (!zctx_interrupted) {
    zmq_pollitem_t items [] = {
        { frontend, 0, ZMQ_POLLIN, 0 },
        { statesub, 0, ZMQ_POLLIN, 0 }
    };
    int time_left = (int) ((send_state_at - zclock_time ()));
    if (time_left < 0)
        time_left = 0;
    int rc = zmq_poll (items, 2, time_left * ZMQ_POLL_MSEC);
    if (rc == -1)
        break;                  //  Context has been shut down

    if (items [0].revents & ZMQ_POLLIN) {
        //  Have a client request
        zmsg_t *msg = zmsg_recv (frontend);
        fsm.event = CLIENT_REQUEST;
        if (s_state_machine (&fsm) == FALSE)
            //  Answer client by echoing request back
            zmsg_send (&msg, frontend);
        else
            zmsg_destroy (&msg);
    }
    if (items [1].revents & ZMQ_POLLIN) {
        //  Have state from our peer, execute as event
        char *message = zstr_recv (statesub);
        fsm.event = atoi (message);
        free (message);
        if (s_state_machine (&fsm))
            break;              //  Error, so exit
        fsm.peer_expiry = zclock_time () + 2 * HEARTBEAT;
    }
    //  If we timed out, send state to peer
    if (zclock_time () >= send_state_at) {
        char message [2];
        sprintf (message, "%d", fsm.state);
        zstr_send (statepub, message);
        send_state_at = zclock_time () + HEARTBEAT;
    }
}
if (zctx_interrupted)
    printf ("W: interrupted\n");

//  Shut down sockets and context
zctx_destroy (&ctx);
return 0;
}
```

Now let's look at the code for the client, beginning with Example 4-66.

Example 4-66. Binary Star client (bstarcli.c)

```
//
//  Binary Star client proof-of-concept implementation. This client does no
//  real work; it just demonstrates the Binary Star failover model.

#include "czmq.h"

#define REQUEST_TIMEOUT     1000    //  msec
#define SETTLE_DELAY        2000    //  Before failing over

int main (void)
{
    zctx_t *ctx = zctx_new ();

    char *server [] = { "tcp://localhost:5001", "tcp://localhost:5002" };
    uint server_nbr = 0;

    printf ("I: connecting to server at %s...\n", server [server_nbr]);
    void *client = zsocket_new (ctx, ZMQ_REQ);
    zsocket_connect (client, server [server_nbr]);

    int sequence = 0;
    while (!zctx_interrupted) {
        //  We send a request, then we work to get a reply
        char request [10];
        sprintf (request, "%d", ++sequence);
        zstr_send (client, request);

        int expect_reply = 1;
        while (expect_reply) {
            //  Poll socket for a reply, with timeout
            zmq_pollitem_t items [] = { { client, 0, ZMQ_POLLIN, 0 } };
            int rc = zmq_poll (items, 1, REQUEST_TIMEOUT * ZMQ_POLL_MSEC);
            if (rc == -1)
                break;          //  Interrupted
```

We use a Lazy Pirate strategy in the client. If there's no reply within our timeout, we close the socket and try again, as seen in Example 4-67. In Binary Star, it's the client vote that decides which server is primary; the client must therefore try to connect to each server in turn.

Example 4-67. Binary Star client (bstarcli.c): main body of client

```
            if (items [0].revents & ZMQ_POLLIN) {
                //  We got a reply from the server, must match sequence
                char *reply = zstr_recv (client);
                if (atoi (reply) == sequence) {
                    printf ("I: server replied OK (%s)\n", reply);
                    expect_reply = 0;
```

```
                sleep (1);  //  One request per second
            }
            else
                printf ("E: bad reply from server: %s\n", reply);
                free (reply);
        }
        else {
            printf ("W: no response from server, failing over\n");

            //  Old socket is confused; close it and open a new one
            zsocket_destroy (ctx, client);
            server_nbr = (server_nbr + 1) % 2;
            zclock_sleep (SETTLE_DELAY);
            printf ("I: connecting to server at %s...\n",
                    server [server_nbr]);
            client = zsocket_new (ctx, ZMQ_REQ);
            zsocket_connect (client, server [server_nbr]);

            //  Send request again, on new socket
            zstr_send (client, request);
        }
    }
}
zctx_destroy (&ctx);
return 0;
}
```

To test our Binary Star implementation, start the servers and client in any order:

```
bstarsrv -p      # Start primary
bstarsrv -b      # Start backup
bstarcli
```

You can then provoke failover by killing the primary server, and recovery by restarting the primary and killing the backup. Note how it's the client vote that triggers failover and recovery.

Binary Star is driven by a finite-state machine (Figure 4-8). States in white accept client requests, and states in gray refuse them. Events are the peer state, so "Peer Active" means the other server has told us it's active. "Client Request" means we've received a client request. "Client Vote" means we've received a client request *and* our peer has been inactive for two heartbeats.

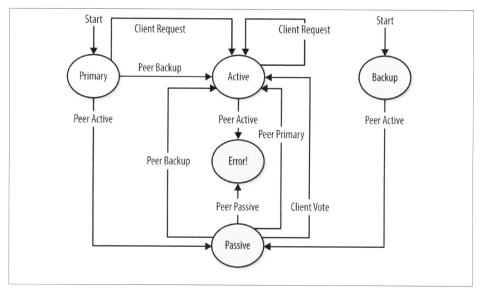

Figure 4-8. Binary Star finite-state machine

Note that the servers use PUB-SUB sockets for state exchange. No other socket combination will work here. PUSH and DEALER block if there is no peer ready to receive a message. PAIR does not reconnect if the peer disappears and comes back. ROUTER needs the address of the peer before it can send it a message.

Binary Star Reactor

Binary Star is useful and generic enough to package up as a reusable reactor class. The reactor then runs and calls our code whenever it has a message to process. This is much nicer than copying/pasting the Binary Star code into each server where we want that capability.

In C, we wrap the CZMQ zloop class that we saw before. zloop lets you register handlers to react on socket and timer events. In the Binary Star reactor, we provide handlers for voters and for state changes (active to passive, and vice versa). Here is the bstar API:

```
// Create a new Binary Star instance, using local (bind) and
// remote (connect) endpoints to set up the server peering
bstar_t *bstar_new (int primary, char *local, char *remote);

// Destroy a Binary Star instance
void bstar_destroy (bstar_t **self_p);

// Return underlying zloop reactor, for timer and reader
// registration and cancelation
zloop_t *bstar_zloop (bstar_t *self);
```

```
// Register voting reader
int bstar_voter (bstar_t *self, char *endpoint, int type,
                 zloop_fn handler, void *arg);

// Register main state change handlers
void bstar_new_active (bstar_t *self, zloop_fn handler, void *arg);
void bstar_new_passive (bstar_t *self, zloop_fn handler, void *arg);

// Start the reactor, which ends if a callback function returns -1,
// or the process received SIGINT or SIGTERM
int bstar_start (bstar_t *self);
```

The class implementation is in Example 4-68.

Example 4-68. Binary Star core class (bstar.c)

```
/*  =====================================================================
 *  bstar - Binary Star reactor
 *  ===================================================================== */

#include "bstar.h"

//  States we can be in at any point in time
typedef enum {
    STATE_PRIMARY = 1,          //  Primary, waiting for peer to connect
    STATE_BACKUP = 2,           //  Backup, waiting for peer to connect
    STATE_ACTIVE = 3,           //  Active, accepting connections
    STATE_PASSIVE = 4           //  Passive, not accepting connections
} state_t;

//  Events, which start with the states our peer can be in
typedef enum {
    PEER_PRIMARY = 1,           //  HA peer is pending primary
    PEER_BACKUP = 2,            //  HA peer is pending backup
    PEER_ACTIVE = 3,            //  HA peer is active
    PEER_PASSIVE = 4,           //  HA peer is passive
    CLIENT_REQUEST = 5          //  Client makes request
} event_t;

//  Structure of our class

struct _bstar_t {
    zctx_t *ctx;                //  Our private context
    zloop_t *loop;              //  Reactor loop
    void *statepub;             //  State publisher
    void *statesub;             //  State subscriber
    state_t state;              //  Current state
    event_t event;              //  Current event
    int64_t peer_expiry;        //  When peer is considered "dead"
    zloop_fn *voter_fn;         //  Voting socket handler
    void *voter_arg;            //  Arguments for voting handler
    zloop_fn *active_fn;        //  Call when become active
    void *active_arg;           //  Arguments for handler
```

```
    zloop_fn *passive_fn;       //  Call when become passive
    void *passive_arg;          //  Arguments for handler
};

    //  The finite-state machine is the same as in the proof-of-concept server.
    //  To understand this reactor in detail, first read the CZMQ zloop class.
...
```

Example 4-69 contains the constructor for our bstar class. We have to tell it whether we're a primary or backup server, as well as providing our local and remote endpoints to bind and connect to.

Example 4-69. Binary Star core class (bstar.c): constructor

```
bstar_t *
bstar_new (int primary, char *local, char *remote)
{
    bstar_t
        *self;

    self = (bstar_t *) zmalloc (sizeof (bstar_t));

    //  Initialize the Binary Star
    self->ctx = zctx_new ();
    self->loop = zloop_new ();
    self->state = primary? STATE_PRIMARY: STATE_BACKUP;

    //  Create publisher for state going to peer
    self->statepub = zsocket_new (self->ctx, ZMQ_PUB);
    zsocket_bind (self->statepub, local);

    //  Create subscriber for state coming from peer
    self->statesub = zsocket_new (self->ctx, ZMQ_SUB);
    zsockopt_set_subscribe (self->statesub, "");
    zsocket_connect (self->statesub, remote);

    //  Set up basic reactor events
    zloop_timer (self->loop, BSTAR_HEARTBEAT, 0, s_send_state, self);
    zmq_pollitem_t poller = { self->statesub, 0, ZMQ_POLLIN };
    zloop_poller (self->loop, &poller, s_recv_state, self);
    return self;
}
```

The destructor (Example 4-70) shuts down the bstar reactor.

Example 4-70. Binary Star core class (bstar.c): destructor

```
void
bstar_destroy (bstar_t **self_p)
{
    assert (self_p);
    if (*self_p) {
        bstar_t *self = *self_p;
```

```
        zloop_destroy (&self->loop);
        zctx_destroy (&self->ctx);
        free (self);
        *self_p = NULL;
    }
}
```

The zloop method (Example 4-71) returns the underlying zloop reactor, so we can add additional timers and readers.

Example 4-71. Binary Star core class (bstar.c): zloop method

```
zloop_t *
bstar_zloop (bstar_t *self)
{
    return self->loop;
}
```

The voter method, shown in Example 4-72, registers a client voter socket. Messages received on this socket provide the CLIENT_REQUEST events for the Binary Star FSM and are passed to the provided application handler. We require exactly one voter per bstar instance.

Example 4-72. Binary Star core class (bstar.c): voter method

```
int
bstar_voter (bstar_t *self, char *endpoint, int type, zloop_fn handler,
             void *arg)
{
    //  Hold actual handler+arg so we can call this later
    void *socket = zsocket_new (self->ctx, type);
    zsocket_bind (socket, endpoint);
    assert (!self->voter_fn);
    self->voter_fn = handler;
    self->voter_arg = arg;
    zmq_pollitem_t poller = { socket, 0, ZMQ_POLLIN };
    return zloop_poller (self->loop, &poller, s_voter_ready, self);
}
```

Next, we register handlers to be called each time there's a state change.

Example 4-73. Binary Star core class (bstar.c): register state-change handlers

```
void
bstar_new_active (bstar_t *self, zloop_fn handler, void *arg)
{
    assert (!self->active_fn);
    self->active_fn = handler;
    self->active_arg = arg;
}

void
```

```
bstar_new_passive (bstar_t *self, zloop_fn handler, void *arg)
{
    assert (!self->passive_fn);
    self->passive_fn = handler;
    self->passive_arg = arg;
}
```

Then we enable/disable verbose tracing, for debugging (Example 4-74).

Example 4-74. Binary Star core class (bstar.c): enable/disable tracing

```
void bstar_set_verbose (bstar_t *self, Bool verbose)
{
    zloop_set_verbose (self->loop, verbose);
}
```

Finally, we start the configured reactor (Example 4-75). It will end if any handler returns -1 to the reactor, or if the process receives a SIGINT or SIGTERM.

Example 4-75. Binary Star core class (bstar.c): start the reactor

```
int
bstar_start (bstar_t *self)
{
    assert (self->voter_fn);
    s_update_peer_expiry (self);
    return zloop_start (self->loop);
}
```

This gives us the short main program for the server shown in Example 4-76.

Example 4-76. Binary Star server, using core class (bstarsrv2.c)

```
//
//  Binary Star server, using bstar reactor
//

//  Lets us build this source without creating a library
#include "bstar.c"

//  Echo service
int s_echo (zloop_t *loop, zmq_pollitem_t *poller, void *arg)
{
    zmsg_t *msg = zmsg_recv (poller->socket);
    zmsg_send (&msg, poller->socket);
    return 0;
}

int main (int argc, char *argv [])
{
    //  Arguments can be either of these:
    //      -p  primary server, at tcp://localhost:5001
    //      -b  backup server, at tcp://localhost:5002
```

```
    bstar_t *bstar;
    if (argc == 2 && streq (argv [1], "-p")) {
        printf ("I: Primary active, waiting for backup (passive)\n");
        bstar = bstar_new (BSTAR_PRIMARY,
            "tcp://*:5003", "tcp://localhost:5004");
        bstar_voter (bstar, "tcp://*:5001", ZMQ_ROUTER, s_echo, NULL);
    }
    else
    if (argc == 2 && streq (argv [1], "-b")) {
        printf ("I: Backup passive, waiting for primary (active)\n");
        bstar = bstar_new (BSTAR_BACKUP,
            "tcp://*:5004", "tcp://localhost:5003");
        bstar_voter (bstar, "tcp://*:5002", ZMQ_ROUTER, s_echo, NULL);
    }
    else {
        printf ("Usage: bstarsrvs { -p | -b }\n");
        exit (0);
    }
    bstar_start (bstar);
    bstar_destroy (&bstar);
    return 0;
}
```

Brokerless Reliability (Freelance Pattern)

It might seem ironic to focus so much on broker-based reliability, when we often explain ØMQ as "brokerless messaging." However, in messaging, as in real life, the middleman is both a burden and a benefit. In practice, most messaging architectures benefit from a mix of distributed and brokered messaging. You get the best results when you can decide freely what trade-offs you want to make. This is why I can drive 20 minutes to a wholesaler to buy five cases of wine for a party, but I can also walk 10 minutes to a corner store to buy one bottle for a dinner. Our highly context-sensitive relative valuations of time, energy, and cost are essential to the real-world economy. And they are essential to an optimal message-based architecture.

This is why ØMQ does not *impose* a broker-centric architecture, though it does give you the tools to build brokers, aka *proxies* (and we've built a dozen or so different ones so far, just for practice).

So, we'll end this chapter by deconstructing the broker-based reliability we've built so far, and turning it back into a distributed peer-to-peer architecture I call the Freelance pattern. Our use case will be a name resolution service. This is a common problem with ØMQ architectures: how do we know which endpoint to connect to? Hard-coding TCP/IP addresses in code is insanely fragile. Using configuration files creates an administration nightmare. Imagine if you had to hand-configure your web browser, on every PC or mobile phone you used, to realize that "google.com" was "74.125.230.82."

A ØMQ name service (we'll make a simple implementation) must do the following:

- Resolve a logical name into at least a bind endpoint and a connect endpoint. A realistic name service would provide multiple bind endpoints, and possibly multiple connect endpoints as well.

- Allow us to manage multiple parallel environments—e.g., "test" versus "production"—without modifying code.

- Be reliable, because if it is unavailable, applications won't be able to connect to the network.

Putting a name service behind a service-oriented Majordomo broker is clever from some points of view. However, it's simpler and much less surprising to just expose the name service as a server to which clients can connect directly. If we do this right, the name service becomes the *only* global network endpoint we need to hard-code in our code or configuration files.

The types of failure we aim to handle are server crashes and restarts, server busy looping, server overload, and network issues. To get reliability, we'll create a pool of name servers so if one crashes or goes away, clients can connect to another, and so on. In practice, two would be enough, but for this example we'll assume the pool can be any size (Figure 4-9).

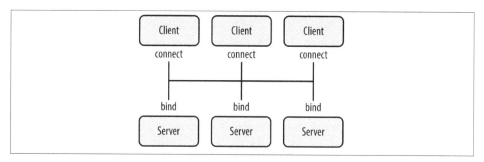

Figure 4-9. The Freelance pattern

In this architecture, a large set of clients connect to a small set of servers directly. The servers bind to their respective addresses. It's fundamentally different from a broker-based approach like Majordomo, where workers connect to the broker. Clients have a couple of options:

- Use REQ sockets and the Lazy Pirate pattern. Easy, but would need some additional intelligence so clients don't stupidly try to reconnect to dead servers over and over.

- Use DEALER sockets and blast out requests (which will be load-balanced to all connected servers) until they get a reply. Effective, but not elegant.

- Use ROUTER sockets so clients can address specific servers. But how does the client know the identity of the server sockets? Either the server has to ping the client first (complex), or the server has to use a hard-coded, fixed identity known to the client (nasty).

We'll develop each of these in the following subsections.

Model One: Simple Retry and Failover

So, our menu appears to offer the following choices: simple, brutal, complex, or nasty. Let's start with simple and then work out the kinks. We'll take Lazy Pirate and rewrite it to work with multiple server endpoints. We'll start one or several servers first, specifying a bind endpoint as the argument (Example 4-77).

Example 4-77. Freelance server, Model One (flserver1.c)

```
//
//  Freelance server - Model One
//  Trivial echo service
//
#include "czmq.h"

int main (int argc, char *argv [])
{
    if (argc < 2) {
        printf ("I: syntax: %s <endpoint>\n", argv [0]);
        exit (EXIT_SUCCESS);
    }
    zctx_t *ctx = zctx_new ();
    void *server = zsocket_new (ctx, ZMQ_REP);
    zsocket_bind (server, argv [1]);

    printf ("I: echo service is ready at %s\n", argv [1]);
    while (true) {
        zmsg_t *msg = zmsg_recv (server);
        if (!msg)
            break;          //  Interrupted
        zmsg_send (&msg, server);
    }
    if (zctx_interrupted)
        printf ("W: interrupted\n");

    zctx_destroy (&ctx);
    return 0;
}
```

Then we'll start the client (Example 4-78), specifying one or more connect endpoints as arguments.

Example 4-78. Freelance client, Model One (flclient1.c)

```
//
//  Freelance client - Model One
//  Uses REQ socket to query one or more services
//
#include "czmq.h"

#define REQUEST_TIMEOUT     1000
#define MAX_RETRIES         3        //  Before we abandon

static zmsg_t *
s_try_request (zctx_t *ctx, char *endpoint, zmsg_t *request)
{
    printf ("I: trying echo service at %s...\n", endpoint);
    void *client = zsocket_new (ctx, ZMQ_REQ);
    zsocket_connect (client, endpoint);

    //  Send request, wait safely for reply
    zmsg_t *msg = zmsg_dup (request);
    zmsg_send (&msg, client);
    zmq_pollitem_t items [] = { { client, 0, ZMQ_POLLIN, 0 } };
    zmq_poll (items, 1, REQUEST_TIMEOUT * ZMQ_POLL_MSEC);
    zmsg_t *reply = NULL;
    if (items [0].revents & ZMQ_POLLIN)
        reply = zmsg_recv (client);

    //  Close socket in any case, we're done with it now
    zsocket_destroy (ctx, client);
    return reply;
}
```

The client uses a Lazy Pirate strategy if it only has one server to talk to. If it has two or more servers to talk to, it will try each server just once. The main client task is in Example 4-79.

Example 4-79. Freelance client, Model One (flclient1.c): client task

```
int main (int argc, char *argv [])
{
    zctx_t *ctx = zctx_new ();
    zmsg_t *request = zmsg_new ();
    zmsg_addstr (request, "Hello world");
    zmsg_t *reply = NULL;

    int endpoints = argc - 1;
    if (endpoints == 0)
        printf ("I: syntax: %s <endpoint> ...\n", argv [0]);
    else
    if (endpoints == 1) {
        //  For one endpoint, we retry N times
        int retries;
        for (retries = 0; retries < MAX_RETRIES; retries++) {
```

```
            char *endpoint = argv [1];
            reply = s_try_request (ctx, endpoint, request);
            if (reply)
                break;          // Successful
            printf ("W: no response from %s, retrying...\n", endpoint);
        }
    }
    else {
        //  For multiple endpoints, try each at most once
        int endpoint_nbr;
        for (endpoint_nbr = 0; endpoint_nbr < endpoints; endpoint_nbr++) {
            char *endpoint = argv [endpoint_nbr + 1];
            reply = s_try_request (ctx, endpoint, request);
            if (reply)
                break;          // Successful
            printf ("W: no response from %s\n", endpoint);
        }
    }
    if (reply)
        printf ("Service is running OK\n");

    zmsg_destroy (&request);
    zmsg_destroy (&reply);
    zctx_destroy (&ctx);
    return 0;
}
```

A sample run is:

```
flserver1 tcp://*:5555 &
flserver1 tcp://*:5556 &
flclient1 tcp://localhost:5555 tcp://localhost:5556
```

Although the basic approach is Lazy Pirate, the client aims to just get one successful reply. It has two techniques, depending on whether we are running a single server or multiple servers:

- With a single server, the client will retry several times, exactly as for Lazy Pirate.

- With multiple servers, the client will try each server at most once until it's received a reply or has tried all servers.

This solves the main weakness of Lazy Pirate, namely that it cannot fail over to backup or alternate servers.

However, this design won't work well in a real application. If we're connecting many sockets and our primary name server is down, we're going to experience this painful timeout each time.

Model Two: Brutal Shotgun Massacre

Let's switch our client to using a DEALER socket. Our goal here is to make sure we get a reply back within the shortest possible time, no matter whether a particular server is up or down. Our client takes this approach:

- We set things up, connecting to all servers.
- When we have a request, we blast it out as many times as we have servers.
- We wait for the first reply, and take that.
- We ignore any other replies.

What will happen in practice is that when all servers are running, ØMQ will distribute the requests so that each server gets one request and sends one reply. When any server is offline and disconnected, ØMQ will distribute the requests to the remaining servers. So, in some cases a server may get the same request more than once.

What's more annoying for the client is that we'll get multiple replies back, but there's no guarantee we'll get a precise number of replies. Requests and replies can get lost (e.g., if the server crashes while processing a request).

So, we have to number requests and ignore any replies that don't match the request number. Our Model One server will work because it's an echo server, but coincidence is not a great basis for understanding, so we'll make a Model Two server here that chews up the message and returns a correctly numbered reply with the content "OK." We'll use messages consisting of two parts: a sequence number and a body.

We'll begin by starting one or more servers, specifying a bind endpoint each time, as in Example 4-80.

Example 4-80. Freelance server, Model Two (flserver2.c)

```
//
//  Freelance server - Model Two
//  Does some work, replies OK, with message sequencing
//
#include "czmq.h"

int main (int argc, char *argv [])
{
    if (argc < 2) {
        printf ("I: syntax: %s <endpoint>\n", argv [0]);
        exit (EXIT_SUCCESS);
    }
    zctx_t *ctx = zctx_new ();
    void *server = zsocket_new (ctx, ZMQ_REP);
    zsocket_bind (server, argv [1]);

    printf ("I: service is ready at %s\n", argv [1]);
```

```
    while (true) {
        zmsg_t *request = zmsg_recv (server);
        if (!request)
            break;              //  Interrupted
        //  Fail nastily if run against wrong client
        assert (zmsg_size (request) == 2);

        zframe_t *identity = zmsg_pop (request);
        zmsg_destroy (&request);

        zmsg_t *reply = zmsg_new ();
        zmsg_add (reply, identity);
        zmsg_addstr (reply, "OK");
        zmsg_send (&reply, server);
    }
    if (zctx_interrupted)
        printf ("W: interrupted\n");

    zctx_destroy (&ctx);
    return 0;
}
```

Then we'll start the client, specifying the connect endpoints as arguments, as in
Example 4-81.

Example 4-81. Freelance client, Model Two (flclient2.c)

```
//
//  Freelance client - Model Two
//  Uses DEALER socket to blast one or more services
//
#include "czmq.h"

//  We design our client API as a class, using the CZMQ style
#ifdef __cplusplus
extern "C" {
#endif

typedef struct _flclient_t flclient_t;
flclient_t *flclient_new (void);
void        flclient_destroy (flclient_t **self_p);
void        flclient_connect (flclient_t *self, char *endpoint);
zmsg_t     *flclient_request (flclient_t *self, zmsg_t **request_p);

#ifdef __cplusplus
}
#endif

//  If not a single service replies within this time, give up
#define GLOBAL_TIMEOUT 2500

int main (int argc, char *argv [])
```

```
{
    if (argc == 1) {
        printf ("I: syntax: %s <endpoint> ...\n", argv [0]);
        exit (EXIT_SUCCESS);
    }
    //  Create new freelance client object
    flclient_t *client = flclient_new ();

    //  Connect to each endpoint
    int argn;
    for (argn = 1; argn < argc; argn++)
        flclient_connect (client, argv [argn]);

    //  Send a bunch of name resolution "requests," measure time
    int requests = 10000;
    uint64_t start = zclock_time ();
    while (requests--) {
        zmsg_t *request = zmsg_new ();
        zmsg_addstr (request, "random name");
        zmsg_t *reply = flclient_request (client, &request);
        if (!reply) {
            printf ("E: name service not available, aborting\n");
            break;
        }
        zmsg_destroy (&reply);
    }
    printf ("Average round trip cost: %d usec\n",
        (int) (zclock_time () - start) / 10);

    flclient_destroy (&client);
    return 0;
}
```

The flclient class implementation is shown in Example 4-82. Each instance has a context, a DEALER socket it uses to talk to the servers, a counter of how many servers it's connected to, and a request sequence number.

Example 4-82. Freelance client, Model Two (flclient2.c): class implementation

```
struct _flclient_t {
    zctx_t *ctx;            //  Our context wrapper
    void *socket;           //  DEALER socket talking to servers
    size_t servers;         //  How many servers we have connected to
    uint sequence;          //  Number of requests ever sent
};

//  -----------------------------------------------------------------
//  Constructor

flclient_t *
flclient_new (void)
{
```

```
        flclient_t
            *self;

    self = (flclient_t *) zmalloc (sizeof (flclient_t));
    self->ctx = zctx_new ();
    self->socket = zsocket_new (self->ctx, ZMQ_DEALER);
    return self;
}

//  ----------------------------------------------------------------
//  Destructor

void
flclient_destroy (flclient_t **self_p)
{
    assert (self_p);
    if (*self_p) {
        flclient_t *self = *self_p;
        zctx_destroy (&self->ctx);
        free (self);
        *self_p = NULL;
    }
}

//  ----------------------------------------------------------------
//  Connect to new server endpoint

void
flclient_connect (flclient_t *self, char *endpoint)
{
    assert (self);
    zsocket_connect (self->socket, endpoint);
    self->servers++;
}
```

The request method in Example 4-83 does the hard work. It sends a request to all connected servers in parallel (for this to work, all connections must be successful and completed by this time). It then waits for a single successful reply, and returns that to the caller. Any other replies are just dropped.

Example 4-83. Freelance client, Model Two (flclient2.c): request method

```
zmsg_t *
flclient_request (flclient_t *self, zmsg_t **request_p)
{
    assert (self);
    assert (*request_p);
    zmsg_t *request = *request_p;

    //  Prefix request with sequence number and empty envelope
    char sequence_text [10];
    sprintf (sequence_text, "%u", ++self->sequence);
```

```
zmsg_pushstr (request, sequence_text);
zmsg_pushstr (request, "");

//  Blast the request to all connected servers
int server;
for (server = 0; server < self->servers; server++) {
    zmsg_t *msg = zmsg_dup (request);
    zmsg_send (&msg, self->socket);
}
//  Wait for a matching reply to arrive from anywhere
//  Because we can poll several times, calculate each one
zmsg_t *reply = NULL;
uint64_t endtime = zclock_time () + GLOBAL_TIMEOUT;
while (zclock_time () < endtime) {
    zmq_pollitem_t items [] = { { self->socket, 0, ZMQ_POLLIN, 0 } };
    zmq_poll (items, 1, (endtime - zclock_time ()) * ZMQ_POLL_MSEC);
    if (items [0].revents & ZMQ_POLLIN) {
        //  Reply is [empty][sequence][OK]
        reply = zmsg_recv (self->socket);
        assert (zmsg_size (reply) == 3);
        free (zmsg_popstr (reply));
        char *sequence = zmsg_popstr (reply);
        int sequence_nbr = atoi (sequence);
        free (sequence);
        if (sequence_nbr == self->sequence)
            break;
    }
}
zmsg_destroy (request_p);
return reply;
}
```

Here are some things to note about the client implementation:

- The client is structured as a nice little class-based API that hides the dirty work of creating ØMQ contexts and sockets and talking to the server. That is, if a shotgun blast to the midriff can be called "talking."

- The client will abandon the chase if it can't find *any* responsive server within a few seconds.

- The client has to create a valid REP envelope (i.e., add an empty message frame to the front of the message).

The client performs 10,000 name resolution requests (fake ones, as our server does essentially nothing) and measures the average cost. On my test box, talking to one server, this requires about 60 microseconds. Talking to three servers, it takes about 80 microseconds.

The pros and cons of our shotgun approach are:

- Pro: it is simple, easy to make and easy to understand.
- Pro: it does the job of failover, and it works rapidly, as long as there is at least one server running.
- Con: it creates redundant network traffic.
- Con: we can't prioritize our servers (i.e., primary, then secondary).
- Con: the server can do at most one request at a time, period.

Model Three: Complex and Nasty

The shotgun approach seems too good to be true. Let's be scientific and work through all the alternatives. We're going to explore the complex/nasty option, even if it's only to finally realize that we preferred the brutal approach. Ah, the story of my life.

We can solve the main problems of the client by switching to a ROUTER socket. That lets us send requests to specific servers, avoid servers we know are dead, and in general be as smart as we want to be. We can also solve the main problem of the server (single-threadedness) by switching to a ROUTER socket.

But doing ROUTER to ROUTER between two anonymous sockets (which haven't set an identity) is not possible. Both sides generate an identity for the other peer only when they receive a first message, and thus neither can talk to the other until it has first received a message. The only way out of this conundrum is to cheat and use hard-coded identities in one direction. The proper way to cheat, in a client/server case, is to let the client "know" the identity of the server. Doing it the other way around would be insane, on top of complex and nasty, because any number of clients should be able to arise independently. Insane, complex, and nasty are great attributes for a genocidal dictator, but terrible ones for software.

Rather than invent yet another concept to manage, we'll use the connection endpoint as the identity. This is a unique string on which both sides can agree without more prior knowledge than they already have for the shotgun model. It's a sneaky and effective way to connect two ROUTER sockets.

Remember how ØMQ identities work. The server ROUTER socket sets an identity before it binds its socket. When a client connects, they do a little handshake to exchange identities before either side sends a real message. The client ROUTER socket, having not set an identity, sends a null identity to the server. The server generates a random UUID to designate the client, for its own use. The server sends its identity (which we've agreed is going to be an endpoint string) to the client.

This means that our client can route a message to the server (i.e., send on its ROUTER socket, specifying the server endpoint as the identity) as soon as the connection is established. That's not *immediately* after doing a zmq_connect(), but at some random time thereafter. Herein lies one problem: we don't know when the server will actually be available and complete its connection handshake. If the server is online, it could be after a few milliseconds. If the server is down, and the sysadmin is out to lunch, it could be an hour from now.

There's a small paradox here. We need to know when servers become connected and available for work. In the Freelance pattern, unlike the broker-based patterns we saw earlier in this chapter, servers are silent until spoken to. Thus, we can't talk to a server until it's told us it's online, which it can't do until we've asked it.

My solution is to mix in a little of the shotgun approach from Model Two, meaning we'll fire (harmless) shots at anything we can, and if anything moves, we know it's alive. We're not going to fire real requests, but rather a kind of ping-pong heartbeat.

 This brings us to the realm of protocols again: you'll find a short spec that defines how a Freelance client and server exchange ping-pong commands and request-reply commands at *http://rfc.zeromq.org/spec: 10.*

This is short and sweet to implement as a server. Example 4-84 presents the code for Model Three of our echo server, now speaking the Freelance Protocol (FLP).

Example 4-84. Freelance server, Model Three (flserver3.c)

```
//
//  Freelance server - Model Three
//  Uses a ROUTER/ROUTER socket but just one thread
//
#include "czmq.h"

int main (int argc, char *argv [])
{
    int verbose = (argc > 1 && streq (argv [1], "-v"));

    zctx_t *ctx = zctx_new ();

    //  Prepare server socket with predictable identity
    char *bind_endpoint = "tcp://*:5555";
    char *connect_endpoint = "tcp://localhost:5555";
    void *server = zsocket_new (ctx, ZMQ_ROUTER);
    zmq_setsockopt (server,
        ZMQ_IDENTITY, connect_endpoint, strlen (connect_endpoint));
    zsocket_bind (server, bind_endpoint);
    printf ("I: service is ready at %s\n", bind_endpoint);

    while (!zctx_interrupted) {
        zmsg_t *request = zmsg_recv (server);
        if (verbose && request)
```

```
        zmsg_dump (request);
    if (!request)
        break;              //  Interrupted

    //  Frame 0: identity of client
    //  Frame 1: PING, or client control frame
    //  Frame 2: request body
    zframe_t *identity = zmsg_pop (request);
    zframe_t *control = zmsg_pop (request);
    zmsg_t *reply = zmsg_new ();
    if (zframe_streq (control, "PING"))
        zmsg_addstr (reply, "PONG");
    else {
        zmsg_add (reply, control);
        zmsg_addstr (reply, "OK");
    }
    zmsg_destroy (&request);
    zmsg_push (reply, identity);
    if (verbose && reply)
        zmsg_dump (reply);
    zmsg_send (&reply, server);
    }
    if (zctx_interrupted)
        printf ("W: interrupted\n");

    zctx_destroy (&ctx);
    return 0;
}
```

The Freelance client, however, has gotten large. For clarity, it's split into an example application and a class that does the hard work. The top-level application is shown in Example 4-85.

Example 4-85. Freelance client, Model Three (flclient3.c)

```
//
//  Freelance client - Model Three
//  Uses flcliapi class to encapsulate Freelance pattern
//
//  Lets us build this source without creating a library
#include "flcliapi.c"

int main (void)
{
    //  Create new freelance client object
    flcliapi_t *client = flcliapi_new ();

    //  Connect to several endpoints
    flcliapi_connect (client, "tcp://localhost:5555");
    flcliapi_connect (client, "tcp://localhost:5556");
    flcliapi_connect (client, "tcp://localhost:5557");
```

```
    //  Send a bunch of name resolution "requests," measure time
    int requests = 1000;
    uint64_t start = zclock_time ();
    while (requests--) {
        zmsg_t *request = zmsg_new ();
        zmsg_addstr (request, "random name");
        zmsg_t *reply = flcliapi_request (client, &request);
        if (!reply) {
            printf ("E: name service not available, aborting\n");
            break;
        }
        zmsg_destroy (&reply);
    }
    printf ("Average round trip cost: %d usec\n",
        (int) (zclock_time () - start) / 10);

    flcliapi_destroy (&client);
    return 0;
}
```

Example 4-86 presents the client API class, which is almost as complex and large as the Majordomo broker.

Example 4-86. Freelance client API (flcliapi.c)

```
/*  =====================================================================
 *  flcliapi - Freelance pattern agent class
 *  Implements the Freelance Protocol at http://rfc.zeromq.org/spec:10
 *  ===================================================================== */

#include "flcliapi.h"

//  If no server replies within this time, abandon request
#define GLOBAL_TIMEOUT  3000    //  msec
//  PING interval for servers we think are alive
#define PING_INTERVAL   2000    //  msec
//  Server considered dead if silent for this long
#define SERVER_TTL      6000    //  msec
```

This API works in two halves—a common pattern for APIs that need to run in the background. One half is a frontend object that our application creates and works with; the other half is a backend "agent" that runs in a background thread. The frontend talks to the backend over an inproc pipe socket. The API structure is shown in Example 4-87.

Example 4-87. Freelance client API (flcliapi.c): API structure

```
//  ---------------------------------------------------------------------
//  Structure of our frontend class

struct _flcliapi_t {
    zctx_t *ctx;        //  Our context wrapper
    void *pipe;         //  Pipe through to flcliapi agent
```

```
};

//  This is the thread that handles our real flcliapi class
static void flcliapi_agent (void *args, zctx_t *ctx, void *pipe);

//  ----------------------------------------------------------------------
//  Constructor

flcliapi_t *
flcliapi_new (void)
{
    flcliapi_t
        *self;

    self = (flcliapi_t *) zmalloc (sizeof (flcliapi_t));
    self->ctx = zctx_new ();
    self->pipe = zthread_fork (self->ctx, flcliapi_agent, NULL);
    return self;
}

//  ----------------------------------------------------------------------
//  Destructor

void
flcliapi_destroy (flcliapi_t **self_p)
{
    assert (self_p);
    if (*self_p) {
        flcliapi_t *self = *self_p;
        zctx_destroy (&self->ctx);
        free (self);
        *self_p = NULL;
    }
}
```

To implement the connect method (Example 4-88), the frontend object sends a multi-part message to the backend agent. The first part is a string "CONNECT", and the second part is the endpoint. It waits 100 msec for the connection to come up, which isn't pretty but saves us from sending all requests to a single server at startup time.

Example 4-88. Freelance client API (flcliapi.c): connect method

```
void
flcliapi_connect (flcliapi_t *self, char *endpoint)
{
    assert (self);
    assert (endpoint);
    zmsg_t *msg = zmsg_new ();
    zmsg_addstr (msg, "CONNECT");
    zmsg_addstr (msg, endpoint);
    zmsg_send (&msg, self->pipe);
```

```
    zclock_sleep (100);        // Allow connection to come up
}
```

To implement the request method, the frontend object sends a message to the backend, specifying a command "REQUEST" and the request message (Example 4-89).

Example 4-89. Freelance client API (flcliapi.c): request method

```
zmsg_t *
flcliapi_request (flcliapi_t *self, zmsg_t **request_p)
{
    assert (self);
    assert (*request_p);

    zmsg_pushstr (*request_p, "REQUEST");
    zmsg_send (request_p, self->pipe);
    zmsg_t *reply = zmsg_recv (self->pipe);
    if (reply) {
        char *status = zmsg_popstr (reply);
        if (streq (status, "FAILED"))
            zmsg_destroy (&reply);
        free (status);
    }
    return reply;
}
```

Now let's look at the backend agent. It runs as an attached thread, talking to its parent over a pipe socket. It is a fairly complex piece of work, so we'll break it down into pieces. First, the agent manages a set of servers, using our familiar class approach (Example 4-90).

Example 4-90. Freelance client API (flcliapi.c): backend agent

```
//  ----------------------------------------------------------------
//  Simple class for one server we talk to

typedef struct {
    char *endpoint;             //  Server identity/endpoint
    uint alive;                 //  1 if known to be alive
    int64_t ping_at;            //  Next ping at this time
    int64_t expires;            //  Expires at this time
} server_t;

server_t *
server_new (char *endpoint)
{
    server_t *self = (server_t *) zmalloc (sizeof (server_t));
    self->endpoint = strdup (endpoint);
    self->alive = 0;
    self->ping_at = zclock_time () + PING_INTERVAL;
    self->expires = zclock_time () + SERVER_TTL;
    return self;
}
```

```
}

void
server_destroy (server_t **self_p)
{
    assert (self_p);
    if (*self_p) {
        server_t *self = *self_p;
        free (self->endpoint);
        free (self);
        *self_p = NULL;
    }
}

int
server_ping (const char *key, void *server, void *socket)
{
    server_t *self = (server_t *) server;
    if (zclock_time () >= self->ping_at) {
        zmsg_t *ping = zmsg_new ();
        zmsg_addstr (ping, self->endpoint);
        zmsg_addstr (ping, "PING");
        zmsg_send (&ping, socket);
        self->ping_at = zclock_time () + PING_INTERVAL;
    }
    return 0;
}

int
server_tickless (const char *key, void *server, void *arg)
{
    server_t *self = (server_t *) server;
    uint64_t *tickless = (uint64_t *) arg;
    if (*tickless > self->ping_at)
        *tickless = self->ping_at;
    return 0;
}
```

We build the agent as a class that's capable of processing messages coming in from its various sockets, as shown in Example 4-91.

Example 4-91. Freelance client API (flcliapi.c): backend agent class

```
//  -----------------------------------------------------------------------
//  Simple class for one background agent

typedef struct {
    zctx_t *ctx;                //  Own context
    void *pipe;                 //  Socket to talk back to application
    void *router;               //  Socket to talk to servers
    zhash_t *servers;           //  Servers we've connected to
    zlist_t *actives;           //  Servers we know are alive
```

```
    uint sequence;              //  Number of requests ever sent
    zmsg_t *request;            //  Current request if any
    zmsg_t *reply;              //  Current reply if any
    int64_t expires;            //  Timeout for request/reply
} agent_t;

agent_t *
agent_new (zctx_t *ctx, void *pipe)
{
    agent_t *self = (agent_t *) zmalloc (sizeof (agent_t));
    self->ctx = ctx;
    self->pipe = pipe;
    self->router = zsocket_new (self->ctx, ZMQ_ROUTER);
    self->servers = zhash_new ();
    self->actives = zlist_new ();
    return self;
}

void
agent_destroy (agent_t **self_p)
{
    assert (self_p);
    if (*self_p) {
        agent_t *self = *self_p;
        zhash_destroy (&self->servers);
        zlist_destroy (&self->actives);
        zmsg_destroy (&self->request);
        zmsg_destroy (&self->reply);
        free (self);
        *self_p = NULL;
    }
}
```

The control_message method, shown in Example 4-92, processes one message from our frontend class (it's going to be "CONNECT" or "REQUEST").

Example 4-92. Freelance client API (flcliapi.c): control messages

```
//  Callback when we remove server from agent "servers" hash table

static void
s_server_free (void *argument)
{
    server_t *server = (server_t *) argument;
    server_destroy (&server);
}

void
agent_control_message (agent_t *self)
{
    zmsg_t *msg = zmsg_recv (self->pipe);
    char *command = zmsg_popstr (msg);
```

```
    if (streq (command, "CONNECT")) {
        char *endpoint = zmsg_popstr (msg);
        printf ("I: connecting to %s...\n", endpoint);
        int rc = zmq_connect (self->router, endpoint);
        assert (rc == 0);
        server_t *server = server_new (endpoint);
        zhash_insert (self->servers, endpoint, server);
        zhash_freefn (self->servers, endpoint, s_server_free);
        zlist_append (self->actives, server);
        server->ping_at = zclock_time () + PING_INTERVAL;
        server->expires = zclock_time () + SERVER_TTL;
        free (endpoint);
    }
    else
    if (streq (command, "REQUEST")) {
        assert (!self->request);    //  Strict request-reply cycle
        //  Prefix request with sequence number and empty envelope
        char sequence_text [10];
        sprintf (sequence_text, "%u", ++self->sequence);
        zmsg_pushstr (msg, sequence_text);
        //  Take ownership of request message
        self->request = msg;
        msg = NULL;
        //  Request expires after global timeout
        self->expires = zclock_time () + GLOBAL_TIMEOUT;
    }
    free (command);
    zmsg_destroy (&msg);
}
```

The `router_message` method, shown in Example 4-93, processes one message from a connected server.

Example 4-93. Freelance client API (flcliapi.c): router messages

```
void
agent_router_message (agent_t *self)
{
    zmsg_t *reply = zmsg_recv (self->router);

    //  Frame 0 is server that replied
    char *endpoint = zmsg_popstr (reply);
    server_t *server =
        (server_t *) zhash_lookup (self->servers, endpoint);
    assert (server);
    free (endpoint);
    if (!server->alive) {
        zlist_append (self->actives, server);
        server->alive = 1;
    }
    server->ping_at = zclock_time () + PING_INTERVAL;
```

```
    server->expires = zclock_time () + SERVER_TTL;

    // Frame 1 may be sequence number for reply
    char *sequence = zmsg_popstr (reply);
    if (atoi (sequence) == self->sequence) {
        zmsg_pushstr (reply, "OK");
        zmsg_send (&reply, self->pipe);
        zmsg_destroy (&self->request);
    }
    else
        zmsg_destroy (&reply);
}
```

Finally, Example 4-94 shows the agent task itself, which polls its two sockets and processes incoming messages.

Example 4-94. Freelance client API (flcliapi.c): backend agent implementation

```
static void
flcliapi_agent (void *args, zctx_t *ctx, void *pipe)
{
    agent_t *self = agent_new (ctx, pipe);

    zmq_pollitem_t items [] = {
        { self->pipe, 0, ZMQ_POLLIN, 0 },
        { self->router, 0, ZMQ_POLLIN, 0 }
    };
    while (!zctx_interrupted) {
        // Calculate tickless timer, up to 1 hour
        uint64_t tickless = zclock_time () + 1000 * 3600;
        if (self->request
        && tickless > self->expires)
            tickless = self->expires;
        zhash_foreach (self->servers, server_tickless, &tickless);

        int rc = zmq_poll (items, 2,
            (tickless - zclock_time ()) * ZMQ_POLL_MSEC);
        if (rc == -1)
            break;                  // Context has been shut down

        if (items [0].revents & ZMQ_POLLIN)
            agent_control_message (self);

        if (items [1].revents & ZMQ_POLLIN)
            agent_router_message (self);

        // If we're processing a request, dispatch to next server
        if (self->request) {
            if (zclock_time () >= self->expires) {
                // Request expired, kill it
                zstr_send (self->pipe, "FAILED");
                zmsg_destroy (&self->request);
```

```
        }
        else {
            //  Find server to talk to, remove any expired ones
            while (zlist_size (self->actives)) {
                server_t *server =
                    (server_t *) zlist_first (self->actives);
                if (zclock_time () >= server->expires) {
                    zlist_pop (self->actives);
                    server->alive = 0;
                }
                else {
                    zmsg_t *request = zmsg_dup (self->request);
                    zmsg_pushstr (request, server->endpoint);
                    zmsg_send (&request, self->router);
                    break;
                }
            }
        }
    }
    //  Disconnect and delete any expired servers
    //  Send heartbeats to idle servers if needed
    zhash_foreach (self->servers, server_ping, self->router);
    }
    agent_destroy (&self);
}
```

This API implementation is fairly sophisticated and uses a couple of techniques that we have not seen before:

Multithreaded API
> The client API consists of two parts: a synchronous flcliapi class that runs in the application thread, and an asynchronous agent class that runs as a background thread. Remember how ØMQ makes it easy to create multithreaded apps. The flcliapi and agent classes talk to each other with messages over an inproc socket. All ØMQ aspects (such as creating and destroying a context) are hidden in the API. The agent in effect acts like a mini-broker, talking to servers in the background, so that when we make a request it can make a best effort to reach a server it believes is available.

Tickless poll timer
> In previous poll loops, we always used a fixed tick interval, such as 1 second. This is simple enough but not excellent on power-sensitive clients (such as notebooks and mobile phones), where waking the CPU costs power. For fun, and to help save the planet, the agent uses a "tickless timer," which calculates the poll delay based on the next timeout we're expecting. A proper implementation would keep an ordered list of timeouts. We just check all timeouts and calculate the poll delay until the next one.

Conclusion

In this chapter, we've seen a variety of reliable request-reply mechanisms, each with certain costs and benefits. The example code is largely ready for real use, though it is not optimized. Of all the different patterns, the two that stand out for production use are the Majordomo pattern, for broker-based reliability, and the Freelance pattern, for brokerless reliability.

## CHAPTER 5

Advanced Publish-Subscribe Patterns

In Chapter 3 and Chapter 4, we looked at advanced uses of ØMQ's request-reply pattern. If you managed to digest all that, congratulations. In this chapter we'll focus on publish-subscribe and extend ØMQ's core pub-sub pattern with higher-level patterns for performance, reliability, state distribution, and monitoring.

We'll cover:

- When to use publish-subscribe
- How to handle too-slow subscribers (the *Suicidal Snail* pattern)
- How to design high-speed subscribers (the *Black Box* pattern)
- How to monitor a publish-subscribe network (the *Espresso* pattern)
- How to build a shared key-value store (the *Clone* pattern)
- How to use reactors to simplify complex servers
- How to use the Binary Star pattern to add failover to a server

Pros and Cons of Publish-Subscribe

ØMQ's low-level patterns have their different characters. Pub-sub addresses an old messaging problem, which is *multicast* or *group messaging*. It has that unique mix of meticulous simplicity and brutal indifference that characterizes ØMQ. It's worth understanding the trade-offs that pub-sub makes, how these benefit us, and how we can work around them if needed.

First, PUB sends each message to "all of many," whereas PUSH and DEALER rotate messages to "one of many." You cannot simply replace PUSH with PUB or vice versa and hope that things will work. This bears repeating, because people seem to quite often suggest doing this.

More profoundly, pub-sub is aimed at scalability. This means large volumes of data, sent rapidly to many recipients. If you need millions of messages per second sent to thousands of points, you'll appreciate pub-sub a lot more than if you need a few messages a second sent to a handful of recipients.

To get scalability, pub-sub uses the same trick as push-pull, which is to get rid of back-chatter. This means that recipients don't talk back to senders. There are some exceptions—e.g., SUB sockets will send subscriptions to PUB sockets—but this is anonymous and infrequent.

Killing back-chatter is essential to real scalability. With pub-sub, it's how the pattern can map cleanly to the Pragmatic General Multicast (PGM) protocol, which is handled by the network switch. In other words, subscribers don't connect to the publisher at all; they connect to a multicast *group* on the switch, to which the publisher sends its messages.

When we remove back-chatter, our overall message flow becomes *much* simpler, which lets us make simpler APIs, simpler protocols, and in general reach many more people. But we also remove any possibility to coordinate senders and receivers. What this means is:

- Publishers can't tell when subscribers are successfully connected, both on initial connections and on reconnections after network failures.
- Subscribers can't tell publishers anything that would allow publishers to control the rate of messages they send. Publishers only have one setting, which is *full speed*, and subscribers must either keep up or lose messages.
- Publishers can't tell when subscribers have disappeared due to processes crashing, networks breaking, and so on.

The downside is that we actually need all of these features if we want to do reliable multicast. The ØMQ pub-sub pattern will lose messages arbitrarily when a subscriber is connecting, when a network failure occurs, or just if the subscriber or network can't keep up with the publisher.

The upside is that there are many use cases where *almost* reliable multicast is just fine. When we need this back-chatter, we can either switch to using ROUTER-DEALER (which I tend to do for most normal-volume cases), or we can add a separate channel for synchronization (we'll see an example of this later in this chapter).

Pub-sub is like a radio broadcast: you miss everything before you join, and then how much information you get depends on the quality of your reception. Surprisingly, this model is useful and widespread because it maps perfectly to real-world distribution of information. Think of Facebook and Twitter, the BBC World Service, and the sports results.

As we did for request-reply, let's define *reliability* in terms of what can go wrong. Here are the classic failure cases for pub-sub:

- Subscribers join late, so they miss messages the server already sent.
- Subscribers can fetch messages too slowly, so queues build up and then overflow.
- Subscribers can drop off and lose messages while they are away.
- Subscribers can crash and restart, and lose whatever data they've already received.
- Networks can become overloaded and drop data (specifically, for PGM).
- Networks can become too slow, so publisher-side queues overflow and publishers crash.

A lot more can go wrong, but these are the typical failures we see in a realistic system. Since v3.x, ØMQ forces default limits on its internal buffers (the so-called high-water mark or HWM), so publisher crashes are rarer unless you deliberately set the HWM to infinite.

All of these failure cases have answers, though not always simple ones. Reliability requires complexity that most of us don't need most of the time, which is why ØMQ doesn't attempt to do this out of the box.

Pub-Sub Tracing (Espresso Pattern)

Let's start this chapter by looking at a way to trace pub-sub networks. In Chapter 2 we saw a simple proxy that used these to do transport bridging. The zmq_proxy() method has three arguments: a *frontend* and *backend* socket that it bridges together, and a *capture* socket to which it will send all messages.

The code is deceptively simple, as you can see in Example 5-1.

Example 5-1. Espresso pattern (espresso.c)

```
//
//  Espresso pattern
//  This shows how to capture data using a pub-sub proxy
//
#include "czmq.h"

//  The subscriber thread requests messages starting with
//  A and B, then reads and counts incoming messages.

static void
subscriber_thread (void *args, zctx_t *ctx, void *pipe)
{
    //  Subscribe to "A" and "B"
    void *subscriber = zsocket_new (ctx, ZMQ_SUB);
    zsocket_connect (subscriber, "tcp://localhost:6001");
```

```
    zsockopt_set_subscribe (subscriber, "A");
    zsockopt_set_subscribe (subscriber, "B");

    int count = 0;
    while (count < 5) {
        char *string = zstr_recv (subscriber);
        if (!string)
            break;              //  Interrupted
        free (string);
        count++;
    }
    zsocket_destroy (ctx, subscriber);
}
```

The publisher sends random messages starting with A–J, as seen in Example 5-2.

Example 5-2. Espresso pattern (espresso.c): publisher thread

```
static void
publisher_thread (void *args, zctx_t *ctx, void *pipe)
{
    void *publisher = zsocket_new (ctx, ZMQ_PUB);
    zsocket_bind (publisher, "tcp://*:6000");

    while (!zctx_interrupted) {
        char string [10];
        sprintf (string, "%c-%05d", randof (10) + 'A', randof (100000));
        if (zstr_send (publisher, string) == -1)
            break;              //  Interrupted
        zclock_sleep (100);     //  Wait for 1/10th second
    }
}
```

The listener, shown in Example 5-3, receives all messages flowing through the proxy on its pipe. In CZMQ, the pipe is a pair of ZMQ_PAIR sockets that connect attached child threads. In other languages, your mileage may vary.

Example 5-3. Espresso pattern (espresso.c): listener thread

```
static void
listener_thread (void *args, zctx_t *ctx, void *pipe)
{
    //  Print everything that arrives on pipe
    while (true) {
        zframe_t *frame = zframe_recv (pipe);
        if (!frame)
            break;              //  Interrupted
        zframe_print (frame, NULL);
        zframe_destroy (&frame);
    }
}
```

The main task (Example 5-4) starts the subscriber and publisher, and then sets itself up as a listening proxy. The listener runs as a child thread.

Example 5-4. Espresso pattern (espresso.c): main thread

```
int main (void)
{
    //  Start child threads
    zctx_t *ctx = zctx_new ();
    zthread_fork (ctx, publisher_thread, NULL);
    zthread_fork (ctx, subscriber_thread, NULL);

    void *subscriber = zsocket_new (ctx, ZMQ_XSUB);
    zsocket_connect (subscriber, "tcp://localhost:6000");
    void *publisher = zsocket_new (ctx, ZMQ_XPUB);
    zsocket_bind (publisher, "tcp://*:6001");
    void *listener = zthread_fork (ctx, listener_thread, NULL);
    zmq_proxy (subscriber, publisher, listener);

    puts (" interrupted");
    //  Tell attached threads to exit
    zctx_destroy (&ctx);
    return 0;
}
```

Espresso works by creating a listener thread that reads a PAIR socket and prints anything it gets. That PAIR socket is one end of a pipe; the other end (another PAIR) is the socket we pass to zmq_proxy(). In practice, you'd filter interesting messages to get the essence of what you want to track (hence the name of the pattern).

The subscriber thread subscribes to "A" and "B," receives five messages, and then destroys its socket. When you run an example, the listener prints two subscription messages, five data messages, two unsubscribe messages, and then silence:

```
[002] 0141
[002] 0142
[007] B-91164
[007] B-12979
[007] A-52599
[007] A-06417
[007] A-45770
[002] 0041
[002] 0042
```

That shows neatly how the publisher socket stops sending data when there are no subscribers for it. The publisher thread is still sending messages. The socket just drops them silently.

Last Value Caching

If you've used commercial publish-subscribe systems, you may be used to some features that are missing in the fast and cheerful ØMQ pub-sub model. One of these is *last value caching* (LVC). This solves the problem of how a new subscriber catches up when it joins the network. The theory is that publishers get notified when a new subscriber joins and subscribes to some specific topics. The publisher can then rebroadcast the last message for those topics.

I've already explained why publishers don't get notified when there are new subscribers: in large pub-sub systems the volumes of data make it pretty much impossible. To make really large-scale pub-sub networks work, you need a protocol like PGM that exploits an upscale Ethernet switch's ability to multicast data to thousands of subscribers. Trying to do a TCP unicast from the publisher to each of thousands of subscribers just doesn't scale. You get weird spikes, unfair distribution (some subscribers getting the message before others), network congestion, and general unhappiness.

PGM is a one-way protocol: the publisher sends a message to a multicast address at the switch, which then rebroadcasts that to all interested subscribers. The publisher never sees when subscribers join or leave: this all happens in the switch, which we don't really want to start reprogramming.

However, in a lower-volume network with a few dozen subscribers and a limited number of topics we *can* use TCP, and then the XSUB and XPUB sockets *do* talk to each other, as we just saw in the Espresso pattern.

Can we make a last value cache using ØMQ? The answer is yes, if we make a proxy that sits between the publisher and subscribers—i.e., an analog for the PGM switch, but one we can program ourselves.

We'll start by making a publisher and subscriber that highlight the worst-case scenario. This publisher is pathological. It starts by immediately sending messages to each of a thousand topics, and then it sends one update a second to a random topic. A subscriber connects and subscribes to a topic. Without LVC, a subscriber would have to wait an average of 500 seconds to get any data. To add some drama, let's pretend there's an escaped convict called Gregor threatening to rip the head off Roger the toy bunny if we can't fix that 8.3-minutes delay.

Example 5-5 presents the publisher code. Note that it has a command-line option to connect to some address, but otherwise binds to an endpoint. We'll use this later to connect to our last value cache.

Example 5-5. Pathological publisher (pathopub.c)

```
//
//  Pathological publisher
//  Sends out 1,000 topics and then one random update per second
```

```
//
#include "czmq.h"

int main (int argc, char *argv [])
{
    zctx_t *context = zctx_new ();
    void *publisher = zsocket_new (context, ZMQ_PUB);
    if (argc == 2)
        zsocket_connect (publisher, argv [1]);
    else
        zsocket_bind (publisher, "tcp://*:5556");

    //  Ensure subscriber connection has time to complete
    sleep (1);

    //  Send out all 1,000 topic messages
    int topic_nbr;
    for (topic_nbr = 0; topic_nbr < 1000; topic_nbr++) {
        zstr_sendfm (publisher, "%03d", topic_nbr, ZMQ_SNDMORE);
        zstr_send (publisher, "Save Roger");
    }
    //  Send one random update per second
    srandom ((unsigned) time (NULL));
    while (!zctx_interrupted) {
        sleep (1);
        zstr_sendfm (publisher, "%03d", randof (1000), ZMQ_SNDMORE);
        zstr_send (publisher, "Off with his head!");
    }
    zctx_destroy (&context);
    return 0;
}
```

The code for the subscriber is in Example 5-6.

Example 5-6. Pathological subscriber (pathosub.c)

```
//
//  Pathological subscriber
//  Subscribes to one random topic and prints received messages
//
#include "czmq.h"

int main (int argc, char *argv [])
{
    zctx_t *context = zctx_new ();
    void *subscriber = zsocket_new (context, ZMQ_SUB);
    if (argc == 2)
        zsocket_connect (subscriber, argv [1]);
    else
        zsocket_connect (subscriber, "tcp://localhost:5556");

    srandom ((unsigned) time (NULL));
    char subscription [5];
```

```
    sprintf (subscription, "%03d", randof (1000));
    zsocket_set_subscribe (subscriber, subscription);

    while (true) {
        char *topic = zstr_recv (subscriber);
        if (!topic)
            break;
        char *data = zstr_recv (subscriber);
        assert (streq (topic, subscription));
        puts (data);
        free (topic);
        free (data);
    }
    zctx_destroy (&context);
    return 0;
}
```

Try building and running these: first the subscriber, then the publisher. You'll see that the subscriber reports getting "Save Roger," as you'd expect:

```
./pathosub &
./pathopub
```

It's when you run a second subscriber that you understand Roger's predicament: you have to leave it an awfully long time before it reports getting any data. Our last value cache is presented in Example 5-7 through 5-9. As I promised, it's a proxy that binds to two sockets and then handles messages on both.

Example 5-7. Last value caching proxy (lvcache.c)

```
//
//  Last value cache
//  Uses XPUB subscription messages to resend data
//
#include "czmq.h"

int main (void)
{
    zctx_t *context = zctx_new ();
    void *frontend = zsocket_new (context, ZMQ_SUB);
    zsocket_bind (frontend, "tcp://*:5557");
    void *backend = zsocket_new (context, ZMQ_XPUB);
    zsocket_bind (backend, "tcp://*:5558");

    //  Subscribe to every single topic from publisher
    zsocket_set_subscribe (frontend, "");

    //  Store last instance of each topic in a cache
    zhash_t *cache = zhash_new ();
```

We route topic updates from frontend to backend, and we handle subscriptions by sending whatever we cached, if anything, as illustrated in Example 5-8.

Example 5-8. Last value caching proxy (lvcache.c): main poll loop

```
zmq_pollitem_t items [] = {
    { frontend, 0, ZMQ_POLLIN, 0 },
    { backend,  0, ZMQ_POLLIN, 0 }
};
if (zmq_poll (items, 2, 1000 * ZMQ_POLL_MSEC) == -1)
    break;                 //  Interrupted

//  Any new topic data we cache and then forward
if (items [0].revents & ZMQ_POLLIN) {
    char *topic = zstr_recv (frontend);
    char *current = zstr_recv (frontend);
    if (!topic)
        break;
    char *previous = zhash_lookup (cache, topic);
    if (previous) {
        zhash_delete (cache, topic);
        free (previous);
    }
    zhash_insert (cache, topic, current);
    zstr_sendm (backend, topic);
    zstr_send (backend, current);
    free (topic);
}
```

When we get a new subscription, we pull data from the cache, as shown in Example 5-9.

Example 5-9. Last value caching proxy (lvcache.c): handle subscriptions

```
        zframe_t *frame = zframe_recv (backend);
        if (!frame)
            break;
        //  Event is one byte, 0=unsub or 1=sub, followed by topic
        byte *event = zframe_data (frame);
        if (event [0] == 1) {
            char *topic = zmalloc (zframe_size (frame));
            memcpy (topic, event + 1, zframe_size (frame) - 1);
            printf ("Sending cached topic %s\n", topic);
            char *previous = zhash_lookup (cache, topic);
            if (previous) {
                zstr_sendm (backend, topic);
                zstr_send (backend, previous);
            }
            free (topic);
        }
        zframe_destroy (&frame);
    }
}
zctx_destroy (&context);
zhash_destroy (&cache);
```

```
        return 0;
}
```

Now, run the proxy, and then the publisher:

```
./lvcache &
./pathopub tcp://localhost:5557
```

Then run as many instances of the subscriber as you want to try, each time connecting to the proxy on port 5558:

```
./pathosub tcp://localhost:5558
```

Each subscriber happily reports "Save Roger," and Gregor the Escaped Convict slinks back to his seat for dinner and a nice cup of hot milk, which is all he really wanted in the first place.

One note: by default, the XPUB socket does not report duplicate subscriptions, which is what you want when you're naively connecting an XPUB to an XSUB. Our example sneakily gets around this by using random topics, so the chance of it not working is one in a million. In a real LVC proxy you'll want to use the ZMQ_XPUB_VERBOSE option that we implement in Chapter 6, *The ØMQ Community* as an exercise.

Slow Subscriber Detection (Suicidal Snail Pattern)

A common problem you will hit when using the pub-sub pattern in real life is the slow subscriber. In an ideal world, we stream data at full speed from publishers to subscribers. In reality, subscriber applications are often written in interpreted languages, or do a lot of work, or are just badly written, to the extent that they can't keep up with publishers.

How do we handle a slow subscriber? The ideal fix is to make the subscriber faster, but that might take a significant amount of work and time. Some of the classic strategies for handling a slow subscriber are:

- *Queue messages on the publisher*. This is what Gmail does when I don't read my email for a couple of hours. But in high-volume messaging, pushing queues upstream has the thrilling but unprofitable result of making publishers run out of memory and then crash—especially if there are lots of subscribers and it's not possible to flush to disk for performance reasons.

- *Queue messages on the subscriber*. This is much better, and it's what ØMQ does by default if the network can keep up with things. If anyone's going to run out of memory and crash, it'll be the subscriber rather than the publisher, which is fair. This is perfect for "peaky" streams where a subscriber can't keep up for a while, but can catch up when the stream slows down. However, it's no answer to a subscriber that's simply too slow in general.

- *Stop queuing new messages after a while.* This is what Gmail does when my mailbox overflows its precious gigabytes of space. New messages just get rejected or dropped. This is a great strategy from the perspective of the publisher, and it's what ØMQ does when the publisher sets an HWM. However, it still doesn't help us fix the slow subscriber—now we just get gaps in our message stream.
- *Punish slow subscribers with a disconnect.* This is what Hotmail (remember that?) did when I didn't log in for two weeks, which is why I was on my fifteenth Hotmail account when it hit me that there was perhaps a better way. It's a nice, brutal strategy that forces subscribers to sit up and pay attention, and it would be ideal for this situation. However, ØMQ doesn't do this, and there's no way to layer it on top because subscribers are invisible to publisher applications.

None of these classic strategies fit, so we need to get creative. Rather than disconnecting the publisher, let's convince the subscriber to kill itself. This is the Suicidal Snail pattern. When a subscriber detects that it's running too slowly (where "too slowly" is presumably a configured option that really means "so slowly that if you ever get here, shout really loudly because I need to know, so I can fix this!"), it croaks and dies.

How can a subscriber detect this? One way would be to sequence messages (number them in order) and use an HWM at the publisher. Now, if the subscriber detects a gap (i.e., the numbering isn't consecutive), it knows something is wrong. We then tune the HWM to the "croak and die if you hit this" level.

There are two problems with this solution. First, if we have many publishers, how do we sequence messages? The solution is to give each publisher a unique ID and add that to the sequencing. Second, if subscribers use ZMQ_SUBSCRIBE filters, they will get gaps by definition. Our precious sequencing will be for nothing.

Some use cases won't use filters, and sequencing will work for them. But a more general solution is that the publisher timestamps each message. When a subscriber gets a message, it checks the time, and if the difference is more than, say, one second, it does the "croak and die" thing, possibly firing off a squawk to some operator console first.

The Suicidal Snail pattern works especially well when subscribers have their own clients and service-level agreements and need to guarantee certain maximum latencies. Aborting a subscriber may not seem like a constructive way to guarantee a maximum latency, but it's the assertion model. Abort today, and the problem will be fixed. Allow late data to flow downstream, and the problem may cause wider damage and take longer to appear on the radar.

Example 5-10 shows a minimal example of a Suicidal Snail.

Example 5-10. Suicidal Snail (suisnail.c)

```
//
//  Suicidal Snail
//
#include "czmq.h"

//  This is our subscriber. It connects to the publisher and subscribes to
//  everything. It sleeps for a short time between messages to simulate doing
//  too much work. If a message is more than one second late, it croaks.

#define MAX_ALLOWED_DELAY    1000    //  msecs

static void
subscriber (void *args, zctx_t *ctx, void *pipe)
{
    //  Subscribe to everything
    void *subscriber = zsocket_new (ctx, ZMQ_SUB);
    zsockopt_set_subscribe (subscriber, "");
    zsocket_connect (subscriber, "tcp://localhost:5556");

    //  Get and process messages
    while (true) {
        char *string = zstr_recv (subscriber);
        printf("%s\n", string);
        int64_t clock;
        int terms = sscanf (string, "%" PRId64, &clock);
        assert (terms == 1);
        free (string);

        //  Suicidal Snail logic
        if (zclock_time () - clock > MAX_ALLOWED_DELAY) {
            fprintf (stderr, "E: subscriber cannot keep up, aborting\n");
            break;
        }
        //  Work for 1 msec plus some random additional time
        zclock_sleep (1 + randof (2));
    }
    zstr_send (pipe, "gone and died");
}
```

Example 5-11 presents our publisher task. It publishes a time-stamped message to its PUB socket every millisecond.

Example 5-11. Suicidal Snail (suisnail.c): publisher task

```
static void
publisher (void *args, zctx_t *ctx, void *pipe)
{
    //  Prepare publisher
    void *publisher = zsocket_new (ctx, ZMQ_PUB);
```

```
    zsocket_bind (publisher, "tcp://*:5556");

    while (true) {
        //  Send current clock (msec) to subscribers
        char string [20];
        sprintf (string, "%" PRId64, zclock_time ());
        zstr_send (publisher, string);
        char *signal = zstr_recv_nowait (pipe);
        if (signal) {
            free (signal);
            break;
        }
        zclock_sleep (1);                   //  1msec wait
    }
}
```

The main task (Example 5-12) simply starts a client and a server, and then waits for the client to signal that it has died.

Example 5-12. Suicidal Snail (suisnail.c): main task

```
int main (void)
{
    zctx_t *ctx = zctx_new ();
    void *pubpipe = zthread_fork (ctx, publisher, NULL);
    void *subpipe = zthread_fork (ctx, subscriber, NULL);
    free (zstr_recv (subpipe));
    zstr_send (pubpipe, "break");
    zclock_sleep (100);
    zctx_destroy (&ctx);
    return 0;
}
```

Here are some things to note about the Suicidal Snail example:

- The message here consists simply of the current system clock as a number of milliseconds. In a realistic application, you'd have at least a message header with the timestamp and a message body with data.

- The example has subscriber and publisher in a single process as two threads. In reality, they would be separate processes. Using threads is just convenient for the demonstration.

High-Speed Subscribers (Black Box Pattern)

Now let's look at one way to make our subscribers faster. A common use case for pub-sub is distributing large data streams, like market data coming from stock exchanges. A typical setup would have a publisher connected to a stock exchange, taking price quotes and sending them out to a number of subscribers. If there were only a handful of subscribers, we could use TCP. With a larger number of subscribers, we'd probably use reliable multicast, i.e., PGM.

Let's imagine our feed has an average of 100,000 100-byte messages a second. That's a typical rate, after filtering market data we don't need to send on to subscribers. Now we decide to record a day's data (maybe 250 GB in 8 hours), and then replay it to a simulation network (i.e., a small group of subscribers). While 100K messages a second is easy for a ØMQ application, we want to replay it *much faster*.

So we set up our architecture with a bunch of boxes—one for the publisher and one for each subscriber. These are well-specified boxes—8 cores, 12 for the publisher.

And as we pump data into our subscribers, we notice two things:

1. When we do even the slightest amount of work with a message, it slows down our subscribers to the point where they can't catch up with the publisher again.

2. We're hitting a ceiling, at both the publisher and the subscribers, of around 6M messages a second, even after careful optimization and TCP tuning.

The first thing we have to do is break our subscriber into a multithreaded design so that we can do work with messages in one set of threads, while reading messages in another. Typically, we don't want to process every message the same way. Rather, the subscriber will filter some messages, perhaps by prefix key. When a message matches some criteria, the subscriber will call a worker to deal with it. In ØMQ terms, this means sending the message to a worker thread.

So, the subscriber looks something like a queue device. We could use various sockets to connect the subscriber and workers. If we assume one-way traffic and workers that are all identical, we can use PUSH and PULL and delegate all the routing work to ØMQ (Figure 5-1). This is the simplest and fastest approach.

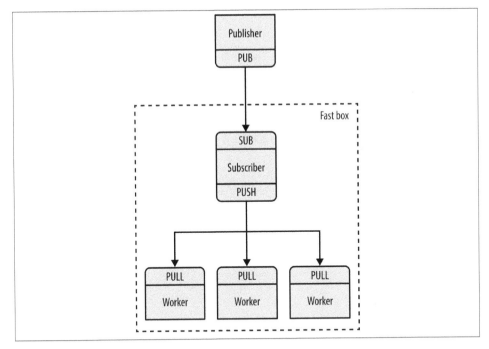

Figure 5-1. The Simple Black Box pattern

The subscriber talks to the publisher over TCP or PGM. The subscriber talks to its workers, which are all in the same process, over inproc.

Now to break that ceiling. The subscriber thread hits 100% of CPU, and because it is one thread, it cannot use more than one core. A single thread will always hit a ceiling, be it at 2M, 6M, or more messages per second. We want to split the work across multiple threads that can run in parallel.

The approach used by many high-performance products, which works here, is *sharding*. Using sharding, we split the work into parallel and independent streams. Half of the topic keys are in one stream, half in another (Figure 5-2). We could use many streams, but performance won't scale unless we have free cores.

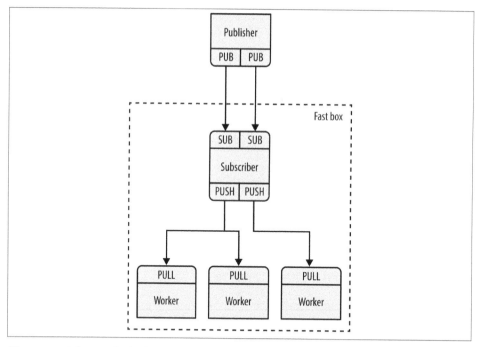

Figure 5-2. The Mad Black Box pattern

With two streams, working at full speed, we would configure ØMQ as follows:

- Two I/O threads, rather than one
- Two network interfaces card (NICs), one per subscriber
- Each I/O thread bound to a specific NIC
- Two subscriber threads, bound to specific cores
- Two SUB sockets, one per subscriber thread
- The remaining cores assigned to worker threads
- Worker threads connected to both subscriber PUSH sockets

Ideally, we want to match the number of fully loaded threads in our architecture with the number of cores. When threads start to fight for cores and CPU cycles, the cost of adding more threads outweighs the benefits.

Reliable Publish-Subscribe (Clone Pattern)

As a larger worked example, we'll take the problem of making a reliable publish-subscribe architecture. We'll develop this in stages. The goal is to allow a set of applications to share some common state. Here are our technical challenges:

- We have a large set of client applications—say, thousands or tens of thousands.
- They will join and leave the network arbitrarily.
- These applications must share a single, eventually consistent *state*.
- Any application can update the state at any point in time.

Let's say that updates are reasonably low-volume, we don't have real time goals, and the whole state can fit into memory. Some plausible use cases are:

- A configuration that is shared by a group of cloud servers
- Some game state shared by a group of players
- Exchange rate data that is updated in real time and available to applications

Centralized Versus Decentralized

A first decision we have to make is whether to work with a central server or not. It makes a big difference in the resulting design. The trade-offs are these:

- Conceptually, a central server is simpler to understand because networks are not naturally symmetrical. With a central server we avoid all questions of discovery, bind versus connect, and so on.
- Generally, a fully distributed architecture is technically more challenging but ends up with simpler protocols. That is, each node must act as server and client in the right way, which is delicate. When done right, the results are simpler than using a central server. We saw this in the Freelance pattern in Chapter 4.
- A central server will become a bottleneck in high-volume use cases. If handling scale on the order of millions of messages a second is required, we should aim for decentralization right away.
- A centralized architecture will scale to more nodes more easily than a decentralized one. That is, it's easier to connect 10,000 nodes to one server than to each other.

So, for the Clone pattern we'll work with a *server* that publishes state updates and a set of *clients* that represent applications.

Representing State as Key-Value Pairs

We'll develop the Clone pattern in stages, solving one problem at a time. First, let's look at how to update a shared state across a set of clients. We need to decide how to represent our state, as well as the updates. The simplest plausible format is a key-value store, where one key-value pair represents an atomic unit of change in the shared state.

We looked at a simple pub-sub example in Chapter 2, the weather server and client. Let's change the server to send key-value pairs, and the client to store these in a hash table. This lets us send updates from one server to a set of clients using the classic pub-sub model (Figure 5-3).

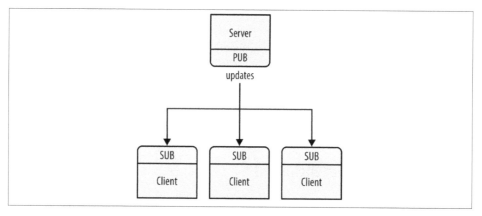

Figure 5-3. Publishing state updates

An update is either a new key-value pair, a modified value for an existing key, or a deleted key. We can assume for now that the whole store fits in memory and that applications access it by key, such as by a hash table or dictionary. For larger stores and some kind of persistence we'd probably store the state in a database, but that's not relevant here.

Our first attempt at the server is shown in Example 5-13.

Example 5-13. Clone server, Model One (clonesrv1.c)

```
//
//  Clone server-Model One
//

//  Lets us build this source without creating a library
#include "kvsimple.c"

int main (void)
{
    //  Prepare our context and publisher socket
    zctx_t *ctx = zctx_new ();
    void *publisher = zsocket_new (ctx, ZMQ_PUB);
    zsocket_bind (publisher, "tcp://*:5556");
    zclock_sleep (200);

    zhash_t *kvmap = zhash_new ();
    int64_t sequence = 0;
    srandom ((unsigned) time (NULL));
```

```
while (!zctx_interrupted) {
    //  Distribute as key-value message
    kvmsg_t *kvmsg = kvmsg_new (++sequence);
    kvmsg_fmt_key  (kvmsg, "%d", randof (10000));
    kvmsg_fmt_body (kvmsg, "%d", randof (1000000));
    kvmsg_send      (kvmsg, publisher);
    kvmsg_store    (&kvmsg, kvmap);
}
printf (" Interrupted\n%d messages out\n", (int) sequence);
zhash_destroy (&kvmap);
zctx_destroy (&ctx);
return 0;
}
```

And our first attempt at the client is shown in Example 5-14.

Example 5-14. Clone client, Model One (clonecli1.c)

```
//
//  Clone client - Model One
//

//  Lets us build this source without creating a library
#include "kvsimple.c"

int main (void)
{
    //  Prepare our context and updates socket
    zctx_t *ctx = zctx_new ();
    void *updates = zsocket_new (ctx, ZMQ_SUB);
    zsockopt_set_subscribe (updates, "");
    zsocket_connect (updates, "tcp://localhost:5556");

    zhash_t *kvmap = zhash_new ();
    int64_t sequence = 0;

    while (true) {
        kvmsg_t *kvmsg = kvmsg_recv (updates);
        if (!kvmsg)
            break;            //  Interrupted
        kvmsg_store (&kvmsg, kvmap);
        sequence++;
    }
    printf (" Interrupted\n%d messages in\n", (int) sequence);
    zhash_destroy (&kvmap);
    zctx_destroy (&ctx);
    return 0;
}
```

Here are some things to note about this first model:

- All the hard work is done in a kvmsg class. This class works with key-value message objects, which are multipart ØMQ messages structured as three frames: a key (a ØMQ string), a sequence number (a 64-bit value, in network byte order), and a binary body (which holds everything else).

- The server generates messages with a randomized four-digit key, which lets us simulate a large but not enormous hash table (10K entries).

- We don't implement deletions in this version: all messages are inserts or updates.

- The server does a 200 msec pause after binding its socket. This is to prevent *slow joiner syndrome*, where the subscriber loses messages as it connects to the server's socket. We'll remove that in later versions of the Clone code.

- We'll use the terms *publisher* and *subscriber* in the code to refer to sockets. This will help later when we have multiple sockets doing different things.

Example 5-15 shows the kvmsg class, in the simplest form that works for now.

Example 5-15. Key-value message class (kvsimple.c)

```
/*  =====================================================================
 *  kvsimple - simple key-value message class for example applications
 *  =====================================================================  */

#include "kvsimple.h"
#include "zlist.h"

//  Keys are short strings
#define KVMSG_KEY_MAX    255

//  Message is formatted on wire as 4 frames:
//  frame 0: key (0MQ string)
//  frame 1: sequence (8 bytes, network order)
//  frame 2: body (blob)
#define FRAME_KEY        0
#define FRAME_SEQ        1
#define FRAME_BODY       2
#define KVMSG_FRAMES     3

//  The kvmsg class holds a single key-value message consisting of a
//  list of 0 or more frames

struct _kvmsg {
    //  Presence indicators for each frame
    int present [KVMSG_FRAMES];
    //  Corresponding 0MQ message frames, if any
    zmq_msg_t frame [KVMSG_FRAMES];
    //  Key, copied into safe C string
    char key [KVMSG_KEY_MAX + 1];
};
```

Example 5-16 contains the code for the constructor and destructor for the class.

Example 5-16. Key-value message class (kvsimple.c): constructor and destructor

```
// Constructor, takes a sequence number for the new kvmsg instance
kvmsg_t *
kvmsg_new (int64_t sequence)
{
    kvmsg_t
        *self;

    self = (kvmsg_t *) zmalloc (sizeof (kvmsg_t));
    kvmsg_set_sequence (self, sequence);
    return self;
}

// zhash_free_fn callback helper that does the low level destruction
void
kvmsg_free (void *ptr)
{
    if (ptr) {
        kvmsg_t *self = (kvmsg_t *) ptr;
        // Destroy message frames, if any
        int frame_nbr;
        for (frame_nbr = 0; frame_nbr < KVMSG_FRAMES; frame_nbr++)
            if (self->present [frame_nbr])
                zmq_msg_close (&self->frame [frame_nbr]);

        // Free object itself
        free (self);
    }
}

// Destructor
void
kvmsg_destroy (kvmsg_t **self_p)
{
    assert (self_p);
    if (*self_p) {
        kvmsg_free (*self_p);
        *self_p = NULL;
    }
}
```

The recv method, shown in Example 5-17, reads a key-value message from the socket and returns a new kvmsg instance.

Example 5-17. Key-value message class (kvsimple.c): recv method

```
kvmsg_t *
kvmsg_recv (void *socket)
{
    assert (socket);
```

```
    kvmsg_t *self = kvmsg_new (0);

    //  Read all frames off the wire, reject if bogus
    int frame_nbr;
    for (frame_nbr = 0; frame_nbr < KVMSG_FRAMES; frame_nbr++) {
        if (self->present [frame_nbr])
            zmq_msg_close (&self->frame [frame_nbr]);
        zmq_msg_init (&self->frame [frame_nbr]);
        self->present [frame_nbr] = 1;
        if (zmq_msg_recv (&self->frame [frame_nbr], socket, 0) == -1) {
            kvmsg_destroy (&self);
            break;
        }
        //  Verify multipart framing
        int rcvmore = (frame_nbr < KVMSG_FRAMES - 1)? 1: 0;
        if (zsockopt_rcvmore (socket) != rcvmore) {
            kvmsg_destroy (&self);
            break;
        }
    }
    return self;
}
```

The send method (Example 5-18) sends a multiframe key-value message to a socket.

Example 5-18. Key-value message class (kvsimple.c): send method

```
void
kvmsg_send (kvmsg_t *self, void *socket)
{
    assert (self);
    assert (socket);

    int frame_nbr;
    for (frame_nbr = 0; frame_nbr < KVMSG_FRAMES; frame_nbr++) {
        zmq_msg_t copy;
        zmq_msg_init (&copy);
        if (self->present [frame_nbr])
            zmq_msg_copy (&copy, &self->frame [frame_nbr]);
        zmq_msg_send (&copy, socket,
            (frame_nbr < KVMSG_FRAMES - 1)? ZMQ_SNDMORE: 0);
        zmq_msg_close (&copy);
    }
}
```

The key methods in Example 5-19 let the caller get and set the message key as a fixed string and as a printf-formatted string.

Example 5-19. Key-value message class (kvsimple.c): key methods

```
char *
kvmsg_key (kvmsg_t *self)
{
```

```
    assert (self);
    if (self->present [FRAME_KEY]) {
        if (!*self->key) {
            size_t size = zmq_msg_size (&self->frame [FRAME_KEY]);
            if (size > KVMSG_KEY_MAX)
                size = KVMSG_KEY_MAX;
            memcpy (self->key,
                zmq_msg_data (&self->frame [FRAME_KEY]), size);
            self->key [size] = 0;
        }
        return self->key;
    }
    else
        return NULL;
}

void
kvmsg_set_key (kvmsg_t *self, char *key)
{
    assert (self);
    zmq_msg_t *msg = &self->frame [FRAME_KEY];
    if (self->present [FRAME_KEY])
        zmq_msg_close (msg);
    zmq_msg_init_size (msg, strlen (key));
    memcpy (zmq_msg_data (msg), key, strlen (key));
    self->present [FRAME_KEY] = 1;
}

void
kvmsg_fmt_key (kvmsg_t *self, char *format, ...)
{
    char value [KVMSG_KEY_MAX + 1];
    va_list args;

    assert (self);
    va_start (args, format);
    vsnprintf (value, KVMSG_KEY_MAX, format, args);
    va_end (args);
    kvmsg_set_key (self, value);
}
```

The two methods in Example 5-20 let the caller get and set the message sequence number.

Example 5-20. Key-value message class (kvsimple.c): sequence methods

```
int64_t
kvmsg_sequence (kvmsg_t *self)
{
    assert (self);
    if (self->present [FRAME_SEQ]) {
        assert (zmq_msg_size (&self->frame [FRAME_SEQ]) == 8);
```

```
        byte *source = zmq_msg_data (&self->frame [FRAME_SEQ]);
        int64_t sequence = ((int64_t) (source [0]) << 56)
                         + ((int64_t) (source [1]) << 48)
                         + ((int64_t) (source [2]) << 40)
                         + ((int64_t) (source [3]) << 32)
                         + ((int64_t) (source [4]) << 24)
                         + ((int64_t) (source [5]) << 16)
                         + ((int64_t) (source [6]) << 8)
                         +  (int64_t) (source [7]);
        return sequence;
    }
    else
        return 0;
}

void
kvmsg_set_sequence (kvmsg_t *self, int64_t sequence)
{
    assert (self);
    zmq_msg_t *msg = &self->frame [FRAME_SEQ];
    if (self->present [FRAME_SEQ])
        zmq_msg_close (msg);
    zmq_msg_init_size (msg, 8);

    byte *source = zmq_msg_data (msg);
    source [0] = (byte) ((sequence >> 56) & 255);
    source [1] = (byte) ((sequence >> 48) & 255);
    source [2] = (byte) ((sequence >> 40) & 255);
    source [3] = (byte) ((sequence >> 32) & 255);
    source [4] = (byte) ((sequence >> 24) & 255);
    source [5] = (byte) ((sequence >> 16) & 255);
    source [6] = (byte) ((sequence >> 8)  & 255);
    source [7] = (byte) ((sequence)       & 255);

    self->present [FRAME_SEQ] = 1;
}
```

The two methods in Example 5-21 let the caller get and set the message body, as a fixed string and as a `printf`-formatted string.

Example 5-21. Key-value message class (kvsimple.c): message body methods

```
byte *
kvmsg_body (kvmsg_t *self)
{
    assert (self);
    if (self->present [FRAME_BODY])
        return (byte *) zmq_msg_data (&self->frame [FRAME_BODY]);
    else
        return NULL;
}
```

```
void
kvmsg_set_body (kvmsg_t *self, byte *body, size_t size)
{
    assert (self);
    zmq_msg_t *msg = &self->frame [FRAME_BODY];
    if (self->present [FRAME_BODY])
        zmq_msg_close (msg);
    self->present [FRAME_BODY] = 1;
    zmq_msg_init_size (msg, size);
    memcpy (zmq_msg_data (msg), body, size);
}

void
kvmsg_fmt_body (kvmsg_t *self, char *format, ...)
{
    char value [255 + 1];
    va_list args;

    assert (self);
    va_start (args, format);
    vsnprintf (value, 255, format, args);
    va_end (args);
    kvmsg_set_body (self, (byte *) value, strlen (value));
}
```

The size method (Example 5-22) returns the body size of the most recently read message, if any exists.

Example 5-22. Key-value message class (kvsimple.c): size method

```
size_t
kvmsg_size (kvmsg_t *self)
{
    assert (self);
    if (self->present [FRAME_BODY])
        return zmq_msg_size (&self->frame [FRAME_BODY]);
    else
        return 0;
}
```

The store method (Example 5-23) stores the key-value message into a hashmap, unless the key and value are both null. It nullifies the kvmsg reference so that the object is owned by the hashmap, not the caller.

Example 5-23. Key-value message class (kvsimple.c): store method

```
void
kvmsg_store (kvmsg_t **self_p, zhash_t *hash)
{
    assert (self_p);
    if (*self_p) {
        kvmsg_t *self = *self_p;
```

```
        assert (self);
        if (self->present [FRAME_KEY]
        &&  self->present [FRAME_BODY]) {
            zhash_update (hash, kvmsg_key (self), self);
            zhash_freefn (hash, kvmsg_key (self), kvmsg_free);
        }
        *self_p = NULL;
    }
}
```

The dump method, shown in Example 5-24, prints the key-value message to stderr for debugging and tracing:

Example 5-24. Key-value message class (kvsimple.c): dump method

```
void
kvmsg_dump (kvmsg_t *self)
{
    if (self) {
        if (!self) {
            fprintf (stderr, "NULL");
            return;
        }
        size_t size = kvmsg_size (self);
        byte  *body = kvmsg_body (self);
        fprintf (stderr, "[seq:%" PRId64 "]", kvmsg_sequence (self));
        fprintf (stderr, "[key:%s]", kvmsg_key (self));
        fprintf (stderr, "[size:%zd] ", size);
        int char_nbr;
        for (char_nbr = 0; char_nbr < size; char_nbr++)
            fprintf (stderr, "%02X", body [char_nbr]);
        fprintf (stderr, "\n");
    }
    else
        fprintf (stderr, "NULL message\n");
}
```

It's good practice to have a self-test method that tests the class; this also shows how it's used in applications. Our self-test method is shown in Example 5-25.

Example 5-25. Key-value message class (kvsimple.c): test method

```
int
kvmsg_test (int verbose)
{
    kvmsg_t
        *kvmsg;

    printf (" * kvmsg: ");

    //  Prepare our context and sockets
    zctx_t *ctx = zctx_new ();
    void *output = zsocket_new (ctx, ZMQ_DEALER);
```

```
int rc = zmq_bind (output, "ipc://kvmsg_selftest.ipc");
assert (rc == 0);
void *input = zsocket_new (ctx, ZMQ_DEALER);
rc = zmq_connect (input, "ipc://kvmsg_selftest.ipc");
assert (rc == 0);

zhash_t *kvmap = zhash_new ();

//  Test send and receive of simple message
kvmsg = kvmsg_new (1);
kvmsg_set_key  (kvmsg, "key");
kvmsg_set_body (kvmsg, (byte *) "body", 4);
if (verbose)
    kvmsg_dump (kvmsg);
kvmsg_send (kvmsg, output);
kvmsg_store (&kvmsg, kvmap);

kvmsg = kvmsg_recv (input);
if (verbose)
    kvmsg_dump (kvmsg);
assert (streq (kvmsg_key (kvmsg), "key"));
kvmsg_store (&kvmsg, kvmap);

//  Shut down and destroy all objects
zhash_destroy (&kvmap);
zctx_destroy (&ctx);

printf ("OK\n");
return 0;
}
```

Later, we'll make a more sophisticated kvmsg class that will work in real applications.

Both the server and the clients maintain hash tables, but this first model only works properly if we start all clients before the server and the clients never crash. That's very artificial.

Getting an Out-of-Band Snapshot

So now we have our second problem: how to deal with late-joining clients or clients that crash and then restart.

For a late (or recovering) client to catch up with a server, it has to get a snapshot of the server's state. Just as we've reduced "message" to mean "a sequenced key-value pair," we can reduce "state" to mean "a hash table." To get the server state, a client opens a DEALER socket and asks for it explicitly (Figure 5-4).

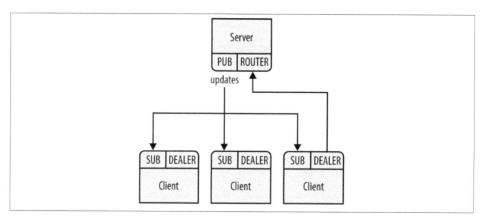

Figure 5-4. State replication

To make this work, we have to solve a problem of timing. Getting a state snapshot will take a certain amount of time, possibly fairly long if the snapshot is large. We need to correctly apply updates to the snapshot, but the server won't know when to start sending us updates. One approach would be to start subscribing, get a first update, and then ask for "state for update N." This would require the server to store one snapshot for each update, though, which isn't practical.

Instead, we will do the synchronization in the client, as follows:

- The client first subscribes to updates and then makes a state request. This guarantees that the state is going to be newer than the oldest update it has.
- The client waits for the server to reply with state, and meanwhile queues all updates. It does this simply by not reading them: ØMQ keeps them queued on the socket queue.
- When the client receives its state update, it begins once again to read updates. However, it discards any updates that are older than the state update (so, if the state update includes updates up to 200, the client will discard updates up to 201).
- The client then applies updates to its own state snapshot.

It's a simple model that exploits ØMQ's own internal queues. Model Two of our Clone server is shown in Example 5-26.

Example 5-26. Clone server, Model Two (clonesrv2.c)

```
//
//  Clone server - Model Two
//

//  Lets us build this source without creating a library
#include "kvsimple.c"
```

```c
static int s_send_single (const char *key, void *data, void *args);
static void state_manager (void *args, zctx_t *ctx, void *pipe);

int main (void)
{
    //  Prepare our context and sockets
    zctx_t *ctx = zctx_new ();
    void *publisher = zsocket_new (ctx, ZMQ_PUB);
    zsocket_bind (publisher, "tcp://*:5557");

    int64_t sequence = 0;
    srandom ((unsigned) time (NULL));

    //  Start state manager and wait for synchronization signal
    void *updates = zthread_fork (ctx, state_manager, NULL);
    free (zstr_recv (updates));

    while (!zctx_interrupted) {
        //  Distribute as key-value message
        kvmsg_t *kvmsg = kvmsg_new (++sequence);
        kvmsg_fmt_key  (kvmsg, "%d", randof (10000));
        kvmsg_fmt_body (kvmsg, "%d", randof (1000000));
        kvmsg_send     (kvmsg, publisher);
        kvmsg_send     (kvmsg, updates);
        kvmsg_destroy (&kvmsg);
    }
    printf (" Interrupted\n%d messages out\n", (int) sequence);
    zctx_destroy (&ctx);
    return 0;
}

//  Routing information for a key-value snapshot
typedef struct {
    void *socket;           //  ROUTER socket to send to
    zframe_t *identity;     //  Identity of peer who requested state
} kvroute_t;

//  Send one state snapshot key-value pair to a socket
//  Hash item data is our kvmsg object, ready to send
static int
s_send_single (const char *key, void *data, void *args)
{
    kvroute_t *kvroute = (kvroute_t *) args;
    //  Send identity of recipient first
    zframe_send (&kvroute->identity,
        kvroute->socket, ZFRAME_MORE + ZFRAME_REUSE);
    kvmsg_t *kvmsg = (kvmsg_t *) data;
    kvmsg_send (kvmsg, kvroute->socket);
    return 0;
}
```

The state manager task, shown in Example 5-27, maintains the state and handles requests from clients for snapshots.

Example 5-27. Clone server, Model Two (clonesrv2.c): state manager

```
static void
state_manager (void *args, zctx_t *ctx, void *pipe)
{
    zhash_t *kvmap = zhash_new ();

    zstr_send (pipe, "READY");
    void *snapshot = zsocket_new (ctx, ZMQ_ROUTER);
    zsocket_bind (snapshot, "tcp://*:5556");

    zmq_pollitem_t items [] = {
        { pipe, 0, ZMQ_POLLIN, 0 },
        { snapshot, 0, ZMQ_POLLIN, 0 }
    };
    int64_t sequence = 0;       //  Current snapshot version number
    while (!zctx_interrupted) {
        int rc = zmq_poll (items, 2, -1);
        if (rc == -1 && errno == ETERM)
            break;              //  Context has been shut down

        //  Apply state update from main thread
        if (items [0].revents & ZMQ_POLLIN) {
            kvmsg_t *kvmsg = kvmsg_recv (pipe);
            if (!kvmsg)
                break;          //  Interrupted
            sequence = kvmsg_sequence (kvmsg);
            kvmsg_store (&kvmsg, kvmap);
        }
        //  Execute state snapshot request
        if (items [1].revents & ZMQ_POLLIN) {
            zframe_t *identity = zframe_recv (snapshot);
            if (!identity)
                break;          //  Interrupted

            //  Request is in second frame of message
            char *request = zstr_recv (snapshot);
            if (streq (request, "ICANHAZ?"))
                free (request);
            else {
                printf ("E: bad request, aborting\n");
                break;
            }
            //  Send state snapshot to client
            kvroute_t routing = { snapshot, identity };

            //  For each entry in kvmap, send kvmsg to client
            zhash_foreach (kvmap, s_send_single, &routing);
```

```
            //  Now send END message with sequence number
            printf ("Sending state shapshot=%d\n", (int) sequence);
            zframe_send (&identity, snapshot, ZFRAME_MORE);
            kvmsg_t *kvmsg = kvmsg_new (sequence);
            kvmsg_set_key  (kvmsg, "KTHXBAI");
            kvmsg_set_body (kvmsg, (byte *) "", 0);
            kvmsg_send      (kvmsg, snapshot);
            kvmsg_destroy (&kvmsg);
        }
    }
    zhash_destroy (&kvmap);
}
```

Model Two of our Clone client is shown in Example 5-28.

Example 5-28. Clone client, Model Two (clonecli2.c)

```
//
//  Clone client - Model Two
//

//  Lets us build this source without creating a library
#include "kvsimple.c"

int main (void)
{
    //  Prepare our context and subscriber
    zctx_t *ctx = zctx_new ();
    void *snapshot = zsocket_new (ctx, ZMQ_DEALER);
    zsocket_connect (snapshot, "tcp://localhost:5556");
    void *subscriber = zsocket_new (ctx, ZMQ_SUB);
    zsockopt_set_subscribe (subscriber, "");
    zsocket_connect (subscriber, "tcp://localhost:5557");

    zhash_t *kvmap = zhash_new ();

    //  Get state snapshot
    int64_t sequence = 0;
    zstr_send (snapshot, "ICANHAZ?");
    while (true) {
        kvmsg_t *kvmsg = kvmsg_recv (snapshot);
        if (!kvmsg)
            break;          //  Interrupted
        if (streq (kvmsg_key (kvmsg), "KTHXBAI")) {
            sequence = kvmsg_sequence (kvmsg);
            printf ("Received snapshot=%d\n", (int) sequence);
            kvmsg_destroy (&kvmsg);
            break;          //  Done
        }
        kvmsg_store (&kvmsg, kvmap);
    }
    //  Now apply pending updates, discard out-of-sequence messages
    while (!zctx_interrupted) {
```

```
        kvmsg_t *kvmsg = kvmsg_recv (subscriber);
        if (!kvmsg)
            break;          // Interrupted
        if (kvmsg_sequence (kvmsg) > sequence) {
            sequence = kvmsg_sequence (kvmsg);
            kvmsg_store (&kvmsg, kvmap);
        }
        else
            kvmsg_destroy (&kvmsg);
    }
    zhash_destroy (&kvmap);
    zctx_destroy (&ctx);
    return 0;
}
```

Here are some things to note about these two programs:

- The server uses two tasks. One thread produces the updates (randomly) and sends these to the main PUB socket, while the other thread handles state requests on the ROUTER socket. The two communicate across PAIR sockets over an inproc connection.

- The client is really simple. In C it consists of about 50 lines of code. A lot of the heavy lifting is done in the kvmsg class. Even so, the basic Clone pattern is easier to implement than it seemed at first.

- We don't use anything fancy for serializing the state. The hash table holds a set of kvmsg objects, and the server sends these, as a batch of messages, to the client requesting state. If multiple clients request state at once, each will get a different snapshot.

- We assume that the client has exactly one server to talk to. The server must be running; we do not try to solve the question of what happens if the server crashes.

Right now, these two programs don't do anything real, but they correctly synchronize state. It's a neat example of how to mix different patterns: PAIR-PAIR, PUB-SUB, and ROUTER-DEALER.

Republishing Updates from Clients

In our second model, changes to the key-value store came from the server itself. This is a centralized model that is useful, for example, if we have a central configuration file we want to distribute, with local caching on each node. A more interesting model takes updates from clients, not the server. The server thus becomes a stateless broker. This gives us a few benefits:

- We're less worried about the reliability of the server. If it crashes, we can start a new instance and feed it new values.

- We can use the key-value store to share knowledge between active peers.

To send updates from clients back to the server, we could use a variety of socket patterns. The simplest plausible solution is a PUSH-PULL combination (Figure 5-5).

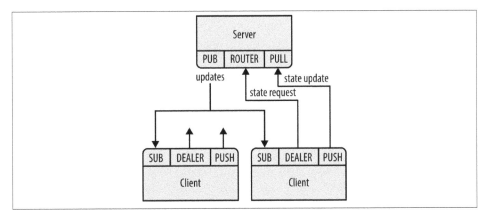

Figure 5-5. Republishing updates

Why don't we allow clients to publish updates directly to each other? While this would reduce latency, it would remove the guarantee of consistency. You can't get consistent shared state if you allow the order of updates to change depending on who receives them. If two clients make changes at the same time, but to different keys, there will be no confusion. But if the two clients try to change the same key at roughly the same time, they'll end up with different notions of its value.

There are a few strategies for obtaining consistency when changes happen in multiple places at once. We'll use the approach of centralizing all change. No matter the precise timing of the changes that clients make, they are all pushed through the server, which enforces a single sequence according to the order in which it gets updates.

By mediating all changes, the server can also add a unique sequence number to all updates. With unique sequencing, clients can detect the nastier failures—network congestion and queue overflow. If a client discovers that its incoming message stream has a hole, it can take action. It seems sensible for the client to contact the server and ask for the missing messages, but in practice that isn't useful. If there are holes, they're caused by network stress, and adding more stress to the network will make things worse. All the client can do is warn its users that it is "unable to continue," stop, and not restart until someone has manually checked the cause of the problem.

In our third model, we'll generate state updates in the client. The server code is in Example 5-29.

Example 5-29. Clone server, Model Three (clonesrv3.c)

```
//
//  Clone server - Model Three
//

//  Lets us build this source without creating a library
#include "kvsimple.c"

//  Routing information for a key-value snapshot
typedef struct {
    void *socket;           //  ROUTER socket to send to
    zframe_t *identity;     //  Identity of peer who requested state
} kvroute_t;

//  Send one state snapshot key-value pair to a socket
//  Hash item data is our kvmsg object, ready to send
static int
s_send_single (const char *key, void *data, void *args)
{
    kvroute_t *kvroute = (kvroute_t *) args;
    //  Send identity of recipient first
    zframe_send (&kvroute->identity,
        kvroute->socket, ZFRAME_MORE + ZFRAME_REUSE);
    kvmsg_t *kvmsg = (kvmsg_t *) data;
    kvmsg_send (kvmsg, kvroute->socket);
    return 0;
}

int main (void)
{
    //  Prepare our context and sockets
    zctx_t *ctx = zctx_new ();
    void *snapshot = zsocket_new (ctx, ZMQ_ROUTER);
    zsocket_bind (snapshot, "tcp://*:5556");
    void *publisher = zsocket_new (ctx, ZMQ_PUB);
    zsocket_bind (publisher, "tcp://*:5557");
    void *collector = zsocket_new (ctx, ZMQ_PULL);
    zsocket_bind (collector, "tcp://*:5558");
```

The body of the main task, shown in Example 5-30, collects updates from clients and publishes them back out to clients.

Example 5-30. Clone server, Model Three (clonesrv3.c): body of main task

```
    int64_t sequence = 0;
    zhash_t *kvmap = zhash_new ();

    zmq_pollitem_t items [] = {
        { collector, 0, ZMQ_POLLIN, 0 },
        { snapshot, 0, ZMQ_POLLIN, 0 }
    };
    while (!zctx_interrupted) {
```

```
            int rc = zmq_poll (items, 2, 1000 * ZMQ_POLL_MSEC);

        //  Apply state update sent from client
        if (items [0].revents & ZMQ_POLLIN) {
            kvmsg_t *kvmsg = kvmsg_recv (collector);
            if (!kvmsg)
                break;          //  Interrupted
            kvmsg_set_sequence (kvmsg, ++sequence);
            kvmsg_send (kvmsg, publisher);
            kvmsg_store (&kvmsg, kvmap);
            printf ("I: publishing update %5d\n", (int) sequence);
        }
        //  Execute state snapshot request
        if (items [1].revents & ZMQ_POLLIN) {
            zframe_t *identity = zframe_recv (snapshot);
            if (!identity)
                break;          //  Interrupted

            //  Request is in second frame of message
            char *request = zstr_recv (snapshot);
            if (streq (request, "ICANHAZ?"))
                free (request);
            else {
                printf ("E: bad request, aborting\n");
                break;
            }
            //  Send state snapshot to client
            kvroute_t routing = { snapshot, identity };

            //  For each entry in kvmap, send kvmsg to client
            zhash_foreach (kvmap, s_send_single, &routing);

            //  Now send END message with sequence number
            printf ("I: sending shapshot=%d\n", (int) sequence);
            zframe_send (&identity, snapshot, ZFRAME_MORE);
            kvmsg_t *kvmsg = kvmsg_new (sequence);
            kvmsg_set_key  (kvmsg, "KTHXBAI");
            kvmsg_set_body (kvmsg, (byte *) "", 0);
            kvmsg_send     (kvmsg, snapshot);
            kvmsg_destroy (&kvmsg);
        }
    }
    printf (" Interrupted\n%d messages handled\n", (int) sequence);
    zhash_destroy (&kvmap);
    zctx_destroy (&ctx);

    return 0;
}
```

The code for Model Three of our client is in Examples 5-31 through 5-33.

Example 5-31. Clone client, Model Three (clonecli3.c)

```
//
//  Clone client - Model Three
//

//  Lets us build this source without creating a library
#include "kvsimple.c"

int main (void)
{
    //  Prepare our context and subscriber
    zctx_t *ctx = zctx_new ();
    void *snapshot = zsocket_new (ctx, ZMQ_DEALER);
    zsocket_connect (snapshot, "tcp://localhost:5556");
    void *subscriber = zsocket_new (ctx, ZMQ_SUB);
    zsockopt_set_subscribe (subscriber, "");
    zsocket_connect (subscriber, "tcp://localhost:5557");
    void *publisher = zsocket_new (ctx, ZMQ_PUSH);
    zsocket_connect (publisher, "tcp://localhost:5558");

    zhash_t *kvmap = zhash_new ();
    srandom ((unsigned) time (NULL));
```

We first request a state snapshot, as shown in Example 5-32.

Example 5-32. Clone client, Model Three (clonecli3.c): getting a state snapshot

```
    zstr_send (snapshot, "ICANHAZ?");
    while (true) {
        kvmsg_t *kvmsg = kvmsg_recv (snapshot);
        if (!kvmsg)
            break;          //  Interrupted
        if (streq (kvmsg_key (kvmsg), "KTHXBAI")) {
            sequence = kvmsg_sequence (kvmsg);
            printf ("I: received snapshot=%d\n", (int) sequence);
            kvmsg_destroy (&kvmsg);
            break;          //  Done
        }
        kvmsg_store (&kvmsg, kvmap);
    }
```

Then we wait for updates from the server and, every so often, send a random key-value update to the server, as shown in Example 5-33.

Example 5-33. Clone client, Model Three (clonecli3.c): processing state updates

```
    int64_t alarm = zclock_time () + 1000;
    while (!zctx_interrupted) {
        zmq_pollitem_t items [] = { { subscriber, 0, ZMQ_POLLIN, 0 } };
        int tickless = (int) ((alarm - zclock_time ()));
        if (tickless < 0)
            tickless = 0;
```

```
        int rc = zmq_poll (items, 1, tickless * ZMQ_POLL_MSEC);
        if (rc == -1)
            break;              //  Context has been shut down

        if (items [0].revents & ZMQ_POLLIN) {
            kvmsg_t *kvmsg = kvmsg_recv (subscriber);
            if (!kvmsg)
                break;          //  Interrupted

            //  Discard out-of-sequence kvmsgs, including heartbeats
            if (kvmsg_sequence (kvmsg) > sequence) {
                sequence = kvmsg_sequence (kvmsg);
                kvmsg_store (&kvmsg, kvmap);
                printf ("I: received update=%d\n", (int) sequence);
            }
            else
                kvmsg_destroy (&kvmsg);

        }
        //  If we timed out, generate a random kvmsg
        if (zclock_time () >= alarm) {
            kvmsg_t *kvmsg = kvmsg_new (0);
            kvmsg_fmt_key  (kvmsg, "%d", randof (10000));
            kvmsg_fmt_body (kvmsg, "%d", randof (1000000));
            kvmsg_send     (kvmsg, publisher);
            kvmsg_destroy (&kvmsg);
            alarm = zclock_time () + 1000;
        }
    }
    printf (" Interrupted\n%d messages in\n", (int) sequence);
    zhash_destroy (&kvmap);
    zctx_destroy (&ctx);
    return 0;
}
```

Here are some things to note about this third design:

- The server has collapsed to a single task. It manages a PULL socket for incoming updates, a ROUTER socket for state requests, and a PUB socket for outgoing updates.

- The client uses a simple tickless timer to send a random update to the server once a second. In a real implementation, we would drive updates from application code.

Working with Subtrees

As we grow the number of clients, the size of our shared store will also grow. Eventually, it stops being reasonable to send everything to every client. This is the classic story with publish-subscribe: when you have a very small number of clients, you can send every message to all clients, but as you grow the architecture this becomes inefficient. Clients specialize in different areas.

So, even when working with a shared store, some clients will want to work only with a part of that store, which we call a *subtree*. The client has to request the subtree when it makes a state request, and it must specify the same subtree when it subscribes to updates.

There are a couple of common syntaxes for trees. One is the *path hierarchy*, and another is the *topic tree*. These look like this:

- Path hierarchy: */some/list/of/paths*
- Topic tree: *some.list.of.topics*

We'll use the path hierarchy and extend our client and server so that a client can work with a single subtree. Once you see how to work with a single subtree, you'll be able to extend this yourself to handle multiple subtrees if your use case demands it.

Example 5-34 shows the server implementing subtrees, a small variation on Model Three.

Example 5-34. Clone server, Model Four (clonesrv4.c)

```
//
//  Clone server - Model Four
//

//  Lets us build this source without creating a library
#include "kvsimple.c"

//  Routing information for a key-value snapshot
typedef struct {
    void *socket;           //  ROUTER socket to send to
    zframe_t *identity;     //  Identity of peer who requested state
    char *subtree;          //  Client subtree specification
} kvroute_t;

//  Send one state snapshot key-value pair to a socket
//  Hash item data is our kvmsg object, ready to send
static int
s_send_single (const char *key, void *data, void *args)
{
    kvroute_t *kvroute = (kvroute_t *) args;
    kvmsg_t *kvmsg = (kvmsg_t *) data;
    if (strlen (kvroute->subtree) <= strlen (kvmsg_key (kvmsg))
    &&  memcmp (kvroute->subtree,
                kvmsg_key (kvmsg), strlen (kvroute->subtree)) == 0) {
        //  Send identity of recipient first
        zframe_send (&kvroute->identity,
            kvroute->socket, ZFRAME_MORE + ZFRAME_REUSE);
        kvmsg_send (kvmsg, kvroute->socket);
```

```
    }
    return 0;
}

//  The main task is identical to clonesrv3 except for where it
//  handles subtrees
...
            //  Request is in second frame of message
            char *request = zstr_recv (snapshot);
            char *subtree = NULL;
            if (streq (request, "ICANHAZ?")) {
                free (request);
                subtree = zstr_recv (snapshot);
            }
...
            //  Send state snapshot to client
            kvroute_t routing = { snapshot, identity, subtree };
...
            //  Now send END message with sequence number
            printf ("I: sending shapshot=%d\n", (int) sequence);
            zframe_send (&identity, snapshot, ZFRAME_MORE);
            kvmsg_t *kvmsg = kvmsg_new (sequence);
            kvmsg_set_key  (kvmsg, "KTHXBAI");
            kvmsg_set_body (kvmsg, (byte *) subtree, 0);
            kvmsg_send     (kvmsg, snapshot);
            kvmsg_destroy (&kvmsg);
            free (subtree);
        }
    }
...
```

The corresponding client code is presented in Example 5-35.

Example 5-35. Clone client, Model Four (clonecli4.c)

```
//
//  Clone client - Model Four
//

//  Lets us build this source without creating a library
#include "kvsimple.c"

//  This client is identical to clonecli3 except for where we
//  handle subtrees
#define SUBTREE "/client/"
...
    zsocket_connect (subscriber, "tcp://localhost:5557");
    zsockopt_set_subscribe (subscriber, SUBTREE);
...
    //  We first request a state snapshot
    int64_t sequence = 0;
    zstr_sendm (snapshot, "ICANHAZ?");
    zstr_send  (snapshot, SUBTREE);
```

```
...
    // If we timed out, generate a random kvmsg
    if (zclock_time () >= alarm) {
        kvmsg_t *kvmsg = kvmsg_new (0);
        kvmsg_fmt_key  (kvmsg, "%s%d", SUBTREE, randof (10000));
        kvmsg_fmt_body (kvmsg, "%d", randof (1000000));
        kvmsg_send     (kvmsg, publisher);
        kvmsg_destroy (&kvmsg);
        alarm = zclock_time () + 1000;
    }
...
```

Ephemeral Values

An ephemeral value is one that expires automatically unless regularly refreshed. If you think of Clone being used for a registration service, then ephemeral values would let you use dynamic values. A node joins the network, publishes its address, and refreshes this regularly. If the node dies, its address eventually gets removed.

The usual abstraction for ephemeral values is to attach them to a *session* and delete them when the session ends. In Clone, sessions would be defined by clients and would end if the client died. A simpler alternative is to attach a *time to live* (TTL) to ephemeral values, which the server uses to expire values that haven't been refreshed in time.

A good design principle that I use whenever possible is to *not invent concepts that are not absolutely essential*. If we have a large quantity of ephemeral values, sessions offer better performance. If we use a handful of ephemeral values, it's fine to set a TTL on each one. If we use masses of ephemeral values, it's more efficient to attach them to sessions and expire them in bulk. This isn't a problem we face at this stage, and we may never face it, so sessions go out the window here.

Now we will implement ephemeral values. First, we need a way to encode the TTL in the key-value message. We could add a frame, but the problem with using ØMQ frames for properties is that each time we want to add a new property, we have to change the message structure. It breaks compatibility. So, let's add a properties frame to the message, and write code to let us get and put property values.

Next we need a way to say, "delete this value." Up until now, servers and clients have always blindly inserted or updated new values into their hash tables. We'll say that if the value is empty, that means "delete this key."

Example 5-36 shows a more complete version of the kvmsg class, which implements a properties frame (and adds a UUID frame, which we'll need later). It also handles empty values by deleting the key from the hash, if necessary.

Example 5-36. Key-value message class: full (kvmsg.c)

```
/* =====================================================================
 * kvmsg - key-value message class for example applications
```

```
 *   ========================================================================= */

#include "kvmsg.h"
#include <uuid/uuid.h>
#include "zlist.h"

//  Keys are short strings
#define KVMSG_KEY_MAX   255

//  Message is formatted on wire as 4 frames:
//  frame 0: key (0MQ string)
//  frame 1: sequence (8 bytes, network order)
//  frame 2: uuid (blob, 16 bytes)
//  frame 3: properties (0MQ string)
//  frame 4: body (blob)
#define FRAME_KEY       0
#define FRAME_SEQ       1
#define FRAME_UUID      2
#define FRAME_PROPS     3
#define FRAME_BODY      4
#define KVMSG_FRAMES    5

//  Structure of our class
struct _kvmsg {
    //  Presence indicators for each frame
    int present [KVMSG_FRAMES];
    //  Corresponding 0MQ message frames, if any
    zmq_msg_t frame [KVMSG_FRAMES];
    //  Key, copied into safe C string
    char key [KVMSG_KEY_MAX + 1];
    //  List of properties, as name=value strings
    zlist_t *props;
    size_t props_size;
};
```

The two helpers in Example 5-37 serialize a list of properties to and from a message frame.

Example 5-37. Key-value message class, full (kvmsg.c): property encoding

```
static void
s_encode_props (kvmsg_t *self)
{
    zmq_msg_t *msg = &self->frame [FRAME_PROPS];
    if (self->present [FRAME_PROPS])
        zmq_msg_close (msg);

    zmq_msg_init_size (msg, self->props_size);
    char *prop = zlist_first (self->props);
    char *dest = (char *) zmq_msg_data (msg);
    while (prop) {
        strcpy (dest, prop);
```

```
        dest += strlen (prop);
        *dest++ = '\n';
        prop = zlist_next (self->props);
    }
    self->present [FRAME_PROPS] = 1;
}

static void
s_decode_props (kvmsg_t *self)
{
    zmq_msg_t *msg = &self->frame [FRAME_PROPS];
    self->props_size = 0;
    while (zlist_size (self->props))
        free (zlist_pop (self->props));

    size_t remainder = zmq_msg_size (msg);
    char *prop = (char *) zmq_msg_data (msg);
    char *eoln = memchr (prop, '\n', remainder);
    while (eoln) {
        *eoln = 0;
        zlist_append (self->props, strdup (prop));
        self->props_size += strlen (prop) + 1;
        remainder -= strlen (prop) + 1;
        prop = eoln + 1;
        eoln = memchr (prop, '\n', remainder);
    }
}
```

The constructor and destructor for the class are shown in Example 5-38.

Example 5-38. Key-value message class, full (kvmsg.c): constructor and destructor

```
//  Constructor, takes a sequence number for the new kvmsg instance
kvmsg_t *
kvmsg_new (int64_t sequence)
{
    kvmsg_t
        *self;

    self = (kvmsg_t *) zmalloc (sizeof (kvmsg_t));
    self->props = zlist_new ();
    kvmsg_set_sequence (self, sequence);
    return self;
}

//  zhash_free_fn callback helper that does the low-level destruction
void
kvmsg_free (void *ptr)
{
    if (ptr) {
        kvmsg_t *self = (kvmsg_t *) ptr;
        //  Destroy message frames, if any
        int frame_nbr;
```

```
        for (frame_nbr = 0; frame_nbr < KVMSG_FRAMES; frame_nbr++)
            if (self->present [frame_nbr])
                zmq_msg_close (&self->frame [frame_nbr]);

        //  Destroy property list
        while (zlist_size (self->props))
            free (zlist_pop (self->props));
        zlist_destroy (&self->props);

        //  Free object itself
        free (self);
    }
}

//  Destructor
void
kvmsg_destroy (kvmsg_t **self_p)
{
    assert (self_p);
    if (*self_p) {
        kvmsg_free (*self_p);
        *self_p = NULL;
    }
}
```

The recv method in Example 5-39 reads a key-value message from the socket and returns a new kvmsg instance.

Example 5-39. Key-value message class, full (kvmsg.c): recv method

```
kvmsg_t *
kvmsg_recv (void *socket)
{
    //  This method is almost unchanged from kvsimple
...
    if (self)
        s_decode_props (self);
    return self;
}


//  --------------------------------------------------------------------
//  Send key-value message to socket; any empty frames are sent as such

void
kvmsg_send (kvmsg_t *self, void *socket)
{
    assert (self);
    assert (socket);

    s_encode_props (self);
```

```
//   The rest of the method is unchanged from kvsimple
...
```

The dup method (Example 5-40) duplicates a kvmsg instance and returns the new instance.

Example 5-40. Key-value message class, full (kvmsg.c): dup method

```
kvmsg_t *
kvmsg_dup (kvmsg_t *self)
{
    kvmsg_t *kvmsg = kvmsg_new (0);
    int frame_nbr;
    for (frame_nbr = 0; frame_nbr < KVMSG_FRAMES; frame_nbr++) {
        if (self->present [frame_nbr]) {
            zmq_msg_t *src = &self->frame [frame_nbr];
            zmq_msg_t *dst = &kvmsg->frame [frame_nbr];
            zmq_msg_init_size (dst, zmq_msg_size (src));
            memcpy (zmq_msg_data (dst),
                    zmq_msg_data (src), zmq_msg_size (src));
            kvmsg->present [frame_nbr] = 1;
        }
    }
    kvmsg->props_size = zlist_size (self->props);
    char *prop = (char *) zlist_first (self->props);
    while (prop) {
        zlist_append (kvmsg->props, strdup (prop));
        prop = (char *) zlist_next (self->props);
    }
    return kvmsg;
}

//   The key, sequence, body, and size methods are the same as in kvsimple
...
```

The methods in Example 5-41 get and set the UUID for the key-value message.

Example 5-41. Key-value message class, full (kvmsg.c): UUID methods

```
byte *
kvmsg_uuid (kvmsg_t *self)
{
    assert (self);
    if (self->present [FRAME_UUID]
    &&  zmq_msg_size (&self->frame [FRAME_UUID]) == sizeof (uuid_t))
        return (byte *) zmq_msg_data (&self->frame [FRAME_UUID]);
    else
        return NULL;
}

//   Set the UUID to a random generated value
void
kvmsg_set_uuid (kvmsg_t *self)
```

```
{
    assert (self);
    zmq_msg_t *msg = &self->frame [FRAME_UUID];
    uuid_t uuid;
    uuid_generate (uuid);
    if (self->present [FRAME_UUID])
        zmq_msg_close (msg);
    zmq_msg_init_size (msg, sizeof (uuid));
    memcpy (zmq_msg_data (msg), uuid, sizeof (uuid));
    self->present [FRAME_UUID] = 1;
}
```

The methods in Example 5-42 get and set a specified message property.

Example 5-42. Key-value message class, full (kvmsg.c): property methods

```
// Get message property, return "" if no such property is defined
char *
kvmsg_get_prop (kvmsg_t *self, char *name)
{
    assert (strchr (name, '=') == NULL);
    char *prop = zlist_first (self->props);
    size_t namelen = strlen (name);
    while (prop) {
        if (strlen (prop) > namelen
        &&  memcmp (prop, name, namelen) == 0
        &&  prop [namelen] == '=')
            return prop + namelen + 1;
        prop = zlist_next (self->props);
    }
    return "";
}


// Set message property. Property name cannot contain '='. Max length of
// value is 255 chars.
void
kvmsg_set_prop (kvmsg_t *self, char *name, char *format, ...)
{
    assert (strchr (name, '=') == NULL);

    char value [255 + 1];
    va_list args;
    assert (self);
    va_start (args, format);
    vsnprintf (value, 255, format, args);
    va_end (args);

    // Allocate name=value string
    char *prop = malloc (strlen (name) + strlen (value) + 2);

    // Remove existing property, if any
    sprintf (prop, "%s=", name);
```

```
        char *existing = zlist_first (self->props);
        while (existing) {
            if (memcmp (prop, existing, strlen (prop)) == 0) {
                self->props_size -= strlen (existing) + 1;
                zlist_remove (self->props, existing);
                free (existing);
                break;
            }
            existing = zlist_next (self->props);
        }
        //  Add new name=value property string
        strcat (prop, value);
        zlist_append (self->props, prop);
        self->props_size += strlen (prop) + 1;
}
```

The store method (Example 5-43) stores the key-value message into a hashmap, unless the key and value are both null. It nullifies the kvmsg reference so that the object is owned by the hashmap, not the caller.

Example 5-43. Key-value message class, full (kvmsg.c): store method

```
void
kvmsg_store (kvmsg_t **self_p, zhash_t *hash)
{
    assert (self_p);
    if (*self_p) {
        kvmsg_t *self = *self_p;
        assert (self);
        if (kvmsg_size (self)) {
            if (self->present [FRAME_KEY]
            &&  self->present [FRAME_BODY]) {
                zhash_update (hash, kvmsg_key (self), self);
                zhash_freefn (hash, kvmsg_key (self), kvmsg_free);
            }
        }
        else
            zhash_delete (hash, kvmsg_key (self));

        *self_p = NULL;
    }
}
```

The dump method (Example 5-44) extends the kvsimple implementation with support for message properties.

Example 5-44. Key-value message class, full (kvmsg.c): dump method

```
void
kvmsg_dump (kvmsg_t *self)
{
...
```

```
        fprintf (stderr, "[size:%zd] ", size);
        if (zlist_size (self->props)) {
            fprintf (stderr, "[");
            char *prop = zlist_first (self->props);
            while (prop) {
                fprintf (stderr, "%s;", prop);
                prop = zlist_next (self->props);
            }
            fprintf (stderr, "]");
        }
...
```

The selftest method, shown in Example 5-45, is the same as in kvsimple, with added support for the UUID and property features of kvmsg.

Example 5-45. Key-value message class, full (kvmsg.c): test method

```
int
kvmsg_test (int verbose)
{
...
    // Test send and receive of simple message
    kvmsg = kvmsg_new (1);
    kvmsg_set_key  (kvmsg, "key");
    kvmsg_set_uuid (kvmsg);
    kvmsg_set_body (kvmsg, (byte *) "body", 4);
    if (verbose)
        kvmsg_dump (kvmsg);
    kvmsg_send (kvmsg, output);
    kvmsg_store (&kvmsg, kvmap);

    kvmsg = kvmsg_recv (input);
    if (verbose)
        kvmsg_dump (kvmsg);
    assert (streq (kvmsg_key (kvmsg), "key"));
    kvmsg_store (&kvmsg, kvmap);

    // Test send and receive of message with properties
    kvmsg = kvmsg_new (2);
    kvmsg_set_prop (kvmsg, "prop1", "value1");
    kvmsg_set_prop (kvmsg, "prop2", "value1");
    kvmsg_set_prop (kvmsg, "prop2", "value2");
    kvmsg_set_key  (kvmsg, "key");
    kvmsg_set_uuid (kvmsg);
    kvmsg_set_body (kvmsg, (byte *) "body", 4);
    assert (streq (kvmsg_get_prop (kvmsg, "prop2"), "value2"));
    if (verbose)
        kvmsg_dump (kvmsg);
    kvmsg_send (kvmsg, output);
    kvmsg_destroy (&kvmsg);

    kvmsg = kvmsg_recv (input);
```

```
    if (verbose)
        kvmsg_dump (kvmsg);
    assert (streq (kvmsg_key (kvmsg), "key"));
    assert (streq (kvmsg_get_prop (kvmsg, "prop2"), "value2"));
    kvmsg_destroy (&kvmsg);
...
```

The Model Five client is almost identical to Model Four. It uses the full kvmsg class now, and sets a randomized ttl property (measured in seconds) on each message:

```
    kvmsg_set_prop (kvmsg, "ttl", "%d", randof (30));
```

Using a Reactor

Up until now, we have used a poll loop in the server. In this next model of the server, we switch to using a reactor. In C, we use CZMQ's zloop class. Using a reactor makes the code more verbose but easier to understand and build out, because each piece of the server is handled by a separate reactor handler.

We use a single thread and pass a server object around to the reactor handlers. We could have organized the server as multiple threads, each handling one socket or timer, but that works better when threads don't have to share data. In this case, all work is centered around the server's hashmap, so one thread is simpler.

There are three reactor handlers:

- One to handle snapshot requests coming on the ROUTER socket
- One to handle incoming updates from clients, coming on the PULL socket
- One to expire ephemeral values that have passed their TTL

The code for Model Five of the Clone server is shown in Example 5-46.

Example 5-46. Clone server, Model Five (clonesrv5.c)

```
//
//  Clone server - Model Five
//

//  Lets us build this source without creating a library
#include "kvmsg.c"

//  zloop reactor handlers
static int s_snapshots (zloop_t *loop, zmq_pollitem_t *poller, void *args);
static int s_collector (zloop_t *loop, zmq_pollitem_t *poller, void *args);
static int s_flush_ttl (zloop_t *loop, zmq_pollitem_t *poller, void *args);

//  Our server is defined by these properties
typedef struct {
    zctx_t *ctx;                    //  Context wrapper
    zhash_t *kvmap;                 //  Key-value store
```

```
    zloop_t *loop;                  //  zloop reactor
    int port;                       //  Main port we're working on
    int64_t sequence;               //  The number of updates we've completed
    void *snapshot;                 //  Handle snapshot requests
    void *publisher;                //  Publish updates to clients
    void *collector;                //  Collect updates from clients
} clonesrv_t;


int main (void)
{
    clonesrv_t *self = (clonesrv_t *) zmalloc (sizeof (clonesrv_t));

    self->port = 5556;
    self->ctx = zctx_new ();
    self->kvmap = zhash_new ();
    self->loop = zloop_new ();
    zloop_set_verbose (self->loop, FALSE);

    //  Set up our Clone server sockets
    self->snapshot  = zsocket_new (self->ctx, ZMQ_ROUTER);
    zsocket_bind (self->snapshot,  "tcp://*:%d", self->port);
    self->publisher = zsocket_new (self->ctx, ZMQ_PUB);
    zsocket_bind (self->publisher, "tcp://*:%d", self->port + 1);
    self->collector = zsocket_new (self->ctx, ZMQ_PULL);
    zsocket_bind (self->collector, "tcp://*:%d", self->port + 2);

    //  Register our handlers with reactor
    zmq_pollitem_t poller = { 0, 0, ZMQ_POLLIN };
    poller.socket = self->snapshot;
    zloop_poller (self->loop, &poller, s_snapshots, self);
    poller.socket = self->collector;
    zloop_poller (self->loop, &poller, s_collector, self);
    zloop_timer (self->loop, 1000, 0, s_flush_ttl, self);

    //  Run reactor until process interrupted
    zloop_start (self->loop);

    zloop_destroy (&self->loop);
    zhash_destroy (&self->kvmap);
    zctx_destroy (&self->ctx);
    free (self);
    return 0;
}
```

We handle ICANHAZ? requests by sending snapshot data to the client that requested it, as shown in Example 5-47.

Example 5-47. Clone server, Model Five (clonesrv5.c): send snapshots

```
//  Routing information for a key-value snapshot
typedef struct {
```

```
    void *socket;          //  ROUTER socket to send to
    zframe_t *identity;    //  Identity of peer who requested state
    char *subtree;         //  Client subtree specification
} kvroute_t;

//  We call this function for each key-value pair in our hash table
static int
s_send_single (const char *key, void *data, void *args)
{
    kvroute_t *kvroute = (kvroute_t *) args;
    kvmsg_t *kvmsg = (kvmsg_t *) data;
    if (strlen (kvroute->subtree) <= strlen (kvmsg_key (kvmsg))
    &&  memcmp (kvroute->subtree,
                kvmsg_key (kvmsg), strlen (kvroute->subtree)) == 0) {
        zframe_send (&kvroute->identity,     //  Choose recipient
            kvroute->socket, ZFRAME_MORE + ZFRAME_REUSE);
        kvmsg_send (kvmsg, kvroute->socket);
    }
    return 0;
}
```

Example 5-48 shows is the reactor handler for the snapshot socket; it accepts just the
ICANHAZ? request and replies with a state snapshot ending with a KTHXBAI message.

Example 5-48. Clone server, Model Five (clonesrv5.c): snapshot handler

```
static int
s_snapshots (zloop_t *loop, zmq_pollitem_t *poller, void *args)
{
    clonesrv_t *self = (clonesrv_t *) args;

    zframe_t *identity = zframe_recv (poller->socket);
    if (identity) {
        //  Request is in second frame of message
        char *request = zstr_recv (poller->socket);
        char *subtree = NULL;
        if (streq (request, "ICANHAZ?")) {
            free (request);
            subtree = zstr_recv (poller->socket);
        }
        else
            printf ("E: bad request, aborting\n");

        if (subtree) {
            //  Send state socket to client
            kvroute_t routing = { poller->socket, identity, subtree };
            zhash_foreach (self->kvmap, s_send_single, &routing);

            //  Now send END message with sequence number
            zclock_log ("I: sending shapshot=%d", (int) self->sequence);
            zframe_send (&identity, poller->socket, ZFRAME_MORE);
            kvmsg_t *kvmsg = kvmsg_new (self->sequence);
```

```
            kvmsg_set_key    (kvmsg, "KTHXBAI");
            kvmsg_set_body (kvmsg, (byte *) subtree, 0);
            kvmsg_send       (kvmsg, poller->socket);
            kvmsg_destroy (&kvmsg);
            free (subtree);
        }
        zframe_destroy(&identity);
    }
    return 0;
}
```

We store each update with a new sequence number and, if necessary, a time to live, as
shown in Example 5-49. We publish updates immediately on our publisher socket.

Example 5-49. Clone server, Model Five (clonesrv5.c): collect updates

```
static int
s_collector (zloop_t *loop, zmq_pollitem_t *poller, void *args)
{
    clonesrv_t *self = (clonesrv_t *) args;

    kvmsg_t *kvmsg = kvmsg_recv (poller->socket);
    if (kvmsg) {
        kvmsg_set_sequence (kvmsg, ++self->sequence);
        kvmsg_send (kvmsg, self->publisher);
        int ttl = atoi (kvmsg_get_prop (kvmsg, "ttl"));
        if (ttl)
            kvmsg_set_prop (kvmsg, "ttl",
                "%" PRId64, zclock_time () + ttl * 1000);
        kvmsg_store (&kvmsg, self->kvmap);
        zclock_log ("I: publishing update=%d", (int) self->sequence);
    }
    return 0;
}
```

At regular intervals, we flush ephemeral values that have expired (Example 5-50). This
could be slow on very large data sets.

Example 5-50. Clone server, Model Five (clonesrv5.c): flush ephemeral values

```
//  If key-value pair has expired, delete it and publish the
//  fact to listening clients
static int
s_flush_single (const char *key, void *data, void *args)
{
    clonesrv_t *self = (clonesrv_t *) args;

    kvmsg_t *kvmsg = (kvmsg_t *) data;
    int64_t ttl;
    sscanf (kvmsg_get_prop (kvmsg, "ttl"), "%" PRId64, &ttl);
    if (ttl && zclock_time () >= ttl) {
        kvmsg_set_sequence (kvmsg, ++self->sequence);
        kvmsg_set_body (kvmsg, (byte *) "", 0);
```

```
        kvmsg_send (kvmsg, self->publisher);
        kvmsg_store (&kvmsg, self->kvmap);
        zclock_log ("I: publishing delete=%d", (int) self->sequence);
    }
    return 0;
}

static int
s_flush_ttl (zloop_t *loop, zmq_pollitem_t *poller, void *args)
{
    clonesrv_t *self = (clonesrv_t *) args;
    if (self->kvmap)
        zhash_foreach (self->kvmap, s_flush_single, args);
    return 0;
}
```

Adding the Binary Star Pattern for Reliability

The Clone models we've explored up until now have been relatively simple. However, we're now going to get into unpleasantly complex territory, which has me getting up for another espresso. You should appreciate the fact that implementing "reliable" messaging is complex enough that you always need to ask, "Do we actually need this?" before jumping into it. If you can get away with being unreliable, or with "good enough" reliability, you can make a huge win in terms of cost and complexity. Sure, you may lose some data now and then. It is often a good trade-off. Having said, that, and... sips... because the espresso is really good, let's jump in.

As you play with the last model, you'll stop and restart the server. It might look like it recovers, but of course it's applying updates to an empty state instead of the proper current state. Any new client joining the network will only get the latest updates instead of the full historical record.

What we want is a way for the server to recover from being killed or crashing. We also need to provide backup in case the server is out of commission for any length of time. When people ask for "reliability," ask them to list the failures they want to handle. In our case, these are:

- The server process crashes and is automatically or manually restarted. The process loses its state and has to get it back from somewhere.

- The server machine dies and is offline for a significant time. Clients have to switch to an alternate server somewhere.

- The server process or machine gets disconnected from the network, such as when a switch dies or a data center gets knocked out. It may come back at some point, but in the meantime clients need an alternate server.

Our first step is to add a second server. We can use the Binary Star pattern from Chapter 6 to organize these into a primary and a backup. Binary Star is a reactor pattern, so it's useful that we've already refactored the last server model into a reactor style.

We need to ensure that updates are not lost if the primary server crashes. The simplest technique is to send them to both servers. The backup server can then act as a client and keep its state synchronized by receiving updates, as all clients do. It'll also get new updates from clients. It can't yet store these in its hash table, but it can hold onto them for a while.

So, Model Six introduces the following changes from Model Five:

- We use a pub-sub flow instead of a push-pull flow for client updates sent to the servers. This takes care of fanning out the updates to both servers. Otherwise, we'd have to use two DEALER sockets.

- We add heartbeats to server updates (to clients), so that a client can detect when the primary server has died. It can then switch over to the backup server.

- We connect the two servers using the Binary Star bstar reactor class. Binary Star relies on the clients to "vote" by making an explicit request to the server they consider "active." We'll use snapshot requests as the voting mechanism.

- We make all update messages uniquely identifiable by adding a UUID field. The client generates this, and the server propagates it back on republished updates.

- The passive server keeps a "pending list" of updates that it has received from clients but not yet from the active server, and updates it's received from the active server but not yet from the clients. The list is ordered from oldest to newest, so that it is easy to remove updates off the head.

It's useful to design the client logic as a finite-state machine. The client cycles through three states:

1. The client opens and connects its sockets, and then requests a snapshot from the first server. To avoid request storms, it will ask any given server only twice. One request might get lost, which would be bad luck. Two getting lost would be carelessness.

2. The client waits for a reply (snapshot data) from the current server and, if it gets it, stores it. If there is no reply within some timeout, it fails over to the next server.

3. When the client has gotten its snapshot, it waits for and processes updates. Again, if it doesn't hear anything from the server within some timeout, it fails over to the next server.

The client loops forever. It's quite likely during startup or failover that some clients may be trying to talk to the primary server while others are trying to talk to the backup server.

The Binary Star state machine handles this (Figure 5-6), hopefully accurately. It's hard to prove software correct; instead, we hammer it until we can't prove it wrong.

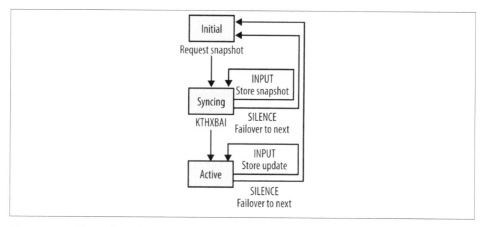

Figure 5-6. Clone client finite-state machine

Failover happens as follows:

- The client detects that primary server is no longer sending heartbeats, and concludes it has died. The client connects to the backup server and requests a new state snapshot.
- The backup server starts to receive snapshot requests from clients, and detects that primary server has gone, so it takes over as primary.
- The backup server applies its pending list to its own hash table, and then starts to process state snapshot requests.

When the primary server comes back online, it will:

- Start up as passive server, and connect to the backup server as a Clone client.
- Start to receive updates from clients, via its SUB socket.

We make a few assumptions:

- At least one server will keep running. If both servers crash, we lose all server state and there's no way to recover it.
- Multiple clients do not update the same hash keys at the same time. Client updates will arrive at the two servers in a different order. Therefore, the backup server may apply updates from its pending list in a different order than the primary server

would or did. Updates from one client will always arrive in the same order on both servers, so that is safe.

Thus the architecture for our high-availability server pair using the Binary Star pattern has two servers and a set of clients that talk to both servers (Figure 5-7).

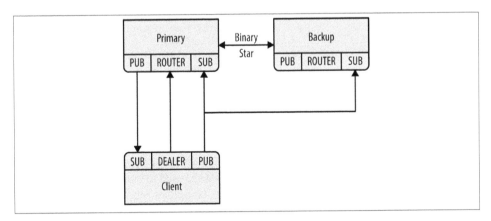

Figure 5-7. High-availability Clone server pair

Examples 5-51 through 5-58 present the sixth and last model of the Clone server.

Example 5-51. Clone server, Model Six (clonesrv6.c)

```
//
//  Clone server - Model Six
//

//  Lets us build this source without creating a library
#include "bstar.c"
#include "kvmsg.c"
```

In Example 5-52, we define a set of reactor handlers and our server object structure.

Example 5-52. Clone server, Model Six (clonesrv6.c): definitions

```
//  bstar reactor handlers
static int s_snapshots   (zloop_t *loop, zmq_pollitem_t *poller, void *args);
static int s_collector   (zloop_t *loop, zmq_pollitem_t *poller, void *args);
static int s_flush_ttl   (zloop_t *loop, zmq_pollitem_t *poller, void *args);
static int s_send_hugz   (zloop_t *loop, zmq_pollitem_t *poller, void *args);
static int s_new_active  (zloop_t *loop, zmq_pollitem_t *poller, void *args);
static int s_new_passive (zloop_t *loop, zmq_pollitem_t *poller, void *args);
static int s_subscriber  (zloop_t *loop, zmq_pollitem_t *poller, void *args);

//  Our server is defined by these properties
typedef struct {
    zctx_t *ctx;                // Context wrapper
```

```
    zhash_t *kvmap;              //  Key-value store
    bstar_t *bstar;              //  bstar reactor core
    int64_t sequence;            //  How many updates we're at
    int port;                    //  Main port we're working on
    int peer;                    //  Main port of our peer
    void *publisher;             //  Publish updates and hugz
    void *collector;             //  Collect updates from clients
    void *subscriber;            //  Get updates from peer
    zlist_t *pending;            //  Pending updates from clients
    Bool primary;                //  TRUE if we're primary
    Bool active;                 //  TRUE if we're active
    Bool passive;                //  TRUE if we're passive
} clonesrv_t;
```

The main task parses the command line to decide whether to start as a primary or backup
server. We're using the Binary Star pattern for reliability. This interconnects the two
servers so they can agree on which one is the primary and which one is the backup. To
allow the two servers to run on the same box, we use different ports for the primary and
backup, as shown in Example 5-53. Ports 5003/5004 are used to interconnect the servers.
Ports 5556/5566 are used to receive voting events (snapshot requests in the clone pattern). Ports 5557/5567 are used by the publisher, and ports 5558/5568 are used by the
collector.

Example 5-53. Clone server, Model Six (clonesrv6.c): main task setup

```
int main (int argc, char *argv [])
{
    clonesrv_t *self = (clonesrv_t *) zmalloc (sizeof (clonesrv_t));
    if (argc == 2 && streq (argv [1], "-p")) {
        zclock_log ("I: primary active, waiting for backup (passive)");
        self->bstar = bstar_new (BSTAR_PRIMARY, "tcp://*:5003",
                                 "tcp://localhost:5004");
        bstar_voter (self->bstar, "tcp://*:5556", ZMQ_ROUTER, s_snapshots, self);
        self->port = 5556;
        self->peer = 5566;
        self->primary = TRUE;
    }
    else
    if (argc == 2 && streq (argv [1], "-b")) {
        zclock_log ("I: backup passive, waiting for primary (active)");
        self->bstar = bstar_new (BSTAR_BACKUP, "tcp://*:5004",
                                 "tcp://localhost:5003");
        bstar_voter (self->bstar, "tcp://*:5566", ZMQ_ROUTER, s_snapshots, self);
        self->port = 5566;
        self->peer = 5556;
        self->primary = FALSE;
    }
    else {
        printf ("Usage: clonesrv4 { -p | -b }\n");
        free (self);
        exit (0);
    }
```

```
}
// Primary server will become first active
if (self->primary)
    self->kvmap = zhash_new ();

self->ctx = zctx_new ();
self->pending = zlist_new ();
bstar_set_verbose (self->bstar, TRUE);

// Set up our clone server sockets
self->publisher = zsocket_new (self->ctx, ZMQ_PUB);
self->collector = zsocket_new (self->ctx, ZMQ_SUB);
zsockopt_set_subscribe (self->collector, "");
zsocket_bind (self->publisher, "tcp://*:%d", self->port + 1);
zsocket_bind (self->collector, "tcp://*:%d", self->port + 2);

// Set up our own clone client interface to peer
self->subscriber = zsocket_new (self->ctx, ZMQ_SUB);
zsockopt_set_subscribe (self->subscriber, "");
zsocket_connect (self->subscriber, "tcp://localhost:%d", self->peer + 1);
```

After we've set up our sockets, we register our Binary Star event handlers and then start the bstar reactor. This finishes when the user presses Ctrl-C or when the process receives a SIGINT interrupt. The main task body is shown in Example 5-54.

Example 5-54. Clone server, Model Six (clonesrv6.c): main task body

```
// Register state change handlers
bstar_new_active (self->bstar, s_new_active, self);
bstar_new_passive (self->bstar, s_new_passive, self);

// Register our other handlers with the bstar reactor
zmq_pollitem_t poller = { self->collector, 0, ZMQ_POLLIN };
zloop_poller (bstar_zloop (self->bstar), &poller, s_collector, self);
zloop_timer  (bstar_zloop (self->bstar), 1000, 0, s_flush_ttl, self);
zloop_timer  (bstar_zloop (self->bstar), 1000, 0, s_send_hugz, self);

// Start the bstar reactor
bstar_start (self->bstar);

// Interrupted, so shut down
while (zlist_size (self->pending)) {
    kvmsg_t *kvmsg = (kvmsg_t *) zlist_pop (self->pending);
    kvmsg_destroy (&kvmsg);
}
zlist_destroy (&self->pending);
bstar_destroy (&self->bstar);
zhash_destroy (&self->kvmap);
zctx_destroy (&self->ctx);
free (self);

return 0;
```

```
}

// We handle ICANHAZ? requests exactly as in the clonesrv5 example.
...
```

The collector (Example 5-55) is more complex than in the *clonesrv5* example because the way in which it processes updates depends on whether the server is active or passive. The active server applies them immediately to its kvmap, whereas the passive one queues them as pending.

Example 5-55. Clone server, Model Six (clonesrv6.c): collect updates

```
// If message was already on pending list, remove it and return TRUE;
// else return FALSE
static int
s_was_pending (clonesrv_t *self, kvmsg_t *kvmsg)
{
    kvmsg_t *held = (kvmsg_t *) zlist_first (self->pending);
    while (held) {
        if (memcmp (kvmsg_uuid (kvmsg),
                    kvmsg_uuid (held), sizeof (uuid_t)) == 0) {
            zlist_remove (self->pending, held);
            return TRUE;
        }
        held = (kvmsg_t *) zlist_next (self->pending);
    }
    return FALSE;
}

static int
s_collector (zloop_t *loop, zmq_pollitem_t *poller, void *args)
{
    clonesrv_t *self = (clonesrv_t *) args;

    kvmsg_t *kvmsg = kvmsg_recv (poller->socket);
    if (kvmsg) {
        if (self->active) {
            kvmsg_set_sequence (kvmsg, ++self->sequence);
            kvmsg_send (kvmsg, self->publisher);
            int ttl = atoi (kvmsg_get_prop (kvmsg, "ttl"));
            if (ttl)
                kvmsg_set_prop (kvmsg, "ttl",
                    "%" PRId64, zclock_time () + ttl * 1000);
            kvmsg_store (&kvmsg, self->kvmap);
            zclock_log ("I: publishing update=%d", (int) self->sequence);
        }
        else {
            // If we already got message from active, drop it; else
            // hold on pending list
            if (s_was_pending (self, kvmsg))
                kvmsg_destroy (&kvmsg);
            else
```

```
            zlist_append (self->pending, kvmsg);
        }
    }
    return 0;
}


//  We purge ephemeral values using exactly the same code as in
//  the previous clonesrv5 example
...
```

We send a HUGZ message once a second to all subscribers so that they can detect if our server dies (Example 5-56). They'll then switch over to the backup server, which will become active.

Example 5-56. Clone server, Model Six (clonesrv6.c): heartbeating

```
static int
s_send_hugz (zloop_t *loop, zmq_pollitem_t *poller, void *args)
{
    clonesrv_t *self = (clonesrv_t *) args;

    kvmsg_t *kvmsg = kvmsg_new (self->sequence);
    kvmsg_set_key  (kvmsg, "HUGZ");
    kvmsg_set_body (kvmsg, (byte *) "", 0);
    kvmsg_send     (kvmsg, self->publisher);
    kvmsg_destroy (&kvmsg);

    return 0;
}
```

When we switch from passive to active, we apply our pending list so that our kvmap is up-to-date. When we switch to passive, we wipe our kvmap and grab a new snapshot from the active process. Example 5-57 illustrates.

Example 5-57. Clone server, Model Six (clonesrv6.c): handling state changes

```
static int
s_new_active (zloop_t *loop, zmq_pollitem_t *unused, void *args)
{
    clonesrv_t *self = (clonesrv_t *) args;

    self->active = TRUE;
    self->passive = FALSE;

    //  Stop subscribing to updates
    zmq_pollitem_t poller = { self->subscriber, 0, ZMQ_POLLIN };
    zloop_poller_end (bstar_zloop (self->bstar), &poller);

    //  Apply pending list to own hash table
    while (zlist_size (self->pending)) {
        kvmsg_t *kvmsg = (kvmsg_t *) zlist_pop (self->pending);
        kvmsg_set_sequence (kvmsg, ++self->sequence);
```

```
        kvmsg_send (kvmsg, self->publisher);
        kvmsg_store (&kvmsg, self->kvmap);
        zclock_log ("I: publishing pending=%d", (int) self->sequence);
    }
    return 0;
}

static int
s_new_passive (zloop_t *loop, zmq_pollitem_t *unused, void *args)
{
    clonesrv_t *self = (clonesrv_t *) args;

    zhash_destroy (&self->kvmap);
    self->active = FALSE;
    self->passive = TRUE;

    //  Start subscribing to updates
    zmq_pollitem_t poller = { self->subscriber, 0, ZMQ_POLLIN };
    zloop_poller (bstar_zloop (self->bstar), &poller, s_subscriber, self);

    return 0;
}
```

When we get an update, we create a new kvmap if necessary, and then add our update
to our kvmap (Example 5-58). We're always passive in this case.

Example 5-58. Clone server, Model Six (clonesrv6.c): subscriber handler

```
static int
s_subscriber (zloop_t *loop, zmq_pollitem_t *poller, void *args)
{
    clonesrv_t *self = (clonesrv_t *) args;
    //  Get state snapshot if necessary
    if (self->kvmap == NULL) {
        self->kvmap = zhash_new ();
        void *snapshot = zsocket_new (self->ctx, ZMQ_DEALER);
        zsocket_connect (snapshot, "tcp://localhost:%d", self->peer);
        zclock_log ("I: asking for snapshot from: tcp://localhost:%d",
                    self->peer);
        zstr_sendm (snapshot, "ICANHAZ?");
        zstr_send (snapshot, ""); // blank subtree to get all
        while (true) {
            kvmsg_t *kvmsg = kvmsg_recv (snapshot);
            if (!kvmsg)
                break;          //  Interrupted
            if (streq (kvmsg_key (kvmsg), "KTHXBAI")) {
                self->sequence = kvmsg_sequence (kvmsg);
                kvmsg_destroy (&kvmsg);
                break;          //  Done
            }
            kvmsg_store (&kvmsg, self->kvmap);
        }
```

```
        zclock_log ("I: received snapshot=%d", (int) self->sequence);
        zsocket_destroy (self->ctx, snapshot);
    }
    //  Find and remove update from pending list
    kvmsg_t *kvmsg = kvmsg_recv (poller->socket);
    if (!kvmsg)
        return 0;

    if (strneq (kvmsg_key (kvmsg), "HUGZ")) {
        if (!s_was_pending (self, kvmsg)) {
            //  If active update came before client update, flip it
            //  around, store active update (with sequence) on pending
            //  list, and use it to clear client update when it comes later
            zlist_append (self->pending, kvmsg_dup (kvmsg));
        }
        //  If update is more recent than our kvmap, apply it
        if (kvmsg_sequence (kvmsg) > self->sequence) {
            self->sequence = kvmsg_sequence (kvmsg);
            kvmsg_store (&kvmsg, self->kvmap);
            zclock_log ("I: received update=%d", (int) self->sequence);
        }
        else
            kvmsg_destroy (&kvmsg);
    }
    else
        kvmsg_destroy (&kvmsg);

    return 0;
}
```

This model is only a few hundred lines of code, but it took quite a while to get working. To be accurate, building Model Six took about a full week of "Sweet god, this is just too complex for the book" hacking. We've assembled pretty much everything and the kitchen sink into this small application. We have failover, ephemeral values, subtrees, and so on. What surprised me was that the up-front design was pretty accurate. Still, the details of writing and debugging so many socket flows are quite challenging.

The reactor-based design removes a lot of the grunt work from the code, and what remains is simpler and easier to understand. We reuse the bstar reactor from Chapter 4. The whole server runs as one thread, so there's no inter-thread weirdness going on—just a structure pointer (self) passed around to all handlers, which can do their thing happily. One nice side effect of using reactors is that the code, being less tightly integrated into a poll loop, is much easier to reuse. Large chunks of Model Six are taken from Model Five.

I built it piece by piece, and got each piece working *properly* before going onto the next one. Because there are four or five main socket flows, that meant quite a lot of debugging and testing. I debugged just by dumping messages to the console. Don't use classic debuggers to step through ØMQ applications; you need to see the message flows to make any sense of what is going on.

For testing, I always try to use valgrind, which catches memory leaks and invalid memory accesses. In C, this is a major concern, as you can't delegate to a garbage collector. Using proper and consistent abstractions like kvmsg and CZMQ helps enormously.

The Clustered Hashmap Protocol

While the Model Six server is pretty much a mashup of the previous model plus the Binary Star pattern, the client is quite a lot more complex. But before we get to that, let's look at the final protocol. I've written this up as a specification on the ZeroMQ RFC website as the Clustered Hashmap Protocol (CHP) (*http://rfc.zeromq.org/spec:12*).

Roughly, there are two ways to design a complex protocol such as this one. One way is to separate each flow into its own set of sockets. This is the approach we used here. The advantage is that each flow is simple and clean. The disadvantage is that managing multiple socket flows at once can be quite complex. Using a reactor makes it simpler, but still, it makes a lot of moving pieces that have to fit together correctly.

The second way to make such a protocol is to use a single socket pair for everything. In this case I'd have used ROUTER for the server and DEALER for the clients, and then done everything over that connection. It makes for a more complex protocol, but at least the complexity is all in one place. In Chapter 7 we'll look at an example of a protocol done over a ROUTER-DEALER combination.

Let's read through the CHP specification now. This text is taken directly from the RFC. Note that "SHOULD" and "MUST" are keywords that we use in protocol specifications to indicate requirement levels.

Goals

CHP is meant to provide a basis for reliable pub-sub across a cluster of clients connected over a ØMQ network. It defines a "hashmap" abstraction consisting of key-value pairs. Any client can modify any key-value pair at any time, and changes are propagated to all clients. A client can join the network at any time.

Architecture

CHP connects a set of client applications and a set of servers. Clients connect to the server. Clients do not see each other. Clients can come and go arbitrarily.

Ports and Connections

The server MUST open three ports as follows:

- A SNAPSHOT port (ØMQ ROUTER socket) at port number P.

- A PUBLISHER port (ØMQ PUB socket) at port number P + 1.
- A COLLECTOR port (ØMQ SUB socket) at port number P + 2.

The client SHOULD open at least two connections:

- A SNAPSHOT connection (ØMQ DEALER socket) to port number P.
- A SUBSCRIBER connection (ØMQ SUB socket) to port number P + 1.

The client MAY open a third connection, if it wants to update the hashmap:

- A PUBLISHER connection (ØMQ PUB socket) to port number P + 2.

This extra frame is not shown in the commands explained below.

State Synchronization

The client MUST start by sending an ICANHAZ command to its snapshot connection. This command consists of two frames as follows:

```
ICANHAZ command
-----------------------------------
        Frame 0: "ICANHAZ?"
        Frame 1: subtree specification
```

Both frames are ØMQ strings. The subtree specification MAY be empty. If not empty, it consists of a slash followed by one or more path segments, ending in a slash.

The server MUST respond to an ICANHAZ command by sending zero or more KVSYNC commands to its snapshot port, followed with a KTHXBAI command. The server MUST prefix each command with the identity of the client, as provided by ØMQ with the ICANHAZ command. The KVSYNC command specifies a single key-value pair as follows:

```
KVSYNC command
-----------------------------------
        Frame 0: key, as 0MQ string
        Frame 1: sequence number, 8 bytes in network order
        Frame 2: <empty>
        Frame 3: <empty>
        Frame 4: value, as blob
```

The sequence number has no significance and may be zero.

The KTHXBAI command takes this form:

```
KTHXBAI command
-----------------------------------
        Frame 0: "KTHXBAI"
        Frame 1: sequence number, 8 bytes in network order
        Frame 2: <empty>
```

```
Frame 3: <empty>
Frame 4: subtree specification
```

The sequence number MUST be the highest sequence number of the KVSYNC commands previously sent.

When the client has received a KTHXBAI command it SHOULD start to receive messages from its subscriber connection, and apply them.

Server-to-Client Updates

When the server has an update for its hashmap it MUST broadcast this on its publisher socket as a KVPUB command. The KVPUB command has this form:

```
KVPUB command
------------------------------------
Frame 0: key, as 0MQ string
Frame 1: sequence number, 8 bytes in network order
Frame 2: UUID, 16 bytes
Frame 3: properties, as 0MQ string
Frame 4: value, as blob
```

The sequence number MUST be strictly incremental. The client MUST discard any KVPUB command whose sequence numbers are not strictly greater than the last KTHXBAI or KVPUB command received.

The UUID is optional and frame 2 MAY be empty (size zero). The properties field is formatted as zero or more instances of *name=value* followed by a newline character. If the key-value pair has no properties, the properties field is empty.

If the value is empty, the client SHOULD delete its key-value entry with the specified key.

In the absence of other updates the server SHOULD send a HUGZ command at regular intervals, e.g., once per second. The HUGZ command has this format:

```
HUGZ command
------------------------------------
Frame 0: "HUGZ"
Frame 1: 00000000
Frame 2: <empty>
Frame 3: <empty>
Frame 4: <empty>
```

The client MAY treat the absence of HUGZ as an indicator that the server has crashed; see "Reliability" below.

Client-to-Server Updates

When the client has an update for its hashmap, it MAY send this to the server via its publisher connection as a KVSET command. The KVSET command has this form:

```
KVSET command
------------------------------------
    Frame 0: key, as 0MQ string
    Frame 1: sequence number, 8 bytes in network order
    Frame 2: UUID, 16 bytes
    Frame 3: properties, as 0MQ string
    Frame 4: value, as blob
```

The sequence number has no significance and may be zero. The UUID SHOULD be a universally unique identifier, if a reliable server architecture is used.

If the value is empty, the server MUST delete its key-value entry with the specified key.

The server SHOULD accept the following properties:

- ttl - specifies a time-to-live in seconds. If the KVSET command has a `ttl` property, the server SHOULD delete the key-value pair and broadcast a KVPUB with an empty value in order to delete this from all clients when the TTL has expired.

Reliability

CHP may be used in a dual-server configuration where a backup server takes over if the primary server fails. CHP does not specify the mechanisms used for this failover, but the Binary Star pattern from Chapter 4 may be helpful.

To assist server reliability, the client MAY:

- Set a UUID in every KVSET command.
- Detect the lack of HUGZ over a time period and use this as an indicator that the current server has failed.
- Connect to a backup server and re-request a state synchronization.

Scalability and Performance

CHP is designed to be scalable to large numbers (thousands) of clients, limited only by system resources on the broker. Since all updates pass through a single server the overall throughput will be limited to some millions of updates per second, at peak, and probably less.

Security

CHP does not implement any authentication, access control, or encryption mechanisms and should not be used in any deployment where these are required.

Building a Multithreaded Stack and API

The client stack we've used so far isn't smart enough to handle this protocol properly. As soon as we start doing heartbeats, we need a client stack that can run in a background thread. In the Freelance pattern at the end of Chapter 4, we used a multithreaded API but didn't explain it in detail. It turns out that multithreaded APIs are quite useful when you start to make more complex ØMQ protocols, like CHP.

If you make a nontrivial protocol and you expect applications to implement it properly, most developers will get it wrong most of the time. You're going to be left with a lot of unhappy people complaining that your protocol is too complex, too fragile, and too hard to use. Whereas if you give them a simple API to call, you have some chance of them buying in.

Our multithreaded API consists of a frontend object and a background agent, connected by two PAIR sockets (Figure 5-8). Connecting two PAIR sockets like this is so useful that your high-level binding should probably do what CZMQ does, which is package a "create new thread with a pipe that I can use to send messages to it" method.

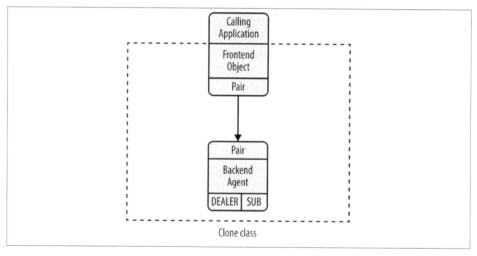

Figure 5-8. Multithreaded API

The multithreaded APIs that we see in this book all take the same form:

- The constructor for the object (clone_new()) creates a context and starts a background thread connected with a pipe. It holds onto one end of the pipe so it can send commands to the background thread.

- The background thread starts an *agent* that is essentially a zmq_poll() loop reading from the pipe socket, and any other sockets (here, the DEALER and SUB sockets).

- The main application thread and the background thread now communicate only via ØMQ messages. By convention, the frontend sends string commands so that each method on the class turns into a message sent to the backend agent, like this:

```
void
clone_connect (clone_t *self, char *address, char *service)
{
    assert (self);
    zmsg_t *msg = zmsg_new ();
    zmsg_addstr (msg, "CONNECT");
    zmsg_addstr (msg, address);
    zmsg_addstr (msg, service);
    zmsg_send (&msg, self->pipe);
}
```

- If the method needs a return code, it can wait for a reply message from the agent.
- If the agent needs to send asynchronous events back to the frontend, we add a recv method to the class, which waits for messages on the frontend pipe.
- We may want to expose the frontend pipe socket handle to allow the class to be integrated into further poll loops. Otherwise, any recv method would block the application.

The clone class has the same structure as the flcliapi class from Chapter 4 and adds the logic from the last model of the Clone client. Without ØMQ, this kind of multi-threaded API design would have required weeks of really hard work. With ØMQ, it only took a day or two of work.

The actual API methods for the clone class are quite simple:

```
// Create a new clone class instance
clone_t *
    clone_new (void);

// Destroy a clone class instance
void
    clone_destroy (clone_t **self_p);

// Define the subtree, if any, for this clone class
void
    clone_subtree (clone_t *self, char *subtree);

// Connect the clone class to one server
void
    clone_connect (clone_t *self, char *address, char *service);

// Set a value in the shared hashmap
void
    clone_set (clone_t *self, char *key, char *value, int ttl);
```

```
        // Get a value from the shared hashmap
        char *
            clone_get (clone_t *self, char *key);
```

Example 5-59 presents the Clone client, which has now become just a thin shell using the clone cl.

Example 5-59. Clone client, Model Six (clonecli6.c)

```
// Clone client Model Six
#include "clone.c"
#define SUBTREE "/client/"
int main (void)
{
    // Create distributed hash instance
    clone_t *clone = clone_new ();
    // Specify configuration
    clone_subtree (clone, SUBTREE);
    clone_connect (clone, "tcp://localhost", "5556");
    clone_connect (clone, "tcp://localhost", "5566");
    // Set random tuples into the distributed hash
    while (!zctx_interrupted) {
        // Set random value, check it was stored
        char key [255];
        char value [10];
        sprintf (key, "%s%d", SUBTREE, randof (10000));
        sprintf (value, "%d", randof (1000000));
        clone_set (clone, key, value, randof (30));
        sleep (1);
    }
    clone_destroy (&clone);
    return 0;
}
```

Note the connect method, which specifies one server endpoint. Under the hood, we're in fact talking to three ports. However, as the CHP specifies, the three ports are on consecutive port numbers:

- The server state router (ROUTER) is at port P.
- The server updates publisher (PUB) is at port P + 1.
- The server updates subscriber (SUB) is at port P + 2.

So we can fold the three connections into one logical operation (which we implement as three separate ØMQ connect calls).

Let's end with the source code for the clone stack. This is a complex piece of code, but it's easier to understand when you break it into the frontend object class and the backend agent. The frontend sends string commands ("SUBTREE", "CONNECT", "SET", "GET") to the agent, which handles these commands as well as talking to the server(s). Here is the agent's logic:

1. Start up by getting a snapshot from the first server.
2. When we get a snapshot, switch to reading from the subscriber socket.
3. If we don't get a snapshot, then fail over to the second server.
4. Poll on the pipe and the subscriber socket.
5. If we got input on the pipe, handle the control message from the frontend object.
6. If we got input on the subscriber, store or apply the update.
7. If we didn't get anything from the server within a certain time, fail over.
8. Repeat until the process is interrupted by Ctrl-C.

And here is the actual clone class implementation. The structure of the class is given in Example 5-60.

Example 5-60. Clone class (clone.c)

```
/*  =====================================================================
 *  clone - clone client API stack (multithreaded)
 *  =====================================================================  */

#include "clone.h"

//  If no server replies within this time, abandon request
#define GLOBAL_TIMEOUT  4000    //  msec


//  =====================================================================
//  Synchronous part, works in our application thread

//  ---------------------------------------------------------------------
//  Structure of our class

struct _clone_t {
    zctx_t *ctx;                //  Our context wrapper
    void *pipe;                 //  Pipe through to clone agent
};

//  This is the thread that handles our real clone class
static void clone_agent (void *args, zctx_t *ctx, void *pipe);
```

Example 5-61 presents the constructor and destructor for the clone class. Note that we create a context specifically for the pipe that connects our frontend to the backend agent.

Example 5-61. Clone class (clone.c): constructor and destructor

```
clone_t *
clone_new (void)
```

```
{
    clone_t
        *self;

    self = (clone_t *) zmalloc (sizeof (clone_t));
    self->ctx = zctx_new ();
    self->pipe = zthread_fork (self->ctx, clone_agent, NULL);
    return self;
}

void
clone_destroy (clone_t **self_p)
{
    assert (self_p);
    if (*self_p) {
        clone_t *self = *self_p;
        zctx_destroy (&self->ctx);
        free (self);
        *self_p = NULL;
    }
}
```

The subtree method in Example 5-62 specifies a subtree for snapshots and updates, which we must do before connecting to a server as the subtree specification is sent as the first command to the server. This method sends a [SUBTREE][subtree] command to the agent.

Example 5-62. Clone class (clone.c): subtree method

```
void clone_subtree (clone_t *self, char *subtree)
{
    assert (self);
    zmsg_t *msg = zmsg_new ();
    zmsg_addstr (msg, "SUBTREE");
    zmsg_addstr (msg, subtree);
    zmsg_send (&msg, self->pipe);
}
```

The connect method (Example 5-63) connects to a new server endpoint. We can connect to at most two servers. This method sends a [CONNECT][endpoint][service] command to the agent.

Example 5-63. Clone class (clone.c): connect method

```
void
clone_connect (clone_t *self, char *address, char *service)
{
    assert (self);
    zmsg_t *msg = zmsg_new ();
    zmsg_addstr (msg, "CONNECT");
    zmsg_addstr (msg, address);
    zmsg_addstr (msg, service);
```

```
    zmsg_send (&msg, self->pipe);
}
```

The set method (Example 5-64) sets a new value in the shared hashmap. It sends a
[SET][key][value][ttl] command through to the agent, which does the actual work.

Example 5-64. Clone class (clone.c): set method

```
void
clone_set (clone_t *self, char *key, char *value, int ttl)
{
    char ttlstr [10];
    sprintf (ttlstr, "%d", ttl);

    assert (self);
    zmsg_t *msg = zmsg_new ();
    zmsg_addstr (msg, "SET");
    zmsg_addstr (msg, key);
    zmsg_addstr (msg, value);
    zmsg_addstr (msg, ttlstr);
    zmsg_send (&msg, self->pipe);
}
```

The get method (Example 5-65) looks up a value in the distributed hash table. It sends
a [GET][key] command to the agent and waits for a value response. If there is no value
available, this method will eventually return NULL.

Example 5-65. Clone class (clone.c): get method

```
char *
clone_get (clone_t *self, char *key)
{
    assert (self);
    assert (key);
    zmsg_t *msg = zmsg_new ();
    zmsg_addstr (msg, "GET");
    zmsg_addstr (msg, key);
    zmsg_send (&msg, self->pipe);

    zmsg_t *reply = zmsg_recv (self->pipe);
    if (reply) {
        char *value = zmsg_popstr (reply);
        zmsg_destroy (&reply);
        return value;
    }
    return NULL;
}
```

The backend agent manages a set of servers, which we implement using our simple class
model, as shown in Example 5-66.

Example 5-66. Clone class (clone.c): working with servers

```
typedef struct {
    char *address;              //  Server address
    int port;                   //  Server port
    void *snapshot;             //  Snapshot socket
    void *subscriber;           //  Incoming updates
    uint64_t expiry;            //  When server expires
    uint requests;              //  How many snapshot requests made?
} server_t;

static server_t *
server_new (zctx_t *ctx, char *address, int port, char *subtree)
{
    server_t *self = (server_t *) zmalloc (sizeof (server_t));

    zclock_log ("I: adding server %s:%d...", address, port);
    self->address = strdup (address);
    self->port = port;

    self->snapshot = zsocket_new (ctx, ZMQ_DEALER);
    zsocket_connect (self->snapshot, "%s:%d", address, port);
    self->subscriber = zsocket_new (ctx, ZMQ_SUB);
    zsocket_connect (self->subscriber, "%s:%d", address, port + 1);
    zsockopt_set_subscribe (self->subscriber, subtree);
    return self;
}

static void
server_destroy (server_t **self_p)
{
    assert (self_p);
    if (*self_p) {
        server_t *self = *self_p;
        free (self->address);
        free (self);
        *self_p = NULL;
    }
}
```

Example 5-67 shows the implementation of the backend agent itself.

Example 5-67. Clone class (clone.c): backend agent class

```
//  Number of servers we will talk to
#define SERVER_MAX      2

//  Server considered dead if silent for this long
#define SERVER_TTL      5000    //  msec

//  States we can be in
#define STATE_INITIAL       0   //  Before asking server for state
#define STATE_SYNCING       1   //  Getting state from server
```

```
#define STATE_ACTIVE        2   //  Getting new updates from server

typedef struct {
    zctx_t *ctx;                    //  Context wrapper
    void *pipe;                     //  Pipe back to application
    zhash_t *kvmap;                 //  Actual key/value table
    char *subtree;                  //  Subtree specification, if any
    server_t *server [SERVER_MAX];
    uint nbr_servers;               //  0 to SERVER_MAX
    uint state;                     //  Current state
    uint cur_server;                //  If active, server 0 or 1
    int64_t sequence;               //  Last kvmsg processed
    void *publisher;                //  Outgoing updates
} agent_t;

static agent_t *
agent_new (zctx_t *ctx, void *pipe)
{
    agent_t *self = (agent_t *) zmalloc (sizeof (agent_t));
    self->ctx = ctx;
    self->pipe = pipe;
    self->kvmap = zhash_new ();
    self->subtree = strdup ("");
    self->state = STATE_INITIAL;
    self->publisher = zsocket_new (self->ctx, ZMQ_PUB);
    return self;
}

static void
agent_destroy (agent_t **self_p)
{
    assert (self_p);
    if (*self_p) {
        agent_t *self = *self_p;
        int server_nbr;
        for (server_nbr = 0; server_nbr < self->nbr_servers; server_nbr++)
            server_destroy (&self->server [server_nbr]);
        zhash_destroy (&self->kvmap);
        free (self->subtree);
        free (self);
        *self_p = NULL;
    }
}
```

The code in Example 5-68 handles the different control messages from the frontend—
SUBTREE, CONNECT, SET, and GET:

Example 5-68. Clone class (clone.c): handling a control message

```
static int
agent_control_message (agent_t *self)
{
```

```
zmsg_t *msg = zmsg_recv (self->pipe);
char *command = zmsg_popstr (msg);
if (command == NULL)
    return -1;        //  Interrupted

if (streq (command, "SUBTREE")) {
    free (self->subtree);
    self->subtree = zmsg_popstr (msg);
}
else
if (streq (command, "CONNECT")) {
    char *address = zmsg_popstr (msg);
    char *service = zmsg_popstr (msg);
    if (self->nbr_servers < SERVER_MAX) {
        self->server [self->nbr_servers++] = server_new (
            self->ctx, address, atoi (service), self->subtree);
        //  We broadcast updates to all known servers
        zsocket_connect (self->publisher, "%s:%d",
            address, atoi (service) + 2);
    }
    else
        zclock_log ("E: too many servers (max. %d)", SERVER_MAX);
    free (address);
    free (service);
}
else
```

When we set a property, we push the new key-value pair onto all our connected servers,
as illustrated in Example 5-69.

Example 5-69. Clone class (clone.c): set and get commands

```
    char *key = zmsg_popstr (msg);
    char *value = zmsg_popstr (msg);
    char *ttl = zmsg_popstr (msg);
    zhash_update (self->kvmap, key, (byte *) value);
    zhash_freefn (self->kvmap, key, free);

    //  Send key-value pair on to server
    kvmsg_t *kvmsg = kvmsg_new (0);
    kvmsg_set_key  (kvmsg, key);
    kvmsg_set_uuid (kvmsg);
    kvmsg_fmt_body (kvmsg, "%s", value);
    kvmsg_set_prop (kvmsg, "ttl", ttl);
    kvmsg_send     (kvmsg, self->publisher);
    kvmsg_destroy (&kvmsg);
    free (ttl);
    free (key);                 //  Value is owned by hash table
}
else
if (streq (command, "GET")) {
    char *key = zmsg_popstr (msg);
```

```
        char *value = zhash_lookup (self->kvmap, key);
        if (value)
            zstr_send (self->pipe, value);
        else
            zstr_send (self->pipe, "");
        free (key);
        free (value);
    }
    free (command);
    zmsg_destroy (&msg);
    return 0;
}
```

The asynchronous agent (Example 5-70) manages a server pool and handles the request-reply dialog when the application asks for it.

Example 5-70. Clone class (clone.c): backend agent

```
static void
clone_agent (void *args, zctx_t *ctx, void *pipe)
{
    agent_t *self = agent_new (ctx, pipe);

    while (true) {
        zmq_pollitem_t poll_set [] = {
            { pipe, 0, ZMQ_POLLIN, 0 },
            { 0,    0, ZMQ_POLLIN, 0 }
        };
        int poll_timer = -1;
        int poll_size = 2;
        server_t *server = self->server [self->cur_server];
        switch (self->state) {
            case STATE_INITIAL:
                //  In this state we ask the server for a snapshot,
                //  if we have a server to talk to...
                if (self->nbr_servers > 0) {
                    zclock_log ("I: waiting for server at %s:%d...",
                        server->address, server->port);
                    if (server->requests < 2) {
                        zstr_sendm (server->snapshot, "ICANHAZ?");
                        zstr_send  (server->snapshot, self->subtree);
                        server->requests++;
                    }
                    server->expiry = zclock_time () + SERVER_TTL;
                    self->state = STATE_SYNCING;
                    poll_set [1].socket = server->snapshot;
                }
                else
                    poll_size = 1;
                break;

            case STATE_SYNCING:
```

```
                // In this state we read from the snapshot and we expect
                // the server to respond, else we fail over
                poll_set [1].socket = server->snapshot;
                break;

        case STATE_ACTIVE:
                // In this state we read from a subscriber and we expect
                // the server to give hugz, else we fail over
                poll_set [1].socket = server->subscriber;
                break;
    }
    if (server) {
        poll_timer = (server->expiry - zclock_time ())
                    * ZMQ_POLL_MSEC;
        if (poll_timer < 0)
            poll_timer = 0;
    }
```

We're now ready to process incoming messages, as shown in Example 5-71. If nothing at all comes from our server within the timeout, that means the server is dead.

Example 5-71. Clone class (clone.c): client poll loop

```
    int rc = zmq_poll (poll_set, poll_size, poll_timer);
    if (rc == -1)
        break;                  // Context has been shut down

    if (poll_set [0].revents & ZMQ_POLLIN) {
        if (agent_control_message (self))
            break;              // Interrupted
    }
    else
    if (poll_set [1].revents & ZMQ_POLLIN) {
        kvmsg_t *kvmsg = kvmsg_recv (poll_set [1].socket);
        if (!kvmsg)
            break;              // Interrupted

        // Anything from server resets its expiration time
        server->expiry = zclock_time () + SERVER_TTL;
        if (self->state == STATE_SYNCING) {
            // Store in snapshot until we're finished
            server->requests = 0;
            if (streq (kvmsg_key (kvmsg), "KTHXBAI")) {
                self->sequence = kvmsg_sequence (kvmsg);
                self->state = STATE_ACTIVE;
                zclock_log ("I: received from %s:%d snapshot=%d",
                    server->address, server->port,
                    (int) self->sequence);
                kvmsg_destroy (&kvmsg);
            }
            else
                kvmsg_store (&kvmsg, self->kvmap);
```

```
        }
        else
        if (self->state == STATE_ACTIVE) {
            //  Discard out-of-sequence updates, including hugz
            if (kvmsg_sequence (kvmsg) > self->sequence) {
                self->sequence = kvmsg_sequence (kvmsg);
                kvmsg_store (&kvmsg, self->kvmap);
                zclock_log ("I: received from %s:%d update=%d",
                    server->address, server->port,
                    (int) self->sequence);
            }
            else
                kvmsg_destroy (&kvmsg);
        }
    }
    else {
        //  Server has died, fail over to next
        zclock_log ("I: server at %s:%d didn't give hugz",
            server->address, server->port);
        self->cur_server = (self->cur_server + 1) % self->nbr_servers;
        self->state = STATE_INITIAL;
    }
}
agent_destroy (&self);
}
```

## PART II

Software Engineering Using ØMQ

The second part of this book is about software engineering using ØMQ. I'll introduce a set of software development techniques and demonstrate them with working examples, starting with ØMQ itself and ending with a general-purpose framework for distributed applications. These techniques are independent of license, though open source amplifies them.

## CHAPTER 6

The ØMQ Community

People sometimes ask me what's so special about ØMQ. My standard answer is true: that ØMQ is arguably the best answer we have to the vexing question, "How do we make the distributed software that the 21st century demands?" But more than that, ØMQ is special because of its community. This is ultimately what separates the wolves from the sheep.

There are three main open source development patterns. The first is the large firm dumping code to break the market for others. This is the Apache Foundation model. The second is tiny teams or small firms building their dreams. This is the most common open source model, which can be very successful commercially. The last is aggressive and diverse communities that swarm over a problem landscape. This is the Linux model, and the one to which we aspire with ØMQ.

It's hard to overemphasize the power and persistence of a working open source community. There really does not seem to be a better way of making software for the long term. Not only does the community choose the best problems to solve, but it solves them minimally, carefully, and then looks after these answers for years—perhaps decades—until they're no longer relevant. Then it quietly puts them away.

To really benefit from ØMQ, you need to understand the community. At some point down the road, you'll want to submit a patch, an issue, or an add-on. You might want to ask someone for help. You will probably want to bet a part of your business on ØMQ, and when I tell you that the community is much, much more important than the company that backs the product—even though I'm CEO of that company—this should be significant.

In this chapter, I'm going to look at our community from several angles. I'll conclude by explaining in detail our contract for collaboration, which we call "C4" (*http://rfc.zeromq.org/spec:16*). You should find the discussion useful for your own work. We've also adapted the ØMQ C4 process for closed source projects with good success.

We'll cover:

- The rough structure of ØMQ as a set of projects
- What "software architecture" is really about
- Why we use the LGPL and not the BSD license
- How we designed and grew the ØMQ community
- The business that backs ØMQ
- Who owns the ØMQ source code
- How to make and submit a patch to ØMQ
- Who controls what patches actually go into ØMQ
- How we guarantee compatibility with old code
- Why we don't use public Git branches
- Who decides on the ØMQ roadmap
- A worked example of a change to libzmq

Architecture of the ØMQ Community

You know that ØMQ is an LGPL-licensed project. In fact, it's a collection of projects built around the core library, libzmq. I'll visualize these projects as an expanding galaxy:

- At the core is libzmq. It's written in C++, with a low-level C API. The code is nasty, mainly because it's highly optimized but also because it's written in C++, a language that lends itself to subtle and deep nastiness. Martin Sustrik originally wrote the bulk of this code. Today, dozens of people maintain different parts of it.

- Around libzmq there are about 50 *bindings*. These are individual projects that create higher-level APIs for ØMQ, or at least map the low-level API into other languages. The bindings vary in quality from experimental to utterly awesome. Probably the most impressive binding is PyZMQ (*https://github.com/zeromq/pyzmq*), which was one of the first community projects built on top of ØMQ. If you are a binding author, you should really study PyZMQ and aspire to making your code and community as great as possible.

- A lot of languages have multiple bindings (Erlang, Ruby, C#, at least), written by different people over time or taking varying approaches. We don't regulate these in any way. There are no "official" bindings. You vote by using one or the other, contributing to it, or ignoring it.

- There are a series of reimplementations of libzmq, starting with JeroMQ, a full Java translation of the library, which is now the basis for NetMQ, a C# stack. These native stacks offer similar or identical APIs and speak the same protocol (ZMTP) as `libzmq`.

- On top of the bindings are a lot of projects that use ØMQ or build on it. See the "Labs" page on the wiki for a long list of projects and proto-projects that use ØMQ in some way. There are frameworks, web servers like Mongrel2, brokers like Majordomo, and enterprise open source tools like Storm.

`libzmq`, most of the bindings, and some of the outer projects sit in the ØMQ community "organization" (*https://github.com/organizations/zeromq*) on GitHub. This organization is "run" by a group consisting of the most senior binding authors. There's actually very little to run, as it's almost all self-managing and there's zero conflict these days.

iMatix, my firm, plays a specific role in the community. We own the trademarks and enforce them discreetly in order to make sure that if you download a package calling itself "ZeroMQ," you can trust what you are getting. People have on rare occasion tried to hijack the name, maybe believing that "free software" means there is no property at stake and no one willing to defend it. One thing you'll understand from this chapter is how seriously we take the process behind our software (and I mean "us" as a community, not a company). iMatix backs the community by enforcing that process on anything calling itself "ZeroMQ" or "ØMQ." We also put money and time into the software and packaging, for reasons I'll explain later.

It is not a charity exercise. ØMQ is a for-profit project, and a very profitable one. The profits are widely distributed among all those who invest in it. It's really that simple: take the time to become an expert in ØMQ, or build something useful on top of ØMQ, and you'll find your value as an individual, or team, or company increasing. iMatix enjoys the same benefits as everyone else in the community. It's win-win for everyone except our competitors, who find themselves facing a threat they can't beat and can't really escape. ØMQ dominates the future world of massively distributed software.

My firm doesn't just have the community's back—we also built the community. This was deliberate work. In the original ØMQ white paper from 2007 there were two projects. One was technical, how to make a better messaging system. The second was how to build a community that could take the software through to dominant success. Software dies, but community survives.

How to Make Really Large Architectures

There are, it has been said (at least by people reading this sentence out loud), two ways to make really large-scale software. Option One is to throw massive amounts of money and problems at empires of smart people, and hope that what emerges is not yet another career killer. If you are building on a lot of experience, have kept your teams solid and are not aiming for technical brilliance, and are furthermore incredibly lucky, it works.

But gambling with hundreds of millions of others' money isn't for everyone. For the rest of us who want to build large-scale software, there's Option Two, which is open source, and more specifically, *free software*. If you're asking how the choice of software license is relevant to the scale of the software you build, that's the right question.

The brilliant and visionary Eben Moglen once said, roughly, that a free software license is the contract on which a community builds. When I heard this, about 10 years ago, the following idea came too: *Can we deliberately grow free software communities?*

Ten years later, the answer is "yes," and there is almost a science to it. I say "almost" because we don't yet have enough evidence of people doing this deliberately with a documented, reproducible process. It is what I'm trying to do with Social Architecture (*http://softwareandsilicon.com/chapter:2#toc5*). ØMQ came after Wikidot, after the Digital Standards Organization (*http://www.digistan.org*) (Digistan), and after the Foundation for a Free Information Infrastructure (*http://www.ffii.org*) (aka the FFII, an NGO that fights against software patents). This all came after a lot of less successful community projects like Xitami and Libero. My main takeaway from a long career of working on projects of every conceivable format is: if you want to build truly large-scale and long-lasting software, aim to build a free software community.

Psychology of Software Architecture

Dirkjan Ochtman pointed me to Wikipedia's definition of software architecture (*http:// en.wikipedia.org/wiki/Software_architecture*) as "the set of structures needed to reason about the system, which comprise software elements, relations among them, and properties of both." For me, this vapid and circular jargon is a good example of how miserably little we understand what actually makes a successful large-scale software architecture.

Architecture is the art and science of making large artificial structures for human use. If there is one thing I've learned and applied successfully in 30 years of making larger and larger software systems, it is this: *software is about people*. Large structures in themselves are meaningless. It's how they function for *human use* that matters. And in software, human use starts with the programmers who make the software itself.

The core problems in software architecture are driven by human psychology, not technology. There are many ways our psychology affects our work. I could point to the way teams seem to get stupider as they get larger or when they have to work across larger distances. Does that mean the smaller the team, the more effective it is? How then does a large global community like ØMQ manage to work successfully?

The ØMQ community wasn't accidental. It was a deliberate design, my contribution to the early days when the code came out of a cellar in Bratislava. The design was based on my pet science of "Social Architecture", which Wikipedia defines (*http://en.wikipe dia.org/wiki/Social_architecture*) as "the conscious design of an environment that encourages a desired range of social behaviors leading towards some goal or set of goals."

My definition is: "the process, and the product, of planning, designing, and growing an online community" by analogy with traditional architecture.

One of the tenets of Social Architecture is that *how we organize* is more significant than *who we are*. The same group, organized differently, can produce wholly different results. We are like peers in a ØMQ network, and our communication patterns have a dramatic impact on our performance. Ordinary people, well connected, can far outperform a team of experts using poor patterns. If you're the architect of a larger ØMQ application, you're going to have to help others find the right patterns for working together. Do this right, and your project can succeed. Do it wrong, and your project will fail.

The two most important psychological elements are that we're really bad at understanding complexity and that we are really good at working together to divide and conquer large problems. We're highly social apes, and kind of smart, but only in the right kind of crowd.

So, here is my short list of the Psychological Elements of Software Architecture:

Stupidity

Our mental bandwidth is limited, so we're all stupid at some point. The architecture has to be simple to understand. This is the number one rule: simplicity beats functionality, every single time. If you can't understand an architecture on a cold gray Monday morning before coffee, it is too complex.

Selfishness

We act only out of self-interest, so the architecture must create space and opportunity for selfish acts that benefit the whole. Selfishness is often indirect and subtle. For example, I'll spend hours helping someone else understand something because that could be worth days to me later.

Laziness

We make lots of assumptions, many of which are wrong. We are happiest when we can spend the least effort to get a result or test an assumption quickly, so the architecture has to make this possible. Specifically, that means it must be simple.

Jealousy

We're jealous of others, which means we'll overcome our stupidity and laziness to prove others wrong and beat them in competition. The architecture thus has to create space for public competition based on fair rules that anyone can understand.

Fear

We're unwilling to take risks, especially if they might make us look stupid. Fear of failure is a major reason people conform and follow the group in mass stupidity. The architecture should make silent experimentation easy and cheap, giving people opportunities for success without punishing failure.

Reciprocity

> We'll pay extra in terms of hard work, even money, to punish cheats and enforce fair rules. The architecture should be heavily rule-based, telling people how to work together, but not what to work on.

Conformity

> We're happiest to conform, out of fear and laziness, which means if the patterns are good, clearly explained and documented, and fairly enforced, we'll naturally choose the right path every time.

Pride

> We're intensely aware of our social status, and we'll work hard to avoid looking stupid or incompetent in public. The architecture has to make sure every piece we make has our name on it, so we'll have sleepless nights stressing about what others will say about our work.

Greed

> We're ultimately economic animals (see *selfishness*), so the architecture has to give us economic incentive to invest in making it happen. Maybe it's polishing our reputation as experts, maybe it's literally making money from contributing some skill or component. It doesn't matter what it is, but there must be economic incentive. Think of architecture as a marketplace, not an engineering design.

These strategies work not only on a large scale but also on a small scale, within an organization or team.

The Contract

Here is a story. It happened to the eldest brother-in-law of the cousin of a friend of mine's colleague at work. His name was, and still is, Patrick.

Patrick was a computer scientist with a PhD in advanced network topologies. He spent two years and his savings building a new product, and chose the BSD license because he believed that would get him more adoption. He worked in his attic, at great personal cost, and proudly published his work. People applauded, for it was truly fantastic, and his mailing lists were soon abuzz with activity and patches and happy chatter. Many companies told him how they were saving millions using his work. Some of them even paid him for consultancy and training. He was invited to speak at conferences and started collecting badges with his name on them. He started a small business, hired a friend to work with him, and dreamed of making it big.

Then one day, someone pointed him to a new project, GPL-licensed, which had forked his work and was improving on it. He was irritated and upset, and asked how people—fellow open sourcers, no less!—would so shamelessly steal his code. There were long arguments on the list about whether it was even legal to relicense the BSD code as GPL code. Turned out, it was. He tried to ignore the new project, but then he soon realized that new patches coming from that project *couldn't even be merged back* into his work!

Worse, the GPL project got popular and some of his core contributors made first small, and then larger patches to it. Again, he couldn't use those changes, and he felt abandoned. Patrick went into a depression, his girlfriend left him for an international currency dealer called, weirdly, Patrice, and he stopped all work on the project. He felt betrayed, and utterly miserable. He fired his friend, who took it rather badly and told everyone that Patrick was a closet banjo player. Finally, Patrick took a job as a project manager for a cloud company, and by the age of 40, he had stopped programming even for fun.

Poor Patrick. I almost felt sorry for him. Then I asked him, "Why didn't you choose the GPL?" "Because it's a restrictive viral license," he replied. I told him, "You may have a PhD, and you maybe the eldest brother-in-law of the cousin of a friend of my colleague, but you are an idiot and Monique was smart to leave you. You published your work inviting people to please steal your code as long as they kept this 'please steal my code' statement in the resulting work, and when people did exactly that, you got upset. Worse, you were a hypocrite because when they did it in secret, you were happy, but when they did it openly, you felt betrayed."

Seeing your hard work captured by a smarter team and then used against you is enormously painful, so why even make that possible? Every proprietary project that uses BSD code is capturing it. A public GPL fork is perhaps more humiliating, but it's fully self-inflicted.

BSD is like food. It literally (and I mean that metaphorically) whispers "eat me" in the little voice one imagines a cube of cheese might use when it's sitting next to an empty bottle of the best beer in the world, which is of course Orval, brewed by an ancient and almost extinct order of silent Belgian monks called Les Gars La-Bas Qui Brassents l'Orval. The BSD license, like its near clone MIT/X11, was designed specifically by a university (Berkeley) with no profit motive, to leak work and effort. It is a way to push subsidized technology at below its cost price, a dumping of underpriced code in the hope that it will break the market for others. BSD is an *excellent* strategic tool, but only if you're a large, well-funded institution that can afford to use Option One. The Apache license is BSD in a suit.

For us small businesses who aim our investments like precious bullets, leaking work and effort is unacceptable. Breaking the market is great, but we cannot afford to subsidize our competitors. The BSD networking stack ended up putting Windows on the Internet. We cannot afford battles with those with whom we should naturally be allies. We cannot afford to make fundamental business errors because in the end, that means we have to fire people.

It comes down to behavioral economics and game theory. *The license we choose modifies the economics of those who use our work.* In the software industry there are friends, foes, and food. BSD makes most people see us as lunch. Closed source makes most people see us as enemies (do you *like* paying people for software?). GPL, however, makes most people, with the exception of the Patricks of the world, our allies. Any fork of ØMQ is license compatible with ØMQ, to the point where we *encourage* forks as a valuable tool for experimentation. Yes, it can be weird to see someone try and run off with the ball, but here's the secret: *I can get it back any time I want.*

The Process

If you've accepted my thesis up to now, great! Now, I'll explain the rough process by which we actually build an open source community. This was how we built (or grew, or gently steered) the ØMQ community into existence.

Your goal as leader of a community is to motivate people to get out there and explore; to ensure they can do so safely and without disturbing others; to reward them when they make successful discoveries; and to ensure they share their knowledge with everyone else (and not because we ask them, not because they feel generous, but because it's The Law).

It is an iterative process. You make a small product, at your own cost, but in public view. You then build a small community around that product. If you have a small but real hit, the community then helps design and build the next version, and grows larger. And then that community builds the next version, and so on. It's evident that you remain part of the community, maybe even a majority contributor, but the more control you try to assert over the material results, the less people will want to participate. Plan your own retirement well before someone decides you are their next problem.

Crazy, Beautiful, and Easy

You need a goal that's crazy and simple enough to get people out of bed in the morning. Your community has to attract the very best people, and that demands something special. With ØMQ, we said we were going to make "the Fastest. Messaging. Ever." which qualifies as a good motivator. If we'd said we were going to make "a smart transport layer that'll connect your moving pieces cheaply and flexibly across your enterprise," we'd have failed.

Then your work must be beautiful, immediately useful, and attractive. Your contributors are users who want to explore just a little beyond where they are now. Make it simple, elegant, and brutally clean. The experience when people run or use your work should be an emotional one. They should *feel* something, and if you've accurately solved even just one big problem that until then they didn't quite realize they faced, you'll have a small part of their soul.

It must also be easy to understand, use, and join. Too many projects have barriers to access: put yourself in the other person's mind and see all the reasons they come to your site, thinking "Um, interesting project, but..." and then leave. You want them to stay, and try it, just once. Use GitHub and put the issue tracker right there.

If you do these things well, your community will be smart, but more importantly, it will be intellectually and geographically diverse. This is really important. A group of like-minded experts cannot explore the problem landscape well. They tend to make big mistakes. Diversity beats education any time.

Stranger, Meet Stranger

How much up-front agreement do two people need to work together on something? In most organizations, a lot. But you can bring this cost down to near zero, and then people can collaborate without having ever met, done a phone conference, or had a meeting or business trip to discuss Roles and Responsibilities over way too many bottles of cheap Korean rice wine.

You need well-written rules that are designed by cynical people like me to force strangers into mutually beneficial collaboration instead of conflict. The GPL is a good start. Git-Hub and its fork/merge strategy is a good follow-up. And then you want something like our C4 rulebook (*http://rfc.zeromq.org/spec:16*) to control how work actually happens.

C4 (which I now use for every new open source project) has detailed and tested answers to a lot of common mistakes people make, such as the sin of working offline in a corner with others "because it's faster." Transparency is essential to get trust, which is essential to get scale. By forcing every single change through a single transparent process, you build real trust in the results.

Another cardinal sin that many open source developers make is to place themselves above others. "I founded this project, thus my intellect is superior to that of others." It's not just immodest and rude, and usually inaccurate; it's also poor business. The rules must apply equally to everyone, without distinction. You are part of the community. Your job, as founder of a project, is not to impose your vision of the product on others, but to make sure the rules are good, honest, and *enforced*.

Infinite Property

One of the saddest myths of the knowledge business is that ideas are a sensible form of property. It's medieval nonsense that should have been junked along with slavery, but sadly it's still making too many powerful people too much money.

Ideas are cheap. What does work sensibly as property is the hard work we do in building a market. "You eat what you kill" is the right model for encouraging people to work hard. Whether it's moral authority over a project, money from consulting, or the sale of a trademark to some large, rich firm: if you make it, you own it. But what you really own is "footfall," participants in your project, which ultimately defines your power.

To do this requires infinite free space. Thankfully, GitHub solved this problem for us, for which I will die a grateful person (there are many reasons to be grateful in life, which I won't list here because we only have a hundred or so pages left, but this is one of them).

You cannot scale a single project with many owners like you can scale a collection of many small projects, each with fewer owners. When we embrace forks, a person can become an "owner" with a single click. Now they just have to convince others to join by demonstrating their unique value.

So, in ØMQ, we aimed to make it easy to write bindings on top of the core library, and we stopped trying to make those bindings ourselves. This created space for others to make them, become their owners, and get that credit.

Care and Feeding

I wish a community could be 100% self-steering, and perhaps one day this will work, but today it's not the case. We're very close with ØMQ, but from my experience a community needs four types of care and feeding:

- First, simply because most people are too nice, we need some kind of symbolic leadership or owners who provide ultimate authority in case of conflict. Usually it's the founders of the community. I've seen it work with self-elected groups of "elders," but old men like to talk a lot. I've seen communities split over the question of who's in charge," and setting up legal entities with boards and such seems to make arguments over control worse, not better—maybe because there seems to be more to fight over. One of the real benefits of free software is that it's always remixable, so instead of fighting over a pie, one simply forks the pie.

- Second, communities need living rules, and thus they need a lawyer able to formulate and write these down. Rules are critical. When done right, they remove friction. When done wrong, or neglected, we see real friction and arguments that can drive away the nice majority, leaving the argumentative core in charge of the burning house. One thing I've tried to do with the ØMQ and previous communities is create reusable rules, which perhaps means we don't need lawyers as much.

- Thirdly, communities need some kind of financial backing. This is the jagged rock that breaks most ships. If you starve a community, it becomes more creative but the core contributors burn out. If you pour too much money into it, you attract the professionals, who never say "no," and the community loses its diversity and creativity. If you create a fund for people to share, they will fight (bitterly) over it. With ØMQ, we (iMatix) spend our time and money on marketing and packaging (like this book), and the basic care, like bug fixes, releases, and websites.

- Lastly, sales and commercial mediation are important. There is a natural market between expert contributors and customers, but both are somewhat incompetent at talking to each other. Customers assume that support is free or very cheap because the software is free. Contributors are shy about asking a fair rate for their work. It makes for a difficult market. A growing part of my work (and my firm's profits) is simply connecting ØMQ users who want help with experts from the community able to provide it, and ensuring both sides are happy with the results.

I've seen communities of brilliant people with noble goals die because the founders got some or all of these four things wrong. The core problem is that you can't expect consistently great leadership from any one company, person, or group. What works today often won't work tomorrow, yet structures become more solid, not more flexible, over time.

The best answer I can find is a mix of two things. The first is the GPL with its guarantee of remixability. No matter how bad the authority is, no matter how much it tries to privatize and capture the community's work, if it's GPL licensed, that work can walk away and find a better authority. Before you say, "all open source offers this," think it through. I can kill a BSD-licensed project by hiring the core contributors and not releasing any new patches. But even with a billion dollars to spend, I *cannot* kill a GPL-licensed project. The second is the philosophical anarchist model of authority, which is that we choose it, it does not own us.

The ØMQ Process: C4

When we say ØMQ, we sometimes mean `libzmq`, the core library. In early 2012, we synthesized the `libzmq` process into a formal protocol for collaboration that we called the Collective Code Construction Contract (*http://rfc.zeromq.org/spec:16*), or C4. You can see this as a layer above the GPL. In fact, `libzmq` doesn't quite stick to C4, because for historic reasons we use Jira instead of the GitHub issue tracker. Apart from that, these are our rules, and I'll explain the reasoning behind each one.

C4 is an evolution of the GitHub Fork + Pull Model (*https://help.github.com/send-pull-requests/*). You may get the feeling I'm a fan of Git and GitHub. This would be accurate: these two tools have made such a positive impact on our work over the last years, especially when it comes to building community.

Language

The keywords "MUST", "MUST NOT", "REQUIRED", "SHALL", "SHALL NOT", "SHOULD", "SHOULD NOT", "RECOMMENDED", "MAY", and "OPTIONAL" in this document are to be interpreted as described in RFC 2119.

By starting with the RFC 2119 language, the C4 text makes very clear its intention to act as a protocol rather than a randomly written set of recommendations. A protocol is a contract between parties that defines the rights and obligations of each party. These can be peers in a network, or they can be strangers working in the same project.

I think C4 is the first time anyone has attempted to codify a community's rulebook as a formal and reusable protocol spec. Previously, our rules were spread out over several wiki pages, and they were quite specific to libzmq in many ways. But experience teaches us that the more formal, accurate, and reusable the rules are, the easier it is for strangers to collaborate up-front. And less friction means a more scalable community. At the time of C4, we also had some disagreement in the libzmq project over precisely what process we were using. Not everyone felt bound by the same rules. Let's just say some people felt they had a special status, which created friction with the rest of the community. Codification made things clear.

It's easy to use C4: just host your project on GitHub, get one other person to join, and open the floor to pull requests. In your README, put a link to C4—that's it. We've done this in quite a few projects and it does seem to work. I've been pleasantly surprised a few times just applying these rules to my own work, like CZMQ. None of us are so amazing that we can work without others.

Goals

> C4 is meant to provide a reusable optimal collaboration model for open source software projects.

The short-term reason for writing C4 was to end arguments over the libzmq contribution process. The dissenters went off elsewhere. The ØMQ community blossomed (*https://github.com/zeromq/libzmq/graphs/contributors*) smoothly and easily, as I'd predicted. Most people were surprised, but gratified. There's been no real criticism of C4 except with regard to its branching policy, which I'll come to later as it deserves its own discussion.

There's a reason I'm reviewing history here: as founder of a community, you are asking people to invest in your property, trademark, and branding. In return, and this is what we do with ØMQ, you can use that branding to set a bar for quality. When you download a product labeled "ØMQ," you know that it's been produced to certain standards. It's a basic rule of quality: write down your process, as otherwise you cannot improve it. Our processes aren't perfect, nor can they ever be. But any flaw in them can be fixed, and tested.

Making C4 reusable is therefore really important. To learn more about the best possible process, we need to get results from the widest possible range of projects.

> It has these specific goals:

> To maximize the scale of the community around a project, by reducing the friction for new Contributors and creating a scaled participation model with strong positive feedbacks;

The number one goal is maximizing the size and health of the community—not technical quality, not profits, not performance, not market share. The goal is simply increasing the number of people who contribute to the project. The science here is simple: the larger the community, the more accurate the results.

> To relieve dependencies on key individuals by separating different skill sets so that there is a larger pool of competence in any required domain;

Perhaps the worst problem we faced in libzmq was dependence on people who could understand the code, manage GitHub branches, and make clean releases—all at the same time. It's like looking for athletes who can run marathons *and* sprint, swim, and also lift weights. We humans are really good at specialization. Asking us to be really good at two contradictory things reduces the number of candidates sharply, which is a Bad Thing for any project. We had this problem severely in libzmq in 2009 or so, and we fixed it by splitting the role of maintainer into two: one person makes patches and another makes releases.

> To allow the project to develop faster and more accurately, by increasing the diversity of the decision making process;

This is theory—not fully proven, but not falsified. The greater the diversity of the community and the number of people who can weigh in on discussions without fear of being criticized or dismissed, the faster and more accurately the software develops. Speed is quite subjective here. Going very fast in the wrong direction is not just useless, it's actively damaging (and we suffered a lot of that in libzmq before we switched to C4).

> To support the natural life-cycle of project versions from experimental through to stable, by allowing safe experimentation, rapid failure, and isolation of stable code;

To be honest, this goal seems to be fading into irrelevance. It's quite an interesting effect of the process: *the Git master is almost always perfectly stable*. This has to do with the size of changes and their latency—i.e., the time between someone writing the code and someone actually using it fully. However, people still expect "stable" releases, so we'll keep this goal there for a while.

> To reduce the internal complexity of project repositories, thus making it easier for Contributors to participate and reducing the scope for error;

Curious observation: people who thrive in complex situations like to create complexity because it keeps their value high. It's the Cobra Effect (Google it). Git made branches easy and left us with the all-too-common statement, "Git is easy once you understand that a Git branch is just a folded five-dimensional lepton space that has a detached history with no intervening cache." Developers should not be made to feel stupid by their tools. I've seen too many top-class developers confused by repository structures to accept conventional wisdom on Git branches. We'll come back to dispose of Git branches shortly, dear reader.

> To enforce collective ownership of the project, which increases economic incentive to Contributors and reduces the risk of hijack by hostile entities.

Ultimately, we're economic creatures, and the sense that "we own this, and our work can never be used against us" makes it much easier for people to invest in an open source project like ØMQ. And it can't be just a feeling, it has to be real. There are a number of aspects to making collective ownership work; we'll see these one by one as we go through C4.

Preliminaries

> The project SHALL use the Git distributed revision control system.

Git has its faults. Its command-line API is horribly inconsistent, and it has a complex, messy internal model that it shoves in your face at the slightest provocation. But despite doing its best to make its users feel stupid, Git does its job really, really well. More pragmatically, I've found that if you stay away from certain areas (branches!), people learn Git rapidly and don't make many mistakes. That works for me.

> The project SHALL be hosted on github.com or equivalent, herein called the "Platform".

I'm sure one day some large firm will buy GitHub and break it, and another platform will rise in its place. GitHub serves up a near-perfect set of minimal, fast, simple tools. I've thrown hundreds of people at it, and they all stick like flies in a dish of honey.

> The project SHALL use the Platform issue tracker.

We made the mistake in `libzmq` of switching to Jira because we hadn't learned yet how to properly use the GitHub issue tracker. Jira is a great example of how to turn something useful into a complex mess because the business depends on selling more "features." But even without criticizing Jira, keeping the issue tracker on the same platform means one less UI to learn, one less login, and smooth integration between issues and patches.

> The project SHOULD have clearly documented guidelines for code style.

This is a protocol plug-in: insert code style guidelines here. If you don't document the code style you use, you have no basis except prejudice to reject patches.

A "Contributor" is a person who wishes to provide a patch, being a set of commits that solve some clearly identified problem.

A "Maintainer" is a person who merges patches to the project. Maintainers are not developers; their job is to enforce process.

Now we move on to definitions of the parties, and the splitting of roles that saved us from the sin of structural dependency on rare individuals. This worked well in libzmq, but as you will see it depends on the rest of the process. C4 isn't a buffet; you will need the whole process (or something very like it), or it won't hold together.

Contributors SHALL NOT have commit access to the repository unless they are also Maintainers.

Maintainers SHALL have commit access to the repository.

What we wanted to avoid was people pushing their changes directly to master. This was the biggest source of trouble in libzmq historically: large masses of raw code that took months or years to fully stabilize. We eventually followed other ØMQ projects like PyZMQ in using pull requests. We even went further, and stipulated that *all* changes had to follow the same path—no exceptions for "special people."

Everyone, without distinction or discrimination, SHALL have an equal right to become a Contributor under the terms of this contract.

We had to state this explicitly. It used to be that the libzmq maintainers would reject patches simply because they didn't like them. Now, that may sound reasonable to the author of a library (though libzmq was not written by any one person), but let's remember our goal of creating a work that is owned by as many people as possible. Saying "I don't like your patch so I'm going to reject it" is equivalent to saying, "I claim to own this and I think I'm better than you, and I don't trust you." Those are toxic messages to give to others who are thinking of becoming your co-investors.

I think this fight between individual expertise and collective intelligence plays out in other areas. It defined Wikipedia, and still does, a decade after that work surpassed anything built by small groups of experts. For me, we make software by synthesizing knowledge, much as we make Wikipedia articles.

Licensing and Ownership

The project SHALL use the GPLv3 or a variant thereof (LGPL, AGPL).

I've already explained how full remixability creates better scale and why the GPL and its variants seem the optimal contract for remixable software. If you're a large business aiming to dump code on the market, you won't want C4, but then you won't really care about community either.

> All contributions to the project source code ("patches") SHALL use the same license as the project.

This removes the need for any specific license or contribution agreement for patches. You fork the GPL code, you publish your remixed version on GitHub, and you or anyone else can then submit that as a patch to the original code. BSD doesn't allow this. Any work that contains BSD code may also contain unlicensed proprietary code, so you need explicit action from the author of the code before you can remix it.

> All patches are owned by their authors. There SHALL NOT be any copyright assignment process.

Here we come to the key reason people trust their investments in ØMQ: it's logistically impossible to buy the copyrights to create a closed-source competitor to ØMQ. iMatix can't do this either. And the more people that send patches, the harder it becomes. ØMQ isn't just free and open today—this specific rule means it will remain so forever. Note that this is not the case in all GPL projects, many of which still ask for copyright transfer back to the maintainers.

> The project SHALL be owned collectively by all its Contributors.

This is perhaps redundant, but worth saying: if everyone owns their patches, then the resulting whole is also owned by every contributor. There's no legal concept of owning lines of code: the "work" is at least a source file.

> Each Contributor SHALL be responsible for identifying themselves in the project Contributor list.

In other words, the maintainers are not karma accountants. Anyone who wants credit has to claim it themselves.

Patch Requirements

In this section, we define the obligations of the contributor: specifically, what constitutes a "valid" patch, so that maintainers have rules they can use to accept or reject patches.

> Maintainers and Contributors MUST have a Platform account and SHOULD use their real names or a well-known alias.

In the worst-case scenario, where someone has submitted toxic code (patented, or owned by someone else), we need to be able to trace who and when, so we can remove the code. Asking for real names or a well-known alias is a theoretical strategy for reducing the risk of bogus patches. We don't know if this actually works because we haven't had the problem yet.

> A patch SHOULD be a minimal and accurate answer to exactly one identified and agreed problem.

This implements the Simplicity Oriented Design process that I'll come to later in this chapter. One clear problem, one minimal solution: apply, test, and repeat.

> A patch MUST adhere to the code style guidelines of the project if these are defined.

This is just sanity. I've spent time cleaning up other peoples' patches because they insisted on putting the "else" beside the "if" instead of just below, as Nature intended. Consistent code is healthier.

> A patch MUST adhere to the "Evolution of Public Contracts" guidelines defined below.

Ah, the pain, the pain. I'm not speaking of the time at age eight when I stepped on a plank with a 4-inch nail protruding from it. That was relatively OK. I'm speaking of 2010–2011, when we had multiple parallel releases of ØMQ, each with different *incompatible* APIs or wire protocols. It was an exercise in bad rules pointlessly enforced. The rule was, "If you change the API or protocol, you SHALL create a new major version." Give me the nail through the foot; that hurt less.

One of the big changes we made with C4 was simply to ban, outright, this kind of sanctioned sabotage. Amazingly, it's not even hard. We just don't allow the breaking of existing public contracts, period, unless everyone agrees, in which case no period. As Linus Torvalds famously put it on December 23, 2012: "WE DO NOT BREAK USER-SPACE!"

> A patch SHALL NOT include non-trivial code from other projects unless the Contributor is the original author of that code.

This rule has two effects. The first is that it forces people to make minimal solutions because they cannot simply import swathes of existing code. In the cases where I've seen this happen to projects, it's always bad unless the imported code is very cleanly separated. The second effect is that it avoids license arguments. You write the patch, you are allowed to publish it as LGPL, and we can merge it back in. But you find a 200-line code fragment on the Web and try to paste that, and we'll refuse.

> A patch MUST compile cleanly on at least the most important target platforms.

This is probably asking a lot because most contributors have only one platform on which to work.

> A "Correct Patch" is one that satisfies the above requirements.

Just in case it wasn't clear, we're back to legalese and definitions.

Development Process

In this section, we aim to describe the actual development process, step-by-step.

> Change on the project SHALL be governed by the pattern of accurately identifying problems and applying minimal, accurate solutions to these problems.

This is an unapologetic ramming through of 30 years' software design experience. It's a profoundly simple approach to design: make minimal, accurate solutions to real problems. Nothing more or less. Note the stress on "accuracy," a rare but essential ingredient. In ØMQ, we don't have feature requests. Treating new features the same as bugs confuses newbies. But this process works, and not just in open source. Enunciating the problem we're trying to solve, with every single change, is key to deciding whether the change is worth making or not.

> To initiate changes, a user SHALL log an issue on the project Platform issue tracker.

This is meant to stop us from going offline and working in a ghetto, either by ourselves or with others. Although we tend to accept pull requests that have clear argumentation, this rule lets us say "stop" to confused or too-large patches.

> The user SHOULD write the issue by describing the problem they face or observe.

"Problem: we need feature X. Solution: make it" is not a good issue. "Problem: user cannot do common tasks A or B except by using a complex workaround. Solution: make feature X" is a decent explanation. Because everyone I've ever worked with has needed to learn this, it seems worth restating: document the real problem first, and the solution second.

> The user SHOULD seek consensus on the accuracy of their observation, and the value of solving the problem.

Because many apparent problems are illusionary, by stating the problem explicitly we give others a chance to correct our logic. "You're only using A and B a lot because function C is unreliable. Solution: make function C work properly."

> Users SHALL NOT log feature requests, ideas, suggestions, or any solutions to problems that are not explicitly documented and provable.

There are several reasons for not logging ideas, suggestions, or feature requests. In our experience, these just accumulate in the issue tracker until someone deletes them. But more profoundly, when we treat all changes as problem solutions, we can prioritize trivially. Either the problem is real and someone wants to solve it now, or it's not on the table. Thus, wish lists are off the table.

Thus, the release history of the project SHALL be a list of meaningful issues logged and solved.

I'd love the GitHub issue tracker to simply list all the issues we solved in each release. Today, we still have to write that by hand. If one puts the issue number in each commit, and if one uses the GitHub issue tracker—which we sadly don't yet do for ØMQ—this release history is easier to produce mechanically.

> To work on an issue, a Contributor SHALL fork the project repository and then work on their forked repository.

Here we explain the GitHub fork + pull request model so that newcomers only have to learn one process (C4) in order to contribute.

> To submit a patch, a Contributor SHALL create a Platform pull request back to the project.

GitHub has made this so simple that we don't need to learn Git commands to do it, for which I'm deeply grateful. Sometimes, I'll tell people whom I don't particularly like that command-line Git is awesome and all they need to do is learn Git's internal model in detail before trying to use it on real work. When I see them several months later, they look... different.

> A Contributor SHALL NOT commit changes directly to the project.

Anyone who submits a patch is a contributor, and all contributors follow the same rules. No special privileges to the original authors, because otherwise we're not building a community, only boosting our egos.

> To discuss a patch, people MAY comment on the Platform pull request, on the commit, or elsewhere.

Randomly distributed discussions may be confusing if you're walking up for the first time, but GitHub solves this for all current participants by sending emails to those who need to follow what's going on. We had the same experience and the same solution in Wikidot, and it works. There's no evidence that discussing in different places has any negative effect.

> To accept or reject a patch, a Maintainer SHALL use the Platform interface.

Working via the GitHub web user interface means pull requests are logged as issues, with workflow and discussion. I'm sure there are more complex ways to work. Complexity is easy; it's simplicity that's incredibly hard.

> Maintainers SHALL NOT accept their own patches.

There was a rule we defined in the FFII years ago to stop people burning out: no less than two people on any project. One-person projects tend to end in tears, or at least bitter silence. We have quite a lot of data on burnout, why it happens, and how to prevent it (even cure it). I'll explore this later in the chapter, because if you work with or on open source projects you need to be aware of the risks. The "no merging your own patch" rule has two goals. First, if you want your project to be C4-certified, you have to get at least one other person to help. If no one wants to help you, perhaps you need to rethink your project. Second, having a control for every patch makes it much more satisfying, keeps us more focused, and stops us breaking the rules because we're in a hurry, or just feeling lazy.

> Maintainers SHALL NOT make value judgments on correct patches.

We already said this, but it's worth repeating: the role of maintainer is not to judge a patch's substance, only its technical quality. The substantive worth of a patch only emerges over time: people use it and like it, or they do not. And if no one is using a patch, eventually it'll annoy someone else, who will remove it, and no one will complain.

> Maintainers SHALL merge correct patches rapidly.

There is a criterion I call *change latency*, which is the round-trip time from identifying a problem to testing a solution. The faster the better. If maintainers cannot respond to pull requests as rapidly as people expect, they're not doing their jobs (or they need more hands).

> The Contributor MAY tag an issue as "Ready" after making a pull request for the issue.

By default, GitHub offers the usual variety of issues, but with C4 we don't use them. Instead, we need just two labels, "Urgent" and "Ready." A contributor who wants another user to test an issue can label it as "Ready."

> The user who created an issue SHOULD close the issue after checking the patch is successful.

When one person opens an issue and another works on it, it's best to allow the original person to close the issue. That acts as a double-check that the issue was properly resolved.

> Maintainers SHOULD ask for improvements to incorrect patches and SHOULD reject incorrect patches if the Contributor does not respond constructively.

Initially, I felt it was worth merging all patches, no matter how poor. There's an element of trolling involved: accepting even obviously bogus patches could, I felt, pull in more contributors. But people were uncomfortable with this, so we defined the "correct patch" rules, and the maintainer's role in checking for quality. On the negative side, I think we didn't take some interesting risks that could have paid off with more participants. On the positive side, this has led to the ØMQ master (and that of all projects that use C4) being practically production quality, practically all the time.

> Any Contributor who has value judgments on a correct patch SHOULD express these via their own patches.

In essence, the goal here is to allow users to try patches rather than to spend time arguing pros and cons. As easy as it is to make a patch, it's as easy to revert it with another patch. You might think this would lead to "patch wars," but that hasn't happened. We've had only a handful of cases in `libzmq` where patches by one contributor were killed by another person who felt the experimentation wasn't going in the right direction. This approach is easier than seeking up-front consensus.

> Maintainers MAY commit changes to non-source documentation directly to the project.

This exit allows maintainers who are making release notes to push those without having to create an issue, which would then affect the release notes, leading to stress on the space-time fabric and possibly involuntary rerouting backwards in the fourth dimension to before the invention of cold beer. Shudder. It is simpler to agree that release notes aren't changes to the software.

Creating Stable Releases

We want some guarantee of stability for a production system. In the past, this meant taking unstable code and then over months hammering out the bugs and faults until it was safe to trust. iMatix's job, for years, has been to do this to `libzmq`, turning raw code into packages by allowing only bug fixes and no new code into a "stabilization branch." It's surprisingly not as thankless as it sounds.

Since we went full speed with C4, we've found that the Git master of `libzmq` is mostly perfect, most of the time. This frees our time to do more interesting things, such as building new open source layers on top of `libzmq`. However, people still want that guarantee: many users will simply not install except from an "official" release. So, a stable release today involves two things: first, a snapshot of the master taken at a time when there have been no new changes for a while and there are no dramatic open bugs; and second, a way to fine-tune that snapshot to fix the critical issues remaining in it.

This is the process we explain in this section.

> The project SHALL have one branch ("master") that always holds the latest in-progress version and SHOULD always build.

This is redundant because every patch always builds, but it's worth restating. If the master doesn't build (and pass its tests), someone needs waking up.

> The project SHALL NOT use topic branches for any reason. Personal forks MAY use topic branches.

I'll come to branches soon. In short (or "tl;dr," as they say on the webs), branches make the repository too complex and fragile, and they require up-front agreement, all of which are expensive and avoidable.

> To make a stable release someone SHALL fork the repository by copying it and thus become maintainer of this repository.

> Forking a project for stabilization MAY be done unilaterally and without agreement of project maintainers.

It's free software. No one has a monopoly on it. If you think the maintainers aren't producing stable releases right, fork the repository and do it yourself. Forking isn't a failure, it's an essential tool for competition. You can't do this with branches, which means a branch-based release policy gives the project maintainers a monopoly. And that's bad because they'll become lazier and more arrogant than if real competition is nipping at their heels.

> Maintainers of the stabilization project SHALL maintain it through pull requests which MAY cherry-pick patches from the forked project.

Perhaps the C4 process should just say that stabilization projects have maintainers and contributors, like any project. That's all this rule means.

> A patch to a repository declared "stable" SHALL be accompanied by a reproducible test case.

Beware of a one-size-fits-all process. New code does not require the same paranoia as code that people are trusting for production use. In the normal development process, we did not mention test cases. There's a reason for this. While I love testable patches, many changes aren't easily (or at all) testable. However, to stabilize a code base you want to fix serious bugs, and you want to be 100% sure every change is accurate. This means before and after tests for every change.

> A stabilization repository SHOULD progress through these phases: "unstable", "candidate", "stable", and then "legacy". That is, the default behavior of stabilization repositories is to die.

This may be too detailed. The key point here is that these forked stabilization repositories all die in the end, as the master continues to evolve and be forked off for production releases.

Evolution of Public Contracts

By "public contracts," I mean APIs and protocols. Up until the end of 2011, libzmq's naturally happy state was marred by broken promises and broken contracts. We stopped making promises (aka "road maps") for libzmq completely, and our dominant theory of change is now that it emerges carefully and accurately over time. At a 2012 Chicago meetup, Garrett Smith and Chuck Remes called this the "drunken stumble to greatness," which is how I think of it now.

We stopped breaking public contracts simply by banning the practice. Before then it had been "OK" (as in, we did it and everyone complained bitterly, and we ignored them) to break the API or protocol so long as we changed the major version number. Sounds fine, until you get ØMQ version 2.0, 3.0, and 4.0 all in development at the same time, and not speaking to each other.

> All Public Contracts (APIs or protocols) SHOULD be documented.

You'd think this was a given for professional software engineers, but no, it's not. So, it's a rule. You want C4 certification for your project, you make sure your public contracts are documented. No "It's specified in the code" excuses. Code is not a contract. (Yes, I intend at some point to create a C4 certification process to act as a quality indicator for open source projects.)

> All Public Contracts SHALL use Semantic Versioning.

This rule is mainly here because people asked for it. I've no real love for it, as semantic versioning is what led to the so-called "Why does ØMQ not speak to itself?!" debacle. I've never seen the problem that this solved. Something about runtime validation of library versions, or some-such.

> All Public Contracts SHOULD have space for extensibility and experimentation.

Now, the real thing is that public contracts *do change*. It's not about not changing them; it's about changing them safely. This means educating (especially protocol) designers to create that space up-front.

> A patch that modifies a Public Contract SHOULD not break existing applications unless there is prior consensus on the value of doing this.

Sometimes the patch is fixing a bad API that no one is using. It's a freedom we need, but it should be based on consensus, not one person's dogma. However, making random changes "just because" is not good. In ØMQ v3.x, did we benefit from renaming ZMQ_NO BLOCK to ZMQ_DONTWAIT? Sure, it's closer to the POSIX socket recv() call, but is that worth breaking thousands of applications? No one ever reported it as an issue. To misquote Richard Stallman: "Your freedom to create an ideal world stops one inch from my application."

> A patch that introduces new features to a Public Contract SHOULD do so using new names.

We had the experience in ØMQ once or twice of new features using old names (or worse, using names that were *still in use* elsewhere). ØMQ v3.0 had a newly introduced "ROUTER" socket that was totally different from the existing ROUTER socket in ØMQ v2.x. Dear lord, you should be face-palming, why? The reason: apparently, even smart people sometimes need regulation to stop them doing silly things.

> Old names SHOULD be deprecated in a systematic fashion by marking new names as "experimental" until they are stable, then marking the old names as "deprecated".

This life-cycle notation has the great benefit of actually telling users what is going on, with a consistent direction. "Experimental" means "we have introduced this and intend to make it stable if it works." It does not mean, "we have introduced this and will remove it at any time if we feel like it." One assumes that code that survives more than one patch cycle is meant to be there. "Deprecated" means "we have replaced this and intend to remove it."

> When sufficient time has passed, old deprecated names SHOULD be marked "legacy" and eventually removed.

In theory, this gives applications time to move on to stable new contracts without risk. You can upgrade first, make sure things work, and then, over time, fix things up to remove dependencies on deprecated and legacy APIs and protocols.

> Old names SHALL NOT be reused by new features.

Ah, yes, the joy when ØMQ v3.x renamed the most-used API functions (`zmq_send()` and `zmq_recv()`) and then recycled the old names for new methods that were utterly incompatible (and which I suspect few people actually use). You should be slapping yourself in confusion again, but really, this is what happened, and I was as guilty as anyone. After all, we did change the version number! The only benefit of that experience was to get this rule.

> When old names are removed, their implementations MUST provoke an exception (assertion) if used by applications.

I've not tested this rule to be certain it makes sense. Perhaps what it means is "if you can't provoke a compile error because the API is dynamic, provoke an assertion."

C4 is not perfect. Few things are. The process for changing it (Digistan's COSS) is a little outdated now: it relies on a single-editor workflow with the ability to fork, but not merge. This seems to work, but it could be better to use C4 for protocols like C4.

A Real-Life Example

In the "XPUB subscription notifications" email thread (*http://lists.zeromq.org/piper mail/zeromq-dev/2012-October/018838.html*), Dan Goes asks how to make a publisher that knows when a new client subscribes and sends out previous matching messages. It's a standard pub-sub technique called "last value caching." Over a one-way transport like pgm (where subscribers literally send no packets back to publishers), this can't be done. But over TCP, it can, if we use an XPUB socket and if that socket didn't cleverly filter out duplicate subscriptions to reduce upstream traffic.

Though I'm not an expert contributor to libzmq, this seemed like a fun problem to solve. How hard could it be? I started by forking the libzmq repository to my own GitHub account, and then cloned it to my laptop, where I built it:

```
Git clone git@github.com:hintjens/libzmq.git
cd libzmq
./autogen.sh
./configure
make
```

Because the libzmq code is neat and well organized, it was quite easy to find the main files to change (*xpub.cpp* and *xpub.hpp*). Each socket type has its own source file and class. They inherit from *socket_base.cpp*, which has this hook for socket-specific options:

```
// First, check whether specific socket type overloads the option.
int rc = xsetsockopt (option_, optval_, optvallen_);
if (rc == 0 || errno != EINVAL)
    return rc;

// If the socket type doesn't support the option, pass it to
// the generic option parser
return options.setsockopt (option_, optval_, optvallen_);
```

Then I checked where the XPUB socket filters out duplicate subscriptions, in its xread_activated() method:

```
bool unique;
if (*data == 0)
    unique = subscriptions.rm (data + 1, size - 1, pipe_);
else
    unique = subscriptions.add (data + 1, size - 1, pipe_);

// If the subscription is not a duplicate, store it so that it can be
// passed to used on next recv call
```

```
if (unique && options.type != ZMQ_PUB)
    pending.push_back (blob_t (data, size));
```

At this stage, I wasn't too concerned with the details of how subscriptions.rm() and subscriptions.()add work. The code seems obvious, except that "subscription" also includes unsubscription, which confused me for a few seconds. If there's anything else weird in the rm and add methods, that's a separate issue to fix later. Now it was time to make an issue for this change. I headed over to the *https://zeromq.jira.com* site, logged in, and created a new entry.

Jira kindly offered me the traditional choice between "bug" and "new feature," and I spent 30 seconds wondering where this counterproductive historical distinction came from. Presumably, the "we'll fix bugs for free but you pay for new features" commercial proposal, which stems from the "you tell us what you want and we'll make it for $X" model of software development, and which generally leads to "we spent three times $X and we got what?!" email Fists of Fury.

Putting such thoughts aside, I created an issue, #443 (*https://zeromq.jira.com/browse/ LIBZMQ-443*), and described the problem and a plausible solution:

> Problem: XPUB socket filters out duplicate subscriptions (deliberate design). However this makes it impossible to do subscription-based intelligence. See http:// lists.zeromq.org/pipermail/zeromq-dev/2012-October/018838.html for a use case.
>
> Solution: make this behavior configurable with a socket option.

Then it was naming time. The API sits in *include/zmq.h*, so this is where I added the option name. When you invent a concept in an API or anywhere, *please* take a moment to choose a name that is explicit and short and obvious. Don't fall back on generic names that require additional context to understand. You have one chance to tell the reader what your concept is and does. A name like ZMQ_SUBSCRIPTION_FORWARDING_FLAG is terrible. It technically kind of aims in the right direction, but it's miserably long and obscure. I chose ZMQ_XPUB_VERBOSE: short and explicit, and clearly an on/off switch, with "off" being the default setting.

Next, it was time to add a private property to the xpub class definition in *xpub.hpp*:

```
// If true, send all subscription messages upstream, not just
// unique ones
bool verbose;
```

and then lift some code from *router.cpp* to implement the xsetsockopt() method. Finally, I changed the xread_activated() method to use this new option, and while I was at it, I made that test on socket type more explicit too:

```
//  If the subscription is not a duplicate, store it so that it can be
//  passed to be used on next recv call
if (options.type == ZMQ_XPUB && (unique || verbose))
    pending.push_back (blob_t (data, size));
```

It built nicely the first time. This made me a little suspicious, but being lazy and jet-lagged, I didn't immediately make a test case to actually try out the change. The process doesn't demand that, even if usually I'd do it just to catch that inevitable 10% of mistakes we all make. I did, however, document this new option on the *doc/zmq_setsockopt.txt* man page. In the worst case, I added a patch that wasn't really useful. But I certainly didn't break anything.

I didn't implement a matching `zmq_getsockopt()` method, because "minimal" means what it says. There's no obvious use case for getting the value of an option that you presumably just set in code. Symmetry isn't a valid reason to double the size of a patch. I did have to document the new option, because the process says, "All Public Contracts SHOULD be documented."

Committing the code, I pushed the patch to my forked repository (the "origin"):

```
Git commit -a -m "Fixed issue #443"
Git push origin master
```

Switching to the GitHub web interface, I went to my `libzmq` fork and pressed the big "Pull Request" button at the top. GitHub asked me for a title, so I entered "Added ZMQ_XPUB_VERBOSE option." I'm not sure why it asks this as I made a neat commit message, but hey, let's go with the flow here.

This made a nice little pull request with two commits: the one I'd made a month ago on the release notes, to prepare for the 3.2.1 release (a month passes so quickly when you spend most of it in airports), and my fix for issue #443 (37 new lines of code). GitHub lets you continue to make commits after you've kicked off a pull request. They get queued up and merged in one go. That simplifies things, but the maintainer may refuse the whole bundle based on one patch that doesn't look valid.

Because Dan was waiting (at least in my highly optimistic imagination) for this fix, I then went back to the *zeromq-dev* list and told him I'd made the patch, with a link to the commit. The faster I get feedback, the better. It was 1 a.m. in South Korea as I made this patch, so early evening in Europe, and morning in the States. You learn to count time zones when you work with people across the world. Ian was in a conference, Mikko was getting on a plane, and Chuck was probably in the office, but three hours later, Ian merged the pull request.

After Ian merged the pull request, I resynchronized my fork with the upstream `libzmq` repository. First, I added a "remote" that tells Git where this repository sits (just once, in the directory where I'm working):

```
Git remote add upstream git://github.com/zeromq/libzmq.git
```

Then I pulled changes back from the upstream master and checked the Git log to verify:

```
Git pull --rebase upstream master
Git log
```

And that is pretty much it, in terms of how much Git one needs to learn and use to contribute patches to libzmq. Six Git commands and some clicking on web pages. Most importantly to me as a naturally lazy, stupid, and easily confused developer, I don't have to learn Git's internal models, and I never have to do anything involving those infernal engines of structural complexity we call "Git branches." Next up, the attempted assassination of those Git branches. Let's live dangerously!

Git Branches Considered Harmful

One of Git's most popular features is its branches. Almost all projects that use Git use branches, and the selection of the "best" branching strategy is like a rite of passage for an open source project. Vincent Driessen's Git-flow (*http://nvie.com/posts/a-successful-git-branching-model/*) is maybe the best known. It has *base branches* (master, develop), *feature branches*, *release branches*, *hotfix branches*, and *support branches*. Many teams have adopted Git-flow, which even has Git extensions to support it. I'm a great believer in popular wisdom, but sometimes you have to recognize mass delusion for what it is.

Here is a section of C4 that might have shocked you when you first read it:

> The project SHALL NOT use topic branches for any reason. Personal forks MAY use topic branches.

To be clear, it's *public branches in shared repositories* that I'm talking about. Using branches for private work, such as to work on different issues, appears to work well enough, though it's more complexity than I personally enjoy. To channel Stallman again: "Your freedom to create complexity ends one inch from our shared workspace."

Like the rest of C4, the rules on branches are not accidental. They came from our experience making ØMQ, starting when Martin Sustrik and I rethought how to make stable releases. We both love and appreciate simplicity (some people seem to have a remarkable tolerance for complexity). We chatted for a while... I asked him, "I'm going to start making a stable release, would it be OK for me to make a branch in the Git you're working in?" Martin didn't like the idea. "OK, if I fork the repository, I can move patches from your repo to that one." That felt much better to both of us.

The response from many in the ØMQ community was shock and horror. People felt we were being lazy and making contributors work harder to find the "right" repository. Still, this seemed simple, and indeed it worked smoothly. The best part was that we each worked as we wanted to, and whereas before the ØMQ repository had felt horribly complex (and it wasn't even anything like Git-flow), this felt simple. And it worked. The only downside was that we lost a single unified history. Now, perhaps historians will feel robbed, but I honestly can't see that the historical minutiae of who changed what and when, including every branch and experiment, are worth any significant pain or friction.

People have gotten used to the "multiple repositories" approach in ØMQ, and we've started using it in other projects quite successfully. My own opinion is that history will judge Git branches and patterns like Git-flow as a complex solution to imaginary problems inherited from the days of Subversion and monolithic repositories.

More profoundly, and perhaps this is why the majority seems to be "wrong": I think the "branches versus forks" argument is really a deeper "design versus evolve" argument about how to make software optimally. I'll address that deeper argument in the next section. For now, I'll try to be scientific about my irrational hatred of branches by looking at a number of criteria and comparing branches and forks in each one.

Simplicity Versus Complexity

The simpler, the better.

There is no inherent reason why branches are more complex than forks. However, Git-flow uses *five types* of branch, whereas C4 uses two types of fork (development and stable) and one branch (master). Circumstantial evidence thus indicates that branches lead to more complexity than forks. For new users, it is definitely—and we've measured this in practice—easier to learn to work with many repositories and no branches except master.

Change Latency

The smaller and more rapid the delivery, the better.

Development branches seem to correlate strongly with large, slow, risky deliveries. "Sorry, I have to merge this branch before we can test the new version" signals a breakdown in process. It's certainly not how C4 works, which is by focusing tightly on individual problems and their minimal solutions. Allowing branches in development raises change latency. Forks have a different outcome: it's up to the forker to ensure that his changes merge cleanly, and to keep them simple so they won't be rejected.

Learning Curve

The smoother the learning curve, the better.

Evidence definitely shows that learning to use Git branches is complex. For some people, this is OK. For most developers, every cycle spent learning Git is a cycle lost on more productive things. I've been told several times, by different people that I do not like branches because I "never properly learned Git." That is fair, but it is a criticism of the tool, not the human.

Cost of Failure

The lower the cost of failure, the better.

Branches demand more perfection from developers, since mistakes potentially affect others. This raises the cost of failure. Forks make failure extremely cheap because literally nothing that happens in a fork can affect others not using that fork.

Up-Front Coordination

The less need for up-front coordination, the better.

You can do a hostile fork. You cannot do a hostile branch. Branches depend on up-front coordination, which is expensive and fragile. One person can veto the desires of a whole group. For example, in the ØMQ community we were unable to agree on a Git branching model for a year. We solved that by using forking instead. The problem went away.

Scalability

The more you can scale a project, the better.

The strong assumption in all branch strategies is that the repository *is* the project. But there is a limit to how many people you can get in agreement to work together in one repository. As I explained, the cost of up-front coordination can become fatal. A more realistic project scales by allowing anyone to start their own repositories, and ensuring these can work together. A project like ØMQ has dozens of repositories. Forking looks more scalable than branching.

Surprise and Expectations

The less surprising, the better.

People expect branches and find forks to be uncommon and thus confusing. This is the one aspect where branches win. If you use branches, a single patch will have the same commit hash tag, whereas across forks the patch will have different hash tags. That makes it harder to track patches as they cross forks, true. But seriously, *having to track hexadecimal hash tags is not a feature*. It's a bug. Sometimes better ways of working are just surprising at first.

Economics of Participation

The more tangible the rewards, the better.

People like to own their work and get credit for it. This is much easier with forks than with branches. Forks create more competition, in a healthy way, while branches suppress competition and force people to collaborate and share credit. This may sound positive, but in my experience it demotivates people. A branch isn't a product you can "own," whereas a fork can be.

Robustness in Conflict

The more a model can survive conflict, the better.

Like it or not, people fight over ego, status, beliefs, and theories of the world. Challenge is a necessary part of science. If your organizational model depends on agreement, you won't survive the first real fight. Branches do not survive real arguments and fights, whereas forks can be hostile and still benefit all parties. And this is indeed how free software works.

Guarantees of Isolation

The stronger the isolation between production code and experiment, the better.

People make mistakes. I've seen experimental code pushed to mainline production by error. I've seen people make bad panic changes under stress. But the real fault is in allowing two entirely separate generations of product to exist in the same protected space. If you can push to random-branch-x, you can push to master. Branches do not guarantee isolation of production-critical code. Forks do.

Visibility

The more visible our work, the better.

Forks have watchers, issues, a README, and a wiki. Branches have none of these. People try forks, build them, break them, patch them. Branches sit there until someone remembers to work on them. Forks have downloads and tarballs. Branches do not. When we look for self-organization, the more visible and declarative the problems, the faster and more accurately we can work.

Conclusions

In this section, I've listed a series of arguments, most of which came from fellow team members. Here's how it seems to break down: Git veterans insist that branches are the way to work, whereas newcomers tend to feel intimidated when asked to navigate Git branches. Git is not an easy tool to master. What we've discovered, accidentally, is that when you stop using branches *at all*, Git becomes trivial to use. It literally comes down to six commands (*clone, remote, commit, log, push, and pull*). Furthermore, a branch-free process actually works; we've used it for a couple of years now with no visible downside except surprise to the veterans, and growth of "single" projects over multiple repositories.

If you can't use forks, perhaps because your firm doesn't trust GitHub's private repositories, then you can perhaps use topic branches, one per issue. However, you'll still suffer the costs of getting up-front consensus, low competitiveness, and risk of human error.

Designing for Innovation

Let's look at innovation, which Wikipedia defines as, "the development of new values through solutions that meet new requirements, inarticulate needs, or old customer and market needs in value adding new ways." This really just means solving problems more cheaply. It sounds straight-forward, but the history of collapsed tech giants proves that it's not. I'll try to explain how teams so often get it wrong, and suggest a way for doing innovation right.

The Tale of Two Bridges

Two old engineers were talking of their lives and boasting of their greatest projects. One of the engineers explained how he had designed one of the greatest bridges ever made.

"We built it across a river gorge," he told his friend. "It was wide and deep. We spent two years studying the land and choosing designs and materials. We hired the best engineers and spent another five years designing the bridge. We contracted the largest engineering firms to build the structures, the towers, the tollbooths, and the roads that would connect the bridge to the main highways. Dozens died during the construction. Under the road level we had trains, and a special path for cyclists. That bridge represented years of my life."

The second man reflected for a while, then spoke. "One evening me and a friend got drunk on vodka, and we threw a rope across a gorge," he said. "Just a rope, tied to two trees. There were two villages, one at each side. At first, people pulled packages across that rope with a pulley and string. Then someone threw a second rope, and built a foot walk. It was dangerous, but the kids loved it. A group of men then rebuilt that, made it solid, and women started to cross, every day, with their produce. A market grew up on one side of the bridge, and slowly that became a large town, since there was a lot of space for houses. The rope bridge got replaced with a wooden bridge, to allow horses and carts to cross. Then the town built a real stone bridge, with metal beams. Later, they replaced the stone part with steel, and today there's a suspension bridge standing in that same spot."

The first engineer was silent. "Funny thing," he said, "my bridge was demolished about 10 years after we built it. Turns out it was built in the wrong place and no one wanted to use it. Some guys had thrown a rope across the gorge, a few miles further downstream, and that's where everyone went."

How ØMQ Lost Its Road Map

Presenting ØMQ at the Mix-IT conference in Lyon in early 2012, I was asked several times for the "road map." My answer was: there is no road map any longer. We had road maps, and we deleted them. Instead of a few experts trying to lay out the next steps, we were allowing this to happen organically. The audience didn't really like my answer. So un-French.

However, the history of ØMQ makes it quite clear why road maps were problematic. In the beginning, we had a small team making the library, with few contributors, and no documented road map. As ØMQ grew more popular, and we switched to more contributors, users asked for road maps. So we collected our plans together and tried to organize them into releases. Here, we wrote, is what will come in the next release.

As we rolled out releases, we hit the problem that it's very easy to promise stuff, and rather harder to make it as planned. For one thing, much of the work was voluntary, and it's not clear how you force volunteers to commit to a road map. But also, priorities can shift dramatically over time. So we were making promises we could not keep, and the real deliveries didn't match the road maps.

The second problem was that by defining the road map, we in effect claimed territory, making it harder for others to participate. People do prefer to contribute to changes they believe were their idea. Writing down a list of things to do turns contribution into a chore rather than an opportunity.

Finally, we saw changes in ØMQ that were quite traumatic (for example, incompatible changes in APIs and protocols), and the road maps didn't help with this, despite a lot of discussion and effort to "do it right." It was quite clear that we needed a different approach for defining the change process.

Software engineers don't like the notion that powerful, effective solutions can come into existence without an intelligent designer actively thinking things through. And yet, no one in that room in Lyon would have questioned evolution. A strange irony, and one I wanted to explore further, as it underpins the direction the ØMQ community has taken since the start of 2012.

In the dominant theory of innovation, brilliant individuals reflect on large problem sets and then carefully and precisely create a solution. Sometimes they have "eureka" moments where they "get" brilliantly simple answers to whole large problem sets. The inventor and the process of invention are rare, precious, and can command a monopoly. History is full of such heroic individuals. We owe them our modern world.

Looking more closely, however, you will see that the facts don't match. History doesn't show lone inventors: it shows lucky people who steal or claim ownership of ideas that are being worked on by many. It shows brilliant people striking lucky once, and then spending decades on fruitless and pointless quests. The best known large-scale inventors, like Thomas Edison, were in fact just very good at managing systematic broad research done by large teams. It's like claiming that Steve Jobs invented every device made by Apple. It is a nice myth, good for marketing, but utterly useless as practical science.

Recent history, much better documented and less easy to manipulate, shows this well. The Internet is surely one of the most innovative and fast-moving areas of technology, and one of the best documented. It has no inventor. Instead, it has a massive economy of people who have carefully and progressively solved a long series of immediate problems, documented their answers, and made those available to all. The innovative nature of the Internet comes not from a small, select band of Einsteins. It comes from RFCs anyone can use and improve, made by hundreds or thousands of smart, but not uniquely smart, individuals. It comes from open source software anyone can use and improve. It comes from sharing, scale of community, and the continuous accretion of good solutions and disposal of bad ones.

Here, thus, is an alternative theory of innovation:

1. There is an infinite problem/solution terrain.
2. This terrain changes over time according to external conditions.
3. We can only accurately perceive problems to which we are close.
4. We can rank the cost/benefit economics of problems using a market for solutions.
5. There is an optimal solution to any solvable problem.
6. We can approach this optimal solution heuristically and mechanically.
7. Our intelligence can make this process faster, but does not replace it.

There are a few corollaries to this:

- *Individual creativity matters less than process.* Smarter people may work faster, but they may work in the wrong direction. It's the collective vision of reality that keeps us honest and relevant.

- *We don't need road maps if we have a good process.* Functionality will emerge and evolve over time as solutions compete for market share.

- *We don't invent solutions so much as discover them.* All sympathies to the creative soul. It's just an information processing machine that likes to polish its own ego and collect karma.

- *Intelligence is a social effect, though it feels personal.* A person cut off from others eventually stops thinking. We can neither collect problems nor measure solutions without other people.

- *The size and diversity of the community is a key factor.* Larger, more diverse communities collect more relevant problems, solve them more accurately, and do this faster than a small expert group.

So, when we trust the solitary experts, we see classic errors: focus on ideas, not problems; focus on the wrong problems; misjudgments about the value of solving problems; not using one's own work; and many other misjudgments of the real market.

Can we turn the preceding theory into a reusable process? In late 2011, I started documenting C4 and similar contracts, and using them both in ØMQ and in closed-source projects. The underlying process is something I call "Simplicity-Oriented Design," or SOD. This is a reproducible way of developing simple and elegant products. It organizes people into flexible supply chains that are able to navigate a problem landscape rapidly and cheaply. They do this by building, testing, and keeping or discarding minimal plausible solutions, called "patches." Living products consist of long series of patches, applied one atop the other.

SOD is relevant first because it's how we evolve ØMQ. It's also the basis for the design process we will use in Chapter 7 to develop larger-scale ØMQ applications. Of course, you can use any software architecture methodology with ØMQ.

To best understand how we ended up with SOD, let's look at the alternatives.

Trash-Oriented Design

The most popular design process in large businesses seems to be *Trash-Oriented Design*, or TOD. TOD feeds off the belief that all we need to make money are great ideas. It's tenacious nonsense, but a powerful crutch for people who lack imagination. The theory goes that ideas are rare, so the trick is to capture them. It's like nonmusicians being awed by a guitar player, not realizing that great talent is so cheap it literally plays on the streets for coins.

The main output of TOD is expensive "ideation": concepts, design documents, and products that go straight into the trash can. It works as follows:

- The Creative People come up with long lists of "we could do X and Y." I've seen endlessly detailed lists of all the amazing things a product could do. We've all been guilty of this. Once the creative work of idea generation has happened, it's just a matter of execution, of course.

- So, the managers and their consultants pass their brilliant ideas to designers, who create acres of preciously refined design documents. The designers take the tens of ideas the managers came up with, and turn them into hundreds of world-changing designs.

- These designs get given to engineers, who scratch their heads and wonder who the heck came up with such nonsense. They start to argue back, but the designs come from up high, and really, it's not up to engineers to argue with creative people and expensive consultants.

- So the engineers creep back to their cubicles, humiliated and threatened into building the gigantic but oh-so-elegant junk heap. It is bone-breaking work because the designs take no account of practical costs. Minor whims might take weeks of work to build. As the project gets delayed, the managers bully the engineers into giving up their evenings and weekends.

- Eventually, something resembling a working product makes it out of the door. It's creaky and fragile, complex and ugly. The designers curse the engineers for their incompetence and pay more consultants to put lipstick onto the pig, and slowly the product starts to look a little nicer.

- By this time, the managers have started to try to sell the product and they find, shockingly, that no one wants it. Undaunted, they courageously build million-dollar websites and ad campaigns to explain to the public why they absolutely need this product. They do deals with other businesses to force the product on the lazy, stupid, and ungrateful market.

- After 12 months of intense marketing, the product still isn't making profits. Worse, it suffers dramatic failures and gets branded in the press as a disaster. The company quietly shelves it, fires the consultants, buys a competing product from a small startup, and rebrands that as its own version 2. Hundreds of millions of dollars end up in the trash.

- Meanwhile, another visionary manager somewhere in the organization drinks a little too much tequila with some marketing people and has a Brilliant Idea.

Trash-Oriented Design would be a caricature if it wasn't so common. Something like 19 out of 20 market-ready products built by large firms are failures (yes, 87% of statistics are made up on the spot). The remaining 1 in 20 probably only succeeds because the competitors are so bad and the marketing is so aggressive.

The main lessons of TOD are quite straightforward, but hard to swallow. They are:

- Ideas are cheap. No exceptions. There are no brilliant ideas. Anyone who tries to start a discussion with "Oooh, we can do this too!" should be beaten down with all the passion one reserves for traveling evangelists. It is like sitting in a cafe at the foot of a mountain, drinking a hot chocolate and telling others, "Hey, I have a great idea, we can climb that mountain! And build a chalet on top! With two saunas! And a garden! Hey, and we can make it solar powered! Dude, that's awesome! What color should we paint it? Green! No, blue! OK, go and make it, I'll stay here and make spreadsheets and graphics!"

- The starting point for a good design process is to collect real problems that confront real people. The second step is to evaluate these problems with the basic question, "How much is it worth to solve this problem?" Having done that, we can collect the set of problems that are worth solving.

- Good solutions to real problems will succeed as products. Their success will depend on how good and cheap the solution is, and how important the problem is (and sadly, how big the marketing budgets are). But their success will also depend on how much they demand in effort to use—in other words, how simple they are.

Now, having slain the dragon of utter irrelevance, we attack the demon of complexity.

Complexity-Oriented Design

Really good engineering teams and small firms can usually build decent products. But the vast majority of products still end up being too complex and less successful than they might be. This is because specialist teams, even the best, often stubbornly apply a process I call *Complexity-Oriented Design*, or COD, which works as follows:

- Management correctly identifies some interesting and difficult problem with economic value. In doing so, they already leapfrog over any TOD team.
- The team, with enthusiasm, starts to build prototypes and core layers. These work as designed, and thus encouraged, the team goes off into intense design and architecture discussions, coming up with elegant schemas that look beautiful and solid.
- Management comes back and challenges the team with yet more difficult problems. We tend to equate cost with value, so the harder and more expensive to solve the problem is, the more the solution should be worth, in their minds.
- The team, being engineers and thus loving to build stuff, build stuff. They build and build and build and end up with massive, perfectly designed complexity.
- The products go to market, and the market scratches its head and asks, "Seriously, is this the best you can do?" People do use the products, especially if they aren't spending their own money in climbing the learning curve.
- Management gets positive feedback from its larger customers, who share the same idea that high cost (in training and use) means high value, and so continues to push the process.
- Meanwhile somewhere across the world, a small team is solving the same problem using a better process, and a year later smashes the market to little pieces.

COD is characterized by a team obsessively solving the wrong problems in a form of collective delusion. COD products tend to be large, ambitious, complex, and unpopular. Much open source software is the output of COD processes. It is insanely hard for engineers to *stop* extending a design to cover more potential problems. They argue, "What if someone wants to do X?" but never ask themselves, "What is the real value of solving X?"

A good example of COD in practice is Bluetooth, a complex, over-designed set of protocols that users hate. It continues to exist only because in a massively patented industry there are no real alternatives. Bluetooth is perfectly secure, which is close to pointless for a proximity protocol. At the same time, it lacks a standard API for developers, meaning it's really costly to use Bluetooth in applications.

On the *#zeromq* IRC channel, Wintre once wrote of how enraged he was many years ago when he "found that XMMS 2 had a working plugin system but could not actually play music."

COD is a form of large-scale "rabbit-holing," in which designers and engineers cannot distance themselves from the technical details of their work. They add more and more features, utterly misreading the economics of their work.

The main lessons of COD are also simple, but hard for experts to swallow. They are:

- Making stuff that you don't immediately have a need for is pointless. It doesn't matter how talented or brilliant you are, if you just sit down and make stuff people are not actually asking for, you are most likely wasting your time.

- Problems are not equal. Some are simple, and some are complex. Ironically, solving the simpler problems often has more value to more people than solving the really hard ones. If you allow engineers to just work on random things, they'll mostly focus on the most interesting but least worthwhile things.

- Engineers and designers love making stuff and decoration, and this inevitably leads to complexity. It is crucial to have a "stop mechanism": a way to set short, hard deadlines that force people to make smaller, simpler answers to just the most crucial problems.

Simplicity-Oriented Design

Finally, we come to the rare but precious *Simplicity-Oriented Design*, or SOD. This process starts with a realization: we do not know what we have to make until after we start making it. Coming up with ideas or large-scale designs isn't just wasteful, it's a direct hindrance to designing the truly accurate solutions. The really juicy problems are hidden like far valleys, and any activity except active scouting creates a fog that hides those distant valleys. You need to keep mobile, pack light, and move fast.

SOD works as follows:

- We collect a set of interesting problems (by looking at how people use technology or other products) and we line these up from simple to complex, looking for and identifying patterns of use.

- We take the simplest, most dramatic problem and we solve this with a minimal plausible solution, or "patch." Each patch solves exactly a genuine and agreed-upon problem in a brutally minimal fashion.
- We apply one measure of quality to patches, namely, "Can this be done any more simply while still solving the stated problem?" We can measure complexity in terms of concepts and models that the user has to learn or guess in order to use the patch. The fewer, the better. A perfect patch solves a problem with zero learning required by the user.
- Our product development consists of a patch that solves the problem "we need a proof of concept" and then evolves in an unbroken line to a mature series of products, through hundreds or thousands of patches piled on top of each other.
- We do not do *anything* that is not a patch. We enforce this rule with formal processes that demand that every activity or task is tied to a genuine and agreed-upon problem, explicitly enunciated and documented.
- We build our projects into a supply chain where each project can provide problems to its "suppliers" and receive patches in return. The supply chain creates the "stop mechanism" because when people are impatiently waiting for an answer, we necessarily cut our work short.
- Individuals are free to work on any projects and provide patches at any place they feel it's worthwhile. No individuals "own" any project, except to enforce the formal processes. A single project can have many variations, each a collection of different, competing patches.
- Projects export formal and documented interfaces so that upstream (client) projects are unaware of changes happening in supplier projects. Thus, multiple supplier projects can compete for client projects, in effect creating a free and competitive market.
- We tie our supply chain to real users and external clients, and we drive the whole process by rapid cycles so that a problem received from outside users can be analyzed, evaluated, and solved with a patch in a few hours.
- At every moment, from the very first patch, our product is shippable. This is essential, because a large proportion of patches will be wrong (10–30%), and only by giving the product to users can we know which patches have become problems that need solving.

SOD is a *hill-climbing algorithm*, a reliable way of finding optimal solutions to the most significant problems in an unknown landscape. You don't need to be a genius to use SOD successfully, you just need to be able to see the difference between the fog of activity and the progress toward new real problems.

People have pointed out that hill-climbing algorithms have known limitations. One gets stuck on local peaks, mainly. But this is nonetheless how life itself works: collecting tiny incremental improvements over long periods of time. There is no intelligent designer. We reduce the risk of local peaks by spreading out widely across the landscape, but it is somewhat moot. The limitations aren't optional, they are physical laws. The theory says, *this is how innovation really works, so it's better to embrace it and work with it than to try to work on the basis of magical thinking.*

And in fact, once you see all innovation as more or less successful hill-climbing, you realize why some teams and companies and products get stuck in a never-never land of diminishing prospects. They simply don't have the diversity and collective intelligence to find better hills to climb. When Nokia killed its open source projects, it cut its own throat.

A really good designer with a good team can use SOD to build world-class products, rapidly and accurately. To get the most out of SOD, the designer has to use the product continuously from day one, and develop his or her ability to smell out problems such as inconsistency, surprising behavior, and other forms of friction. We naturally overlook many annoyances, but a good designer picks these up and thinks about how to patch them. Design is about removing friction in the use of a product.

In an open source setting, we do this work in public. There's no "let's open the code" moment. Projects that do this are in my view missing the point of open source, which is to engage your users in your exploration, and to build community around the seed of the architecture.

Burnout

The ØMQ community has been and still is heavily dependent on pro bono individual efforts. I'd like to think that everyone was compensated in some way for their contributions, and I believe that with ØMQ, contributing means gaining expertise in an extraordinarily valuable technology, which leads to improved professional options.

However, not all projects will be so lucky, and if you work with or in open source, you should understand the risk of burnout that volunteers face. This applies to all pro bono communities. In this section, I'll explain what causes burnout, how to recognize it, how to prevent it, and (if it happens) how to try to treat it. Disclaimer: I'm not a psychiatrist and this section is based on my own experiences of working in pro bono contexts for the last 20 years, including on free software projects and NGOs such as the FFII (*http://www.ffii.org*).

In a pro bono context, we're expected to work without direct or obvious economic incentive. That is, we sacrifice family life, professional advancement, free time, and health in order to accomplish some goal we have decided to accomplish. In any project, we need some kind of reward to make it worth continuing each day. In most pro bono projects the rewards are very indirect, superficially not economical at all. Mostly, we do things because people say, "Hey, great!" Karma is a powerful motivator.

However, we are economic beings, and sooner or later, if a project costs us a great deal and does not bring economic rewards of some kind (money, fame, a new job...), we start to suffer. At a certain stage, it seems our subconscious simply gets disgusted and says, "Enough is enough!" and refuses to go any further. If we try to force ourselves, we can literally get sick.

This is what I call "burnout," though the term is also used for other kinds of exhaustion. Too much investment in a project with too little economic reward, for too long. We are great at manipulating ourselves and others, and this is often part of the process that leads to burnout. We tell ourselves that it's for a good cause and that the other guy is doing OK, so we should be able to as well.

When I got burned out on open source projects like Xitami, I remember clearly how I felt. I simply stopped working on the project, refused to answer any more emails, and told people to forget about it. You can tell when someone's burned out. They go offline, and everyone starts saying, "He's acting strange... depressed, or tired...."

Diagnosis is simple. Have the victims worked a lot on a project that was not paying back in any way? Did they make exceptional sacrifices? Did they lose or abandon their jobs or studies to work on the project? If you're answering "yes," it's burnout.

There are three simple tenets I've developed over the years to reduce the risk of burnout in the teams I work with:

- *No one is irreplaceable.* Working solo on a critical or popular project—the concentration of responsibility on one person who cannot set her own limits—is probably the main factor in burnout. It's a management truism: if someone in your organization is irreplaceable, get rid of him or her.

- *We need day jobs to pay the bills.* This can be hard, but it seems necessary. Getting money from somewhere else makes it much easier to sustain a sacrificial project.

- *People must be taught about burnout.* This should be a basic course in colleges and universities, as pro bono work becomes a more common way for young people to experiment professionally.

When a person is working alone on a critical project, you *know* he is going blow his fuse sooner or later. It's actually fairly predictable: it will happen in something like 18–36 months, depending on the individuals and how much economic stress they face in their private lives. I've not seen anyone burn out after half a year, nor last five years working on an unrewarding project.

There is a simple cure for burnout that works in at least some cases: get paid decently for your work. However, this pretty much destroys the freedom of movement (across that infinite problem landscape) that the volunteer enjoys.

Patterns for Success

I'll end this code-free chapter with a series of patterns for success in software engineering. They aim to capture the essence of what divides glorious success from tragic failure. They were described as "religious maniacal dogma" by a manager, and "anything else would be effing insane" by a colleague, in a single day. For me, they are science. But treat the Lazy Perfectionist and others as tools to use, sharpen, and throw away if something better comes along.

The Lazy Perfectionist

Never design anything that's not a precise, minimal answer to a problem we can identify and have to solve.

The Lazy Perfectionist spends his idle time observing others and identifying problems that are worth solving. He looks for agreement on those problems, always asking, "What is the *real* problem?" Then he moves, precisely and minimally, to build (or get others to build) a usable answer to one problem. He uses, or gets others to use, those solutions. And he repeats this until there are no problems left to solve, or time or money runs out.

The Benevolent Tyrant

The control of a large force is the same principle as the control of a few men: it is merely a question of dividing up their numbers. — Sun Tzu

The Benevolent Tyrant divides large problems into smaller ones and throws them at groups to focus on. He brokers contracts between these groups, in the form of APIs and the "unprotocols" we'll read about in the next chapter. The Benevolent Tyrant constructs a supply chain that starts with problems and results in usable solutions. He is ruthless about how the supply chain works, but does not tell people what to work on, or how to do their work.

The Earth and Sky

The ideal team consists of two sides: one writing code, and one providing feedback.

The Earth and Sky work together as a whole, in close proximity, but they communicate formally through issue tracking. Sky seeks out problems from others and from personal use of the product and feeds these to Earth. Earth rapidly answers with testable solutions. Earth and Sky can work through dozens of issues in a day. Sky talks to other users, and Earth talks to other developers. Earth and Sky may be two people, or two small groups.

The Open Door

The accuracy of knowledge comes from diversity.

The Open Door accepts contributions from almost anyone. She does not argue quality or direction, instead allowing others to argue that and to get more engaged. She calculates that even a troll will bring more diverse opinions to the group. She lets the group form its opinion about what goes into stable code, and she enforces this opinion with the help of a Benevolent Tyrant.

The Laughing Clown

Perfection precludes participation.

The Laughing Clown, often acting as the Happy Failure, makes no claim to high competence. Instead, his antics and bumbling attempts provoke others into rescuing him from his own tragedy. Somehow, however, he always identifies the right problems to solve. People are so busy proving him wrong, they don't realize they're doing valuable work.

The Mindful General

Make no plans. Set goals, develop strategies and tactics.

The Mindful General operates in unknown territory, solving problems that are hidden until they are nearby. Thus he makes no plans, but seeks opportunities, then exploits them rapidly and accurately. He develops tactics and strategies in the field, and teaches these to his men so they can move independently, and together.

The Social Engineer

If you know the enemy and know yourself, you need not fear the result of a hundred battles. — Sun Tzu

The Social Engineer reads the hearts and minds of those she works with and for. She asks of everyone, "What makes this person angry, insecure, argumentative, calm, happy?" She studies their moods and dispositions. With this knowledge she can encourage those who are useful, and discourage those who are not. The Social Engineer never acts on her own emotions.

The Constant Gardener

He will win whose army is animated by the same spirit throughout all its ranks. — Sun Tzu

The Constant Gardener grows a process from a small seed, step-by-step, as more people come into the project. He makes every change for a precise reason, with agreement from everyone. He never imposes a process from above, but lets others come to consensus, and then he enforces that consensus. In this way, everyone owns the process together, and by owning it, they are attached to it.

The Rolling Stone

After crossing a river, you should get far away from it. — Sun Tzu

The Rolling Stone accepts her own mortality and transience. She has no attachment to her past work. She accepts that all that we make is destined for the trash can; it is just a matter of time. With precise, minimal investments, she can move rapidly away from the past and stay focused on the present and near future. Above all, she has no ego and no pride to be hurt by the actions of others.

The Pirate Gang

Code, like all knowledge, works best as collective—not private—property.

The Pirate Gang organizes freely around problems. It accepts authority insofar as authority provides goals and resources. The Pirate Gang owns and shares all it makes: every work is fully remixable by others in the Pirate Gang. The gang moves rapidly as new problems emerge, and it is quick to abandon old solutions if those stop being relevant. No persons or groups can monopolize any part of the supply chain.

The Flash Mob

Water shapes its course according to the nature of the ground over which it flows. — Sun Tzu

The Flash Mob comes together in space and time as needed, then disperses as soon as it can. Physical closeness is essential for high-bandwidth communications, but over time it creates technical ghettos, where Earth gets separated from Sky. The Flash Mob tends to collect a lot of frequent flier miles.

The Canary Watcher

Pain is not, generally, a Good Sign.

The Canary Watcher measures the quality of an organization by his own pain level, and the observed pain levels of those with whom he works. He brings new participants into existing organizations so they can express the raw pain of the innocent. He may use alcohol to get others to verbalize their pain points. He asks others, and himself, "Are you happy in this process, and if not, why not?" When an organization causes pain in himself or others, he treats that as a problem to be fixed. People should feel joy in their work.

The Hangman

Never interrupt others when they are making mistakes.

The Hangman knows that we learn only by making mistakes, and he gives others copious rope with which to learn. He only pulls the rope gently, when it's time. A little tug to remind the other of her precarious position. Allowing others to learn by failure gives the good reason to stay, and the bad an excuse to leave. The Hangman is endlessly patient, because there is no shortcut to the learning process.

The Historian

Keeping the public record may be tedious, but it's the only way to prevent collusion.

The Historian forces discussion into the public view, to prevent collusion to own areas of work. The Pirate Gang depends on full and equal communications that do not depend on momentary presence. No one really reads the archives, but the simple possibility stops most abuses. The Historian encourages the right tool for the job: email for transient discussions, IRC for chatter, wikis for knowledge, issue tracking for recording opportunities.

The Provocateur

When a man knows he is to be hanged in a fortnight, it concentrates his mind wonderfully. — Samuel Johnson

The Provocateur creates deadlines, enemies, and the occasional impossibility. Teams work best when they don't have time for the crap. Deadlines bring people together and focus the collective mind. An external enemy can move a passive team into action. The Provocateur never takes the deadline too seriously. The product is *always* ready to ship. But she gently reminds the team of the stakes: fail, and we all look for other jobs.

The Mystic

When people argue or complain, just write them a Sun Tzu quotation. — Mikko Koppanen

The Mystic never argues directly. He knows that to argue with an emotional person only creates more emotion. Instead, he sidesteps the discussion. It's hard to be angry at a Chinese general, especially when he has been dead for 2,400 years. The Mystic plays Hangman when people insist on the right to get it wrong.

## CHAPTER 7

Advanced Architecture Using ØMQ

One of the effects of using ØMQ at a large scale is that because we can build distributed architectures so much faster than before, the limitations of our software engineering processes become more visible. Mistakes in slow motion are often harder to see (or rather, easier to rationalize away).

My experience when teaching ØMQ to groups of engineers is that it's rarely sufficient to just explain how ØMQ works and then expect them to start building successful products. Like any technology that removes friction, ØMQ opens the door to big blunders. If ØMQ is the ACME rocket-propelled shoe of distributed software development, a lot of us are like Wile E. Coyote, slamming full speed into the proverbial desert cliff.

We saw in Chapter 6that ØMQ itself uses a formal process for changes. One reason we built this process, over some years, was to stop the repeated cliff-slamming that happened in the library itself.

Partially it's about slowing down, and partially it's about ensuring that when you move fast, you go—and this is essential, dear reader—in the *right direction*. It's my standard interview riddle: what's the rarest property of any software system, the absolute hardest thing to get right, the lack of which causes the slow or fast death of the vast majority of projects? The answer is not code quality, funding, performance, or even (though it's a close answer) popularity. The answer is *accuracy*.

Accuracy is half the challenge, and that applies to any engineering work. The other half is specific distributed computing itself, which sets up a whole range of problems that we need to solve if we are going to create large architectures. We need to encode and decode data, and we need to define protocols to connect clients and servers; we need to secure these protocols against attackers, and we need to make stacks that are robust. Asynchronous messaging is hard to get right.

This chapter will tackle these challenges, starting with a basic reappraisal of how to design and build software and ending with a fully formed example of a distributed application for large-scale file distribution.

We'll cover the following juicy topics:

- How to go from idea to working prototype safely (the MOPED pattern)
- Different ways to serialize your data as ØMQ messages
- How to code-generate binary serialization codecs
- How to build custom code generators using the GSL tool
- How to write and license a protocol specification
- How to perform fast restartable file transfer over ØMQ
- How to accomplish credit-based flow control
- How to build protocol servers and clients as state machines
- How to make a secure protocol over ØMQ
- A large-scale file publishing system (FileMQ)

Message-Oriented Pattern for Elastic Design

In this section I'll introduce the *Message-Oriented Pattern for Elastic Design* (MOPED), a software engineering pattern for ØMQ architectures. It was either "MOPED" or "BIKE," the Backronym-Induced Kinetic Effect. That's short for "BICICLE," the Backronym-Inflated See if I Care Less Effect. In life, one learns to go with the least embarrassing choice.

If you've been reading the book carefully, you'll have seen MOPED in action already. The development of the Majordomo pattern in Chapter 4 is a near-perfect case. But cute names are worth a thousand words.

The goal of MOPED is to define a process by which we can take a rough use case for a new distributed application, and go from "Hello World" to fully working prototype in any language in under a week.

Using MOPED, you grow, more than build, a working ØMQ architecture from the ground up with minimal risk of failure. By focusing on the contracts rather than the implementations, you avoid the risk of premature optimization. By driving the design process through ultra-short test-based cycles, you can be more certain that what you have works before you add more.

We can turn this into five real steps:

1. Internalize the ØMQ semantics.

2. Draw a rough architecture.

3. Decide on the contracts.

4. Make a minimal end-to-end solution.

5. Solve one problem and repeat.

Step 1: Internalize the Semantics

You must learn and digest ØMQ's "language," that is, the socket patterns and how they work. The only way to learn a language is to use it. There's no way to avoid this investment, no tapes you can play while you sleep, no chips you can plug in to magically become smarter. Read Part I of this book, work through the code examples, understand what's going on, and (most importantly) write some examples yourself, and then throw them away.

At a certain point, you'll feel a clicking noise in your brain. Maybe you'll have a weird chili-induced dream where little ØMQ tasks run around trying to eat you alive. Maybe you'll just think, "Aaahh, so *that's* what it means!" If we did our work right, it should take two to three days. However long it takes, until you start thinking in terms of ØMQ sockets and patterns, you're not ready for step 2.

Step 2: Draw a Rough Architecture

From my experience, it's essential to be able to draw the core of your architecture. This helps others understand what you are thinking, but it also helps you think through your ideas. There is really no better way to explain your ideas to your colleagues than using a whiteboard.

You don't need to get it right, and you don't need to make it complete. What you do need to do is break your architecture into pieces that make sense. The nice thing about software architecture (as compared to constructing bridges) is that you really can replace entire layers cheaply, if you've isolated them.

Start by choosing the core problem that you are going to solve. Ignore anything that's not essential to that problem: you will add it in later. The problem should be an end-to-end problem: the rope across the gorge.

For example, a client asked us to make a supercomputing cluster with ØMQ. Clients create bundles of work, which are sent to a broker that distributes them to workers (running on fast graphics processors), collects the results back, and returns them to the client.

The rope across the gorge is one client talking to a broker talking to one worker. We draw three boxes: client, broker, and worker. We draw arrows from box to box showing the request flowing one way, and the response flowing back. It's just like the many diagrams we saw in earlier chapters.

Be minimalistic. Our goal is not to define a *real* architecture, but to throw a rope across the gorge to bootstrap our process. We'll make the architecture progressively more complete and realistic over time: e.g., adding multiple workers, adding client and worker APIs, handling failures, and so on.

Step 3: Decide on the Contracts

A good software architecture depends on contracts, and the more explicit they are, the better things scale. You don't care *how* things happen; you only care about the results. If I send an email, I don't care how it arrives at its destination, as long as the contract is respected (it arrives within a few minutes, it's not modified, and it doesn't get lost).

And to build a large system that works well, you must focus on the contracts before the implementations. It may sound obvious, but all too often people forget or ignore this, or are just too shy to impose themselves. I wish I could say ØMQ had done this properly, but for years our public contracts were second-rate afterthoughts instead of primary in-your-face pieces of work.

So what is a contract in a distributed system? There are, in my experience, two types of contract:

- The APIs to client applications. Remember the Psychological Elements of Software Architecture from Chapter 6. The APIs need to be as absolutely *simple, consistent,* and *familiar* as possible. Yes, you can generate API documentation from code, but you must first design it, and designing an API is often hard.
- The protocols that connect the pieces. It sounds like rocket science, but it's really just a simple trick, and one that ØMQ makes particularly easy. In fact, they're so simple to write, and need so little bureaucracy, that I call them "unprotocols."

You'll write minimal contracts that are mostly just place markers. Most messages and most API methods will be missing or empty. You'll also want to write down any known technical requirements in terms of throughput, latency, reliability, etc. These are the criteria on which you will accept, or reject, any particular piece of work.

Step 4: Write a Minimal End-to-End Solution

The goal is to test out the overall architecture as rapidly as possible. Make skeleton applications that call the APIs, and skeleton stacks that implement both sides of every protocol. You want to get a working end-to-end "Hello World" as soon as you can. You want to be able to test code as you write it and to weed out the broken assumptions and inevitable errors you make. Do not go off and spend six months writing a test suite! Instead, make a minimal bare-bones application that uses your still-hypothetical API.

If you design an API wearing the hat of the person who implements it, you'll start to think of performance, features, options, and so on. You'll make it more complex, more irregular, and more surprising than it should be. But—and here's the trick (it's a cheap one, was big in Japan)—if you design an API while wearing the hat of the person who has to actually write apps that use it, you'll use all that laziness and fear to your advantage.

Write down the protocols on a wiki or shared document in such a way that you can explain every command clearly, without too much detail. Strip off any real functionality, because it'll only create inertia that makes it harder to move stuff around. You can always add weight. Don't spend effort defining formal message structures: pass the minimum around in the simplest possible fashion using ØMQ's multipart framing.

Our goal is to get the simplest test case working, without any avoidable functionality. Everything you can chop off the list of things to do, you chop. Ignore the groans from colleagues and bosses. I'll repeat this once again: you can *always* add functionality, that's relatively easy. But aim to keep the overall weight to a minimum.

Step 5: Solve One Problem and Repeat

You're now in the happy cycle of issue-driven development, where you can start to solve tangible problems instead of adding features. Write issues that state a clear problem, and propose a solution for each. As you design the API, keep in mind your standards for names, consistency, and behavior. Writing these down in prose often helps keep them sane.

From here, every single change you make to the architecture and code can be proven by running the test case, watching it not work, making the change, and then watching it work.

Now you can go through the whole cycle (extending the test case, fixing the API, updating the protocol, extending the code, as needed), taking problems one at a time and testing the solutions individually. It should take about 10–30 minutes for each cycle, with the occasional spike due to random confusion.

Unprotocols

When this man thinks of protocols, this man thinks of massive documents written by committees, over years. This man thinks of the IETF, W3C, ISO, Oasis, regulatory capture, FRAND patent license disputes... and soon after, this man thinks of retirement to a nice little farm in northern Bolivia, up in the mountains where the only other needlessly stubborn beings are the goats chewing up the coffee plants.

Now, I've nothing personal against committees. The useless folk need a place to sit out their lives with minimal risk of reproducing; after all, that only seems fair. But most committee protocols tend toward complexity (the ones that work), or trash (the ones we don't talk about). There are a few reasons for this. One is the amount of money at stake. More money means more people who want their particular prejudices and assumptions expressed in prose. But the second reason is the lack of good abstractions on which to build. People have tried to build reusable protocol abstractions, like BEEP. Most did not stick, and those that did, like SOAP and XMPP, are on the complex side of things.

It used to be, decades ago, when the Internet was a young and modest thing, that protocols were short and sweet. They weren't even "standards," but "requests for comments," which is as modest as you can get. It's been one of my goals since we started iMatix in 1995 to find a way for ordinary people like me to write small, accurate protocols without the overhead of the committees.

Now, ØMQ does appear to provide a living, successful protocol abstraction layer with its "we'll carry multipart messages over random transports" way of working. Because ØMQ deals silently with framing, connections, and routing, it's surprisingly easy to write full protocol specs on top of ØMQ, and in Chapter 4 and Chapter 5 I showed how to do this.

Somewhere around mid-2007, I kicked off the Digital Standards Organization to define new, simpler ways of producing little standards, protocols, and specifications. In my defense, it was a quiet summer. At the time, I wrote that (*http://www.digistan.org/spec:1*) a new specification should take "minutes to explain, hours to design, days to write, weeks to prove, months to become mature, and years to replace."

In 2010, we started calling such little specifications "unprotocols," which some people might mistake for a dastardly plan for world domination by a shadowy international organization, but which really just means "protocols without the goats."

Contracts Are Hard

Writing contracts is perhaps the most difficult part of large-scale architecture. With unprotocols, we remove as much of the unnecessary friction as possible. What remains is still a hard set of problems to solve. A good contract (be it an API, a protocol, or a rental agreement) has to be simple, unambiguous, technically sound, and easy to enforce.

Like any technical skill, it's something you have to learn and practice. There are a series of specifications on the ØMQ RFC site (*http://rfc.zeromq.org*), which are worth reading and using as a basis for your own specifications when you find yourself in need.

I'll try to summarize what I've learned from my experience as a protocol writer:

- Start simple, and develop your specifications step-by-step. Don't solve problems you don't have in front of you.

- Use very clear and consistent language. A protocol may often break down into commands and fields; use clear, short names for these entities.

- Try to avoid inventing concepts. Reuse anything you can from existing specifications. Use terminology that is obvious and clear to your audience.

- Make *nothing* for which you cannot demonstrate an immediate need. Your specification solves problems; it does not provide features. Make the simplest plausible solution for each problem that you identify.

- Implement your protocol *as you build it*, so that you are aware of the technical consequences of each choice. Use a language that makes it hard (like C) and not one that makes it easy (like Python).

- Test your specification on other people *as you build it* . Your best feedback on a specification is when someone else tries to implement it without the assumptions and knowledge that you have in your head.

- Cross-test rapidly and consistently, throwing others' clients against your servers and vice versa.

- Be prepared to throw it out and start again as often as needed. Plan for this, by layering your architecture so that, e.g., you can keep an API but change the underlying protocols.

- Only use constructs that are independent of programming language and operating system.

- Solve a large problem in layers, making each layer an independent specification. Beware of creating monolithic protocols. Think about how reusable each layer is. Think about how different teams could build competing specifications at each layer.

And above all, *write it down*. Code is not a specification. The point about a written specification is that no matter how weak it is, it can be systematically improved. By writing down a specification you will be able to spot inconsistencies and gray areas that are impossible to see in code.

If this sounds hard, don't worry too much. One of the less obvious benefits of using ØMQ is that it reduces the effort necessary to write a protocol spec by perhaps 90% or more, because it already handles framing, routing, queuing, and so on. This means that you can experiment rapidly, make mistakes cheaply, and thus learn rapidly.

How to Write Unprotocols

When you start to write an unprotocol specification document, stick to a consistent structure so that your readers know what to expect. Here is the structure I use:

- Cover section: with a one-line summary, URL to the spec, formal name, version, who to blame.

- License for the text: absolutely needed for public specifications.
- The change process: i.e., how can I as a reader fix problems in the specification?
- Use of language: MUST, MAY, SHOULD, etc., with a reference to RFC 2119.
- Maturity indicator: is this an experimental, draft, stable, legacy, or retired version?
- Goals of the protocol: what problems is it trying to solve?
- Formal grammar: prevents arguments due to different interpretations of the text.
- Technical explanation: semantics of each message, error handling, etc.
- Security discussion: explicitly, how secure the protocol is.
- References: to other documents, protocols, etc.

Writing clear, expressive text is hard. Do avoid trying to describe implementations of the protocol. Remember that you're writing a contract. Describe in clear language the obligations and expectations of each party, the level of obligation, and the penalties for breaking the rules. Do not try to define *how* each party honors its part of the deal.

Here are some key points about unprotocols:

- As long as your process is open, you don't need a committee: just make clean, minimal designs and make sure anyone is free to improve them.
- If you use an existing license, you won't have legal worries afterwards. I use GPLv3 for my public specifications and advise you to do the same. For in-house work, standard copyright is perfect.
- Formality is valuable. That is, learn to write a formal grammar such as ABNF (Augmented Backus-Naur Form) and use this to fully document your messages.
- Use a market-driven life-cycle process like Digistan's COSS (*http://www.digistan.org/spec:1*) so that people place the right weight on your specs as they mature (or don't).

Why Use the GPLv3 for Public Specifications?

The license you choose is particularly crucial for public specifications. Traditionally, protocols are published under custom licenses, where the authors own the text and derived works are forbidden. This sounds great (after all, who wants to see a protocol forked?), but it is in fact highly risky. A protocol committee is vulnerable to capture, and if the protocol is important and valuable, the incentive for capture grows.

Once captured, like some wild animals, an important protocol will often die. The real problem is that there's no way to *free* a captive protocol published under a conventional license. The word "free" isn't just an adjective to describe speech or air, it's also a verb, and the right to fork a work *against the wishes of the owner* is essential to avoiding capture.

Let me explain this in shorter words. Imagine that iMatix writes a protocol today, that's really amazing and popular. We publish the spec, and many people implement it. Those implementations are fast and awesome, and free as in beer. They start to threaten an existing business, whose expensive commercial product is slower and can't compete. So one day some representatives of that business come to our iMatix office in Maetang-Dong, South Korea, and offer to buy our firm. Because we're spending vast amounts on sushi and beer, we accept gratefully. With evil laughter, the new owners of the protocol stop improving the public version, close the specification, and add patented extensions. Their new products support this, and they take over the whole market.

When you contribute to an open source project, you really want to know your hard work won't be used against you by a closed-source competitor. This is why the GPL beats the "more permissive" BSD/MIT/X11 licenses. These licenses give permission to cheat. This applies just as much to protocols as to source code.

When you implement a GPLv3 specification, your applications are, of course, yours, and they can be licensed any way you like. But you can be certain of two things. First, that specification will *never* be embraced and extended into proprietary forms. Any derived forms of the specification must also be GPLv3. And second, no one who ever implements or uses the protocol will ever launch a patent attack on anything it covers.

Using ABNF

My advice when writing protocol specs is to learn, and use, a formal grammar. It's just less hassle than allowing others to interpret what you mean, and then recover from the inevitable false assumptions. The target of your grammar is other people: engineers, not compilers.

My favorite grammar is ABNF, as defined by RFC 2234 (*http://www.ietf.org/rfc/rfc2234.txt*), because it is probably the simplest and most widely used formal language for defining bidirectional communications protocols. Most IETF (Internet Engineering Task Force) specifications use ABNF, which is good company to be in.

I'll give a 30-second crash course in writing ABNF here. It may remind you of regular expressions. You write the grammar as rules. Each rule takes the form "name = elements". An element can be another rule (which you define below as another rule), or a pre-defined "terminal" (like CRLF, OCTET), or a number. The RFC (*http://www.ietf.org/rfc/rfc2234.txt*) lists all the terminals. To define alternative elements, use "element / element". To define repetition, use "*" (read the RFC, because it's not intuitive). To group elements, use parentheses.

I'm not sure if this extension is proper, but I then prefix elements with "C:" and "S:" to indicate whether they come from the client or server.

Here's a piece of ABNF for an unprotocol called NOM that we'll come back to later in this chapter:

```
nom-protocol    = open-peering *use-peering

open-peering    = C:OHAI ( S:OHAI-OK / S:WTF )

use-peering     = C:ICANHAZ
                / S:CHEEZBURGER
                / C:HUGZ S:HUGZ-OK
                / S:HUGZ C:HUGZ-OK
```

I've actually used these keywords (OHAI, WTF) in commercial projects. They make developers giggly and happy. They confuse management. They're good in first drafts that you want to throw away later.

The Cheap or Nasty Pattern

There is a general lesson I've learned over a couple of decades of writing protocols small and large. I call this the "Cheap or Nasty" pattern: you can often split your work into two aspects or layers, and solve these separately—one using a "cheap" approach, the other using a "nasty" approach.

The key insight to making Cheap or Nasty work is to realize that many protocols mix a low-volume chatty part for control, and a high-volume asynchronous part for data. For instance, HTTP has a chatty dialog to authenticate and get pages, and an asynchronous dialog to stream data. FTP actually splits this over two ports; one port for control and one port for data.

Protocol designers who don't separate control from data tend to make horrid protocols, because the trade-offs in the two cases are almost totally opposed. What is perfect for control is bad for data, and what's ideal for data just doesn't work for control. This is especially true when we want high performance at the same time as extensibility and good error checking.

Let's break this down using a classic client/server use case. The client connects to the server and authenticates. It then asks for some resource. The server chats back, then starts to send data back to the client. Eventually, the client disconnects or the server finishes, and the conversation is over.

Now, before starting to design these messages, stop and think, and let's compare the control dialog and the data flow:

- The control dialog lasts a short time and involves very few messages. The data flow could last for hours or days and involve billions of messages.

- The control dialog is where all the "normal" errors happen, e.g., not authenticated, not found, payment required, censored, and so on. Any errors that happen during the data flow are exceptional (disk full, server crashed).
- The control dialog is where things will change over time as we add more options, parameters, and so on. The data flow should barely change over time because the semantics of a resource are fairly constant over time.
- The control dialog is essentially a synchronous request-reply dialog. The data flow is essentially a one-way asynchronous flow.

These differences are critical. Thus, when we talk about performance, it applies *only* to data flows. It's pathological to design a one-time control dialog to be fast. When we talk about the cost of serialization, this only applies to the data flow. The cost of encoding/decoding the control flow could be huge, and for many cases it would not change a thing. So, we encode control using Cheap, and we encode data flows using Nasty.

Cheap is essentially synchronous, verbose, descriptive, and flexible. A Cheap message is full of rich information that can change for each application. Your goal as designer is to make this information easy to encode and parse, trivial to extend for experimentation or growth, and highly robust against change, both forwards and backwards. The Cheap part of a protocol looks like this:

- It uses a simple self-describing structured encoding for data, be it XML, JSON, HTTP-style headers, or some other. Any encoding is fine, so as long as there are standard simple parsers for it in your target languages.
- It uses a straight request-reply model where each request has a success/failure reply. This makes it trivial to write correct clients and servers for a Cheap dialog.
- It doesn't try, even marginally, to be fast. Performance doesn't matter when you do something only once or a few times per session.

A Cheap parser is something you take off the shelf and throw data at. It shouldn't crash, shouldn't leak memory, should be highly tolerant, and should be relatively simple to work with. That's it.

Nasty, however, is essentially asynchronous, terse, silent, and inflexible. A Nasty message carries minimal information that practically never changes. Your goal as designer is to make this information ultra-fast to parse, and possibly even impossible to extend and experiment with. The ideal Nasty pattern looks like this:

- It uses a hand-optimized binary layout for data, where every bit is precisely crafted.
- It uses a pure asynchronous model, where one or both peers send data without acknowledgments (or if they do use these, they use sneaky asynchronous techniques like credit-based flow control).

- It doesn't try, even marginally, to be friendly. Performance is all that matters when you are doing something several million times per second.

A Nasty parser is something you write by hand, which writes or reads bits, bytes, words, and integers individually and precisely. It rejects anything it doesn't like, does no memory allocations at all, and never crashes.

Cheap or Nasty isn't a universal pattern; not all protocols have this dichotomy. Also, how you use Cheap or Nasty will depend on your circumstances. In some cases, it can be two parts of a single protocol. In other cases it can be two protocols, one layered on top of the other.

Error handling

Using Cheap or Nasty makes error handling rather simpler. You have two kinds of commands and two ways to signal errors:

Synchronous control commands
> Errors are normal: every request has a response that is either OK or an error response.

Asynchronous data commands
> Errors are exceptional: bad commands either are discarded silently or cause the whole connection to be closed.

It's usually good to distinguish a few kinds of errors, but as always keep it minimal and add only what you need.

Serializing Your Data

When we start to design a protocol, one of the first questions we face is how to encode data on the wire. There is no universal answer. There are a half-dozen different ways to serialize data, each with pros and cons. We'll explore some of these.

ØMQ Framing

The simplest and most widely used serialization format for ØMQ applications is ØMQ's own multipart framing. For example, here is how the Majordomo Protocol (*http://rfc.zeromq.org/spec:7*) defines a request:

```
Frame 0: Empty frame
Frame 1: "MDPW01" (six bytes, representing MDP/Worker v0.1)
Frame 2: 0x02 (one byte, representing REQUEST)
Frame 3: Client address (envelope stack)
Frame 4: Empty (zero bytes, envelope delimiter)
Frames 5+: Request body (opaque binary)
```

Reading and writing this in code is easy. But this is a classic example of a control flow (the whole of MDP is a classic example, really, as it's a chatty request-reply protocol). When we came to improve MDP for the second version, we had to change this framing. Excellent, we broke all existing implementations!

Backward compatibility is hard, but using ØMQ framing for control flows *does not help*. Here's how I should have designed this protocol if I'd followed my own advice (and I'll fix this in the next version). It's split into a Cheap part and a Nasty part, and it uses the ØMQ framing to separate these:

```
Frame 0: "MDP/2.0" for protocol name and version
Frame 1: command header
Frame 2: command body
```

Where we'd expect to parse the command header in the various intermediaries (client API, broker, and worker API), and pass the command body untouched from application to application.

Serialization Languages

Serialization languages have their fashions. XML used to be big as in popular, then it got big as in overengineered, and then it fell into the hands of "Enterprise Information Architects" and it's not been seen alive since. Today's XML is the epitome of "somewhere in that mess is a small, elegant language trying to escape."

Still, XML was way, way better than its predecessors, which included such monsters as the Standard Generalized Markup Language (SGML), which in turn were a cool breeze compared to mind-torturing beasts like EDIFACT. So, the history of serialization languages seems to be one of gradually emerging sanity, hidden by waves of revolting EIAs doing their best to hold onto their jobs.

JSON popped out of the JavaScript world as a quick-and-dirty "I'd rather resign than use XML here" way to throw data onto the wire and get it back again. JSON is just minimal XML expressed, sneakily, as JavaScript source code.

Here's a simple example of using JSON in a Cheap protocol:

```
"protocol": {
    "name": "MTL",
    "version": 1
},
"virtual-host": "test-env"
```

The same example in XML would be (XML forces us to invent a single top-level entity):

```
<command>
    <protocol name = "MTL" version = "1" />
    <virtual-host>test-env</virtual-host>
</command>
```

And using plain-old HTTP-style headers:

```
Protocol: MTL/1.0
Virtual-host: test-env
```

These are all pretty equivalent, so as long as you don't go overboard with validating parsers, schemas, and other "trust us, this is all for your own good" nonsense. A Cheap serialization language gives you space for experimentation for free ("ignore any elements/attributes/headers that you don't recognize"), and it's simple to write generic parsers that, for example, thunk a command into a hash table, or vice versa.

However, it's not all roses. While modern scripting languages support JSON and XML easily enough, older languages do not. If you use XML or JSON, you create nontrivial dependencies. It's also somewhat of a pain to work with tree-structured data in a language like C.

So, you can drive your choice according to the languages you're aiming for. If your universe is a scripting language, then go for JSON. If you are aiming to build protocols for wider system use, keep things simple for C developers and stick to HTTP-style headers.

Serialization Libraries

The *msgpack.org* site says this about the MessagePack serialization library:

> It's like JSON, but fast and small. MessagePack is an efficient binary serialization format. It lets you exchange data among multiple languages like JSON, but it's faster and smaller. For example, small integers (like flags or error code) are encoded into a single byte, and typical short strings only require an extra byte in addition to the strings themselves.

I'm going to make the perhaps unpopular claim that "fast and small" are features that solve non-problems. The only real problem that serialization libraries solve is, as far as I can tell, the need to document the message contracts and actually serialize data to and from the wire.

Let's start with the "fast and small" claim. It's based on a two-part argument: first, that making your messages smaller and reducing CPU cost for encoding and decoding will make a significant difference to your application's performance; and second, that this will be equally valid across the board, for all messages.

But most real applications tend to fall into one of two categories: either the speed of serialization and size of encoding are marginal compared to other costs, such as database access or application code performance, or network performance really is critical, and then all significant costs occur in a few specific message types.

Thus, aiming for "fast and small" across the board is a false optimization. You get neither the easy flexibility of Cheap for your infrequent control flows, nor the brutal efficiency of Nasty for your high-volume data flows. Worse, the assumption that all messages are equal in some way can corrupt your protocol design. Cheap or Nasty isn't only about serialization strategies; it's also about synchronous versus asynchronous, error handling, and the cost of change.

My experience is that most performance problems in message-based applications can be solved by (a) improving the application itself and (b) hand-optimizing the high-volume data flows. And to hand-optimize your most critical data flows, you need to cheat and to know and exploit facts about your data, which is something general-purpose serializers cannot do.

Now let us address documentation: the need to write our contracts explicitly and formally, not only in code. This is a valid problem to solve: indeed, one of the main ones if we're to build a long-lasting, large-scale, message-based architecture.

Here is how we describe a typical message using the MessagePack interface definition language (IDL):

```
message Person {
    1: string surname
    2: string firstname
    3: optional string email
}
```

Now, here's the same message using the Google protocol buffers IDL:

```
message Person {
    required string surname = 1;
    required string firstname = 2;
    optional string email = 3;
}
```

It works, but in most practical cases wins you little over a serialization language backed by decent specifications written by hand or produced mechanically (we'll come to this). The price you'll pay is an extra dependency and, quite probably, worse overall performance than if you used Cheap or Nasty.

Handwritten Binary Serialization

As you'll gather from this book, my preferred language for systems programming is C (upgraded to C99, with a constructor/destructor API model and generic containers). There are two reasons I like this modernized C language. First, I'm too weak-minded to learn a big language like C++. Life just seems filled with more interesting things to understand. Second, I find that this specific level of manual control lets me produce better results, faster.

The point here isn't C versus C++, but the value of manual control for high-end professional users. It's no accident that the best cars, cameras, and espresso machines in the world have manual controls. That level of on-the-spot fine-tuning often makes the difference between world-class success and being second best.

When you are really, truly concerned about the speed of serialization and/or the size of the result (often these contradict each other), you need handwritten binary serialization. In other words, let's hear it for Mr. Nasty!

Your basic process for writing an efficient Nasty encoder/decoder (codec) is:

- Build representative data sets and test applications that can stress-test your codec.
- Write a first dumb version of the codec.
- Test, measure, improve, and repeat until you run out of time and/or money.

Here are some of the techniques we use to make our codecs better:

- *Use a profiler.* There's simply no way to know what your code is doing until you've profiled it for function counts and for CPU cost per function. When you find your hot spots, fix them.
- *Eliminate memory allocations.* The heap is very fast on a modern Linux kernel, but it's still the bottleneck in most naive codecs. On older kernels, the heap can be tragically slow. Use local variables (the stack) instead of the heap where you can.
- *Test on different platforms and with different compilers and compiler options.* Apart from the heap, there are many other differences. You need to learn the main ones, and allow for them.
- *Use state to compress better.* If you are concerned about codec performance, you are almost definitely sending the same kinds of data many times. There will be redundancy between instances of data. You can detect these and use that to compress (for example, a short value that means "same as last time").
- *Know your data.* The best compression techniques (in terms of CPU cost for compactness) require knowing about the data. For example, the techniques used to compress a word list, a video, and a stream of stock market data are all different.
- *Be ready to break the rules.* Do you really need to encode integers in big-endian network byte order? x86 and ARM account for almost all modern CPUs, yet they use little-endian byte order (ARM is actually bi-endian, but Android, like Windows and iOS, is little-endian).

Code Generation

Reading the previous two sections, you might have wondered, "Could I write my own IDL generator that's better than a general-purpose one?" If this thought wandered into your mind, it probably left pretty soon after, chased by dark calculations about how much work that would actually involve.

What if I told you of a way to build custom IDL generators cheaply and quickly? You can have a way to get perfectly documented contracts, code that is as evil and domain-specific as you need, and all you need to do is sign away your soul (*who ever really used that, amirite?*) right here....

At iMatix, until a few years ago, we used code generation to build ever larger and more ambitious systems; then we decided the technology (the Generator Script Language, or GSL) was too dangerous for common use, and we sealed the archive and locked it away, with heavy chains, in a deep dungeon. In reality, we actually posted it on GitHub. If you want to try the examples that are coming up, grab the repository (*https://github.com/imatix/gsl*) and build yourself a *gsl* command. Typing "make" in the *src* subdirectory should do it (and if you're that guy who loves Windows, I'm sure you'll send a patch with project files).

This section isn't really about GSL at all, but about a useful and little-known trick that's handy for ambitious architects who want to scale themselves, as well as their work. Once you learn the trick, you can whip up your own code generators in a short time. The code generators most software engineers know about come with a single hard-coded model. For instance, Ragel (*http://www.complang.org/ragel/*) "compiles executable finite state machines from regular languages" (i.e., Ragel's model is a regular language). This certainly works for a good set of problems, but it's far from universal. How do you describe an API in Ragel? Or a project makefile? Or even a finite-state machine like the one we used to design the Binary Star pattern in Chapter 4?

All of these would benefit from code generation, but there's no universal model. So, the trick is to design your own models as you need them, and then make code generators as cheap compilers for those models. You need some experience in how to make good models, and you need a technology that makes it cheap to build custom code generators. Scripting languages like Perl and Python are a good option. However, we actually built GSL specifically for this, and that's what I prefer.

Let's take a simple example that ties into what we already know. We'll see more extensive examples later, because I really do believe that code generation is crucial knowledge for large-scale work. In Chapter 4, we developed the Majordomo Protocol (MDP) (*http://rfc.zeromq.org/spec:7*) and wrote clients, brokers, and workers for that. Now, could we generate those pieces mechanically, by building our own interface description language and code generators?

When we write a GSL model, we can use *any* semantics we like. In other words, we can invent domain-specific languages on the spot. I'll invent a couple—see if you can guess what they represent:

```
slideshow
    name = Cookery level 3
    page
        title = French Cuisine
        item = Overview
        item = The historical cuisine
        item = The nouvelle cuisine
        item = Why the French live longer
    page
        title = Overview
        item = Soups and salads
        item = Le plat principal
        item = Béchamel and other sauces
        item = Pastries, cakes, and quiches
        item = Soufflé - cheese to strawberry
```

Now, how about this one?

```
table
    name = person
    column
        name = firstname
        type = string
    column
        name = lastname
        type = string
    column
        name = rating
        type = integer
```

The first we could compile into a presentation. The second, we could compile into SQL to create and work with a database table. So, for this exercise our domain language—our model—consists of "classes" that contain "messages" that contain "fields" of various types. It's deliberately familiar. Here is the MDP client protocol:

```
<class name = "mdp_client">
    MDP/Client
    <header>
        <field name = "empty" type = "string" value = ""
            >Empty frame</field>
        <field name = "protocol" type = "string" value = "MDPC01"
            >Protocol identifier</field>
    </header>
    <message name = "request">
        Client request to broker
        <field name = "service" type = "string">Service name</field>
        <field name = "body" type = "frame">Request body</field>
    </message>
    <message name = "reply">
        Response back to client
        <field name = "service" type = "string">Service name</field>
        <field name = "body" type = "frame">Response body</field>
```

```
        </message>
    </class>
```

And here is the MDP worker protocol:

```
<class name = "mdp_worker">
    MDP/Worker
    <header>
        <field name = "empty" type = "string" value = ""
            >Empty frame</field>
        <field name = "protocol" type = "string" value = "MDPW01"
            >Protocol identifier</field>
        <field name = "id" type = "octet">Message identifier</field>
    </header>
    <message name = "ready" id = "1">
        Worker tells broker it is ready
        <field name = "service" type = "string">Service name</field>
    </message>
    <message name = "request" id = "2">
        Client request to broker
        <field name = "client" type = "frame">Client address</field>
        <field name = "body" type = "frame">Request body</field>
    </message>
    <message name = "reply" id = "3">
        Worker returns reply to broker
        <field name = "client" type = "frame">Client address</field>
        <field name = "body" type = "frame">Request body</field>
    </message>
    <message name = "hearbeat" id = "4">
        Either peer tells the other it's still alive
    </message>
    <message name = "disconnect" id = "5">
        Either peer tells other the party is over
    </message>
</class>
```

GSL uses XML as its modeling language. XML has a poor reputation, having been dragged through too many enterprise sewers to smell sweet, but it has some strong positives, as long as you keep it simple. Any way to write a self-describing hierarchy of items and attributes would work.

Now, here is a short IDL generator written in GSL that turns our protocol models into documentation:

```
.#  Trivial IDL generator (specs.gsl)
.#
.output "$(class.name).md"
## The $(string.trim (class.?''):left) Protocol
.for message
.   frames = count (class->header.field) + count (field)

A $(message.NAME) command consists of a multipart message of $(frames)
frames:
```

```
.    for class->header.field
.          if name = "id"
* Frame $(item ()): 0x$(message.id:%02x) (1 byte, $(message.NAME))
.          else
* Frame $(item ()): "$(value:)" ($(string.length ("$(value)")) \
bytes, $(field.:))
.          endif
.    endfor
.    index = count (class->header.field) + 1
.    for field
* Frame $(index): $(field.?'') \
.          if type = "string"
(printable string)
.          elsif type = "frame"
(opaque binary)
.                index += 1
.          else
.                echo "E: unknown field type: $(type)"
.          endif
.          index += 1
.    endfor
.endfor
```

The XML models and this script are in the subdirectory *examples/models*. To do the code generation, I give this command:

```
gsl -script:specs mdp_client.xml mdp_worker.xml
```

Here is the Markdown text we get for the worker protocol:

```
## The MDP/Worker Protocol

A READY command consists of a multipart message of 4 frames:

* Frame 1: "" (0 bytes, Empty frame)
* Frame 2: "MDPW01" (6 bytes, Protocol identifier)
* Frame 3: 0x01 (1 byte, READY)
* Frame 4: Service name (printable string)

A REQUEST command consists of a multipart message of 5 frames:

* Frame 1: "" (0 bytes, Empty frame)
* Frame 2: "MDPW01" (6 bytes, Protocol identifier)
* Frame 3: 0x02 (1 byte, REQUEST)
* Frame 4: Client address (opaque binary)
* Frame 6: Request body (opaque binary)

A REPLY command consists of a multipart message of 5 frames:

* Frame 1: "" (0 bytes, Empty frame)
* Frame 2: "MDPW01" (6 bytes, Protocol identifier)
* Frame 3: 0x03 (1 byte, REPLY)
```

```
* Frame 4: Client address (opaque binary)
* Frame 6: Request body (opaque binary)
```

A HEARBEAT command consists of a multipart message of 3 frames:

```
* Frame 1: "" (0 bytes, Empty frame)
* Frame 2: "MDPW01" (6 bytes, Protocol identifier)
* Frame 3: 0x04 (1 byte, HEARBEAT)
```

A DISCONNECT command consists of a multipart message of 3 frames:

```
* Frame 1: "" (0 bytes, Empty frame)
* Frame 2: "MDPW01" (6 bytes, Protocol identifier)
* Frame 3: 0x05 (1 byte, DISCONNECT)
```

Which, as you can see, is close to what I wrote by hand in the original spec. Now, if you have cloned the book repository and you are looking at the code in *examples/models*, you can generate the MDP client and worker codecs. We pass the same two models to a different code generator:

```
gsl -script:codec_c mdp_client.xml mdp_worker.xml
```

Which gives us mdp_client and mdp_worker classes. Actually, MDP is so simple that it's barely worth the effort of writing the code generator. The profit comes when we want to change the protocol (which we did for the standalone Majordomo project). We modify the protocol, run the command, and out pops more perfect code.

The *codec_c.gsl* code generator is not short, but the resulting codecs are much better than the handwritten code I originally put together for Majordomo. For instance, the handwritten code had no error checking, and would die if you passed it bogus messages.

I'm now going to explain the pros and cons of GSL-powered model-oriented code generation. Power does not come for free, and one of the greatest traps in our business is the ability to invent concepts out of thin air. GSL makes this particularly easy, so it can be an equally dangerous tool.

Do not invent concepts. The job of a designer is to remove problems, not add features.

First, I will lay out the advantages of model-oriented code generation:

- You can create "perfect" abstractions that map to your real world. So, our protocol model maps 100% to the "real world" of Majordomo. This would be impossible without the freedom to tune and change the model in any way.
- You can develop these perfect models quickly and cheaply.
- You can generate *any* text output. From a single model, you can create documentation, code in any language, test tools—literally any output you can think of.
- You can generate (and I mean this literally) *perfect* output, since it's cheap to improve your code generators to any level you want.

- You get a single source that combines specifications and semantics.
- You can leverage a small team to a massive size. At iMatix, we produced the million-line OpenAMQ messaging product out of perhaps 85K lines of input models, including the code generation scripts themselves.

Now, let's look at the disadvantages:

- You add tool dependencies to your project.
- You may get carried away and create models for the pure joy of creating them.
- You may alienate newcomers, who will see "strange stuff," from your work.
- You may give people a strong excuse to not invest in your project.

Cynically, model-oriented abuse works great in environments where you want to produce huge amounts of perfect code that you can maintain with little effort, and which *no one can ever take away from you*. Personally, I like to cross my rivers and move on. But if long-term job security is your thing, this is almost perfect.

So, if you do use GSL and want to create open communities around your work, here is my advice:

- Use it only where you would otherwise be writing tiresome code by hand.
- Design natural models that are what people would expect to see.
- Write the code by hand first so you know what to generate.
- Do not overuse. Keep it simple! *Do not get too meta*!!
- Introduce it gradually into a project.
- Put the generated code into your repositories.

We're already using GSL in some projects around ØMQ. For example the high-level C binding, CZMQ, uses GSL to generate the socket options class (`zsockopt`). A 300-line code generator turns 78 lines of XML model into 1,500 lines of perfect but really boring code. That's a good win.

Transferring Files

Let's take a break from the lecturing and get back to our first love and the reason for doing all of this: code.

"How do I send a file?" is a common question on the ØMQ mailing lists. Not surprisingly, file transfer is perhaps the oldest and most obvious type of messaging. Sending files around networks has lots of use cases, apart from annoying the copyright cartels.

ØMQ is very good out of the box at sending events and tasks, but less good at sending files.

I've promised, for a year or two, to write a proper explanation. Here's a gratuitous piece of information to brighten your morning: the word "proper" comes from the archaic French *propre*, which means "clean." English common folk in the Dark Ages, not being familiar with hot water and soap, changed the word to mean "foreign" or "upper-class," as in "that's proper food!"; later it came to mean just "real," as in "that's a proper mess you've gotten us into!"

So, file transfer. There are several reasons why you can't just pick up a random file, blindfold it, and shove it whole into a message. The most obvious reason is that despite decades of determined growth in RAM sizes (and who among us old-timers doesn't fondly remember saving up for that 1,024-byte memory extension card?!), disk sizes obstinately remain much larger. Even if we could send a file with one instruction (say, using a system call like *sendfile*), we'd hit the reality that networks are neither infinitely fast, nor perfectly reliable. After trying to upload a large file several times on a slow, flaky network (WiFi, anyone?), you'll realize that a proper file transfer protocol needs a way to recover from failures. That is, it needs a way to send only the part of a file that hasn't yet been received.

Finally, after all this, if you build a proper file server you'll notice that simply sending massive amounts of data to lots of clients creates that situation we like to call, in the technical parlance, "server went belly-up due to all available heap memory being eaten by a poorly designed application." A proper file transfer protocol needs to pay attention to memory use.

We'll solve these problems properly, one by one, which should hopefully get us to a good and proper file transfer protocol running over ØMQ. First, let's generate a 1 GB test file with random data (real power-of-two-giga-like-Von-Neumman-intended, not the fake silicon ones the memory industry likes to sell):

```
dd if=/dev/urandom of=testdata bs=1M count=1024
```

This is large enough to be troublesome when we have lots of clients asking for the same file at once, and on many machines, 1 GB is going to be too large to allocate in memory anyhow. As a base reference, let's measure how long it takes to copy this file from disk back to disk. This will tell us how much our file transfer protocol adds on top (including network costs):

```
$ time cp testdata testdata2

real    0m7.143s
user    0m0.012s
sys     0m1.188s
```

The four-figure precision is misleading; expect variations of 25% either way. This is just an "order of magnitude" measurement.

Example 7-1 shows our first cut at the code, where the client asks for the test data and the server just sends it, without stopping for breath, as a series of messages, where each message holds one "chunk."

Example 7-1. File transfer test, model 1 (fileio1.c)

```
//  File Transfer model #1
//
//  In which the server sends the entire file to the client in
//  large chunks with no attempt at flow control.

#include <czmq.h>
#define CHUNK_SIZE  250000

static void
client_thread (void *args, zctx_t *ctx, void *pipe)
{
    void *dealer = zsocket_new (ctx, ZMQ_DEALER);
    zsocket_connect (dealer, "tcp://127.0.0.1:6000");

    zstr_send (dealer, "fetch");
    size_t total = 0;       //  Total bytes received
    size_t chunks = 0;      //  Total chunks received

    while (true) {
        zframe_t *frame = zframe_recv (dealer);
        if (!frame)
            break;              //  Shutting down, quit
        chunks++;
        size_t size = zframe_size (frame);
        zframe_destroy (&frame);
        total += size;
        if (size == 0)
            break;              //  Whole file received
    }
    printf ("%zd chunks received, %zd bytes\n", chunks, total);
    zstr_send (pipe, "OK");
}

static void
free_chunk (void *data, void *arg)
{
    free (data);
}
```

The server thread, shown in Example 7-2, reads the file from the disk in chunks and sends each chunk to the client as a separate message. We only have one test file, so we'll open that once and then serve it out as needed.

Example 7-2. File transfer test, model 1 (fileio1.c): file server thread

```
static void
server_thread (void *args, zctx_t *ctx, void *pipe)
{
    FILE *file = fopen ("testdata", "r");
    assert (file);

    void *router = zsocket_new (ctx, ZMQ_ROUTER);
    //  Default HWM is 1000, which will drop messages here
    //  since we send more than 1,000 chunks of test data,
    //  so set an infinite HWM as a simple, stupid solution
    zsocket_set_hwm (router, 0);
    zsocket_bind (router, "tcp://*:6000");
    while (true) {
        //  First frame in each message is the sender identity
        zframe_t *identity = zframe_recv (router);
        if (!identity)
            break;                 //  Shutting down, quit

        //  Second frame is "fetch" command
        char *command = zstr_recv (router);
        assert (streq (command, "fetch"));
        free (command);

        while (true) {
            byte *data = malloc (CHUNK_SIZE);
            assert (data);
            size_t size = fread (data, 1, CHUNK_SIZE, file);
            zframe_t *chunk = zframe_new_zero_copy (data, size, free_chunk, NULL);
            zframe_send (&identity, router, ZFRAME_REUSE + ZFRAME_MORE);
            zframe_send (&chunk, router, 0);
            if (size == 0)
                break;             //  Always end with a zero-size frame
        }
        zframe_destroy (&identity);
    }
    fclose (file);
}
```

The main task, shown in Example 7-3, starts the client and server threads; it's easier to test this as a single process with threads than as multiple processes.

Example 7-3. File transfer test, model 1 (fileio1.c): file main thread

```
int main (void)
{
    //  Start child threads
    zctx_t *ctx = zctx_new ();
    zthread_fork (ctx, server_thread, NULL);
    void *client =
    zthread_fork (ctx, client_thread, NULL);
    //  Loop until client tells us it's done
```

```
    char *string = zstr_recv (client);
    free (string);
    //  Kill server thread
    zctx_destroy (&ctx);
    return 0;
}
```

It's pretty simple, but we already run into a problem: if we send too much data to the
ROUTER socket, we can easily overflow it. The simple but stupid solution is to put an
infinite high-water mark on the socket. It's stupid because we now have no protection
against exhausting the server's memory. Yet without an infinite HWM, we risk losing
chunks of large files.

Try this: set the HWM to 1,000 (in ØMQ v3.x, this is the default) and then reduce the
chunk size to 100K so we send 10K chunks in one go. Run the test, and you'll see it never
finishes. As the zmq_socket() man page says with cheerful brutality, for the ROUTER
socket: "ZMQ_HWM option action: Drop."

We have to control the amount of data the server sends up-front. There's no point in it
sending more than the network can handle. Let's try sending one chunk at a time. In
this version of the protocol, the client will explicitly say, "Give me chunk N," and the
server will fetch that specific chunk from disk and send it.

Example 7-4 presents the improved second model, where the client asks for one chunk
at a time, and the server only sends one chunk for each request it gets from the client.

Example 7-4. File transfer test, model 2 (fileio2.c)

```
//  File Transfer model #2
//
//  In which the client requests each chunk individually, thus
//  eliminating server queue overflows, but at a cost in speed.

#include <czmq.h>
#define CHUNK_SIZE  250000

static void
client_thread (void *args, zctx_t *ctx, void *pipe)
{
    void *dealer = zsocket_new (ctx, ZMQ_DEALER);
    zsocket_set_hwm (dealer, 1);
    zsocket_connect (dealer, "tcp://127.0.0.1:6000");

    size_t total = 0;        //  Total bytes received
    size_t chunks = 0;       //  Total chunks received

    while (true) {
        //  Ask for next chunk
        zstr_sendfm (dealer, "fetch");
        zstr_sendfm (dealer, "%ld", total);
        zstr_sendf  (dealer, "%ld", CHUNK_SIZE);
```

```
    zframe_t *chunk = zframe_recv (dealer);
    if (!chunk)
        break;                  // Shutting down, quit
    chunks++;
    size_t size = zframe_size (chunk);
    zframe_destroy (&chunk);
    total += size;
    if (size < CHUNK_SIZE)
        break;                  // Last chunk received; exit
    }
    printf ("%zd chunks received, %zd bytes\n", chunks, total);
    zstr_send (pipe, "OK");
}

static void
free_chunk (void *data, void *arg)
{
    free (data);
}
```

The server thread (Example 7-5) waits for a chunk request from a client, reads that chunk, and sends it back to the client.

Example 7-5. File transfer test, model 2 (fileio2.c): file server thread

```
static void
server_thread (void *args, zctx_t *ctx, void *pipe)
{
    FILE *file = fopen ("testdata", "r");
    assert (file);

    void *router = zsocket_new (ctx, ZMQ_ROUTER);
    zsocket_set_hwm (router, 1);
    zsocket_bind (router, "tcp://*:6000");
    while (true) {
        // First frame in each message is the sender identity
        zframe_t *identity = zframe_recv (router);
        if (!identity)
            break;              // Shutting down, quit

        // Second frame is "fetch" command
        char *command = zstr_recv (router);
        assert (streq (command, "fetch"));
        free (command);

        // Third frame is chunk offset in file
        char *offset_str = zstr_recv (router);
        size_t offset = atoi (offset_str);
        free (offset_str);

        // Fourth frame is maximum chunk size
```

```
        char *chunksz_str = zstr_recv (router);
        size_t chunksz = atoi (chunksz_str);
        free (chunksz_str);

        //  Read chunk of data from file
        fseek (file, offset, SEEK_SET);
        byte *data = malloc (chunksz);
        assert (data);

        //  Send resulting chunk to client
        size_t size = fread (data, 1, chunksz, file);
        zframe_t *chunk = zframe_new_zero_copy (data, size, free_chunk, NULL);
        zframe_send (&identity, router, ZFRAME_MORE);
        zframe_send (&chunk, router, 0);
    }
    fclose (file);
}

//  The main task is just the same as in the first model
...
```

It is much slower now, because of the to-and-fro chatting between client and server. We pay about 300 microseconds for each request-reply round-trip, on a local loop connection (client and server on the same box). It doesn't sound like much, but it adds up quickly:

```
$ time ./fileio1
4296 chunks received, 1073741824 bytes

real    0m0.669s
user    0m0.056s
sys     0m1.048s

$ time ./fileio2
4295 chunks received, 1073741824 bytes

real    0m2.389s
user    0m0.312s
sys     0m2.136s
```

There are two valuable lessons here. First, while request-reply is easy, it's also too slow for high-volume data flows. Paying that 300 microseconds once would be fine. Paying it for every single chunk isn't acceptable, particularly on real networks with latencies perhaps 1,000 times higher.

The second point is something I've said before but will repeat: it's incredibly easy to experiment, measure, and improve a protocol over ØMQ. And when the cost of something comes way down, you can afford a lot more of it. Do learn to develop and prove your protocols in isolation: I've seen teams waste a lot of time trying to improve poorly designed protocols that are too deeply embedded in applications to be easily testable or fixable.

Our model 2 file transfer protocol isn't so bad, apart from performance:

- It completely eliminates any risk of memory exhaustion. To prove that, we set the high-water mark to 1 in both the sender and the receiver.
- It lets the client choose the chunk size, which is useful because if there's any tuning of the chunk size to be done (for network conditions, for file types, or to reduce memory consumption further), it's the client that should be doing this.
- It gives us fully restartable file transfers.
- It allows the client to cancel the file transfer at any point in time.

If we just didn't have to do a request for each chunk, it'd be a usable protocol. What we need is a way for the server to send multiple chunks without waiting for the client to request or acknowledge each one. What are our choices?

- The server could send 10 chunks at once, then wait for a single acknowledgment. That's exactly like multiplying the chunk size by 10, though, so it's pointless. And yes, it's just as pointless for all multiples of 10.
- The server could send chunks without any chatter from the client but with a slight delay between each send, so that it would send chunks only as fast as the network could handle them. This would require the server to know what's happening at the network layer, though, which sounds like hard work. It also breaks layering horribly. And what happens if the network is really fast, but the client itself is slow? Where are chunks queued then?
- The server could try to spy on the sending queue—i.e., see how full it is, and send only when the queue isn't full. ØMQ doesn't allow that, though, because it doesn't work, for the same reason as throttling doesn't work. The server and network may be more than fast enough, but the client may be a slow little device.
- We could modify libzmq to take some other action on reaching the HWM. Perhaps it could block? That would mean that a single slow client would block the whole server, so no thank you. Maybe it could return an error to the caller? Then the server could do something smart like... well, there isn't really anything it could do that's any better than dropping the message.

Apart from being complex and variously unpleasant, none of these options would even work. What we need is a way for the client to tell the server, asynchronously and in the background, that it's ready for more. We need some kind of asynchronous flow control. If we do this right, data should flow without interruption from the server to the client, but only as long as the client is reading it. Let's review our protocols. This was the first one:

```
C: fetch
S: chunk 1
S: chunk 2
S: chunk 3
...
```

And the second introduced a request for each chunk:

```
C: fetch chunk 1
S: send chunk 1
C: fetch chunk 2
S: send chunk 2
C: fetch chunk 3
S: send chunk 3
C: fetch chunk 4
...
```

Now—waves hands mysteriously—here's a changed protocol that fixes the performance problem:

```
C: fetch chunk 1
C: fetch chunk 2
C: fetch chunk 3
S: send chunk 1
C: fetch chunk 4
S: send chunk 2
S: send chunk 3
....
```

It looks suspiciously similar to the second protocol. In fact, it's identical, except that we send multiple requests without waiting for a reply for each one. This is a technique called "pipelining," and it works because our DEALER and ROUTER sockets are fully asynchronous.

Example 7-6 presents the third model of our file transfer test-bench, with pipelining. The client sends a number of requests ahead (the "credit"), and then each time it processes an incoming chunk, it sends one more credit. The server will never send more chunks than the client has asked for.

Example 7-6. File transfer test, model 3 (fileio3.c)

```
//  File Transfer model #3
//
//  In which the client requests each chunk individually, using
//  command pipelining to give us a credit-based flow control.

#include <czmq.h>
#define CHUNK_SIZE  250000
#define PIPELINE    10

static void
client_thread (void *args, zctx_t *ctx, void *pipe)
{
```

```
        void *dealer = zsocket_new (ctx, ZMQ_DEALER);
        zsocket_connect (dealer, "tcp://127.0.0.1:6000");

        //  Up to this many chunks in transit
        size_t credit = PIPELINE;

        size_t total = 0;        //  Total bytes received
        size_t chunks = 0;       //  Total chunks received
        size_t offset = 0;       //  Offset of next chunk request

        while (true) {
            while (credit) {
                //  Ask for next chunk
                zstr_sendfm (dealer, "fetch");
                zstr_sendfm (dealer, "%ld", offset);
                zstr_sendf  (dealer, "%ld", CHUNK_SIZE);
                offset += CHUNK_SIZE;
                credit--;
            }
            zframe_t *chunk = zframe_recv (dealer);
            if (!chunk)
                break;              //  Shutting down, quit
            chunks++;
            credit++;
            size_t size = zframe_size (chunk);
            zframe_destroy (&chunk);
            total += size;
            if (size < CHUNK_SIZE)
                break;              //  Last chunk received; exit
        }
        printf ("%zd chunks received, %zd bytes\n", chunks, total);
        zstr_send (pipe, "OK");
}

//  The rest of the code is exactly the same as in model 2, except
//  that we set the HWM on the server's ROUTER socket to PIPELINE
//  to act as a sanity check
...
```

That tweak gives us full control over the end-to-end pipeline, including all network buffers and ØMQ queues at the sender and receiver. We ensure the pipeline is always filled with data while never growing beyond a predefined limit. More than that, the client decides exactly when to send a "credit" to the sender. It could be when it receives a chunk, or when it has fully processed a chunk. And this happens asynchronously, with no significant performance cost.

In the third model, I chose a pipeline size of 10 messages (each message is a chunk). This will cost a maximum of 2.5 MB of memory per client, so with 1 GB of memory we can handle at least 400 clients. We can try to calculate the ideal pipeline size. It takes about 0.7 seconds to send the 1 GB file, which is about 160 microseconds for a chunk.

A round-trip is 300 microseconds, so the pipeline needs to be at least 3–5 messages to keep the server busy. In practice, I still got performance spikes with a pipeline of 5, probably because the credit messages sometimes get delayed by outgoing data. At 10, it works consistently:

```
$ time ./fileio3
4291 chunks received, 1072741824 bytes

real    0m0.777s
user    0m0.096s
sys     0m1.120s
```

Do measure rigorously. Your calculations may be good, but the real world tends to have its own opinions.

What we've made is clearly not yet a real file transfer protocol, but it proves the pattern, and I think it is the simplest plausible design. For a real working protocol, we might want to add some or all of the following:

- Authentication and access controls, even without encryption: the point isn't to protect sensitive data, but to catch errors like sending test data to production servers.

- A Cheap-style request including the file path, optional compression, and other stuff we've learned is useful from HTTP (such as If-Modified-Since).

- A Cheap-style response, at least for the first chunk, that provides meta-data such as file size (so the client can preallocate and avoid unpleasant disk-full situations).

- The ability to fetch a set of files in one go; otherwise the protocol becomes inefficient for large sets of small files.

- Confirmation from the client when it's fully received a file, to recover from chunks that might be lost if the client disconnects unexpectedly.

So far, our semantic has been "fetch"; that is, the recipient knows (somehow) that it needs a specific file, so it asks for it. The knowledge of which files exist, and where they are, is then passed out-of-band (e.g., in HTTP, by links in the HTML page).

How about a "push" semantic? There are two plausible use cases for this. First, if we adopt a centralized architecture with files on a main "server" (not something I'm advocating, but people do sometimes like this), then it's very useful to allow clients to upload files to the server. Second, it lets us do a kind of pub-sub for files, where the client asks for all new files of some type; as the server gets these, it forwards them to the client.

A fetch semantic is synchronous, while a push semantic is asynchronous. Asynchronous is less chatty, so faster. Also, you can do cute things like "subscribe to this path," thus creating a publish-subscribe file transfer architecture. That is so obviously awesome that I shouldn't need to explain what problem it solves.

Still, here is the problem with the fetch semantic: that out-of-band route to tell clients what files exist. No matter how you do this, it ends up being complex. Either clients have to poll, or you need a separate pub-sub channel to keep clients up-to-date, or you need user interaction.

Thinking this through a little more, though, we can see that fetch is just a special case of publish-subscribe. So, we can get the best of both worlds. Here is the general design:

- Fetch this path
- Here is credit (repeat)

To make this work (and we will, my dear readers), we need to be a little more explicit about how we send credit to the server. The cute trick of treating a pipelined "fetch chunk" request as credit won't fly because the client doesn't know any longer what files actually exist, how large they are, or anything. If the client says, "I'm good for 250,000 bytes of data," this should work equally for 1 file of 250K bytes, or 100 files of 2,500 bytes.

And this gives us "credit-based flow control," which effectively removes the need for high-water marks and any risk of memory overflow.

State Machines

Software engineers tend to think of (finite) state machines as a kind of intermediary interpreter. That is, you take a regular language and compile that into a state machine, then execute the state machine. The state machine itself is rarely visible to the developer: it's an internal representation—optimized, compressed, and bizarre.

However, it turns out that state machines are also valuable as first-class modeling languages for protocol handlers, such as ØMQ clients and servers. ØMQ makes it rather easy to design protocols, but we've never defined a good pattern for writing those clients and servers properly.

A protocol has at least two levels:

- How we represent individual messages on the wire
- How messages flow between peers, and the significance of each message

We've seen in this chapter how to produce codecs that handle serialization. That's a good start. But if we leave the second job to developers, that gives them a lot of room to interpret. As we make more ambitious protocols (file transfer + heartbeating + credit + authentication), it becomes less and less sane to try to implement clients and servers by hand.

Yes, people do this almost systematically. But the costs are high, and they're avoidable. In this section I'll explain how to model protocols using state machines, and how to generate neat and solid code from those models.

My initial experience with using state machines as a software construction tool dates back to 1985 and my first real job making tools for application developers. In 1991 I turned that knowledge into a free software tool called Libero, which spat out executable state machines from a simple text model.

The thing about Libero's model was that it was readable. That is, you described your program logic as named states, each accepting a set of events, each doing some real work. The resulting state machine hooked into your application code, driving it like a boss.

Libero was charmingly good at its job, fluent in many languages, and modestly popular, given the enigmatic nature of state machines. We used Libero in anger in dozens of large distributed applications, one of which was finally switched off in 2011 after 20 years of operation. State-machine-driven code construction worked so well that it's somewhat impressive that this approach never hit the mainstream of software engineering.

So, in this section I'm going to explain Libero's model, and show how to use it to generate ØMQ clients and servers. We'll use GSL again, but like I said, the principles are general and you can put together code generators using any scripting language.

As a worked example, let's see how to carry on a stateful dialog with a peer on a ROUTER socket. We'll develop the server using a state machine (and the client by hand). We have a simple protocol that I'll call "NOM." I'm using the oh-so-very-serious "Keywords for Unprotocols" (*http://unprotocols.org/blog:2*) proposal:

```
nom-protocol    = open-peering *use-peering

open-peering    = C:OHAI ( S:OHAI-OK / S:WTF )

use-peering     = C:ICANHAZ
                / S:CHEEZBURGER
                / C:HUGZ S:HUGZ-OK
                / S:HUGZ C:HUGZ-OK
```

I've not found a quick way to explain the true nature of state machine programming. In my experience, it invariably takes a few days of practice. After three or four days' exposure to the idea there is a near-audible "click!" as something in the brain connects all the pieces together. We'll make it concrete by looking at the state machine for our NOM server.

A useful thing about state machines is that you can read them state by state. Each state has a unique descriptive name and one or more *events*, which we list in any order. For each event we perform zero or more *actions*, and we then move to a *next state* (or stay in the same state).

In a ØMQ protocol server, we have a state machine instance *per client*. That sounds complex, but it isn't, as we'll see. We describe our first state (Start) as having one valid event, "OHAI." We check the user's credentials and then arrive in the Authenticated state (Figure 7-1).

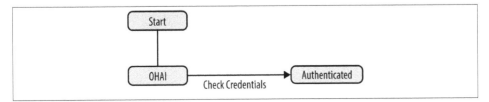

Figure 7-1. The "Start" state

The Check Credentials action produces either an "OK" or an "error" event. It's in the Authenticated state that we handle these two possible events, by sending an appropriate reply back to the client (Figure 7-2). If authentication failed, we return to the Start state where the client can try again.

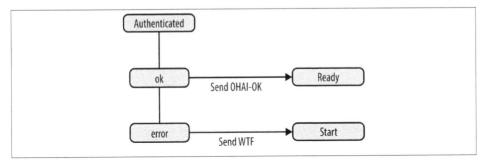

Figure 7-2. The "Authenticated" state

When authentication has succeeded, we arrive in the Ready state. Here we have three possible events: an ICANHAZ or HUGZ message from the client, or a heartbeat timer event (Figure 7-3).

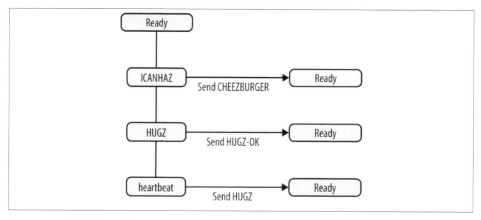

Figure 7-3. The "Ready" state

There are a few more things about this state machine model that are worth knowing:

- Events in upper-case (like "HUGZ") are "external events" that come from the client as messages.

- Events in lower-case (like "heartbeat") are "internal events," produced by code in the server.

- The "Send SOMETHING" actions are shorthand for sending a specific reply back to the client.

- Events that aren't defined in a particular state are silently ignored.

Now, the original source for these pretty pictures is an XML model:

```
<class name = "nom_server" script = "server_c">

<state name = "start">
    <event name = "OHAI" next = "authenticated">
        <action name = "check credentials" />
    </event>
</state>

<state name = "authenticated">
    <event name = "ok" next = "ready">
        <action name = "send" message ="OHAI-OK" />
    </event>
    <event name = "error" next = "start">
        <action name = "send" message = "WTF" />
    </event>
</state>

<state name = "ready">
    <event name = "ICANHAZ">
        <action name = "send" message = "CHEEZBURGER" />
```

```
        </event>
        <event name = "HUGZ">
            <action name = "send" message = "HUGZ-OK" />
        </event>
        <event name = "heartbeat">
            <action name = "send" message = "HUGZ" />
        </event>
    </state>
</class>
```

The code generator is in *examples/models/server_c.gsl*. It is a fairly complete tool that I'll use and expand for more serious work later. It generates:

- A server class in C (*nom_server.c, nom_server.h*) that implements the whole protocol flow
- A selftest method that runs the self-test steps listed in the XML file
- Documentation in the form of graphics (the pretty pictures)

Here's a simple main program that starts the generated NOM server:

```
#include "czmq.h"
#include "nom_server.h"

int main (int argc, char *argv [])
{
    printf ("Starting NOM protocol server on port 5670...\n");
    nom_server_t *server = nom_server_new ();
    nom_server_bind (server, "tcp://*:5670");
    nom_server_wait (server);
    nom_server_destroy (&server);
    return 0;
}
```

The generated nom_server class is a fairly classic model. It accepts client messages on a ROUTER socket, so the first frame of every request is the client's connection identity. The server manages a set of clients, each with state. As messages arrive, it feeds these as "events" to the state machine. Here's the core of the state machine, as a mix of GSL commands and the C code we intend to generate:

```
client_execute (client_t *self, int event)
{
    self->next_event = event;
    while (self->next_event) {
        self->event = self->next_event;
        self->next_event = 0;
        switch (self->state) {
.for class.state
            case $(name:c)_state:
.    for event
.        if index () > 1
```

```
                  else
    .      endif
                      if (self->event == $(name:c)_event) {
    .      for action
    .          if name = "send"
                          zmsg_addstr (self->reply, "$(message:)");
    .          else
                          $(name:c)_action (self);
    .          endif
    .      endfor
    .      if defined (event.next)
                          self->state = $(next:c)_state;
    .      endif
                      }
    .  endfor
                      break;
    .endfor
              }
              if (zmsg_size (self->reply) > 1) {
                  zmsg_send (&self->reply, self->router);
                  self->reply = zmsg_new ();
                  zmsg_add (self->reply, zframe_dup (self->address));
              }
          }
      }
  }
```

Each client is held as an object with various properties, including the variables we need to represent a state machine instance:

```
event_t next_event;       //  Next event
state_t state;            //  Current state
event_t event;            //  Current event
```

You will see by now that we are generating technically perfect code that has the precise design and shape we want. The only clue that the nom_server class isn't handwritten is that the code is *too good*. People who complain that code generators produce poor code are used to poor code generators.

It is trivial to extend our model as we need it. For example, here's how we generate the self-test code. First, we add a "selftest" item to the state machine and write our tests. We're not using any XML grammar or validation, so it really is just a matter of opening the editor and adding a half-dozen lines of text:

```
<selftest>
    <step send = "OHAI" body = "Sleepy" recv = "WTF" />
    <step send = "OHAI" body = "Joe" recv = "OHAI-OK" />
    <step send = "ICANHAZ" recv = "CHEEZBURGER" />
    <step send = "HUGZ" recv = "HUGZ-OK" />
    <step recv = "HUGZ" />
</selftest>
```

Designing on the fly, I decided that "send" and "recv" were a nice way to express "send this request, then expect this reply." Here's the GSL code that turns this model into real code:

```
.for class->selftest.step
.    if defined (send)
     msg = zmsg_new ();
     zmsg_addstr (msg, "$(send:)");
.        if defined (body)
     zmsg_addstr (msg, "$(body:)");
.        endif
     zmsg_send (&msg, dealer);

.    endif
.    if defined (recv)
     msg = zmsg_recv (dealer);
     assert (msg);
     command = zmsg_popstr (msg);
     assert (streq (command, "$(recv:)"));
     free (command);
     zmsg_destroy (&msg);

.    endif
.endfor
```

Finally, one of the more tricky but absolutely essential parts of any state machine generator is *how do I plug this into my own code?* As a minimal example for this exercise, I wanted to implement the "check credentials" action by accepting all OHAIs from my friend Joe (Hi Joe!) and rejecting everyone else's OHAIs. After some thought I decided to grab code directly from the state machine model—i.e., embed action bodies in the XML file. So, in *nom_server.xml*, you'll see this:

```
<action name = "check credentials">
    char *body = zmsg_popstr (self->request);
    if (body && streq (body, "Joe"))
        self->next_event = ok_event;
    else
        self->next_event = error_event;
    free (body);
</action>
```

And the code generator grabs that C code and inserts it into the generated *nom_server.c* file:

```
.for class.action
static void
$(name:c)_action (client_t *self) {
$(string.trim (.):)
}
.endfor
```

Now we have something quite elegant: a single source file that describes my server state machine, and which also contains the native implementations for my actions. A nice mix of high-level and low-level that is about 90% smaller than the C code.

Beware, as your head spins with notions of all the amazing things you could produce with such leverage: while this approach gives you real power, it also moves you away from your peers, and if you go too far, you'll find yourself working alone.

By the way, this simple little state machine design exposes just three variables to our custom code:

- `self->next_event`
- `self->request`
- `self->reply`

In the Libero state machine model there are a few more concepts that we haven't used here but that we will need when we write larger state machines:

- Exceptions, which let us write terser state machines. When an action raises an exception, further processing on the event stops. The state machine can then define how to handle exception events.

- Default state, where we can define default handling for events (especially useful for exception events).

Authentication Using SASL

When we designed AMQP in 2007, we chose the Simple Authentication and Security Layer (*http://en.wikipedia.org/wiki/Simple_Authentication_and_Security_Layer*) (SASL) for the authentication layer, one of the ideas we took from the BEEP protocol framework (*http://www.rfc-editor.org/rfc/rfc3080.txt*). SASL looks complex at first, but it's actually simple and fits neatly into a ØMQ-based protocol. What I especially like about SASL is that it's scalable. You can start with anonymous access or plain text authentication and no security, and grow to more secure mechanisms over time, without changing your protocol.

I'm not going to give a deep explanation now, since we'll see SASL in action a bit later. But I'll explain the principle so you're already somewhat prepared.

In the NOM protocol the client started with an OHAI command, which the server either accepted ("Hi Joe!") or rejected. This is simple but not scalable, since the server and client have to agree up-front on what kind of authentication they're going to do.

What SASL introduces, which is genius, is a fully abstracted and negotiable security layer that's still easy to implement at the protocol level. It works as follows:

1. The client connects.

2. The server challenges the client, passing a list of security "mechanisms" that it knows about.

3. The client chooses a security mechanism that it knows about, and answers the server's challenge with a blob of opaque data that (and here's the neat trick) some generic security library calculates and gives to the client.

4. The server takes the security mechanism the client chose, and that blob of data, and passes it to its own security library.

5. Either the library accepts the client's answer, or the server challenges again.

There are a number of free SASL libraries. When we come to real code, we'll implement just two mechanisms, ANONYMOUS and PLAIN, which don't need any special libraries.

To support SASL we have to add an optional challenge/response step to our "open-peering" flow. Here is what the resulting protocol grammar looks like (I'm modifying NOM to do this):

```
secure-nom      = open-peering *use-peering

open-peering    = C:OHAI *( S:ORLY C:YARLY ) ( S:OHAI-OK / S:WTF )

ORLY            = 1*mechanism challenge
mechanism       = string
challenge       = *OCTET

YARLY           = mechanism response
response        = *OCTET
```

where ORLY and YARLY each contain a string (a list of mechanisms in ORLY, one mechanism in YARLY) and a blob of opaque data. Depending on the mechanism, the initial challenge from the server may be empty. We don't care a jot: we just pass this to the security library to deal with.

The SASL RFC (*http://tools.ietf.org/html/rfc4422*) goes into detail about other features (that we don't need), the kinds of ways SASL could be attacked, and so on.

Large-Scale File Publishing: FileMQ

Let's put all these techniques together into a file distribution system that I'll call FileMQ. This is going to be a real product, living on GitHub (*https://github.com/hintjens/filemq*). What we'll make here is a first version of FileMQ, as a training tool. If the concept works, the real thing may eventually get its own book.

Why Make FileMQ?

Why make a file distribution system? I already explained how to send large files over ØMQ, and it's really quite simple. But if you want to make messaging accessible to a million times more people than can use ØMQ, you need another kind of API. An API that my five-year-old son can understand. An API that is universal, requires no programming, and works with just about every single application.

Yes, I'm talking about the filesystem. It's the DropBox pattern: chuck your files somewhere, and they get magically copied somewhere else, when the network connects again.

However, what I'm aiming for is a fully decentralized architecture that looks more like Git, that doesn't need any cloud services (though we could put FileMQ in the cloud), and that does multicast (i.e., can send files to many places at once).

FileMQ has to be secure(able), has to be easily hooked into random scripting languages, and has to be as fast as possible across our domestic and office networks.

I want to use it to back up photos from my mobile phone to my laptop, over WiFi. To share presentation slides in real time across 50 laptops in a conference. To share documents with colleagues in a meeting. To send earthquake data from sensors to central clusters. To back up video from my phone as I take it, during protests or riots. To synchronize configuration files across a cloud of Linux servers.

A visionary idea, isn't it? Well, ideas are cheap. The hard part is making this, and making it simple.

Initial Design Cut: The API

Here's the way I see the first design. FileMQ has to be distributed, so every node can be a server and a client at the same time. But I don't want the protocol to be symmetrical, because that seems forced. We have a natural flow of files from point A to point B, where A is the "server" and B is the "client." If files flow back the other way, we have two flows. FileMQ is not yet a directory synchronization protocol, but we'll bring it quite close.

Thus, I'm going to build FileMQ as two pieces: a client and a server. Then, I'll put these together in a main application (the "filemq" tool) that can act both as client and server. The two pieces will look quite similar to the nom_server, with the same kind of API:

```
fmq_server_t *server = fmq_server_new ();
fmq_server_bind (server, "tcp://*:5670");
fmq_server_publish (server, "/home/ph/filemq/share", "/public");
fmq_server_publish (server, "/home/ph/photos/stream", "/photostream");

fmq_client_t *client = fmq_client_new ();
fmq_client_connect (client, "tcp://pieter.filemq.org:5670");
fmq_client_subscribe (server, "/public/", "/home/ph/filemq/share");
fmq_client_subscribe (server, "/photostream/", "/home/ph/photos/stream");
```

```
    while (!zctx_interrupted)
        sleep (1);

    fmq_server_destroy (&server);
    fmq_client_destroy (&client);
```

If we wrap this C API in other languages, we can easily script FileMQ, embed it applications, port it to smartphones, and so on.

Initial Design Cut: The Protocol

The full name for the protocol is the File Message Queuing Protocol, or FILEMQ (in
uppercase, to distinguish it from the software). To start with, we write down the protocol
as an ABNF grammar. Our grammar starts with the flow of commands between the
client and server. You should recognize these as a combination of the various techniques
we've seen already:

```
filemq-protocol = open-peering *use-peering [ close-peering ]

open-peering   = C:OHAI *( S:ORLY C:YARLY ) ( S:OHAI-OK / error )

use-peering    = C:ICANHAZ ( S:ICANHAZ-OK / error )
               / C:NOM
               / S:CHEEZBURGER
               / C:HUGZ S:HUGZ-OK
               / S:HUGZ C:HUGZ-OK

close-peering  = C:KTHXBAI / S:KTHXBAI

error          = S:SRSLY / S:RTFM
```

Here are the commands to and from the server:

```
;   The client opens peering to the server
OHAI            = signature %x01 protocol version
signature       = %xAA %xA3
protocol        = string        ; Must be "FILEMQ"
string          = size *VCHAR
size            = OCTET
version         = %x01

;   The server challenges the client using the SASL model
ORLY            = signature %x02 mechanisms challenge
mechanisms      = size 1*mechanism
mechanism       = string
challenge       = *OCTET        ; 0MQ frame

;   The client responds with SASL authentication information
YARLY           = %signature x03 mechanism response
response        = *OCTET        ; 0MQ frame

;   The server grants the client access
```

```
OHAI-OK          = signature %x04

;   The client subscribes to a virtual path
ICANHAZ          = signature %x05 path options cache
path             = string          ; Full path or path prefix
options          = dictionary
dictionary       = size *key-value
key-value        = string          ; Formatted as name=value
cache            = dictionary      ; File SHA-1 signatures

;   The server confirms the subscription
ICANHAZ-OK       = signature %x06

;   The client sends credit to the server
NOM              = signature %x07 credit
credit           = 8OCTET          ; 64-bit integer, network order
sequence         = 8OCTET          ; 64-bit integer, network order

;   The server sends a chunk of file data
CHEEZBURGER      = signature %x08 sequence operation filename
                   offset headers chunk
sequence         = 8OCTET          ; 64-bit integer, network order
operation        = OCTET
filename         = string
offset           = 8OCTET          ; 64-bit integer, network order
headers          = dictionary
chunk            = FRAME

;   Client or server sends a heartbeat
HUGZ             = signature %x09

;   Client or server responds to a heartbeat
HUGZ-OK          = signature %x0A

;   Client closes the peering
KTHXBAI          = signature %x0B
```

And here are the different ways the server can tell the client things went wrong:

```
;   Server error reply - refused due to access rights
S:SRSLY          = signature %x80 reason

;   Server error reply - client sent an invalid command
S:RTFM           = signature %x81 reason
```

FILEMQ lives on the ØMQ unprotocols website (*http://rfc.zeromq.org/spec:19*) and has a registered TCP port with IANA (the Internet Assigned Numbers Authority), which is port 5670.

Building and Trying FileMQ

The FileMQ stack is on GitHub (*https://github.com/hintjens/filemq*). It works like a classic C/C++ project:

```
git clone git://github.com/hintjens/filemq.git
cd filemq
./autogen.sh
./configure
make check
```

You want to be using the latest CZMQ master for this. Now try running the *track* command, which is a simple tool that uses FileMQ to track changes in one directory in another:

```
cd src
./track ./fmqroot/send ./fmqroot/recv
```

Open two file navigator windows, one into *src/fmqroot/send* and one into *src/fmqroot/recv*. Drop files into the *send* folder, and you'll see them arrive in the *recv* folder. The server checks once per second for new files. Delete files in the *send* folder, and they're deleted in the *recv* folder simultaneously.

I use *track* for things like updating my MP3 player, mounted as a USB drive. As I add or remove files in my laptop's *Music* folder, the same changes happen on the MP3 player. FILEMQ isn't a full replication protocol yet, but we'll fix that later.

Internal Architecture

To build FileMQ I used a lot of code generation, possibly too much for a tutorial. However, the code generators are all reusable in other stacks and will be important for our final project in Chapter 8. They are an evolution of the set we saw earlier:

- *codec_c.gsl* generates a message codec for a given protocol.
- *server_c.gsl* generates a server class for a protocol and state machine.
- *client_c.gsl* generates a client class for a protocol and state machine.

The best way to learn to use GSL code generation is to translate these into a language of your choice and make your own demo protocols and stacks. You'll find it fairly easy. FileMQ itself doesn't try to support multiple languages. It could, but it'd make things needlessly complex.

The FileMQ architecture actually slices into two layers. There's a generic set of classes to handle chunks, directories, files, patches, SASL security, and configuration files. Then, there's the generated stack: messages, client, and server. If I was creating a new project I'd fork the whole FileMQ project, and go and modify the three models:

- *fmq_msg.xml*, which defines the message formats
- *fmq_client.xml*, which defines the client state machine, API, and implementation
- *fmq_server.xml*, which does the same for the server

You'd want to rename things to avoid confusion. Why didn't I make the reusable classes into a separate library? The answer is twofold. First, no one actually needs this (yet). Second, it'd make things more complex for you as you build and play with FileMQ. It's never worth adding complexity to solve a theoretical problem.

Although I wrote FileMQ in C, it's easy to map to other languages. It is quite amazing how nice C becomes when you add CZMQ's generic zlist and zhash containers, and class style. Let me go through the classes quickly:

- fmq_sasl encodes and decodes a SASL challenge. I only implemented the PLAIN mechanism, which is enough to prove the concept.
- fmq_chunk works with variable-sized blobs. These are not as efficient as ØMQ's messages, but they do less weirdness and so are easier to understand. The chunk class has methods to read and write chunks from/to disk.
- fmq_file works with files, which may or may not exist on disk. It gives you information about a file (like size) and lets you read from and write to files, remove files, check if a file exists, and check if a file is "stable" (more on that later).
- fmq_dir works with directories, reading them from disk and comparing two directories to see what's changed. When there are changes, it returns a list of "patches."
- fmq_patch works with one patch, which really just says "create this file" or "delete this file" (referring to an fmq_file item each time).
- fmq_config works with configuration data. I'll come back to client and server configuration later.

Every class has a test method, and the main development cycle is "edit, test." These are mostly simple self-tests, but they make the difference between code I can trust and code I know will still break. It's a safe bet that any code that isn't covered by a test case will have undiscovered errors. I'm not a fan of external test harnesses, but internal test code that you write as you write your functionality... that's like the handle on a knife.

You should, really, be able to read the source code and rapidly understand what these classes are doing. If you can't read the code happily, tell me. If you want to port the FileMQ implementation into other languages, start by forking the whole repository, and later we'll see if it's possible to do this in one overall repo.

Public API

The public API consists of two classes (as we sketched earlier):

- `fmq_client` provides the client API, with methods to connect to a server, configure the client, and subscribe to paths.
- `fmq_server` provides the server API, with methods to bind to a port, configure the server, and publish a path.

These classes provide a *multithreaded API*, a model we've used a few times now. When you create an API instance (i.e., `fmq_server_new()` or `fmq_client_new()`), this method kicks off a background thread that does the real work—that is, runs the server or the client. The other API methods then talk to this thread over ØMQ sockets (a "pipe" consisting of two PAIR sockets over `inproc`).

If I was a keen young developer eager to use FileMQ in another language, I'd probably spend a happy weekend writing a binding for this public API, then stick it in a subdirectory of the *filemq* project called, say, "bindings/," and make a pull request.

The actual API methods come from the state machine description, like this (for the server):

```
<method name = "publish">
<argument name = "location" type = "string" />
<argument name = "alias" type = "string" />
mount_t *mount = mount_new (location, alias);
zlist_append (self->mounts, mount);
</method>
```

Which gets turned into this code:

```
void
fmq_server_publish (fmq_server_t *self, const char *location, const char *alias)
{
    assert (self);
    assert (location);
    assert (alias);
    zstr_sendm (self->pipe, "PUBLISH");
    zstr_sendfm (self->pipe, "%s", location);
    zstr_sendf (self->pipe, "%s", alias);
}
```

Design Notes

The hardest part of making FileMQ wasn't implementing the protocol, but maintaining accurate state internally. An FTP or HTTP server is essentially stateless, but a publish-subscribe server *has* to maintain subscriptions, at least.

So, I'll go through some of the design aspects:

- The client detects if the server has died by the lack of heartbeats (HUGZ) coming from the server. It then restarts its dialog by sending an OHAI. There's no timeout on the OHAI since the ØMQ DEALER socket will queue an outgoing message indefinitely.

- The server detects if a client has died by its lack of response (HUGZ-OK) to a heartbeat. In that case, it deletes all state for the client, including its subscriptions.

- The client API holds subscriptions in memory and replays them when it has connected successfully. This means the caller can subscribe at any time (and doesn't care when connections and authentication actually happen).

- The server and client use virtual paths, much like an HTTP or FTP server. You publish one or more "mount points," each corresponding to a directory on the server. Each of these maps to some virtual path; for instance, "/" if you have only one mount point. Clients then subscribe to virtual paths, and files arrive in an inbox directory. We don't send physical filenames across the network.

- There are some timing issues: if the server is creating its mount points while clients are connected and subscribing, the subscriptions won't attach to the right mount points. So, we bind the server port as the last thing.

- Clients can reconnect at any point; if the client sends OHAI, that signals the end of any previous conversation and the start of a new one. I might one day make subscriptions durable so that they survive a disconnection. The client stack, after reconnecting, replays any subscriptions the caller application has already made.

Configuration

I've built several large server products, like the Xitami web server that was popular in the late '90s, and the OpenAMQ messaging server (*http://www.openamq.org*). Getting configuration easy and obvious was a large part of making these servers fun to use.

We typically aim to solve a number of problems:

- Ship default configuration files with the product.
- Allow users to add custom configuration files that are never overwritten.
- Allow users to configure from the command line.

And then layer these one on top of the other, so command-line settings override custom settings, which override default settings. It can be a lot of work to do this right. For FileMQ, I've taken a somewhat simpler tack: all configuration is done from the API.

This is how we start and configure the server, for example:

```
server = fmq_server_new ();
fmq_server_configure (server, "server_test.cfg");
fmq_server_publish (server, "./fmqroot/send", "/");
fmq_server_publish (server, "./fmqroot/logs", "/logs");
fmq_server_bind (server, "tcp://*:5670");
```

We do use a specific format for the config files—the ZeroMQ Property Language (ZPL (*http://rfc.zeromq.org/spec:4*)), a minimalist syntax that we started using for ØMQ "devices" a few years ago, but which works well for any server:

```
#    Configure server for plain access
#
server
    monitor = 1            #   Check mount points
    heartbeat = 1          #   Heartbeat to clients

publish
    location = ./fmqroot/logs
    virtual = /logs

security
    echo = I: use guest/guest to login to server
    #    These are SASL mechanisms we accept
    anonymous = 0
    plain = 1
        account
            login = guest
            password = guest
            group = guest
        account
            login = super
            password = secret
            group = admin
```

One cute thing (which seems useful) that the generated server code does is to parse this config file (when you use the `fmq_server_configure()` method) and execute any section that matches an API method. Thus, the "publish" section works as an `fmq_serv er_publish()` method.

File Stability

It is quite common to poll a directory for changes and then do something "interesting" with new files. But as one process is writing to a file, other processes have no idea when the file has been fully written. One solution is to add a second "indicator" file that we create after creating the first file. This is intrusive, however.

There is a neater way, which is to detect when a file is "stable" (i.e., no one is writing to it any longer). FileMQ does this by checking the modification time of the file. If it's more than a second old, then the file is considered stable—at least, stable enough to be shipped off to clients. If a process comes along after five minutes and appends to the file, it'll be shipped off again.

For this to work, and this is a requirement for any application hoping to use FileMQ successfully, do not buffer more than a second's worth of data in memory before writing. If you use very large block sizes, the file may look stable when it's not.

Delivery Notifications

One of the nice things about the multithreaded API model we're using is that it's essentially message-based. This makes it ideal for returning events back to the caller. A more conventional API approach would be to use callbacks, but callbacks that cross thread boundaries are somewhat delicate. Here's how the client sends a message back when it has received a complete file:

```
zstr_sendm (self->pipe, "DELIVER");
zstr_sendm (self->pipe, filename);
zstr_sendf (self->pipe, "%s/%s", inbox, filename);
```

We can now add a _recv() method to the API that waits for events back from the client. It makes a clean style for the caller: create the client object, configure it, and then receive and process any events it returns.

Symbolic Links

While using a staging area is a nice, simple API, it also creates costs for senders. If I already have a 2 GB video file on a camera and I want to send it via FileMQ, the current implementation asks that I copy it to a staging area before it will be sent to subscribers.

One option is to mount the whole content directory (e.g., */home/me/Movies*), but this is fragile since it means the application can't decide to send individual files. It's everything or nothing.

A simple answer is to implement portable symbolic links. As Wikipedia (*http://en.wiki pedia.org/wiki/Symbolic_link*) explains:

> A symbolic link contains a text string that is automatically interpreted and followed by the operating system as a path to another file or directory. This other file or directory is called the "target". The symbolic link is a second file that exists independently of its target. If a symbolic link is deleted, its target remains unaffected.

This doesn't affect the protocol in any way; it's an optimization in the server implementation. Let's make a simple portable implementation:

- A symbolic link consists of a filename with the extension *.ln*.
- The filename without *.ln* is the published filename.
- The link file contains one line, which is the real path to the file.

Since we've collected all operations on files in a single class (fmq_file), it's a clean change. When we create a new file object we check if it's a symbolic link; if so, all read-only actions (get file size, read file) operate on the target file, not the link.

Recovery and Late Joiners

As it stands now, FileMQ has one major remaining problem: it provides no way for clients to recover from failures. The scenario is that a client, connected to a server, starts to receive files, and then disconnects for some reason. The network may be too slow, or break. The client may be on a laptop that is shut down, then resumed. The WiFi may be disconnected. As we move to a more mobile world (see Chapter 8), this use case becomes more and more frequent. In some ways it's becoming a dominant use case.

In the classic ØMQ publish-subscribe pattern, there are two strong underlying assumptions, both of which are usually wrong in FileMQ's real world: first, that data expires very rapidly, so there's no interest in asking for old data; and second, that networks are stable and rarely break (so it's better to invest more in improving the infrastructure and less in addressing recovery).

Take any FileMQ use case, and you'll see that if the client disconnects and reconnects, it should get anything it missed. A further improvement would be to recover from partial failures, like HTTP and FTP do. But one thing at a time.

One answer to recovery is "durable subscriptions." The first drafts of the FILEMQ protocol aimed to support this, with client identifiers that the server could hold onto and store so that if a client reappeared after a failure, the server would know what files it had not received.

Stateful servers are, however, nasty to make and difficult to scale. How do we, for example, fail over to a secondary server? Where does it get its subscriptions from? It's far nicer if each client connection works independently and carries all necessary state with it.

Another nail in the coffin of durable subscriptions is that this approach requires up-front coordination. Up-front coordination is always a red flag, whether it's in a team of people working together or a bunch of processes talking to each other. What about late joiners? In the real world, clients do not neatly line up and then all say "Ready!" at the same time. In the real world they come and go arbitrarily, and it's valuable if we can treat a brand new client in the same way as a client that has gone away and come back.

To deal with this I will add two concepts to the protocol: a resync option and a cache field (a dictionary). If the client wants recovery, it sets the resync option and tells the server what files it already has via the cache field. We need both, because there's no way in the protocol to distinguish between an empty field and a null field. The FILEMQ RFC describes these fields as follows:

> The 'options' field provides additional information to the server. The server SHOULD implement these options:

- RESYNC=1 - if the client sets this, the server SHALL send the full contents of the virtual path to the client, except files the client already has, as identified by their SHA-1 digest in the 'cache' field.

When the client specifies the RESYNC option, the 'cache' dictionary field tells the server which files the client already has. Each entry in the 'cache' dictionary is a "filename=digest" key/value pair where the digest SHALL be a SHA-1 digest in printable hexadecimal format. If the filename starts with '/' then it SHOULD start with the path, otherwise the server MUST ignore it. If the filename does not start with '/' then the server SHALL treat it as relative to the path.

Clients that know they are in the classic pub-sub use case just don't provide any cache data, and clients that want recovery provide their cache data. It requires no state in the server, no up-front coordination, and works equally well for brand new clients (which may have received files via some out-of-band means) and clients that have received some files and were then disconnected for a while.

I decided to use SHA-1 digests for several reasons. First, SHA-1 is fast enough: 150 msec to digest a 25 MB core dump on my laptop. Second, it's reliable: the chance of getting the same hash for different versions of one file is close enough to zero. Third, it's the widest supported digest algorithm. A cyclic-redundancy check (such as CRC-32) is faster but not reliable. More recent SHA versions (SHA-256, SHA-512) are more secure but take 50% more CPU cycles, and are overkill for our needs.

Here is what a typical ICANHAZ message looks like when we use both caching and resyncing (this is output from the dump method of the generated codec class):

```
ICANHAZ:
    path='/photos'
    options={
        RESYNC=1
    }
    cache={
        DSCF0001.jpg=1FABCD4259140ACA99E991E7ADD2034AC57D341D
        DSCF0006.jpg=01267C7641C5A22F2F4B0174FFB0C94DC59866F6
        DSCF0005.jpg=698E88C05B5C280E75C055444227FEA6FB60E564
        DSCF0004.jpg=F0149101DD6FEC13238E6FD9CA2F2AC62829CBD0
        DSCF0003.jpg=4A49F25E2030B60134F109ABD0AD9642C8577441
        DSCF0002.jpg=F84E4D69D854D4BF94B5873132F9892C8B5FA94E
    }
```

Although we don't do this in FileMQ, the server can use the cache information to help the client catch up with deletions that it has missed. To do this it would have to log deletions, and then compare this log with the client cache when a client subscribes.

Test Use Case: The Track Tool

To properly test something like FileMQ we need a test case that plays with live data. One of my sysadmin tasks is to manage the MP3 tracks on my music player. That is, by the way, a Sansa Clip reflashed with Rock Box, which I highly recommend. As I download tracks into my *Music* folder, I want to copy these to my player, and as I find tracks that annoy me, I delete them in the *Music* folder and want those gone from my player, too.

I could write this using a bash or Perl script—a powerful file distribution protocol is kind of overkill—but to be honest the hardest work in FileMQ was the directory comparison code, and I want to benefit from that. So I put together a simple tool called "track" that calls the FileMQ API. From the command line this runs with two arguments, the sending and receiving directories:

```
./track /home/ph/Music /media/3230-6364/MUSIC
```

The code is a neat example of how to use the FileMQ API to do local file distribution. Here is the full program, minus the license text (it's MIT/X11 licensed):

```
#include "czmq.h"
#include "../include/fmq.h"

int main (int argc, char *argv [])
{
    fmq_server_t *server = fmq_server_new ();
    fmq_server_configure (server, "anonymous.cfg");
    fmq_server_publish (server, argv [1], "/");
    fmq_server_set_anonymous (server, true);
    fmq_server_bind (server, "tcp://*:5670");

    fmq_client_t *client = fmq_client_new ();
    fmq_client_connect (client, "tcp://localhost:5670");
    fmq_client_set_inbox (client, argv [2]);
    fmq_client_set_resync (client, true);
    fmq_client_subscribe (client, "/");

    while (true) {
        //  Get message from fmq_client API
        zmsg_t *msg = fmq_client_recv (client);
        if (!msg)
            break;              //  Interrupted
        char *command = zmsg_popstr (msg);
        if (streq (command, "DELIVER")) {
            char *filename = zmsg_popstr (msg);
            char *fullname = zmsg_popstr (msg);
            printf ("I: received %s (%s)\n", filename, fullname);
            free (filename);
            free (fullname);
        }
        free (command);
        zmsg_destroy (&msg);
```

```
    }
    fmq_server_destroy (&server);
    fmq_client_destroy (&client);
    return 0;
}
```

Note how we work with physical paths in this tool. The server publishes the physical path "/home/ph/Music" and maps this to the virtual path "/". The client subscribes to "/" and receives all files in "/media/3230-6364/MUSIC". I could use any structure within the server directory, and it would be copied faithfully to the client's inbox. Note the API method `fmq_client_set_resync()`, which causes a server-to-client synchronization.

Getting an Official Port Number

We've been using port 5670 in the examples for FILEMQ. Unlike all the previous examples in this book, this port isn't arbitrary but was assigned (*http://www.iana.org/ assignments/service-names-port-numbers/service-names-port-numbers.txt*) by the Internet Assigned Numbers Authority (*http://www.iana.org*), which "is responsible for the global coordination of the DNS Root, IP addressing, and other Internet protocol resources."

I'll explain very briefly when and how to request registered port numbers for your application protocols. The main reason is to ensure that your applications can run in the public domain without conflict with other protocols. Technically, if you ship any software that uses port numbers between 1024 and 49151, you should be using only IANA-registered port numbers. Many products don't bother with this, however, and tend instead to use the IANA list as "ports to avoid."

If you aim to make a public protocol of any importance, such as FILEMQ, you're going to want an IANA-registered port. Briefly, here's how to do this:

- Document your protocol clearly, as IANA will want a specification of how you intend to use the port. It's not a formal agreement but must be solid enough to pass expert review.

- Decide what transport protocols you want: UDP, TCP, SCTP, etc. Usually with ØMQ you will want just TCP.

- Fill in the application on *iana.org*, providing all the necessary information.

- IANA will then continue the process by email until your application is either accepted or rejected.

Note that you don't request a specific port number; IANA will assign you one. It's therefore wise to start this process before you ship software, not afterwards.

## CHAPTER 8

A Framework for Distributed Computing

We've gone though a journey of understanding ØMQ in its many aspects. By now you may have started to build your own products using the techniques I've explained, as well as others you've figured out yourself. You will start to face questions about how to make these products work in the real world.

But what is that "real world"? I'll argue that it is becoming a world of ever-increasing numbers of moving pieces. Some people use the phrase "the Internet of Things," suggesting that we'll soon see a new category of devices that are more numerous, but also more stupid than our current smartphones, tablets, laptops, and servers. However, I don't think the data points this way at all. Yes, there are more and more devices, but they're not stupid at all. They're smart and powerful, and getting more so all the time.

The mechanism at work is something I call "cost gravity," and it has the effect of reducing the cost of technology by half every 18–24 months. Put another way, our global computing capacity doubles every two years, over and over and over. The future is filled with trillions of devices that are fully powerful multicore computers: they don't run a cut-down "operating system for things," but full operating systems and full applications.

And this is the world at which we're aiming with ØMQ. When we talk of "scale," we don't mean hundreds of computers, or even thousands. Think of clouds of tiny, smart, and perhaps self-replicating machines surrounding every person, filling every space, covering every wall, filling the cracks and, eventually, becoming so much a part of us that we get them before birth and they follow us to death.

These clouds of tiny machines talk to each other, all the time, over short-range wireless links using the Internet Protocol. They create mesh networks, pass information and tasks around like nervous signals. They augment our memory, our vision, every aspect of our communications, and our physical functions. And it's ØMQ that powers their conversations and events and exchanges of work and information.

Now, to make even a thin imitation of this vision come true today, we need to solve a set of technical problems. These include: How do peers discover each other? How do they talk to existing networks like the Web? How do they protect the information they carry? How do we track and monitor them, to get some idea of what they're doing? Then we need to do what most engineers forget about: package this solution into a framework that is dead easy for ordinary developers to use.

This is what we'll attempt in this chapter: to build a framework for distributed applications, as an API, protocols, and implementations. It's not a small challenge, but I've claimed often that ØMQ makes such problems simple, so let's see if that's still true.

We'll cover:

- Requirements for distributed computing
- The pros and cons of WiFi for proximity networking
- Discovery using UDP and TCP
- A message-based API
- Creating a new open source project
- Peer-to-peer connectivity (the Harmony pattern)
- Tracking peer presence and disappearance
- Group messaging without central coordination
- Large-scale testing and simulation
- Dealing with high-water marks and blocked peers
- Distributed logging and monitoring

Design for the Real World

Whether we're connecting a roomful of mobile devices over WiFi or a cluster of virtual boxes over simulated Ethernet, we will hit the same kinds of problems. These are:

Discovery
How do we learn about other nodes on the network? Do we use a discovery service, centralized mediation, or some kind of broadcast beacon?

Presence
How do we track when other nodes come and go? Do we use some kind of central registration service, or heartbeating or beacons?

Connectivity
How do we actually connect one node to another? Do we use local networking, wide-area networking, or do we use a central message broker to do the forwarding?

Point-to-point messaging

How do we send a message from one node to another? Do we send this to the node's network address, or do we use some indirect addressing via a centralized message broker?

Group messaging

How do we send a message from one node to a group of others? Do we work via a centralized message broker, or do we use a publish-subscribe model like ØMQ?

Testing and simulation

How do we simulate large numbers of nodes so we can test performance properly? Do we have to buy two dozen Android tablets, or can we use pure software simulation?

Distributed logging

How do we track what this cloud of nodes is doing so we can detect performance problems and failures? Do we create a main logging service, or do we allow every device to log the world around it?

Content distribution

How do we send content from one node to another? Do we use server-centric protocols like FTP or HTTP, or do we use decentralized protocols like FileMQ?

If we can solve these problems reasonably well, and the further problems that will emerge (like security and wide-area bridging), we'll get something like a framework for what I might call "Really Cool Distributed Applications" and my grandkids might call "the software our world runs on."

You should have guessed from my rhetorical questions that there are two broad directions in which we can go. One is to centralize everything. The other is to distribute everything. I'm going to bet on decentralization. If you want centralization, you don't really need ØMQ; there are other options you can use.

So, very roughly, here's the story. One, the number of moving pieces increases exponentially over time (it doubles every 24 months). Two, these pieces stop using wires because dragging cables everywhere gets *really* boring. Three, future applications run across clusters of these pieces using the Benevolent Tyrant pattern from Chapter 6. Four, today it's really difficult—nay, still rather impossible—to build such applications. Five, let's make it cheap and easy using all the techniques and tools we've built up. Six, partay!

The Secret Life of WiFi

The future is clearly wireless, and while many big businesses live by concentrating data in their clouds, the future doesn't look quite so centralized. The devices at the edges of our networks get smarter every year, not dumber. They're hungry for work and information to digest and profit from. And they don't drag cables around, except once a night for power. It's all wireless and more and more, it's 802.11-branded WiFi of different alphabetical flavors.

Why Mesh Isn't Here Yet

As such a vital part of our future, WiFi has a big problem that's not often discussed, but that anyone betting on it needs to be aware of. The phone companies of the world have built themselves nice, profitable mobile phone cartels in nearly every country with a functioning government, based on convincing governments that without monopoly rights to airwaves and ideas, the world would fall apart. Technically, we call this "regulatory capture" and "patents," but in fact it's just a form of blackmail and corruption. If you, the state, give me, a business, the right to overcharge, tax the market, and ban all real competitors, I'll give you 5%. Not enough? How about 10%? OK, 15% plus snacks. If you refuse, we pull service.

But WiFi snuck past this, borrowing unlicensed airspace and riding on the back of the open and unpatented and remarkably innovative Internet Protocol stack. So today, we have the curious situation where it costs me several euros a minute to call from Seoul to Brussels if I use the state-backed infrastructure that we've subsidized over decades, but nothing at all if I can find an unregulated WiFi access point. Oh, and I can do video, send files and photos, and download entire home movies all for the same amazing price point of precisely zero point zero zero (in any currency you like). God help me if I try to send just one photo to my home using the service for which I actually pay. That would cost me more than the camera I took it on.

This is the price we pay for having tolerated the "trust us, we're the experts" patent system for so long. But more than that, it's a massive economic incentive to chunks of the technology sector—and especially chipset makers who own patents on the anti-Internet GSM, GPRS, 3G, and LTE stacks, and who treat the telcos as prime clients—to actively throttle WiFi development. And of course, it's these firms that bulk out the IEEE committees that define WiFi.

The reason for this rant against lawyer-driven "innovation" is to steer your thinking toward the question, "What if WiFi were really free?" This will happen one day, not too far off, and it's worth betting on. We'll see several things happen: first, much more aggressive use of airspace, especially for near-distance communications where there is no risk of interference; second, big capacity improvements as we learn to use more airspace in parallel; third, acceleration of the standardization process; and last, broader support in devices for really interesting connectivity.

Right now, streaming a movie from your phone to your TV is considered "leading edge." This is ridiculous. Let's get truly ambitious. How about a stadium of people watching a game, sharing photos and HD video with each other in real time, creating an ad hoc event that literally saturates the airspace with a digital frenzy? I should be able to collect terabytes of imagery from those around me, in an hour. Why does this have to go through Twitter or Facebook and that tiny, expensive mobile data connection? How about a home with hundreds of devices all talking to each other over mesh, so when someone rings the doorbell, the porch lights stream video through to your phone or TV? How about a car that can talk to your phone and play your dubstep playlist *without you plugging in wires*?

To get more serious, why is our digital society in the hands of central points that are monitored, censored, logged, used to track who we talk to and to collect evidence against us, and then shut down when the authorities decide we have too much free speech? The loss of privacy we're living through is only a problem when it's one-sided, but then the problem is calamitous. A truly wireless world would bypass all central censorship. It's how the Internet was designed, and it's quite feasible, technically.

Some Physics

Naive developers of distributed software treat the network as infinitely fast and perfectly reliable. While this is approximately true for simple applications running over Ethernet, WiFi rapidly proves the difference between magical thinking and science. That is, WiFi breaks so easily and dramatically under stress that I sometimes wonder how anyone would dare use it for real work. The ceiling moves up as WiFi gets better, but never fast enough to stop us hitting it.

To understand how WiFi performs technically, you need to understand a basic law of physics: the power required to connect two points increases according to the square of the distance. People who grow up in larger houses have exponentially louder voices, as I learned in Dallas. For a WiFi network this means that as two radios get further apart, they have to either use more power or lower their signal rate.

There's only so much power you can pull out of a battery before users treat the device as hopelessly broken. Thus, even though a WiFi network may be rated at a certain speed, the real bit rate between the access point (AP) and a client depends on how far apart the two are. As you move your WiFi-enabled phone away from the AP, the two radios trying to talk to each other will first increase their power and then reduce their bit rate.

This effect has some consequences of which we should be aware if we want to build robust distributed applications that don't dangle wires behind them like puppets:

- If you have a group of devices talking to an AP, when the AP is talking to the slowest device, the *whole network has to wait*. It's like having to repeat a joke at a party to the designated driver who has no sense of humor, is still fully and tragically sober, and has a poor grasp of language.
- If you use unicast TCP and send a message to multiple devices, the AP must send the packets to each device separately, Yes, you knew this; it's also how Ethernet works. But now understand that one distant (or low-powered) device will force everything to wait for that slowest device to catch up.

- If you use multicast or broadcast (which work the same, in most cases), the AP will send single packets to the whole network at once, which is awesome, but it will do it at the slowest possible bit rate (usually 1 Mbps). You can adjust this rate manually in some APs, but that just reduces the reach of your AP. You can also buy more expensive APs that have a little more intelligence and will figure out the highest bit rate they can safely use, or you can use enterprise APs with Internet Group Management Protocol (IGMP) support and ØMQ's PGM transport to send only to subscribed clients. I would not, however, bet on such APs being widely available, ever.

As you try to put more devices onto an AP, performance rapidly gets worse, to the point where adding one more device can break the whole network for everyone. Many APs solve this by randomly disconnecting clients when they reach some limit, such as 4–8 devices for a mobile hotspot, 30–50 devices for a consumer AP, or perhaps 100 devices for an enterprise AP.

What's the Current Status?

Despite its uncomfortable role as enterprise technology that somehow escaped into the wild, WiFi is already useful for more than making a free Skype call. It's not ideal, but it works well enough to let us solve some interesting problems. Let me give you a rapid status report.

First, point-to-point versus AP-to-client. Traditional WiFi is all AP-client. Every packet has to go from client A to AP, then to client B. You cut your bandwidth by 50%—but that's only half the problem. I explained about the inverse power law. If A and B are very close together but both are far from the AP, they'll both be using a low bit rate. Imagine your AP is in the garage, and you're in the living room trying to stream video from your phone to your TV. Good luck!

There is an old "ad hoc" mode that lets A and B talk to each other, but it's way too slow for anything fun, and of course, it's disabled on all mobile chipsets. Actually, it's disabled in the top-secret drivers that the chipset makers kindly provide to hardware makers. There is also a new Tunneled Direct Link Setup (TDLS) protocol that lets two devices create a direct link, using an AP for discovery but not for traffic. And there's a "5G" WiFi standard (it's a marketing term, so it goes in quotes) that boosts link speeds to a gigabit. TDLS and 5G together make HD movie streaming from your phone to your TV a plausible reality. I assume TDLS will be restricted in various ways so as to placate the telcos.

Furthermore, we saw standardization of the 802.11s mesh protocol in 2012, after a remarkably speedy 10 years or so of work. Mesh removes the access point completely, at least in the imaginary future where it exists and is widely used. Devices talk to each other directly and maintain little routing tables of neighbors that let them forward packets. Imagine the AP software embedded into every device, but smart enough (it's not as impressive as it sounds) to do multiple hops.

No one who is making money from the mobile data extortion racket wants to see 802.11s available, because citywide mesh is such a nightmare for the bottom line, so it's happening as slowly as possible. The only large organization with the power (and, I assume the surface-to-surface missiles) to get mesh technology into wide use is the US Army. But mesh will emerge, and I'd bet on 802.11s being widely available in consumer electronics by 2020 or so.

Second, if we don't have point-to-point, how far can we trust APs today? Well, if you go to a Starbucks in the US and try the ØMQ "Hello World" example using two laptops connected via the free WiFi, you'll find they cannot connect. Why? The answer is in the name: "attwifi." AT&T is a good old incumbent telco that hates WiFi and presumably provides the service cheaply to Starbucks and others so that independents can't get into the market. But any access point you buy will support client-AP-client access, and outside the US I've never found a public AP locked down the AT&T way.

Third, performance. The AP is clearly a bottleneck; you cannot get better than half of its advertised speed even if you put A and B literally beside the AP. Worse, if there are other APs in the same airspace, they'll shout each other out. In my home, WiFi barely works at all because the neighbors two houses down have an AP that they've amplified. Even on a different channel, it interferes with our home WiFi. In the cafe where I'm sitting now there are over a dozen networks. Realistically, as long as we're dependent on AP-based WiFi, we're subject to random interference and unpredictable performance.

Fourth, battery life. There's no inherent reason that WiFi, when idle, is hungrier than Bluetooth, for example. They use the same radio waves and low-level framing. The main difference is in tuning and in the protocols. For wireless power-saving to work well, devices have to mostly sleep, and beacon out to other devices only once every so often. For this to work, they need to synchronize their clocks. This happens properly for the mobile phone part, which is why my old flip phone can run five days on a charge. When WiFi is working, it will use more power. Current power amplifier technology is also inefficient, meaning you draw a lot more energy from your battery than you pump into the air (the waste turns into a hot phone). Power amplifiers are improving as people focus more on mobile WiFi.

Lastly, mobile access points. If we can't trust centralized APs, and if our devices are smart enough to run full operating systems, can't we make them work as APs? I'm *so glad* you asked that question. Yes, we can, and it works quite nicely. Especially since we can switch this on and off in software, on a modern OS like Android. Again, the villains of the piece are the US telcos, who mostly detest this feature and kill it or cripple it on the phones they control. Smarter telcos realize that it's a way to amplify their "last mile" and bring higher-value products to more users, but crooks don't compete on smarts.

Conclusions

WiFi is not Ethernet, and although I believe future ØMQ applications will have a very important decentralized wireless presence, it's not going to be an easy road. Much of the basic reliability and capacity that you expect from Ethernet is missing. When you run a distributed application over WiFi you have to allow for frequent timeouts, random latencies, arbitrary disconnections, whole interfaces going down and coming up, and so on.

The technological evolution of wireless networking is best described as "slow and joyless." Applications and frameworks that try to exploit decentralized wireless are mostly absent or poor. The only existing open source framework for proximity networking is AllJoyn (*https://www.alljoyn.org*) from Qualcomm. But with ØMQ we proved that the inertia and decrepit incompetence of existing players was no reason for us to sit still. When we accurately understand problems, we can solve them. What we imagine, we can make real.

Discovery

One of the great things about short-range wireless is the proximity. WiFi maps closely to the physical space, which maps closely to how we naturally organize. In fact, the Internet is quite abstract, and this confuses a lot of people who "kind of get it" but in fact don't really. With WiFi, we have technical connectivity that is potentially super-tangible. You see what you get and you get what you see. Tangible means easy to understand, and that should mean love from users instead of the typical frustration and quiet seething hatred.

Proximity is the key. Say we have a bunch of WiFi radios in a room, happily beaconing to each other. For lots of applications it makes sense that they can find each other and start chatting, without any user input. After all, most real-world data isn't private, it's just highly localized.

As a first step toward ØMQ-based proximity networking, let's look at how to do discovery. There exist libraries that do this. I don't like them. They seem too complex and too specific and somehow to date from a prehistoric era before people realized that distributed computing could be *fundamentally simple*.

Preemptive Discovery over Raw Sockets

I'm in a hotel room in Gangnam, Seoul, with a 4G wireless hotspot, a Linux laptop, and a couple of Android phones. The phones and laptop are talking to the hotspot. The *ifconfig* command says my IP address is 192.168.1.2. Let me try some *ping* commands. Dynamic Host Control Protocol (DHCP) servers tend to dish out addresses in sequence, so my phones are probably close by, numerically speaking:

```
$ ping 192.168.1.1
PING 192.168.1.1 (192.168.1.1) 56(84) bytes of data.
64 bytes from 192.168.1.1: icmp_req=1 ttl=64 time=376 ms
64 bytes from 192.168.1.1: icmp_req=2 ttl=64 time=358 ms
64 bytes from 192.168.1.1: icmp_req=4 ttl=64 time=167 ms
^C
--- 192.168.1.1 ping statistics ---
3 packets transmitted, 2 received, 33% packet loss, time 2001ms
rtt min/avg/max/mdev = 358.077/367.522/376.967/9.445 ms
```

Found one! 150–300 msec round-trip latency... that's a surprisingly high figure, something to keep in mind for later. Now I *ping* myself, just to try to double-check things:

```
$ ping 192.168.1.2
PING 192.168.1.2 (192.168.1.2) 56(84) bytes of data.
64 bytes from 192.168.1.2: icmp_req=1 ttl=64 time=0.054 ms
64 bytes from 192.168.1.2: icmp_req=2 ttl=64 time=0.055 ms
64 bytes from 192.168.1.2: icmp_req=3 ttl=64 time=0.061 ms
^C
--- 192.168.1.2 ping statistics ---
3 packets transmitted, 3 received, 0% packet loss, time 1998ms
rtt min/avg/max/mdev = 0.054/0.056/0.061/0.009 ms
```

The response time is a bit faster now, which is what we'd expect. Let's try the next couple of addresses:

```
$ ping 192.168.1.3
PING 192.168.1.3 (192.168.1.3) 56(84) bytes of data.
64 bytes from 192.168.1.3: icmp_req=1 ttl=64 time=291 ms
64 bytes from 192.168.1.3: icmp_req=2 ttl=64 time=271 ms
64 bytes from 192.168.1.3: icmp_req=3 ttl=64 time=132 ms
^C
--- 192.168.1.3 ping statistics ---
3 packets transmitted, 3 received, 0% packet loss, time 2001ms
rtt min/avg/max/mdev = 132.781/231.914/291.851/70.609 ms
```

That's the second phone, with the same kind of latency as the first one. Let's continue, and see if there are any other devices connected to the hotspot:

```
$ ping 192.168.1.4
PING 192.168.1.4 (192.168.1.4) 56(84) bytes of data.
^C
--- 192.168.1.4 ping statistics ---
3 packets transmitted, 0 received, 100% packet loss, time 2016ms
```

And that is it. Now, *ping* uses raw IP sockets to send ICMP_ECHO messages. The useful thing about ICMP_ECHO is that it gets a response from any IP stack that has not deliberately had echo switched off. That's still a common practice on corporate websites who fear the old "ping of death" exploit, where malformed messages could crash the machine.

I call this *pre-emptive discovery* since it doesn't take any cooperation from the device. We don't rely on any cooperation from the phones to see them sitting there; as long as they're not actively ignoring us, we can see them.

You might ask why this is useful. We don't know that the peers responding to `ICMP_ECHO` run ØMQ, that they are interested in talking to us, that they have any services we can use, or even what kinds of devices they are. However, knowing that there's *something* on address 192.168.1.3 is already useful. We also know how far away the device is (relatively), we know how many devices are on the network, and we know the rough state of the network (as in, good, poor, or terrible).

It isn't even hard to create `ICMP_ECHO` messages and send them. It only takes a few dozen lines of code, and we could use ØMQ multithreading to do this in parallel for addresses stretching out above and below our own IP address. Could be kind of fun.

However, sadly, there's a fatal flaw in my idea of using `ICMP_ECHO` to discover devices. Opening a raw IP socket requires root privileges on a POSIX box. This stops rogue programs getting data meant for others. We can get the power to open raw sockets on Linux by giving *sudo* privileges to our command (*ping* has the so-called *sticky bit* set). But on a mobile OS like Android, it requires root access (i.e., rooting the phone or tablet). That's out of the question for most people, so `ICMP_ECHO` is out of reach for most devices.

Expletive deleted! Let's try something in user space. The next step most people take is UDP multicast or broadcast. Let's follow that trail.

Cooperative Discovery Using UDP Broadcasts

Multicast tends to be seen as more modern and "better" than broadcast. In IPv6, broadcast doesn't work at all: you always have to use multicast. Nonetheless, all IPv4 local network discovery protocols end up using UDP broadcast anyhow. The reason: broadcast and multicast end up working much the same, except broadcast is simpler and less risky. Multicast is seen by network admins as kind of dangerous, as it can leak over network segments.

If you've never used UDP, you'll discover it's quite a nice protocol. In some ways it reminds me of ØMQ, sending whole messages to peers using two different patterns: one-to-one and one-to-many. The main problems with UDP are that (a) the POSIX socket API was designed for universal flexibility, not simplicity, (b) UDP messages are limited for practical purposes to about 512 bytes, and (c) when you start to use UDP for real data you'll find that a lot of messages get dropped, especially as infrastructure tends to favor TCP over UDP.

Example 8-1 is a minimal *ping* program that uses UDP instead of `ICMP_ECHO`.

Example 8-1. UDP discovery, model 1 (udpping1.c)

```
//
//  UDP ping command
//  Model 1, does UDP work inline
//
```

```
#include <czmq.h>
#define PING_PORT_NUMBER 9999
#define PING_MSG_SIZE    1
#define PING_INTERVAL    1000  //  Once per second

static void
derp (char *s)
{
    perror (s);
    exit (1);
}

int main (void)
{
    zctx_t *ctx = zctx_new ();

    //  Create UDP socket
    int fd;
    if ((fd = socket (AF_INET, SOCK_DGRAM, IPPROTO_UDP)) == -1)
        derp ("socket");

    //  Ask operating system to let us do broadcasts from socket
    int on = 1;
    if (setsockopt (fd, SOL_SOCKET, SO_BROADCAST, &on, sizeof (on)) == -1)
        derp ("setsockopt (SO_BROADCAST)");

    //  Bind UDP socket to local port so we can receive pings
    struct sockaddr_in si_this = { 0 };
    si_this.sin_family = AF_INET;
    si_this.sin_port = htons (PING_PORT_NUMBER);
    si_this.sin_addr.s_addr = htonl (INADDR_ANY);
    if (bind (fd, &si_this, sizeof (si_this)) == -1)
        derp ("bind");

    byte buffer [PING_MSG_SIZE];
```

We use zmq_poll() to wait for activity on the UDP socket, since this function works on non-ØMQ file handles. We send a beacon once a second, and we collect and report beacons that come in from other nodes. Example 8-2 shows the main *ping* loop.

Example 8-2. UDP discovery, model 1 (udpping1.c): main ping loop

```
    zmq_pollitem_t pollitems [] = {{ NULL, fd, ZMQ_POLLIN, 0 }};
    //  Send first ping right away
    uint64_t ping_at = zclock_time ();

    while (!zctx_interrupted) {
        long timeout = (long) (ping_at - zclock_time ());
        if (timeout < 0)
            timeout = 0;
        if (zmq_poll (pollitems, 1, timeout * ZMQ_POLL_MSEC) == -1)
            break;                  //  Interrupted
```

```
        // Someone answered our ping
        if (pollitems [0].revents & ZMQ_POLLIN) {
            struct sockaddr_in si_that;
            socklen_t si_len;
            ssize_t size = recvfrom (fd, buffer, PING_MSG_SIZE, 0, &si_that,       &si_len);
            if (size == -1)
                derp ("recvfrom");
            printf ("Found peer %s:%d\n",
                inet_ntoa (si_that.sin_addr), ntohs (si_that.sin_port));
        }
        if (zclock_time () >= ping_at) {
            // Broadcast our beacon
            puts ("Pinging peers...");
            buffer [0] = '!';
            struct sockaddr_in si_that = si_this;
            inet_aton ("255.255.255.255", &si_that.sin_addr);
            if (sendto (fd, buffer, PING_MSG_SIZE, 0, &si_that,       sizeof (struct sockadd
                derp ("sendto");
            ping_at = zclock_time () + PING_INTERVAL;
        }
    }
    close (fd);
    zctx_destroy (&ctx);
    return 0;
}
```

This code uses a single socket to broadcast 1-byte messages and receive anything that
other nodes are broadcasting. When I run it, it shows just one node, which is itself:

```
Pinging peers...
Found peer 192.168.1.2:9999
Pinging peers...
Found peer 192.168.1.2:9999
```

If I switch off all networking and try again, sending a message fails, as I'd expect:

```
Pinging peers...
sendto: Network is unreachable
```

Working on the basis of *solve the problems currently aiming at your throat*, let's fix the
most urgent issues in this first model. These issues are:

- Using the 255.255.255.255 broadcast address is a bit dubious. On the one hand, this
  broadcast address means precisely "send to all nodes on the local network, and don't
  forward." However, if you have several interfaces (wired Ethernet, WiFi), broadcasts
  will go out on your default route only, and via just one interface. What we want to
  do is either send our broadcast on each interface's broadcast address, or find the
  WiFi interface and its broadcast address.

- Like many aspects of socket programming, getting information on network interfaces is not portable. Do we want to write nonportable code in our applications? No, this is better hidden in a library.

- There's no handling for errors except "abort," which is too brutal for transient problems like "your WiFi is switched off." The code should distinguish between soft errors (ignore and retry) and hard errors (assert).

- The code needs to know its own IP address and ignore beacons that it sent out. Like finding the broadcast address, this requires inspecting the available interfaces.

The simplest answer to these issues is to push the UDP code into a separate library that provides a clean API, like this:

```
// Constructor
static udp_t *
    udp_new (int port_nbr);

// Destructor
static void
    udp_destroy (udp_t **self_p);

// Returns UDP socket handle
static int
    udp_handle (udp_t *self);

// Send message using UDP broadcast
static void
    udp_send (udp_t *self, byte *buffer, size_t length);

// Receive message from UDP broadcast
static ssize_t
    udp_recv (udp_t *self, byte *buffer, size_t length);
```

Example 8-3 shows the refactored UDP *ping* program that calls this library, which is much cleaner and nicer.

Example 8-3. UDP discovery, model 2 (udpping2.c)

```
//
//  UDP ping command
//  Model 2, uses separate UDP library
//
#include <czmq.h>
#include "udplib.c"

#define PING_PORT_NUMBER 9999
#define PING_MSG_SIZE    1
#define PING_INTERVAL    1000  // Once per second

int main (void)
{
```

```
zctx_t *ctx = zctx_new ();
udp_t *udp = udp_new (PING_PORT_NUMBER);

byte buffer [PING_MSG_SIZE];
zmq_pollitem_t pollitems [] = {{ NULL, udp_handle (udp), ZMQ_POLLIN, 0 }};

// Send first ping right away
uint64_t ping_at = zclock_time ();

while (!zctx_interrupted) {
    long timeout = (long) (ping_at - zclock_time ());
    if (timeout < 0)
        timeout = 0;
    if (zmq_poll (pollitems, 1, timeout * ZMQ_POLL_MSEC) == -1)
        break;                  // Interrupted

    // Someone answered our ping
    if (pollitems [0].revents & ZMQ_POLLIN)
        udp_recv (udp, buffer, PING_MSG_SIZE);

    if (zclock_time () >= ping_at) {
        puts ("Pinging peers...");
        buffer [0] = '!';
        udp_send (udp, buffer, PING_MSG_SIZE);
        ping_at = zclock_time () + PING_INTERVAL;
    }
}
udp_destroy (&udp);
zctx_destroy (&ctx);
return 0;
}
```

The library, udplib, hides a lot of the unpleasant code (which will become uglier as we make this work on more systems). I'm not going to print that code here, but you can read it in the repository (*https://github.com/imatix/zguide/blob/master/examples/C/ udplib.c*).

Now there are more problems sizing us up and wondering if they can make lunch out of us. First, IPv4 versus IPv6 and multicast versus broadcast. In IPv6, broadcast doesn't exist at all; one uses multicast. From my experience with WiFi, IPv4 multicast and broadcast work identically except that multicast breaks in some situations where broadcast works fine. The problem is that some access points do not forward multicast packets. When you have a device (e.g., a tablet) that acts as a mobile AP, it's possible it won't get multicast packets, meaning it won't see other peers on the network.

The simplest plausible solution is simply to ignore IPv6 for now, and use broadcast. A perhaps smarter solution would be to use multicast, and deal with asymmetric beacons if they happen.

We'll stick with stupid and simple for now. There's always time to make it more complex.

Multiple Nodes on One Device

So, we can discover nodes on the WiFi network, as long as they're sending out beacons as we expect. But when I try to test this with two processes, running *udpping2* twice, the second instance complains "'Address already in use' on bind" and exits. Oh, right. UDP and TCP both return an error if you try to bind two different sockets to the same port. This is correct; the semantics of two readers on one socket would be weird, to say the least. Odd/even bytes? You get all the 1s, I get all the 0s?

However, a quick check of stackoverflow.com and some memory of a socket option called SO_REUSEADDR turns up gold. If I use that, I can bind several processes to the same UDP port, and they will all receive any message arriving on that port. It's almost as if the guys who designed this were reading my mind! (That's way more plausible than me reinventing the wheel.)

A quick test shows that SO_REUSEADDR works as promised. This is great because the next thing I want to do is design an API and then start dozens of nodes to see them discovering each other. It would be really cumbersome to have to test each node on a separate device. And when we get to testing how real traffic behaves on a large, flaky network, the two alternatives are simulation or temporary insanity.

And I speak from experience: we were, this summer, testing on dozens of devices at once. It takes about an hour to set up a full test run, and you need a space shielded from WiFi interference if you want any kind of reproducibility (unless your test case is "prove that interference kills WiFi networks faster than Orval can kill a thirst").

If I was a whizz Android developer with a free weekend I'd immediately (as in, it would take me two days) port this code to my phone and get it sending beacons to my PC. But sometimes being lazy is more profitable. I *like* my Linux laptop. I like being able to start a dozen threads from one process, and have each thread act like an independent node. I like not having to work in a real Faraday cage when I can simulate one on my laptop.

Designing the API

I'm going to run N nodes on a device, and they are going to have to discover each other, and also discover a bunch of other nodes out there on the local network. I can use UDP for local discovery as well as remote discovery. It's arguably not as efficient as using, e.g., the ØMQ inproc transport, but it has the great advantage that the exact same code will work in simulation and in real deployment.

If I have multiple nodes on one device, I clearly can't use the IP address and port number as the node address. I need some logical node identifier. Arguably, the node identifier only has to be unique within the context of the device. My mind fills with complex stuff I could make, like supernodes that sit on real UDP ports and forward messages to internal nodes. I hit my head on the table until the idea of *inventing new concepts* leaves it.

Experience tells us that WiFi does things like disappear and reappear while applications are running. Users click on things, with interesting results like changing the IP address halfway through a session. We cannot depend on IP addresses, nor on established connections (in the TCP fashion). We need some long-lasting addressing mechanism that survives interfaces and connections being torn down and then recreated.

Here's the simplest solution I can see: we give every node a UUID, and we specify that nodes, represented by their UUIDs, can appear or reappear at certain *IP address:port* endpoints, and then disappear again. We'll deal with recovery from lost messages later. A UUID is 16 bytes. So if I have 100 nodes on a WiFi network, that's (double it for other random stuff) 3,200 bytes a second of beacon data that the air has to carry just for discovery and presence. Seems acceptable.

Back to concepts. We do need some names for our API. At the least, we need a way to distinguish between the node object that is "us," and node objects that are our peers. We'll be doing things like creating an "us" and then asking it how many peers it knows about, and who they are. The term "peer" is clear enough.

From the developer's point of view, a node (the application) needs a way to talk to the outside world. Let's borrow a term from networking and call this an "interface." The interface represents us to the rest of the world and presents the rest of the world to us, as a set of other peers. It automatically does whatever discovery it has to. When we want to talk to a peer, we get the interface to do that for us. And when a peer talks to us, it's the interface that delivers us the message.

This seems like a clean API design. How about the internals?

- The interface has to be multithreaded, so that one thread can do I/O in the background, while the foreground API talks to the application. We used this design in the Clone and Freelance client APIs.

- The interface background thread does the discovery business: bind to the UDP port, send out UDP beacons, and receive beacons.

- We need to at least send UUIDs in the beacon message so that we can distinguish our own beacons from those of our peers.

- We need to track peers that appear and that disappear. For this I'll use a hash table that stores all known peers, and expire peers after some timeout.

- We need a way to report peers and events to the caller. Here we get into a juicy question. How does a background I/O thread tell a foreground API thread that stuff is happening? Callbacks, maybe? *Heck no.* We'll use ØMQ messages, of course.

The third iteration of the UDP *ping* program, shown in Example 8-4, is even simpler and more beautiful than the second. The main body, in C, is just 10 lines of code.

Example 8-4. UDP discovery, model 3 (udpping3.c)

```
//
//  UDP ping command
//  Model 3, uses abstract network interface
//
#include <czmq.h>
#include "interface.c"

int main (void)
{
    interface_t *interface = interface_new ();
    while (true) {
        zmsg_t *msg = interface_recv (interface);
        if (!msg)
            break;                  //  Interrupted
        zmsg_dump (msg);
    }
    interface_destroy (&interface);
    return 0;
}
```

The interface code (Example 8-5) should be familiar if you've studied how we make multithreaded API classes.

Example 8-5. UDP ping interface (interface.c)

```
//  Interface class
//  This implements an "interface" to our network of nodes

#include <czmq.h>
#include <uuid/uuid.h>
#include "udplib.c"


//  =====================================================================
//  Synchronous part, works in our application thread

//  ---------------------------------------------------------------------
//  Structure of our class

typedef struct {
    zctx_t *ctx;                //  Our context wrapper
    void *pipe;                 //  Pipe through to agent
} interface_t;

//  This is the thread that handles our real interface class
static void
    interface_agent (void *args, zctx_t *ctx, void *pipe);
```

Example 8-6 presents the constructor and destructor for the interface class. Note that the class has barely any properties; it is just an excuse to start the background thread, and a wrapper around zmsg_recv().

Example 8-6. UDP ping interface (interface.c): constructor and destructor

```
interface_t *
interface_new (void)
{
    interface_t
        *self;

    self = (interface_t *) zmalloc (sizeof (interface_t));
    self->ctx = zctx_new ();
    self->pipe = zthread_fork (self->ctx, interface_agent, NULL);
    return self;
}

void
interface_destroy (interface_t **self_p)
{
    assert (self_p);
    if (*self_p) {
        interface_t *self = *self_p;
        zctx_destroy (&self->ctx);
        free (self);
        *self_p = NULL;
    }
}
```

In Example 8-7, we wait for a message from the interface. This returns us a zmsg_t object, or NULL if interrupted.

Example 8-7. UDP ping interface (interface.c): receive message

```
static zmsg_t *
interface_recv (interface_t *self)
{
    assert (self);
    zmsg_t *msg = zmsg_recv (self->pipe);
    return msg;
}


//  =========================================================================
//  Asynchronous part, works in the background
```

The structure in Example 8-8 defines each peer that we discover and track.

Example 8-8. UDP ping interface (interface.c): peer class

```
typedef struct {
    uuid_t uuid;                    //  Peer's UUID as binary blob
```

```
    char *uuid_str;              //  UUID as printable string
    uint64_t expires_at;
} peer_t;

#define PING_PORT_NUMBER 9999
#define PING_INTERVAL    1000  //  Once per second
#define PEER_EXPIRY      5000  //  Five seconds and it's gone

//  Convert binary UUID to freshly allocated string

static char *
s_uuid_str (uuid_t uuid)
{
    char hex_char [] = "0123456789ABCDEF";
    char *string = zmalloc (sizeof (uuid_t) * 2 + 1);
    int byte_nbr;
    for (byte_nbr = 0; byte_nbr < sizeof (uuid_t); byte_nbr++) {
        string [byte_nbr * 2 + 0] = hex_char [uuid [byte_nbr] >> 4];
        string [byte_nbr * 2 + 1] = hex_char [uuid [byte_nbr] & 15];
    }
    return string;
}
```

The constructor and destructor for the peer class are shown in Example 8-9.

Example 8-9. UDP ping interface (interface.c): peer constructor and destructor

```
static peer_t *
peer_new (uuid_t uuid)
{
    peer_t *self = (peer_t *) zmalloc (sizeof (peer_t));
    memcpy (self->uuid, uuid, sizeof (uuid_t));
    self->uuid_str = s_uuid_str (self->uuid);
    return self;
}

//  Destroy peer object

static void
peer_destroy (peer_t **self_p)
{
    assert (self_p);
    if (*self_p) {
        peer_t *self = *self_p;
        free (self->uuid_str);
        free (self);
        *self_p = NULL;
    }
}
```

The methods in Example 8-10 return the peer's UUID in binary format or as a printable string.

Example 8-10. UDP ping interface (interface.c): peer methods

```
static byte *
peer_uuid (peer_t *self)
{
    assert (self);
    return self->uuid;
}

static char *
peer_uuid_str (peer_t *self)
{
    assert (self);
    return self->uuid_str;
}

//  Just resets the peer's expiration time; we call this method
//  whenever we get any activity from a peer

static void
peer_is_alive (peer_t *self)
{
    assert (self);
    self->expires_at = zclock_time () + PEER_EXPIRY;
}

//  Peer hash calls this handler automatically whenever we delete
//  peer from agent peers, or destroy that hash table

static void
peer_freefn (void *argument)
{
    peer_t *peer = (peer_t *) argument;
    peer_destroy (&peer);
}
```

The structure in Example 8-11 holds the context for our agent, so we can pass that around cleanly to methods that need it.

Example 8-11. UDP ping interface (interface.c): agent class

```
typedef struct {
    zctx_t *ctx;            //  CZMQ context
    void *pipe;             //  Pipe back to application
    udp_t *udp;             //  UDP object
    uuid_t uuid;            //  Our UUID as binary blob
    zhash_t *peers;         //  Hash of known peers, fast lookup
} agent_t;
```

The constructor and destructor for our agent are presented in Example 8-12. Each interface has one agent object, which implements its background thread.

Example 8-12. UDP ping interface (interface.c): agent constructor and destructor

```
static agent_t *
agent_new (zctx_t *ctx, void *pipe)
{
    agent_t *self = (agent_t *) zmalloc (sizeof (agent_t));
    self->ctx = ctx;
    self->pipe = pipe;
    self->udp = udp_new (PING_PORT_NUMBER);
    self->peers = zhash_new ();
    uuid_generate (self->uuid);
    return self;
}

static void
agent_destroy (agent_t **self_p)
{
    assert (self_p);
    if (*self_p) {
        agent_t *self = *self_p;
        zhash_destroy (&self->peers);
        udp_destroy (&self->udp);
        free (self);
        *self_p = NULL;
    }
}
...
```

Example 8-13 shows how we handle a beacon coming into our UDP socket; this may be from other peers or an echo of our own broadcast beacon.

Example 8-13. UDP ping interface (interface.c): handle beacon

```
static int
agent_handle_beacon (agent_t *self)
{
    uuid_t uuid;
    ssize_t size = udp_recv (self->udp, uuid, sizeof (uuid_t));

    //  If we got a UUID and it's not our own beacon, we have a peer
    if (size == sizeof (uuid_t)
    && memcmp (uuid, self->uuid, sizeof (uuid))) {
        char *uuid_str = s_uuid_str (uuid);

        //  Find or create peer via its UUID string
        peer_t *peer = (peer_t *) zhash_lookup (self->peers, uuid_str);
        if (peer == NULL) {
            peer = peer_new (uuid);
            zhash_insert (self->peers, uuid_str, peer);
            zhash_freefn (self->peers, uuid_str, peer_freefn);

            //  Report peer joined the network
            zstr_sendm (self->pipe, "JOINED");
```

```
            zstr_send (self->pipe, uuid_str);
        }
        //  Any activity from the peer means it's alive
        peer_is_alive (peer);
        free (uuid_str);
    }
    return 0;
}
```

The method in Example 8-14 checks one peer item for expiry; if the peer hasn't sent us anything by now, it's "dead" and we can delete it.

Example 8-14. UDP ping interface (interface.c): reap peers

```
static int
agent_reap_peer (const char *key, void *item, void *argument)
{
    agent_t *self = (agent_t *) argument;
    peer_t *peer = (peer_t *) item;
    if (zclock_time () >= peer->expires_at) {
        //  Report peer left the network
        zstr_sendm (self->pipe, "LEFT");
        zstr_send (self->pipe, peer_uuid_str (peer));
        zhash_delete (self->peers, peer_uuid_str (peer));
    }
    return 0;
}
```

The main loop for the background agent is shown in Example 8-15. It uses zmq_poll() to monitor the frontend pipe (commands from the API) and the backend UDP handle (beacons).

Example 8-15. UDP ping interface (interface.c): agent main loop

```
static void
interface_agent (void *args, zctx_t *ctx, void *pipe)
{
    //  Create agent instance to pass around
    agent_t *self = agent_new (ctx, pipe);

    //  Send first beacon immediately
    uint64_t ping_at = zclock_time ();
    zmq_pollitem_t pollitems [] = {
        { self->pipe, 0, ZMQ_POLLIN, 0 },
        { 0, udp_handle (self->udp), ZMQ_POLLIN, 0 }
    };

    while (!zctx_interrupted) {
        long timeout = (long) (ping_at - zclock_time ());
        if (timeout < 0)
            timeout = 0;
        if (zmq_poll (pollitems, 2, timeout * ZMQ_POLL_MSEC) == - 1)
```

```
        break;                    //  Interrupted

        //  If we had activity on the pipe, go handle the control
        //  message. Current code never sends control messages.
        if (pollitems [0].revents & ZMQ_POLLIN)
            agent_control_message (self);

        //  If we had input on the UDP socket, go process that
        if (pollitems [1].revents & ZMQ_POLLIN)
            agent_handle_beacon (self);

        //  If we passed the 1-second mark, broadcast our beacon
        if (zclock_time () >= ping_at) {
            udp_send (self->udp, self->uuid, sizeof (uuid_t));
            ping_at = zclock_time () + PING_INTERVAL;
        }
        //  Delete and report any expired peers
        zhash_foreach (self->peers, agent_reap_peer, self);
    }
    agent_destroy (&self);
}
```

When I run this in two windows, it reports one peer joining the network. If kill that peer, a few seconds later it tells me the peer has left:

```
----------------------------------------
[006] JOINED
[032] 418E98D4B7184844B7D5E0EE5691084C
----------------------------------------
[004] LEFT
[032] 418E98D4B7184844B7D5E0EE5691084C
```

What's nice about a ØMQ-message-based API is that I can wrap this any way I like. For instance, I can turn it into callbacks if I really want those. I can also trace all activity on the API very easily.

Some notes about tuning. On Ethernet, five seconds (the expiry time I used in this code) seems like a lot. On a badly stressed WiFi network you can get ping latencies of 30 seconds or more. If you use a too-aggressive value for the expiry, you'll disconnect nodes that are still there. On the other side, end user applications expect a certain liveliness. If it takes 30 seconds to report that a node has gone, users will get annoyed.

A decent strategy is to detect and report disappeared nodes rapidly, but only delete them after a longer interval. Visually, a node would be green when it's alive, then gray for a while as it went out of reach, then finally disappear. We're not doing this now, but we will do it in the real implementation of the as-yet-unnamed framework we're making.

As we will also see later, we have to treat any input from a node, not just UDP beacons, as a sign of life. UDP may get squashed when there's a lot of TCP traffic. This is perhaps the main reason we're not using an existing UDP discovery library: we have to integrate this tightly with our ØMQ messaging for it to work.

More About UDP

So, we have discovery and presence working over UDP IPv4 broadcasts. It's not ideal, but it works for the local networks we have today. However, we can't use UDP for real work, not without additional work to make it reliable. There's a joke about UDP, but sometimes you'll get it, and sometimes you won't.

We'll stick to TCP for all one-to-one messaging. There is one more use case for UDP after discovery, which is multicast file distribution. I'll explain why and how, then shelve that for another day. The why is simple: what we call "social networks" are just augmented culture. We create culture by sharing, and this means more and more sharing works that we make or remix—photos, documents, contracts, tweets. The clouds of devices we're aiming toward do more of this, not less.

Now, there are two principal patterns for sharing content. One is the pub-sub pattern, where one node sends out content to a set of other nodes, all at the same time. The second is the late joiner pattern, where a node arrives somewhat later and wants to catch up to the conversation. We can deal with the late joiner using TCP unicast, but doing TCP unicast to a group of clients at the same time has some disadvantages. First, it can be slower than multicast. Second, it's unfair since some will get the content before others.

Before you jump off to design a UDP multicast protocol, realize that it's not a simple calculation. When you send a multicast packet, the WiFi access point uses a low bit rate, to ensure that even the furthest devices will get it safely. Most normal APs don't do the obvious optimization, which is to measure the distance to the furthest device and use that bit rate. Instead, they just use a fixed value. So, if you have a few devices close to the AP, multicast will be insanely slow. But if you have a roomful of devices that all want to get the next chapter of the book, multicast can be insanely effective.

The curves cross at around 6–12 devices, depending on the network. You could in theory measure the curves in real time and create an adaptive protocol. That would be cool, but probably too hard for even the smartest of us.

If you do sit down and sketch out a UDP multicast protocol, realize that you need a channel for recovery, to get lost packets. You'd probably want to do this over TCP, using ØMQ. For now, however, we'll forget about multicast UDP, and assume all traffic goes over TCP.

Spinning Off a Library Project

At this stage the code is growing larger than an example should be, so it's time to create a proper GitHub project. It's a rule: build your projects in public view and tell people about them as you go, so your marketing and community building efforts start on day one. I'll walk through what this involves. I explained in Chapter 6 about growing communities around projects. We need a few things:

- A name
- A slogan
- A public GitHub repository
- A README that links to the C4 process
- License files
- An issue tracker
- Two maintainers
- A first bootstrap version

The name and slogan first. The trademarks of the 21st century are domain names, so the first thing I do when spinning off a project is to look for a domain name that might work. Quite randomly, one of our old mobile projects was called "Zyre," and I have the domain names for it.

I'm somewhat shy about pushing new projects into the ØMQ community too aggressively, and normally I would start a project in either my personal account or the iMatix organization. But we've learned that moving projects after they become popular is counter-productive. My predictions of a future filled with moving pieces are either valid, or wrong. If this chapter is valid, we might as well launch this as a ØMQ project from the start. If it's wrong, we can delete the repository later, or let it sink to the bottom of a long list of forgotten starts.

Let's start with the basics. The protocol (UDP and ØMQ/TCP) will be ZRE (the ZeroMQ Realtime Exchange protocol) and the project will be Zyre. I need a second maintainer, so I invite my friend Dong Min (the Korean hacker behind JeroMQ, a pure-Java ØMQ stack) to join. He's been working on very similar ideas so is enthusiastic. We discuss this and we get the idea of building Zyre on top of JeroMQ as well as on top of CZMQ and libzmq. This will make it a lot easier to run Zyre on Android. It will also give us two fully separate implementations from the start, always a good thing for a protocol.

So, we take the FileMQ project we built in Chapter 7 as a template for a new GitHub project. The GNU autoconf tools are quite decent but have a painful syntax. It's easiest to copy existing project files, and modify them. The FileMQ project builds a library and has test tools, license files, man pages, and so on. It's not too large, so it's a good starting point.

I put together a README to summarize the goals of the project and point to C4. The issue tracker is enabled by default on new GitHub projects, so once we've pushed the

UDP *ping* code as a first version, we're ready to go. However, it's always good to recruit more maintainers, so I create an issue, "Call for maintainers," that says:

> If you'd like to help click that lovely green "Merge Pull Request" button, and get eternal karma, add a comment confirming that you've read and understand the C4 process at http://rfc.zeromq.org/spec:16.

Finally, I change the issue tracker labels. By default, GitHub offers the usual variety of issue types, but with C4 we don't use them. Instead, we need just two labels ("Urgent," in red, and "Ready," in black).

Point-to-Point Messaging

We're going to take our last UDP *ping* program and build a point-to-point messaging layer on top of that. Our goal is to be able to detect peers as they join and leave the network, send messages to them, and get replies. It is a nontrivial problem to solve, and it takes Min and me two days to get a "Hello World" version working.

We had to solve a number of issues:

- What information to send in the UDP beacon, and how to format it
- What ØMQ socket types to use to interconnect nodes
- What ØMQ messages to send, and how to format them
- How to send a message to a specific node
- How to know the sender of any message so we could send a reply
- How to recover from lost UDP beacons
- How to avoid overloading the network with beacons

I'll explain these in enough detail that you understand why we made each choice we did, with some code fragments to illustrate. We tagged this code as version 0.1.0 (*https://github.com/zeromq/zyre/zipball/v0.1.0*) so you can look at the code: most of the hard work is done in *zre_interface.c*.

UDP Beacon Framing

Sending UUIDs across the network is the bare minimum for a logical addressing scheme. However, we have a few more aspects to get working before this will work in real use:

- We need some protocol identification so that we can check for, and reject, invalid packets.
- We need some version information so that we can change this protocol over time.

- We need to tell other nodes how to reach us via TCP; i.e., a ØMQ port they can talk to us on.

Let's start with the beacon message format. We probably want a fixed protocol header that will never change in future versions, and a body that depends on the version (Figure 8-1).

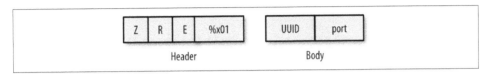

Figure 8-1. ZRE discovery message

The version can be a 1-byte counter starting at 1. The UUID is 16 bytes, and the port is a 2-byte port number, since UDP nicely tells us the sender's IP address for every message we receive. This gives us a 22-byte frame.

The C language (and a few others, like Erlang) makes it simple to read and write binary structures. We define the beacon frame structure as follows:

```
#define BEACON_PROTOCOL     "ZRE"
#define BEACON_VERSION      0x01

typedef struct {
    byte protocol [3];
    byte version;
    uuid_t uuid;
    uint16_t port;
} beacon_t;
```

which makes sending and receiving beacons quite simple. Here is how we send a beacon, using the zre_udp class to do the non-portable network calls:

```
// Beacon object
beacon_t beacon;

// Format beacon fields
beacon.protocol [0] = 'Z';
beacon.protocol [1] = 'R';
beacon.protocol [2] = 'E';
beacon.version = BEACON_VERSION;
memcpy (beacon.uuid, self->uuid, sizeof (uuid_t));
beacon.port = htons (self->port);

// Broadcast the beacon to anyone who is listening
zre_udp_send (self->udp, (byte *) &beacon, sizeof (beacon_t));
```

When we receive a beacon, we need to guard against bogus data. We're not going to be paranoid against, for example, denial-of-service attacks. We just want to make sure we're not going to crash when a bad ZRE implementation sends us erroneous frames.

To validate a frame we check its size and header. If those are OK, we assume the body is usable. When we get a UUID that isn't ourselves (recall, we'll get our own UDP broadcasts back), we can treat this as a peer:

```
// Get beacon frame from network
beacon_t beacon;
ssize_t size = zre_udp_recv (self->udp, (byte *) &beacon, sizeof (beacon_t));

// Basic validation on the frame
if (size != sizeof (beacon_t)
||  beacon.protocol [0] != 'Z'
||  beacon.protocol [1] != 'R'
||  beacon.protocol [2] != 'E'
||  beacon.version != BEACON_VERSION)
    return 0;                   // Ignore invalid beacons

// If we got a UUID and it's not our own beacon, we have a peer
if (memcmp (beacon.uuid, self->uuid, sizeof (uuid_t))) {
    char *identity = s_uuid_str (beacon.uuid);
    s_require_peer (self, identity,
        zre_udp_from (self->udp), ntohs (beacon.port));
    free (identity);
}
```

True Peer Connectivity (Harmony Pattern)

Since ØMQ is designed to make distributed messaging easy, people often ask how to interconnect a set of true peers (as compared to obvious clients and servers). It is a thorny question, and ØMQ doesn't really provide a single clear answer.

TCP, which is the most commonly used transport in ØMQ, is not symmetric; one side must bind and one must connect, and though ØMQ tries to be neutral about this, it's not. When you connect, you create an outgoing message pipe. When you bind, you do not. When there is no pipe, you cannot write messages (ØMQ will return EAGAIN).

Developers who study ØMQ and then try to create N-to-N connections between sets of equal peers often try a ROUTER-to-ROUTER flow. It's obvious why: each peer needs to address a set of peers, which requires ROUTER. It usually ends with a plaintive email to the list.

Experience teaches us that ROUTER-to-ROUTER is particularly difficult to use successfully. At a minimum, one peer must bind and one must connect, meaning the architecture is not symmetrical. But also, you simply can't tell when you are allowed to safely send a message to a peer. It's a Catch-22: you can talk to a peer after it's talked to you, but the peer can't talk to you until you've talked to it. One side or the other will be losing messages and thus has to retry, which means the peers cannot be equal.

I'm going to explain the Harmony pattern, which solves this problem, and which we use in Zyre.

We want a guarantee that when a peer "appears" on our network, we can talk to it safely, without ØMQ dropping messages. For this, we have to use a DEALER or PUSH socket that *connects out to the peer* so that even if that connection takes some nonzero time, there is immediately a pipe, and ØMQ will accept outgoing messages.

A DEALER socket cannot address multiple peers individually. But if we have one DEALER per peer, and we connect that DEALER to the peer, we can safely send messages to a peer as soon as we've connected to it.

Now, the next problem is to know who sent us a particular message. We need a reply address, which is the UUID of the node that sent any given message. DEALER can't do this unless we prefix every single message with that 16-byte UUID, which would be wasteful. ROUTER can, if we set the identity properly before connecting to the router.

And so the Harmony pattern comes down to:

- One ROUTER socket that we bind to an ephemeral port, which we broadcast in our beacons
- One DEALER socket *per peer* that we connect to the peer's ROUTER socket
- Reading from our ROUTER socket
- Writing to the peer's DEALER socket

The next problem is that discovery isn't neatly synchronized. We can get the first beacon from a peer *after* we start to receive messages from it. A message comes in on the ROUTER socket and has a nice UUID attached to it, but no physical IP address and port. We have to force discovery over TCP. To do this, our first command to any new peer we connect to is an OHAI command with our IP address and port. This ensures that the receiver connects back to us before trying to send us any command.

Breaking this down into steps:

- If we receive a UDP beacon, we connect to the peer.
- We read messages from our ROUTER socket, and each message comes with the UUID of the sender.
- If it's an OHAI message, we connect back to that peer (if we're not already connected to it).
- If it's any other message, we *must* already be connected to the peer (this is a good place for an assertion).

- We send messages to each peer using a dedicated per-peer DEALER socket, which *must* be connected.
- When we connect to a peer, we also tell our application that the peer exists.
- Every time we get a message from a peer, we treat that as a heartbeat (it's alive).

If we were not using UDP but some other discovery mechanism, I'd still use the Harmony pattern for a true peer network: one ROUTER for input from all peers, and one DEALER per peer for output. Bind the ROUTER, connect the DEALER, and start each conversation with an OHAI equivalent that provides the return IP address and port. We would need some external mechanism to bootstrap each connection.

Detecting Disappearances

Heartbeating sounds simple, but it's not. UDP packets get dropped when there's a lot of TCP traffic, so if we depend on UDP beacons we'll get false disconnections. TCP traffic can be delayed for 5, 10, even 30 seconds if the network is really busy. So if we kill peers when they go quiet, we'll have false disconnections.

Since UDP beacons aren't reliable, it's tempting to add in TCP beacons. After all, TCP will deliver them reliably. However, there's one little problem. Imagine you have 100 nodes on a network, and each node sends a TCP beacon once a second. Each beacon is 22 bytes, not counting TCP's framing overhead. That is 100 * 99 * 22 bytes per second, or 217,000 bytes/second just for heartbeating. That's about 1–2% of a typical WiFi network's ideal capacity, which sounds OK. But when a network is stressed, or fighting other networks for airspace, that extra 200K a second will break what's left. UDP broadcasts are at least low cost.

So what we do is switch to TCP heartbeats only when a specific peer hasn't sent us any UDP beacons in a while. And then, we send TCP heartbeats only to that one peer. If the peer continues to be silent, we conclude it's gone away. If the peer comes back, with a different IP address and/or port, we have to disconnect our DEALER socket and reconnect to the new port.

This gives us a set of states for each peer, though at this stage the code doesn't use a formal state machine:

- Peer visible thanks to UDP beacon (we connect using IP address and port from beacon)
- Peer visible thanks to OHAI command (we connect using IP address and port from command)
- Peer seems alive (we got a UDP beacon or command over TCP recently)
- Peer seems quiet (no activity in some time, so we send a HUGZ command)

- Peer has disappeared (no reply to our HUGZ commands, so we destroy peer)

There's one remaining scenario we haven't addressed in the code at this stage. It's possible for a peer to change IP addresses and ports without actually triggering a disappearance event. For example, if the user switches off WiFi and then switches it back on, then the the access point can assign the peer a new IP address. We'll need to handle a disappeared WiFi interface on our node by unbinding the ROUTER socket and rebinding it when we can. Since this is not central to the design now, I decided to log an issue on the GitHub tracker and leave it for a rainy day.

Group Messaging

Group messaging is a common and very useful pattern. The concept is simple: instead of talking to a single node, you talk to a "group" of nodes. The group is just a name, a string that you agree on in the application. It's precisely like using the publish-subscribe prefixes in PUB and SUB sockets. In fact, the only reason I say "group messaging" and not "pub-sub" is to prevent confusion, since we're not going to use PUB-SUB sockets for this.

PUB-SUB sockets would almost work. But we've just done such a lot of work to solve the late joiner problem. Applications are inevitably going to wait for peers to arrive before sending messages to groups, so we have to build on the Harmony pattern rather than start again beside it.

Let's look at the operations we want to do on groups:

- We want to join and leave groups.
- We want to know what other nodes are in any given group.
- We want to send a message to (all nodes in) a group.

These will look familiar to anyone who's used Internet Relay Chat (IRC), except we have no server. Every node will need to keep track of what each group represents. This information will not always be fully consistent across the network, but it will be close enough.

Our interface will track a set of groups (each an object). These are all the known groups with one or more member node, excluding ourselves. We'll track nodes as they leave and join groups. Since nodes can join the network at any time, we have to tell new peers what groups we're in. When a peer disappears, we'll remove it from all groups we know about.

This gives us some new protocol commands:

JOIN
    We send this to all peers when we join a group.

LEAVE
   We send this to all peers when we leave a group.

Plus, we add a `groups` field to the first command we send (renamed from OHAI to HELLO at this point because I need a larger lexicon of command verbs).

Lastly, let's add a way for peers to double-check the accuracy of their group data. The risk is that we miss one of the above messages. Though we are using Harmony to avoid the typical message loss at startup, it's worth being paranoid. For now, all we need is a way to detect such a failure. We'll deal with recovery later, if the problem actually happens.

We'll use the UDP beacon for this. What we want is a rolling counter that simply tells us how many join and leave operations ("transitions") there have been for a node. It starts at 0 and increments for each group we join or leave. We can use a minimal 1-byte value since that will catch all failures except the astronomically rare "we lost precisely 256 messages in a row" failure (this is the one that hits during the first demo). We will also put the transitions counter into the JOIN, LEAVE, and HELLO commands. And to try to provoke the problem, we'll test by joining/leaving several hundred groups, with a high-water mark set to 10 or so.

Time to choose verbs for the group messaging. We need a command that means "talk to one peer" and one that means "talk to many peers." After some attempts, my best choices are WHISPER and SHOUT, and this is what the code uses. The SHOUT command needs to tell the user the group name, as well as the sender peer.

Since groups are like publish-subscribe, you might be tempted to use this to broadcast the JOIN and LEAVE commands as well, perhaps by creating a "global" group that all nodes join. My advice is to keep groups purely as user-space concepts, for two reasons. First, how do you join the global group if you need the global group to send out a JOIN command? Second, it creates special cases (reserved names) that are messy.

It's simpler just to send JOINs and LEAVEs explicitly to all connected peers, period.

I'm not going to work through the implementation of group messaging in detail, since it's fairly pedantic and not exciting. The data structures for group and peer management aren't optimal, but they're workable. We need:

- A list of groups for our interface, which we can send to new peers in a HELLO command

- A hash of groups for other peers, which we update with information from HELLO, JOIN, and LEAVE commands

- A hash of peers for each group, which we update with the same three commands

At this stage I'm starting to get pretty happy with the binary serialization (our codec generator from Chapter 7), which handles lists and dictionaries as well as strings and integers.

This version is tagged in the repository as v0.2.0, and you can download the tarball (*https://github.com/zeromq/zyre/tags*) if you want to check what the code looked like at this stage.

Testing and Simulation

When you build a product out of pieces, and this includes a distributed framework like Zyre, the only way to know that it will work properly in real life is to simulate real activity on each piece.

On Assertions

The proper use of assertions is one of the hallmarks of a professional programmer.

Our confirmation bias as creators makes it hard to test our work properly. We tend to write tests to prove the code works, rather than trying to prove it doesn't. There are many reasons for this. We pretend to ourselves and others that we can be (could be) perfect, when in fact we consistently make mistakes. Bugs in code are seen as "bad" rather than "inevitable," so psychologically we want to see fewer of them, not uncover more of them. "He writes perfect code" is seen as a compliment, rather than a euphemism for "He never takes risks, so his code is as boring and heavily used as cold spaghetti."

Some cultures teach us to aspire to perfection, and punish mistakes, in education and work, which makes this attitude worse. To accept that we're fallible, and then to learn how to turn that into profit rather than shame, is one of the hardest intellectual exercises in any profession. We leverage our fallibilities by working with others, and by challenging our own work sooner, not later.

One trick that makes it easier is to use assertions. Assertions are not a form of error handling. They are executable theories of fact. The code asserts, "At this point, such and such must be true," and if the assertion fails, the code kills itself.

The faster you can prove code incorrect, the faster and more accurately you can fix it. Believing that code works and proving that it behaves as expected is less science, and more magical thinking. It's far better to be able to say, "libzmq has 500 assertions and despite all my efforts, not one of them fails."

So, the Zyre code base is scattered with assertions, and particularly a couple on the code that deals with the state of peers. This is the hardest aspect to get right: peers need to track each other and exchange state accurately, or things stop working. The algorithms depend on asynchronous messages flying around, and I'm pretty sure the initial design has flaws. They always do.

And as I test the original Zyre code by starting and stopping instances of `zre_ping` by hand, every so often I get an assertion failure. Running by hand doesn't reproduce these often enough, so let's make a proper tester tool.

On Up-Front Testing

Being able to fully test the real behavior of individual components in the laboratory can make a 10x or 100x difference to the cost of your project. That confirmation bias engineers have to their own work makes up-front testing incredibly profitable, and late-stage testing incredibly expensive.

I'll tell you a short story about a project we worked on in the late 1990s. We provided the software, and other teams the hardware, for a factory automation project. Three or four teams brought their experts on-site, which was a remote factory (funny how the polluting factories are always in a remote border country).

One of these teams, a firm specializing in industrial automation, built ticket machines: kiosks, and software to run on them. Nothing unusual: swipe a badge, choose an option, receive a ticket. They assembled two of these kiosks on-site, each week bringing some more bits and pieces. Ticket printers, monitor screens, special keypads from Israel. The stuff had to be resistant against dust since the kiosks sat outside. Nothing worked. The screens were unreadable in the sun. The ticket printers continually jammed and misprinted. The internals of the kiosk were just sat on wooden shelving. The kiosk software crashed regularly. It was comedic, except that the project really, *really* had to work, so we spent weeks—months—on-site helping the other teams debug their bits and pieces until it worked.

A year later, a second factory, and the same story. By this time the client was getting impatient. So when it came to the third and largest factory, a year later, we jumped up and said, "Please let us make the kiosks and the software and everything."

We made a detailed design for the software and hardware and found suppliers for all the pieces. It took us three months to search the Internet for each component, and another two months to get them assembled into stainless-steel bricks, each weighing about 20 kilos. These bricks were 60cm square and 20cm deep, with a large flat-screen panel behind unbreakable glass, and two connectors: one for power, one for Ethernet. You loaded up the paper bin with enough for six months, then screwed the brick into a housing, and it automatically booted, found its DNS server, and loaded its Linux OS and then the application software. It connected to the real server and showed the main menu. You got access to the configuration screens by swiping a special badge and then entering a code.

The software was portable, so we could test that as we wrote it, and as we collected the pieces from our suppliers we kept one of each so we had a disassembled kiosk to play with. When we got our finished kiosks, they all worked immediately. We shipped them to the client, who plugged them into their housings, switched them on, and got to business. We spent a week or so on-site, and in 10 years, only one kiosk broke (the screen died and was replaced).

The lesson is, test up-front so that when you plug the thing in, you know precisely how it's going to behave. If you haven't tested it up-front, you're going to be spending weeks or months in the field, ironing out problems that should never have been there.

The Zyre Tester

During manual testing I did, rarely, hit an assertion. It then disappeared. Since I don't believe in magic, that meant the code was still wrong somewhere. So, the next step was heavy-duty testing of the Zyre v0.2.0 code to try to break its assertions, and get a good idea of how it would behave in the field.

We packaged the discovery and messaging functionality as an *interface* object that the main program creates, works with, and then destroys. We don't use any global variables. This makes it easy to start large numbers of interfaces and simulate real activity, all within one process. And if there's one thing we've learned from writing lots of examples, it's that ØMQ's ability to orchestrate multiple threads in a single process is *much* easier to work with than multiple processes.

The first version of the tester consists of a main thread that starts and stops a set of child threads, each running one interface, each with a ROUTER, DEALER, and UDP socket (R, D, and U in Figure 8-2).

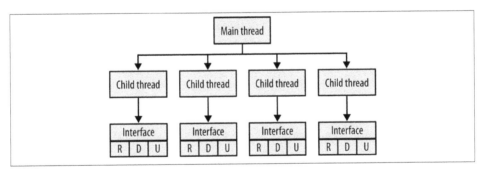

Figure 8-2. Zyre tester tool

The nice thing is that when I am connected to a WiFi access point, all Zyre traffic (even between two interfaces in the same process) goes across the AP. This means I can fully stress-test any WiFi infrastructure with just a couple of PCs running in a room. It's hard to emphasize how valuable this is: if we had built Zyre as, say, a dedicated service for Android, we'd literally need dozens of Android tablets or phones to do any large-scale testing. Kiosks, and all that.

The focus is now on breaking the current code, trying to prove it wrong. There's *no point* at this stage in testing how well it runs, how fast it is, how much memory it uses, or anything else. We'll work up to trying (and failing) to break each individual functionality, but first we'll try to break some of the core assertions I've put into the code.

These are:

- The first command that any node receives from a peer MUST be HELLO. In other words, messages *cannot* be lost during the peer-to-peer connection process.

- The state each node calculates for its peers matches the state each peer calculates for itself. In other words, again, no messages are lost in the network.

- When the application sends a message to a peer, we have a connection to that peer. In other words, the application only "sees" a peer after we have established a ØMQ connection to it.

With ØMQ, there are several cases where we may lose messages. One is the "late joiner" syndrome. Two is when we close sockets without sending everything. Three is when we overflow the high-water mark on a ROUTER or PUB socket. Four is when we use an unknown address with a ROUTER socket.

Now, I *think* Harmony gets around all these potential cases. But we're also adding UDP to the mix. So, the first version of the tester simulates an unstable and dynamic network, where nodes come and go randomly. It's here that things will break.

Here is the main thread of the tester, which manages a pool of 100 threads, starting and stopping each one randomly. Every ~750 msec it either starts or stops one random thread. We randomize the timing so that threads aren't all synchronized. After a few minutes we have an average of 50 threads happily chatting to each other like Korean teenagers in Gangnam subway station:

```
int main (int argc, char *argv [])
{
    //  Initialize context for talking to tasks
    zctx_t *ctx = zctx_new ();
    zctx_set_linger (ctx, 100);

    //  Get number of interfaces to simulate (default 100)
    int max_interface = 100;
    int nbr_interfaces = 0;
    if (argc > 1)
        max_interface = atoi (argv [1]);

    //  We address interfaces as an array of pipes
    void **pipes = zmalloc (sizeof (void *) * max_interface);

    //  We will randomly start and stop interface threads
    while (!zctx_interrupted) {
        uint index = randof (max_interface);
```

```
        // Toggle interface thread
        if (pipes [index]) {
            zstr_send (pipes [index], "STOP");
            zsocket_destroy (ctx, pipes [index]);
            pipes [index] = NULL;
            zclock_log ("I: Stopped interface (%d running)", --nbr_interfaces);
        }
        else {
            pipes [index] = zthread_fork (ctx, interface_task, NULL);
            zclock_log ("I: Started interface (%d running)", ++nbr_interfaces);
        }
        // Sleep ~750 msec randomly so we smooth out activity
        zclock_sleep (randof (500) + 500);
    }
    zctx_destroy (&ctx);
    return 0;
}
```

Note that we maintain a *pipe* to each child thread (CZMQ creates the pipe automatically when we use the `zthread_fork()` method). It's via this pipe that we tell child threads to stop, when it's time for them to leave. The child threads do the following (I'm switching to pseudo-code for clarity):

```
create an interface
while true:
    poll on pipe to parent, and on interface
    if parent sent us a message:
        break
    if interface sent us a message:
        if message is ENTER:
            send a WHISPER to the new peer
        if message is EXIT:
            send a WHISPER to the departed peer
        if message is WHISPER:
            send back a WHISPER 1/2 of the time
        if message is SHOUT:
            send back a WHISPER 1/3 of the time
            send back a SHOUT 1/3 of the time
    once per second:
        join or leave one of 10 random groups
destroy interface
```

Test Results

Yes, we broke the code. Several times, in fact. This was satisfying. I'll work through the different things we found.

Getting nodes to agree on consistent group status was the most difficult. Every node needs to track the group membership of the whole network, as I already explained in the section "Group Messaging." Group messaging is a publish-subscribe pattern. JOINs and LEAVEs are analogous to subscribe and unsubscribe messages. It's essential that none of these ever get lost, or we'll find nodes dropping randomly off groups.

So, each node counts the total number of JOINs and LEAVEs it's ever done, and broadcasts this status (as a 1-byte rolling counter) in its UDP beacon. Other nodes pick up the status and compare it to their own calculations, and if there's a difference, the code asserts.

The first problem was that UDP beacons get delayed randomly, so they're useless for carrying the status. When a beacon arrives late, the status is inaccurate and we get a *false negative.* To fix this we moved the status information into the JOIN and LEAVE commands. We also added it to the HELLO command. The logic then becomes:

- Get initial status for a peer from its HELLO command.
- When getting a JOIN or LEAVE from a peer, increment the status counter.
- Check that the new status counter matches the value in the JOIN or LEAVE command.
- If it doesn't, assert.

The next problem we got was that messages were arriving unexpectedly on new connections. The Harmony pattern connects, then sends HELLO as the first command. This means the receiving peer should always get a HELLO as the first command from a new peer. Instead, we were seeing PING, JOIN, and other commands arriving first.

This turned out to be due to CZMQ's ephemeral port logic. An ephemeral port is just a dynamically assigned port that a service can get rather than asking for a fixed port number. A POSIX system usually assigns ephemeral ports in the range 0xC000 to 0xFFFF. CZMQ's logic is to look for a free port in this range, bind to that, and return the port number to the caller.

Which sounds fine, until you get one node stopping and another node starting close together, and the new node getting the port number of the old node. Remember that ØMQ tries to re-establish a broken connection. So, when the first node stops, its peers will retry to connect. When the new node appears on that same port, suddenly all the peers connect to it, and start chatting like they're old buddies.

It's a general problem that affects any larger-scale dynamic ØMQ application. There are a number of plausible solutions. One is to not reuse ephemeral ports, which is easier said than done when you have multiple processes on one system. Another solution would be to select a random port each time, which at least reduces the risk of hitting a just-freed port. This brings the risk of a garbage connection down to perhaps 1/1,000, but it's still there. Perhaps the best solution is to accept that this can happen, understand the causes, and deal with it on the application level.

We have a stateful protocol that always starts with a HELLO command. We know that it's possible for peers to connect to us, thinking we're an existing node that went away and came back, and send us other commands. Step one is, when we discover a new peer, to destroy any existing peer connected to the same endpoint. It's not a full answer, but it's polite, at least. Step two is to ignore anything coming in from a new peer until that peer says HELLO.

This doesn't require any change to the protocol, but it has to be specified in the protocol when we come to it: due to the way ØMQ connections work, it's possible to receive unexpected commands from a *well-behaving* peer and there is no way to return an error code, or otherwise tell that peer to reset its connection. Thus, a peer must discard any command from a peer until it receives a HELLO.

In fact, if you draw this on a piece of paper and think it through, you'll see that you never get a HELLO from such a connection. The peer will send PINGs and JOINs and LEAVEs and then eventually time out and close, as it fails to get any heartbeats back from us.

You'll also see that there's no risk of confusion, no way for commands from two peers to get mixed into a single stream on our DEALER socket.

When you are satisfied this works, we're ready to move on. This version is tagged in the repository as v0.3.0 and you can download the tarball (*https://github.com/zeromq/zyre/tags*) if you want to check what the code looked like at this stage.

Note that doing heavy simulation of lots of nodes will probably cause your process to run out of file handles, giving an assertion failure in libzmq. I raised the per-process limit to 30,000 by running (on my Linux box):

```
ulimit -n 30000
```

Tracing Activity

To debug the kinds of problems we saw here, we need extensive logging. There's a lot happening in parallel, but every problem can be traced down to a specific exchange between two nodes, consisting of a set of events that happen in strict sequence. We know how to make very sophisticated logging, but as usual it's wiser to make just what we need, no more. We have to capture:

- The time and date for each event
- In which node the event occurred
- The peer node, if any
- What the event was (e.g., which command arrived)
- Event data, if any

The very simplest technique is to print the necessary information to the console, with a timestamp. That's the approach I used. Then it's simple to find the nodes affected by a failure, filter the log file for only messages referring to them, and see exactly what happened.

Dealing with Blocked Peers

In any performance-sensitive ØMQ architecture you need to solve the problem of flow control. You cannot simply send unlimited messages to a socket and hope for the best. At the one extreme, you can exhaust memory. This is a classic failure pattern for a message broker: one slow client stops receiving messages; the broker starts to queue them, and eventually exhausts memory and the whole process dies. At the other extreme, the socket drops messages, or blocks, as you hit the high-water mark.

With Zyre we want to distribute messages to a set of peers, and we want to do this fairly. Using a single ROUTER socket for output would be problematic, since any one blocked peer would block outgoing traffic to all peers. TCP does have good algorithms for spreading the network capacity across a set of connections. And we're using a separate DEALER socket to talk to each peer, so in theory each DEALER socket will send its queued messages in the background reasonably fairly.

The normal behavior of a DEALER socket that hits its high-water mark is to block. This is usually ideal, but it's a problem for us here. Our current interface design uses one thread that distributes messages to all peers. If one of those send calls were to block, all output would block.

There are a few options to avoid blocking. One is to use `zmq_poll()` on the whole set of DEALER sockets, and only write to sockets that are ready. I don't like this, for a couple of reasons. First, the DEALER socket is hidden inside the peer class, and it is cleaner to allow each class to handle this opaquely. Second, what do we do with messages we can't yet deliver to a DEALER socket? Where do we queue them? Third, it seems to be side-stepping the issue. If a peer is really so busy it can't read its messages, something is wrong. Most likely, it's dead.

So, no polling for output. The second option is to use one thread per peer. I quite like the idea of this, since it fits into the ØMQ design pattern of "do one thing in one thread." But this is going to create a *lot* of threads (the square of the number of nodes we start) in the simulation, and we're already running out of file handles.

A third option is to use a non-blocking send. This is nicer, and it's the solution I chose. We can then provide each peer with a reasonable outgoing queue (the HWM) and, if that gets full, treat it as a fatal error on that peer. This will work for smaller messages. If we're sending large chunks—e.g., for content distribution—we'll need a credit-based flow control mechanism on top.

Therefore, the first step is to prove to ourselves that we can turn the normal blocking DEALER socket into a non-blocking socket. Example 8-16 creates a normal DEALER socket, connects it to some endpoint (so there's an outgoing pipe and the socket will accept messages), sets the high-water mark to 4, and then sets the send timeout to 0.

Example 8-16. Checking EAGAIN on DEALER socket (eagain.c)

```
//
//  Shows how to provoke EAGAIN when reaching HWM
//
#include <czmq.h>

int main (void) {
    zctx_t *ctx = zctx_new ();

    void *mailbox = zsocket_new (ctx, ZMQ_DEALER);
    zsocket_set_sndhwm (mailbox, 4);
    zsocket_set_sndtimeo (mailbox, 0);
    zsocket_connect (mailbox, "tcp://localhost:9876");

    int count;
    for (count = 0; count < 10; count++) {
        printf ("Sending message %d\n", count);
        int rc = zstr_sendf (mailbox, "message %d", count);
        if (rc == -1) {
            printf ("%s\n", strerror (errno));
            break;
        }
    }
    zctx_destroy (&ctx);
    return 0;
}
```

When we run this, we send four messages successfully (they go nowhere, the socket just queues them), and then we get a nice EAGAIN error:

```
Sending message 0
Sending message 1
Sending message 2
Sending message 3
Sending message 4
Resource temporarily unavailable
```

The next step is to decide what a reasonable high-water mark would be for a peer. Zyre is meant for human interactions; that is, applications that chat at a low frequency, such as two games or a shared drawing program. I'd expect a hundred messages per second to be quite a lot. Our "peer is really dead" timeout is 10 seconds, so a high-water mark of 1,000 seems fair.

Rather than set a fixed HWM, or use the default (which randomly also happens to be 1,000), we calculate it as 100 * the timeout. Here's how we configure a new DEALER socket for a peer:

```
// Create new outgoing socket (drop any messages in transit)
self->mailbox = zsocket_new (self->ctx, ZMQ_DEALER);

// Set our caller "From" identity so that receiving node knows
// who each message came from
zsocket_set_identity (self->mailbox, reply_to);

// Set a high-water mark that allows for reasonable activity
zsocket_set_sndhwm (self->mailbox, PEER_EXPIRED * 100);

// Send messages immediately or return EAGAIN
zsocket_set_sndtimeo (self->mailbox, 0);

// Connect through to peer node
zsocket_connect (self->mailbox, "tcp://%s", endpoint);
```

And finally, what do we do when we get an EAGAIN on a peer? We don't need to go through all the work of destroying the peer since the interface will do this automatically if it doesn't get any message from the peer within the expiry timeout. Just dropping the last message seems very weak, though: it will give the receiving peer gaps.

I'd prefer a more brutal response. Brutal is good because it forces the design to a "good" or "bad" decision rather than a fuzzy "should work, but to be honest there are a lot of edge cases so let's worry about it later." Destroy the socket, disconnect the peer, and stop sending anything to it. The peer will eventually have to reconnect and reinitialize any state. It's kind of an assertion that 100 messages a second is enough for anyone. So, in the zre_peer_send() method, we do this:

```
int
zre_peer_send (zre_peer_t *self, zre_msg_t **msg_p)
{
    assert (self);
    if (self->connected) {
        if (zre_msg_send (msg_p, self->mailbox) && errno == EAGAIN) {
            zre_peer_disconnect (self);
            return -1;
        }
    }
    return 0;
}
```

Where the disconnect method looks like this:

```
void
zre_peer_disconnect (zre_peer_t *self)
{
    // If connected, destroy socket and drop all pending messages
```

```
    assert (self);
    if (self->connected) {
        zsocket_destroy (self->ctx, self->mailbox);
        free (self->endpoint);
        self->endpoint = NULL;
        self->connected = false;
    }
}
```

Distributed Logging and Monitoring

Let's look at logging and monitoring. If you've ever managed a real server (like a web server) you know how vital it is to have a capture of what is going on. There's a long list of reasons, not least:

- To measure the performance of the system over time
- To see what kinds of work are done the most, to optimize performance
- To track errors and how often they occur
- To do postmortems of failures
- To provide an audit trail in case of dispute

Let's scope this in terms of the problems we think we'll have to solve:

- We want to track key events (such as nodes leaving and rejoining the network).
- For each event, we want to track a consistent set of data: the date/time, node that observed the event, peer that created the event, type of the event itself, and other event data.
- We want to be able to switch logging on and off at any time.
- We want to be able to process log data mechanically, since it will be sizable.
- We want to be able to monitor a running system; that is, collect logs and analyze them in real time.
- We want log traffic to have minimal effect on the network.
- We want to be able to collect log data at a single point on the network.

As in any design, some of these requirements are hostile to each other. For example, collecting log data in real time means sending it over the network, which will affect network traffic to some extent. However, as in any design these requirements are also hypothetical until we have running code, so we can't take them too seriously. We'll aim for *plausibly good enough* and improve over time.

A Plausible Minimal Implementation

Arguably, just dumping log data to disk is one solution, and it's what most mobile applications do (using "debug logs"). But most failures require correlation of events from two nodes. This means searching lots of debug logs by hand to find the ones that matter. It's not a very clever approach.

We want to send log data somewhere central, either immediately or opportunistically (i.e., store and forward). For now, let's focus on immediate logging. My first idea, when it comes to sending data, is to use Zyre for this: just send log data to a group called "LOG," and hope someone collects it.

But using Zyre to log Zyre itself is a Catch-22. Who logs the logger? What if we want a verbose log of every message sent? Do we include logging messages in that, or not? It quickly gets messy. We want a logging protocol that's independent of Zyre's main ZRE protocol. The simplest approach is a PUB-SUB protocol, where all nodes publish log data on a PUB socket and a collector picks that up via a SUB socket (Figure 8-3).

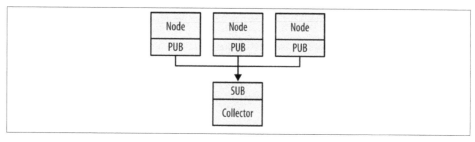

Figure 8-3. Distributed log collection

The collector can, of course, run on any node. This gives us a nice range of use cases:

- A passive log collector that stores log data on disk for eventual statistical analysis. This would be a PC with sufficient hard disk space for weeks or months of log data.

- A collector that stores log data into a database where it can be used in real time by other applications. This might be overkill for a small workgroup but would be snazzy for tracking the performance of larger groups. The collector could collect log data over WiFi and then forward it over Ethernet to a database somewhere.

- A live meter application that joins the Zyre network and then collects log data from nodes, showing events and statistics in real time.

The next question is how to interconnect the nodes and the collector. Which side binds, and which connects? Both ways will work here, but it's marginally better if the PUB sockets connect to the SUB socket. If you recall, ØMQ's internal buffers only pop into existence when there are connections. That means as soon as a node connects to the collector it can start sending log data without loss.

How do we tell nodes what endpoint to connect to? We may have any number of collectors on the network, and they'll be using arbitrary network addresses and ports. We need some kind of service announcement mechanism, and here we can use Zyre to do the work for us. We could use group messaging, but it seems neater to build service discovery into the ZRE protocol itself. It's nothing complex: if a node provides a service X, it can tell other nodes about that when it sends them a HELLO command.

We'll extend the HELLO command with a *headers* field that holds a set of name=value pairs. Let's define that the header X-ZRELOG specifies the collector endpoint (the SUB socket). A node that acts as a collector can add a header like this (for example):

```
X-ZRELOG=tcp://192.168.1.122:9992
```

When another node sees this header, it simply connects its PUB socket to that endpoint. Log data now gets distributed to all collectors (zero or more) on the network.

Making this first version was fairly simple and took half a day. Here are the pieces we had to make or change:

- We made a new class, `zre_log`, that accepts log data and manages the connection to the collector, if any.
- We added some basic management for peer headers, taken from the HELLO command.
- When a peer has the X-ZRELOG header, we connect to the endpoint it specifies.
- Where we were logging to stdout, we switched to logging via the `zre_log` class.
- We extended the interface API with a method that lets the application set headers.
- We wrote a simple logger application that manages the SUB socket and sets the X-ZRELOG header.
- We send our own headers when we send a HELLO command.

This version is tagged in the Zyre repository as v0.4.0, and you can download the tarball (*https://github.com/zeromq/zyre/tags*) if you want to check what the code looked like at this stage.

At this point the log message is just a string. We'll make more professionally structured log data in a little while.

First, a note on dynamic ports. In the *zre_tester* app that we use for testing, we create and destroy interfaces aggressively. One consequence is that a new interface can easily reuse a port that was just freed by another application. If there's a ØMQ socket somewhere trying to connect to this port, the results can be hilarious.

Here's the scenario I had, which caused a few minutes' confusion. The logger was running on a dynamic port:

1. Start logger application.
2. Start tester application.
3. Stop logger.
4. Tester receives invalid message (and asserts as designed).

As the tester created a new interface, that reused the dynamic port freed by the (just stopped) logger, and suddenly the interface began to receive log data from nodes on its mailbox. We saw a similar situation before, where a new interface could reuse the port freed by an old interface and start getting old data.

The lesson is, if you use dynamic ports, be prepared to receive random data from ill-informed applications that are reconnecting to you. Switching to a static port stopped the misbehaving connection. That's not a full solution, though. There are two more weaknesses:

- As I write this, libzmq doesn't check socket types when connecting. The ZMTP/2.0 protocol (*http://rfc.zeromq.org/spec:15*) does announce each peer's socket type, so this check is doable.

- The ZRE protocol has no fail-fast (assertion) mechanism; we need to read and parse a whole message before realizing that it's invalid.

Let's address the second one. Socket pair validation wouldn't solve this fully anyhow.

Protocol Assertions

As Wikipedia (*http://en.wikipedia.org/wiki/Fail_Fast*) puts it, "Fail-fast systems are usually designed to stop normal operation rather than attempt to continue a possibly flawed process." A protocol like HTTP has a fail-fast mechanism in that the first four bytes that a client sends to an HTTP server must be "HTTP". If they're not, the server can close the connection without reading anything more.

Our ROUTER socket is not connection-oriented, so there's no way to "close the connection" when we get bad incoming messages. However, we can throw out the entire message if it's not valid. The problem is going to be worse when we use ephemeral ports, but it applies broadly to all protocols.

So, let's define a *protocol assertion* as being a unique signature that we place at the start of each message, which identities the intended protocol. When we read a message, we check the signature, and if it's not what we expect we discard the message silently. A good signature should be hard to confuse with regular data and give us enough space for a number of protocols.

I'm going to use a 16-bit signature consisting of a 12-bit pattern and a 4-bit protocol ID (Figure 8-4). The pattern %xAAA is meant to stay away from values we might otherwise expect to see at the start of a message: %x00, %xFF, and printable characters.

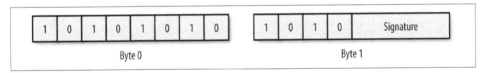

Figure 8-4. Protocol signature

As our protocol codec is generated, it's relatively easy to add this assertion. The logic is:

- Get first frame of message.
- Check if first two bytes are %xAAA with expected 4-bit signature.
- If so, continue to parse rest of message.
- If not, skip all "more" frames, get first frame, and repeat.

To test, I switched the logger back to using an ephemeral port. The interface now properly detects and discards any messages that don't have a valid signature. If the message has a valid signature and is *still* wrong, that's a proper bug.

Binary Logging Protocol

Now that we have the logging framework working properly, let's look at the protocol itself. Sending strings around the network is simple, but when it comes to WiFi we really cannot afford to waste bandwidth. We have the tools to work with efficient binary protocols, so let's design one for logging.

This is going to be a PUB-SUB protocol, and in ØMQ v3.x we do publisher-side filtering. This means we can do multilevel logging (errors, warnings, information), if we put the logging level at the start of the message. So, our message starts with a protocol signature (two bytes), a logging level (one byte), and an event type (one byte).

In the first version we send UUID strings to identify each node. As text, these are 32 characters each. We can send binary UUIDs, but it's still verbose and wasteful. In the log files we don't care about the node identifiers. All we need is some way to correlate events. So what's the shortest identifier we can use that's going to be unique enough for logging? I say "unique enough" because while we really want zero chance of duplicate UUIDs in the live code, log files are not so critical.

The simplest plausible answer is to hash the IP address and port into a 2-byte value. We'll get some collisions, but they'll be rare. How rare? As a quick sanity check I wrote a small program that generates a bunch of addresses and hashes them into 16-bit values, looking for collisions. To be sure, I generated 10,000 addresses across a small number of IP addresses (matching a simulation setup), and then across a large number of addresses (matching a real-life setup). The hashing algorithm is a *modified Bernstein*:

```
uint16_t hash = 0;
while (*endpoint)
    hash = 33 * hash ^ *endpoint++;
```

Over several runs I didn't get any collisions, so this will work as an identifier for the log data. This adds four bytes (two for the node recording the event, and two for its peer in events that come from a peer).

Next, we want to store the date and time of the event. The POSIX time_t type used to be 32 bits but since this will overflow in 2038, it's now a 64-bit value. We'll use this, as there's no need for millisecond resolution in a log file: events are sequential, clocks are unlikely to be that tightly synchronized, and network latencies mean that precise times aren't that meaningful.

We're up to 16 bytes, which is decent. Finally, we want to allow some additional data, formatted as text and depending on the type of event. Putting this all together gives the following message specification:

```
<class
    name = "zre_log_msg"
    script = "codec_c.gsl"
    signature = "2"
>
This is the ZRE logging protocol - raw version.
<include filename = "license.xml" />

<!-- Protocol constants -->
<define name = "VERSION" value = "1" />

<define name = "LEVEL_ERROR" value = "1" />
<define name = "LEVEL_WARNING" value = "2" />
<define name = "LEVEL_INFO" value = "3" />

<define name = "EVENT_JOIN" value = "1" />
<define name = "EVENT_LEAVE" value = "2" />
<define name = "EVENT_ENTER" value = "3" />
<define name = "EVENT_EXIT" value = "4" />

<message name = "LOG" id = "1">
    <field name = "level" type = "number" size = "1" />
    <field name = "event" type = "number" size = "1" />
    <field name = "node" type = "number" size = "2" />
    <field name = "peer" type = "number" size = "2" />
    <field name = "time" type = "number" size = "8" />
    <field name = "data" type = "string" />
Log an event
</message>
```

```
</class>
```

Which generates us 800 lines of perfect binary codec (the `zre_log_msg` class). The codec does protocol assertions just like the main ZRE protocol does. Code generation has a fairly steep starting curve, but it makes it so much easier to push your designs past "amateur" into "professional."

Content Distribution

We now have a robust framework for creating groups of nodes, letting them chat to each other, and monitoring the resulting network. The next step is to allow them to distribute content as files.

As usual, we'll aim for the very simplest plausible solution and then improve that step-by-step. At the very least we want the following:

- An application can tell the Zyre API, "Publish this file," and provide the path to a file that exists somewhere in the filesystem.
- Zyre will distribute that file to all peers—both those that are on the network at that time, and those that arrive later.
- Each time an interface receives a file, it tells its application, "Here is this file."

We might eventually want more discrimination—e.g., publishing to specific groups—but we can add that later, if it's needed.

In Chapter 7 we developed a file distribution system (FileMQ) designed to be plugged into ØMQ applications. Let's use that.

Each node is going to be a file publisher, and a file subscriber. We bind the publisher to an ephemeral port (if we use the standard FileMQ port 5670, we can't run multiple interfaces on one box), and we broadcast the publisher's endpoint in the HELLO message, as we did for the log collector. This lets us interconnect all nodes so that all subscribers talk to all publishers.

We need to ensure that each node has its own directory for sending and receiving files (the outbox and the inbox). Again, this is so we can run multiple nodes on one box. Since we already have a unique ID per node, we just use that in the directory name.

Here's how we set up the FileMQ API when we create a new interface:

```
sprintf (self->fmq_outbox, ".outbox/%s", self->identity);
mkdir (self->fmq_outbox, 0775);

sprintf (self->fmq_inbox, ".inbox/%s", self->identity);
mkdir (self->fmq_inbox, 0775);
```

```
self->fmq_server = fmq_server_new ();
self->fmq_service = fmq_server_bind (self->fmq_server, "tcp://*:*");
fmq_server_publish (self->fmq_server, self->fmq_outbox, "/");
fmq_server_set_anonymous (self->fmq_server, true);
char publisher [32];
sprintf (publisher, "tcp://%s:%d", self->host, self->fmq_service);
zhash_update (self->headers, "X-FILEMQ", strdup (publisher));

// Client will connect as it discovers new nodes
self->fmq_client = fmq_client_new ();
fmq_client_set_inbox (self->fmq_client, self->fmq_inbox);
fmq_client_set_resync (self->fmq_client, true);
fmq_client_subscribe (self->fmq_client, "/");
```

And when we process a HELLO command, we check for the X-FILEMQ header field:

```
// If peer is a FileMQ publisher, connect to it
char *publisher = zre_msg_headers_string (msg, "X-FILEMQ", NULL);
if (publisher)
    fmq_client_connect (self->fmq_client, publisher);
```

The last thing is to expose content distribution in the Zyre API. We need two things:

- A way for the application to say, "Publish this file."
- A way for the interface to tell the application, "We received this file."

In theory the application can publish a file just by creating a symbolic link in the outbox directory, but as we're using a hidden outbox, this is a little difficult. So we add an API method, publish:

```
// Publish file into virtual space
void
zre_interface_publish (zre_interface_t *self, char *pathname, char *virtual)
{
    zstr_sendm (self->pipe, "PUBLISH");
    zstr_sendm (self->pipe, pathname);
    zstr_send  (self->pipe, virtual);
}
```

which the API passes to the interface thread, which creates the file in the outbox directory so that the FileMQ server will pick it up and broadcast it. We could literally copy file data into this directory, but since FileMQ supports symbolic links, we use that instead. The file has an ".ln" extension and contains one line, the actual pathname.

Finally, how do we notify the recipient that a file has arrived? The FileMQ fmq_client API has a message for this (DELIVER), so all we have to do in zre_interface is grab this message from the fmq_client API and pass it on to our own API:

```
zmsg_t *msg = fmq_client_recv (fmq_client_handle (self->fmq_client));
zmsg_send (&msg, self->pipe);
```

This is complex code that does a lot at once. But we're only at around 10K lines of code for FileMQ and Zyre together. The most complex Zyre class, `zre_interface`, is 800 lines of code. This is compact. Message-based applications do keep their shape, if you're careful to organize them properly.

Writing the Unprotocol

We have all the pieces for a formal protocol specification, and it's time to put the protocol on paper. There are two reasons for this: first, to make sure that any other implementations talk to each other properly; and second, because I want to get an official port for the UDP discovery protocol, and that means doing the paperwork.

Like all the other unprotocols we've developed in this book, the protocol lives on the ØMQ RFC site (*http://rfc.zeromq.org/spec:20*). The core of the protocol specification is the ABNF grammar for the commands and fields:

```
zre-protocol    = greeting *traffic

greeting        = S:HELLO
traffic         = S:WHISPER
                / S:SHOUT
                / S:JOIN
                / S:LEAVE
                / S:PING R:PING-OK

;    Greet a peer so it can connect back to us
S:HELLO         = header %x01 ipaddress mailbox groups status headers
header          = signature sequence
signature       = %xAA %xA1
sequence        = 2OCTET        ; Incremental sequence number
ipaddress       = string        ; Sender IP address
string          = size *VCHAR
size            = OCTET
mailbox         = 2OCTET        ; Sender mailbox port number
groups          = strings       ; List of groups sender is in
strings         = size *string
status          = OCTET         ; Sender group status sequence
headers         = dictionary    ; Sender header properties
dictionary      = size *key-value
key-value       = string        ; Formatted as name=value

; Send a message to a peer
S:WHISPER       = header %x02 content
content         = FRAME         ; Message content as 0MQ frame

; Send a message to a group
S:SHOUT         = header %x03 group content
group           = string        ; Name of group
content         = FRAME         ; Message content as 0MQ frame
```

```
; Join a group
S:JOIN          = header %x04 group status
status          = OCTET        ; Sender group status sequence

; Leave a group
S:LEAVE         = header %x05 group status

; Ping a peer that has gone silent
S:PING          = header %06

; Reply to a peer's ping
R:PING-OK       = header %07
```

Conclusions

Building applications for unstable, decentralized networks is one of the endgames for ØMQ. As the cost of computing falls every year, such networks (be they computer electronics or virtual boxes in the cloud) become more and more common. In this chapter we've pulled together many of the techniques from the book to build Zyre, a framework for proximity computing over a local network. Zyre isn't unique; there are and have been many attempts to open this area for applications (ZeroConf, SLP, SSDP, UPnP, DDS). But these all seem to end up too complex or otherwise hard for application developers to build on.

Zyre isn't finished. Like many of the projects in this book, it's an icebreaker for others. There are some major areas that are unfinished, which we may address in later editions of this book or versions of the software:

High-level APIs

The message-based API that Zyre offers now is usable but still rather more complex than I'd like for average developers. If there's one target we absolutely cannot miss, it's raw *simplicity*. This means we should build high-level APIs, in lots of languages, that hide all the messaging and come down to simple methods like start, join/leave group, get message, publish file, and stop.

Security

How do we build a fully decentralized security system? We might be able to leverage public key infrastructure for some work, but that requires that nodes have their own Internet access, which isn't guaranteed. The answer is, as far as we can tell, to use any existing secure peer-to-peer link (TLS, Bluetooth, perhaps NFC) to exchange a session key, a symmetric cipher. Symmetric ciphers have their advantages and disadvantages.

Nomadic content

How do I, as a user, manage my content across multiple devices? The Zyre + FileMQ combination might help for local network use, but I'd like to be able to do this across the Internet too. Are there cloud services I could use? Something to make using ØMQ?

Federation

How do we scale a local-area distributed application across the globe? One plausible answer is federation, which means creating clusters of clusters. If 100 nodes can join together to create a local cluster, then perhaps 100 clusters can join together to create a wide-area cluster. The challenges are then quite similar: discovery, presence, group messaging.

## CHAPTER 9

Postface

Tales from Out There

I asked some of the contributors to this book to tell us what they were doing with ØMQ. Here are their stories.

Rob Gagnon's Story

"We use ØMQ to assist in aggregating thousands of events occurring every minute across our global network of telecommunications servers so that we can accurately report and monitor for situations that require our attention. ØMQ made the development of the system not only easier, but faster to develop and more robust and fault-tolerant than we had originally planned in our original design.

"We're able to easily add and remove clients from the network without the loss of any message. If we need to enhance the server portion of our system, we can stop and restart it as well, without having to worry about stopping all of the clients first. The built-in buffering of ØMQ makes this all possible."

Tom van Leeuwen's Story

"I was looking at creating some kind of service bus connecting all kinds of services together. There were already some products that implemented a broker, but they did not have the functionality I needed. By accident, I stumbled upon ØMQ, which is awesome. It's very lightweight, lean, simple, and easy to follow since the book is very complete and reads very well. I've actually implemented the Titanic pattern and the Majordomo broker with some additions (client/worker authentication and workers sending a catalog explaining what they provide and how they should be addressed).

"The beautiful thing about ØMQ is the fact that it is a library and not an application. You can mold it however you like and it simply puts boring things like queuing, reconnecting, TCP sockets and such to the background, making sure you can concentrate on what is important for you. I've implemented all kinds of workers/clients and the broker in Ruby, because that is the main language we use for development, but also some PHP clients to connect to the bus from existing PHP webapps. We use this service bus for cloud services connecting all kinds of platform devices to a service bus exposing functionality for automation.

"ØMQ is very easy to understand and if you spend a day in this book, you'll have good knowledge of how it works. I'm a network engineer, not a software developer, but managed to create a very nice solution for our automation needs! ØMQ: Thank you very much!"

Michael Jakl's Story

"We use ØMQ for distributing millions of documents per day in our distributed processing pipeline. We started out with big message queuing brokers that had their own respective issues and problems. In the quest of simplifying our architecture, we chose ØMQ to do the wiring. So far it's had a huge impact on how our architecture scales and how easy it is to change and move the components. The plethora of language bindings lets us choose the right tool for the job without sacrificing interoperability in our system. We don't use a lot of sockets (less than 10 in our whole application), but that's all we needed to split a huge monolithic application into small independent parts.

"All in all, ØMQ lets me keep my sanity and helps my customers to stay within budget."

Vadim Shalts's Story

"I am team leader in the company ActForex, which develops software for financial markets. Due to the nature of our domain, we need to process large volumes of prices quickly. In addition, it's extremely critical to minimize latency in processing orders and prices. Achieving a high throughput is not enough. Everything must be handled in a soft real time with a predictable ultra-low latency per price. The system consists of multiple components exchanging messages. Each price can take a lot of processing stages, each of which increases total latency. As a consequence, low and predictable latency of messaging between components becomes a key factor of our architecture.

"We investigated different solutions to find one suitable for our needs. We tried different message brokers (RabbitMQ, ActiveMQ Apollo, Kafka), but failed to reach a low and predictable latency with any of them. In the end, we chose ØMQ used in conjunction with ZooKeeper for service discovery. Complex coordination with ØMQ requires a relatively large effort and a good understanding, as a result of the natural complexity of multithreading. We found that an external agent like ZooKeeper is a better choice for service discovery and coordination while ØMQ can be used primarily for simple messaging. ØMQ perfectly fit into our architecture. It allowed us to achieve the desired latency using minimal efforts. It saved us from a bottleneck in the processing of messages and made processing time very stable and predictable.

"I can decidedly recommend ØMQ for solutions where low latency is important."

How This Book Happened

When I set out to write a ØMQ book, we were still debating the pros and cons of forks and pull requests in the ØMQ community. Today, for what it's worth, this argument seems settled: the "liberal" policy we adopted for libzmq in early 2012 broke our dependency on a single prime author and opened the floor to dozens of new contributors. More profoundly, it allowed us to move to a gently organic evolutionary model that was very different from the older forced-march model.

The reason I was confident this would work was that our work on the guide had, for a year or more, shown the way. True, the text is my own work, which is perhaps as it should be. Writing is not programming. When we write, we tell a story, and one doesn't want different voices telling one tale; it feels strange.

For me the real long-term value of this project is the repository of examples: about 65,000 lines of code in 24 different languages. It's partly about making ØMQ accessible to more people. People already refer to the Python and PHP example repositories—two of the most complete—when they want to tell others how to learn ØMQ. But it's also about learning programming languages.

For example, here's a loop of code in Tcl:

```tcl
while {1} {
    # Process all parts of the message
    zmq message message
    frontend recv_msg message
    set more [frontend getsockopt RCVMORE]
    backend send_msg message [expr {$more?"SNDMORE":""}]
    message close
    if {!$more} {
        break ; # Last message part
    }
}
```

And the same loop in Lua:

```lua
while true do
    -- Process all parts of the message
    local msg = frontend:recv()
    if (frontend:getopt(zmq.RCVMORE) == 1) then
        backend:send(msg, zmq.SNDMORE)
    else
        backend:send(msg, 0)
        break;      -- Last message part
```

```
        end
    end
```

This particular example (*rrbroker*) is also included in the online version of this book in C#, C++, CL, Clojure, Erlang, F#, Go, Haskell, Haxe, Java, Lua, Node.js, Perl, PHP, Python, Ruby, Scala, Tcl, and of course C. This code base, all licensed as open source under the MIT/X11 license, may form the basis for other books or projects.

But what this collection of translations says most profoundly is this: the language you choose is a detail, even a distraction. The power of ØMQ lies in the patterns it gives you and lets you build, and these transcend the comings and goings of languages. My goal as a software and social architect is to build structures that can last generations. There seems no point in aiming for mere decades.

Removing Friction

I'll explain the technical toolchain we used in terms of the friction we removed. With this book we're telling a story, and the goal is to reach as many people as possible, as cheaply and smoothly as we can.

The core idea was to host this book on GitHub and make it easy for anyone to contribute. It turned out to be more complex than that, however.

Let's start with the division of labor. I'm a good writer and can produce endless amounts of decent text quickly. But what was impossible for me was to provide the examples in other languages. Because the core ØMQ API is in C, it seemed logical to write the original examples in C. Also, C is a neutral choice; it's perhaps the only language that doesn't create strong emotions.

How to encourage people to make translations of the examples? We tried a few approaches and finally what worked best was to offer a "choose your language" link on every single example, in the text, which took people either to the translation or to a page explaining how they could contribute. The way it usually works is that as people learn ØMQ in their preferred language, they contribute a handful of translations, or fixes to the existing ones.

At the same time I noticed a few people quite determinedly translating *every single* example. This was mainly binding authors who'd realized that the examples were a great way to encourage people to use their bindings. For their efforts, I extended the scripts to produce language-specific versions of the book online. Instead of including the C code, we'd include the Python, or PHP code. Lua and Haxe also got their dedicated books.

Once we have an idea of who works on what, we know how to structure the work itself. It's clear that to write and test an example, what you want to work on is *source code*. So we import this source code when we build the book, and that's how we make language-specific versions.

I like to write in a plain text format. It's fast and works well with source control systems like Git. Since the main platform for our websites is Wikidot, I write using Wikidot's very readable markup format.

At least in the first chapters, it was important to draw pictures to explain the flow of messages between peers. I found Ditaa, a lovely tool that chews up line drawings and spits out elegant graphics. Having the graphics in the text, as text, makes it remarkably easy to work.

By now you'll realize that the toolchain we use is highly customized, though it uses a lot of external tools. All are available on Ubuntu, which is a mercy, and the whole toolchain is in the *zguide* repository in the *bin* subdirectory.

Let's walk through the editing and publishing process. Here is how we produce the online version:

```
bin/mkguide
```

Which works as follows:

- The original text sits in a series of text files (one per chapter).
- The examples sit in the *examples* subdirectory, classified per language.
- We take the text and process this into a set of Wikidot-ready files, for each of the languages that get their own version.
- We extract the graphics and call Ditaa on each one to produce image files, which are stored in the *images* subdirectory.
- We extract inline listings (which are not translated) and store these in the *listings* subdirectory.
- We use *pygmentize* on each example and listing to create a marked-up page in Wikidot format.
- We upload all changed files to the book wiki using the Wikidot API.

Doing this from scratch takes a while. So, we store the SHA-1 signatures of every image, listing, example, and text file and only process and upload changes, and that makes it easy to publish a new version of the book when people make new contributions.

To produce the PDF and Epub formats, we do this:

```
bin/mkpdfs
```

Which works as follows:

- We use the *mkbook* script on all the input files to produce a DocBook output.

- We push the DocBook format through *docbook2ps* and *ps2pdf* to create clean PDFs, in each language.
- We push the DocBook format though *db2epub* to create Epub books, in each language.
- We upload the PDFs to the wiki using the Wikidot API.

When creating a community project, it's important to lower the "change latency," which is the time it takes for people to see their work live or, at least, to see that you've accepted their pull requests. If that is more than a day or two, you've often lost your contributor's interest.

Licensing

I want people to reuse this text in their own work: in presentations, articles, and even other books. However, the deal is that if they remix my work, others can remix theirs. I'd like credit, and have no argument against others making money from their remixes. Thus, this text is licensed under cc-by-sa.

For the examples, we started with GPL, but it rapidly became clear this wasn't workable. The point of examples is to give people reusable code fragments so they will use ØMQ more widely, and if these are GPL that won't happen. So we switched to MIT/X11, even for the larger and more complex examples that conceivably would work as LGPL.

However, when we started turning the examples into standalone projects (as with Majordomo), we used LGPL. Again, remixability trumps dissemination. Licenses are tools; use them with intent, not ideology.

Index

We'd like to hear your suggestions for improving our indexes. Send email to index@oreilly.com.

M

Majordomo Management Interface (MMI), 192
Majordomo pattern, 38, 164–186
Majordomo pattern, Asynchronous, 186–191
MDP (Majordomo Protocol), 164–165, 185, 382
memory leaks, detecting, 62–63
message queues, overflowing, 37, 142, 247, 255
Message-Oriented Pattern for Elastic Design
    (MOPED), 372–375
MessagePack, 384–385
messages, 39–41
    benefits of ZeroMQ for, 23–27
    best practices for, 22
    content of, accessing, 39
    envelopes for, 75–76, 81–86
    flow control for, 77
    high-water mark for, 77–78
    losing, causes of, 78
    multipart, 40–41, 44–45, 382
    patterns for sending (see patterns)
    reading, 39
    receiving, 32, 34–35
    releasing, 39
    sending, 32, 34–35, 39, 40
    size of, 39
    string format for, 10–11
    as structures, 32, 39
    TCP for, 23
    writing, 39
    zero-length, 41
Mindful General role, 367
MIT/X11 license, 484
MMI (Majordomo Management Interface), 192
monitoring, in distributed environment, 467–
    473
MOPED (Message-Oriented Pattern for Elastic
    Design), 372–375
multicast messaging (see publish-subscribe pat-
    tern)
multicast transports, 35
multipart messages, 40–41, 44–45, 382
    envelopes for, 75–76
    high water mark for, 78
    zero-copy used with, 74
Multiple Socket Reader/Poller example, 41–44
Multithreaded Hello World example, 65–67
Multithreaded Relay example, 68–70
multithreading, 63–67
    best practices for, 64

for client stack, 310–320
exiting, best practices for, 22
I/O threads, 36
for increasing subscriber speed, 258–260
portable thread management, 104
signaling between threads, 68–70
Mystic role, 369

N

Nagle's algorithm, 186
networks
    asynchronous disconnected, 194–206
    failure of, 142
    plugging sockets into, 32–34
nodes, coordination between, 70–74
    (see also client node; server node)
non-blocking reads, 41
non-blocking request-reply, 48–54

O

one-way data distribution pattern (see publish-
    subscribe pattern)
one-way heartbeats, 160
Open Door role, 367
open source software
    licensing for, 330–332
    models for, 325, 328
    reasons for, 325, 328
OpenAMQ server, 206
optimization
    hand-optimizing high-volume data flows,
        385
    with heartbeats, 160
    zero-copy for, 74–74

P

PAIR socket, 38, 68–70
Parallel Task Ventilator example, 16–20, 57–59
Paranoid Pirate pattern, 151–159, 161–163
path hierarchy, 282
patterns, 37–38
    asynchronous client/server (see asynchro-
        nous client/server pattern)
    Asynchronous Majordomo pattern, 186–191
    Binary Star pattern, 206–222
    Black Box pattern, 258–260
    Clone (see Clone pattern)

About the Author

Pieter Hintjens started his first business making video games 30 years ago and has been building software products ever since. Taking as his principle the idea that "the real physics of software is the physics of people," he focuses now on building communities through "Social Architecture," writing, and helping others use ØMQ profitably.

For two years Pieter was president of the FFII, a large NGO fighting software patents. He was CEO of Wikidot, founder of the European Patent Conference, and founder of the Digital Standards Organization. Pieter speaks English, French, Dutch, and bits and pieces of a dozen other languages. He lives with his beautiful wife and three lovely children in Brussels, Belgium, where he plays with a West African drumming group; he also travels extensively.

Colophon

The animal on the cover of *ZeroMQ* is the fourhorn sculpin (*Myoxocephalus quadricornis*). The fourhorn sculpin is mostly found in arctic coastal waters around North America and northern Eurasia, but it can also be found in some freshwater lakes in Europe. This fish is named for its four bony protuberances on its head.

The fourhorn sculpin has a dark and slightly flattened body with eyes close to the top of its heads, a large pelvis, and a distinctive large mouth. It usually reaches about 30 cm in length. One way to distinguish between males and females of this species is that males have a yellowish brown belly and females have a white belly. This fish mostly feeds on organisms at the bottom of the sea, crustaceans, and fish eggs.

The fourhorn sculpin reproduces in the winter. During this time males will typically dig a pit that females will put all their eggs into. Once eggs are laid into a pit, males will guard the eggs during the three month incubation period.

The cover image is from Johnson's Natural History. The cover font is Adobe ITC Garamond. The text font is Adobe Minion Pro; the heading font is Adobe Myriad Condensed; and the code font is Dalton Maag's Ubuntu Mono.

Get even more for your money.

Join the O'Reilly Community, and register the O'Reilly books you own. It's free, and you'll get:

- $4.99 ebook upgrade offer
- 40% upgrade offer on O'Reilly print books
- Membership discounts on books and events
- Free lifetime updates to ebooks and videos
- Multiple ebook formats, DRM FREE
- Participation in the O'Reilly community
- Newsletters
- Account management
- 100% Satisfaction Guarantee

Signing up is easy:

1. **Go to: oreilly.com/go/register**
2. **Create an O'Reilly login.**
3. **Provide your address.**
4. **Register your books.**

Note: English-language books only

To order books online:
oreilly.com/store

For questions about products or an order:
orders@oreilly.com

To sign up to get topic-specific email announcements and/or news about upcoming books, conferences, special offers, and new technologies:
elists@oreilly.com

For technical questions about book content:
booktech@oreilly.com

To submit new book proposals to our editors:
proposals@oreilly.com

O'Reilly books are available in multiple DRM-free ebook formats. For more information:
oreilly.com/ebooks